SOCIAL AND ECONOMIC RIGHTS IN THE SOVIET BLOC

SOCIAL AND ECONOMIC RIGHTS IN THE SOVIET BLOC

A Documentary Review Seventy Years After the Bolshevik Revolution

Edited with an introduction by George R. Urban

Preface by Max M. Kampelman

Transaction Books
New Brunswick (U.S.A.) and Oxford (U.K.)

Library of Congress Catalog Number: 88-1157
ISBN: 0-88738-186-3
Printed in the United States of America

Library of Congress Cataloging in Publication Data

Social and economic rights in the Soviet bloc.

1. Soviet Union—Social conditions—1970-
2. Europe, Eastern—Social conditions. 3. Soviet Union—Politics and government—1945— 4. Europe, Eastern—Politics and government—1945- I. Urban, G. R. (George R), 1921-
HN523.5.S57 1988 306′.0947 88-1157
ISBN 0-88738-186-3

Contents

2. Rights—Views From the West

Some Western Accounts of the State and Social and Economic Rights in the Soviet Union and Eastern Europe

3. Rights—Views From the Bridge

Soviet and East European Accounts (Including *Samizdat*) of the State of Social and Economic Rights in the Soviet Bloc

Some of the materials in this issue are taken from "Social and Economic Rights in Soviet and East European Societies," prepared by Radio Free Europe/Radio Liberty, with additional materials selected, collated and edited, and an introduction, by G. R. Urban for this publication in *Survey* and subsequently in book form from Transaction Publishers, New Brunswick, New Jersey, USA.

G. R. Urban expresses his gratitude to the President and Research Departments of RFE/RL Inc. for cooperation generously given in preparing this symposium.

Preface

This year (1987), the U.S. and U.S.S.R. are each celebrating important anniversaries. These are celebrations of very different events. For the United States, it is 200 years since our Constitution, which formalized and protected our system of democracy, came into being. For the Soviet Union, the October Revolution of 1917 introduced a period of prolonged repression; and its commemoration is today taking place against a background of wide-ranging internal debate and official efforts to bring about more openness, "democratization," and rebuilding of the Soviet economy. The bicentennial of the United States Constitution—a document as revolutionary in its day as the 1917 events—has also been the occasion for renewed attention and commitment to the fundamental sources of American political beliefs and institutions.

Celebrations of our respective pasts have brought more sharply into focus the challenge of the future. To face that future realistically, both societies must come to understand and manage a new revolution—one which is even more profound than those which accompanied the founding of our respective states. It is a revolution in technology and information which is dramatically transforming the world before our eyes and stretching our minds to the limits of our capacity to understand and absorb the changes that are enveloping us.

New computers and the accompanying research fueled by them are constantly expanding our knowledge of the world, and simultaneously changing that world. Information moves more swiftly and relentlessly than our ability to organize it. We are truly living in an age in which no society and no country can effectively isolate itself from these currents. A flash of insight or discovery may begin one place on the globe, but will inevitably spread out and reach kindred spirits elsewhere.

The implications of this technology revolution are not yet fully understood, but it is clear that the society which is best able to initiate, absorb, and reflect these tremendous developments will be the one which will best meet the challenge and prosper. The changes present opportunities for quantum steps in improving the quality of life on earth, but they also pose the threat of annihilating civilization as we know it today.

In this nuclear age, there can be *absolutely* no justification for mass violence and terror in order to achieve ideological goals, no matter how noble those goals may appear to be. One's faith must not today be propagated by the sword. Unilateral security can no longer be achieved either by withdrawing from the world or by attempting to attain national impregnability. We must learn to accept a mutual responsibility for the lives of people in all of our countries.

For this reason, too, securing respect for human rights remains an international imperative. It certainly is an abiding concern of the American people and an essential element of any developing relationship with the Soviet Union. On the threshold of the twenty-first century, we must be particularly appalled that, despite the gigantic strides man has made in opening the universe of space and finding cures for dread diseases, millions of our fellow men still suffer gross abuses of their rights and dignity as human beings. To those who would argue that the pursuit of greater justice and freedom for the peoples of the Soviet Union and Eastern Europe is secondary to the political pursuit of arms control, we must say that history has taught us that the cause of peace and human freedom are indivisible. Respect for human rights is essential to stability and peace on earth. We seek neither the peace of the graveyard nor the peace of the gulag. It is peace with liberty and human dignity that men and women seek for themselves and their families. Furthermore, a strong case can be made for the view that governments that must answer to their peoples do not launch wars of aggression.

To realize the full potential of our shared stake in peace requires that we look fully and frankly upon the issues which trouble us to discern common ground where we can, and do, acknowledge differences. Those differences are a matter of deep-seated values and beliefs about the dignity of man, the rights of the individual, and the role of government. In the United States we find particularly abhorrent the notion that the rights of the individual must be subordinate to the interests of a self-selected elite who purport to speak for the rest of their society. By contrast, advocates of the so-called dictatorship of the proletariat claim that, while their system does not correspond to Western notions of democracy and political rights, it does guarantee what they consider to be the most basic human rights, such as the "right" to health care, housing, work, and, above all, the "right" to peace. It is this Soviet claim that requires analysis.

This extraordinarily significant volume examines the Soviet record in the economic and social areas presumably emphasized by the Soviet system. It proves that seventy years after the October Revolution the record of achievement remains a dismally poor one. In making this review, the authors and editors have provided an impressive service in the cause of human rights and dignity. The work assesses the Soviet system's actual *performance* in fulfilling its citizens' economic and social needs against the *claims* made for it. Seventy years after the Bolsheviks took power, the inconsistency is more apparent than ever between a system which limits its citizens' freedoms and rights of self-expression while asserting but not fulfilling their claims to material well being. The demonstrated gap between Soviet living standards and that of the industrialized countries of the West and Japan tells a vital story.

George Urban effectively notes in his introduction to this volume the fundamental relationship between political rights and economic progress; that, for example, political freedom is the vehicle for social progress and that the Soviet effort to list desirable social or economic goals as "rights" is nothing but an effort to obfuscate the absence of the fundamental "rights of man" in their society. What this volume unmistakably demonstrates is that governments which deny their people the freedom to use their creative talents are falling further behind in the race for the future, while those which have loosened the binds of central control on individual freedom are flourishing and providing their people with a higher standard of living. The current Soviet leadership seems aware of the system's material shortcomings. The world has a stake in inducing the Soviet leaders to make the changes necessary to bring their country into the ranks of those nations which provide for their citizens the full benefits of liberty, self-determination and extensive material benefits.

The spread of democracy in virtually every continent attests to its strength. Only a few years ago, for example, democracy was under attack throughout Latin America. Today, more than 90 percent of the people living in Latin America and the Caribbean live in democracies or countries well on their way toward democracy. In the Philippines, Haiti, Brazil, Argentina, South Korea, and even the People's Republic of China, efforts to secure more openness and relaxation of restrictions on individual initiative are prompted not only by an abstract love of justice—although this is undoubtedly present among the peoples—but by the pragmatic realization that democracy works. Governments which, under the influence of the statist mystique introduced centralized command models in Africa, Asia and elsewhere are turning away from that experiment which left their economies bankrupt and impoverished their people.

In the Soviet Union and Eastern Europe, the implicit recognition of the relationship between freedom and economic dynamism has resulted in new experimentation with more openness and the relaxation of some restrictions on individual economic initiative. It is fair to say that much of the new Soviet leadership's impetus to modernize comes from an appreciation of the fact that a closed, tightly-controlled society cannot compete in a world in which economic development, and the power which it produces, is the result of rapid technological advances stimulated by an information explosion which knows no national boundaries.

The present collection of articles and documents represents, in the main, the work of the research departments of Radio Free Europe and Radio Liberty, the largest single repository of research on conditions within the Soviet Union and Eastern Europe. I have often been the beneficiary of that research. Radio Free Europe and Radio Liberty are symbols of the U.S. commitment to freedom and democracy in the postwar era. They speak for and to the majority of those who would speak freely and claim their human rights if the Soviet Union and its allies abided by the international treaties and accords they have voluntarily signed. The presence of hundreds of thousands of Soviet troops watching over the enforced orthodoxy of the East Europeans and the absence of free and open discussion of these issues is not only a source of concern to those who value freedom throughout the world, but is a source of weakness and inefficiency for those who would accept the challenge of the future.

In an age of unparalleled technological change, when satellite dishes can bring in the remotest corners of the world at the flick of a dial, no state or government can long hope to maintain a monopoly on information nor restrict ideas to narrow boundaries. Today, those satellite dishes can fit on rooftops. Tomorrow, they will be no larger than the radios which bring us our morning news; and they will be in our living rooms and bedrooms—in all of our countries and of value to all of our peoples.

It is a privilege for me to be a part of this important symposium by Radio Liberty-Radio Free Europe.

Max M. Kampelman
Washington, D.C.
October, 1987

With minor changes, this book is an enlarged version of the August 1987 issue (No. 127) of *Survey* magazine. The editor would like to express his thanks to Rebecca Penrose, the magazine's assistant editor, for her generous assistance.

Introduction

G. R. Urban

Communist governments of the Soviet type make one crucial claim when comparing their system with "burgeois" or "capitalist" societies. They say that their performance "in the service of Man" is superior to their opponents' because socialism guarantees the satisfaction of every citizen's social and economic needs such as Health Care, Housing and Employment. They call these social and economic "rights" and aver that "human rights" as advocated in the West can have no meaning unless the rights to be fed, housed, employed and medically looked after are first duly met. These rights, they insist, are the true barometer of what kind of social justice, equity and "democracy" society offers to its members; and they have frequently suggested that their worth as a new civilization should be measured by their performance in these areas.

This volume sets out to do just that. It examines the Communist record over the past several years, applying, without accepting, the Communist governments' own terms of reference and drawing its documentary evidence from both official and unofficial sources.

If it is true, as Communist doctrine proclaims, that Man is the measure of all things, no task could be more important. Have the Communist systems, in fact, satisfied those social and economic needs that form the very basis of their claim to legitimacy? Has radical social change produced radical change in the level of social satisfaction? If they have, something may, perhaps, be said in extenuation of the sacrifices exacted; if they have not, the whole Communist experiment collapses under the weight of its own failures. A socialism that excels in manufacturing bacteria and nuclear arms but cannot house and feed its population, cancels out its reason to exist. Mikhail Gorbachev understands the reality of the problem. He also understands the difficulty of answering it and the dangers of leaving it unanswered.

The conclusions emerging from this volume are a tribute to the long-suffering peoples of the Soviet Union and East and Central Europe —and an indictment of their rulers. After 70 years of "scientific socialism" in the USSR, and some 40 years in Central and Eastern Europe, Communist achievements in the field of economic and social "rights" vary from the banal to the minuscule. The sacrifices have been stupendous—the results commonplace and often shaming in the context of the rapid modernization and growing affluence of the rest of the industrialized world. Never has so much blood and sweat been shed to attain what the Japanese, for example, starting from a comparably backward economic base, attained and more than attained without a

Stalin, without Show-Trials, without Gulags or the starvation of millions.

It is not that Communist governments were reluctant to promote the social and economic rights of their citizens, but rather that the perverse priorities and organizational handicaps they imposed on themselves in pursuit of the millennium and in preparation for non-existing threats, made it impossible for them to do better. The utopian character of the system entailed the pursuit of utopian objectives. To the fanciful readings of human nature was added an obsessive determination to change it, and bring forth that class-conscious and clean-living New Man that, defying the Marxist forecast, History would not. The system allowed one factor to escape its attention—the stubborn reality of weak, fickle, irrational, selfish and sluggish human beings who spoke and felt Polish because they were Poles, or Hungarian because they were Hungarians, and would not dissolve in the melting pot of socialism. The Soviet authorities in particular acted as though the New Man had become a reality—but found themselves confronted by Soviet Man who looked like nothing so much as the Old Adam. It was the rights of this imperfect human being Communist governments had to satisfy.

There was never a very good chance that they would. An unspoken resolve in the minds of Communist purists that unregenerate man shall not be rewarded, was one factor that held them back. More important, the wasteful outlays of "building socialism," supporting an outsize military establishment and acquiring a Continental and then a maritime empire stood in the way. Massive repercussions (at least in the Soviet Union) did not have to be feared because Soviet Man had been disenfranchised and the security apparatus was all-powerful. So it happened that the social and economic rights of the citizen were allowed to go begging under socialism, and 70 years after the Revolution that is said to have changed the course of human history, they are still begging all the way from Sofia to Vladivostok. "Life has become better, comrades, life has become gayer," Stalin observed in 1935 on the eve of the great terror. 50 years on and despite many changes, those lapidary words have lost none of their irony.

The facts are simply told. Housing in the Communist countries is extremely poor if not downright degrading; health care inadequate and subject to almost universal corruption; the care of the old and disabled callous by any standard of human dignity, and the protection of the environment conspicuous by its virtual absence. The despoliation of nature in East Germany, the Czech lands and Silesia is a massive menace to that "common house of Europe" that Mikhail Gorbachov says he is anxious to protect. Even providing the population with a proper diet represents a serious problem, especially in the underdeveloped parts of the Communist community such as Romania (where electricity and heating fuels are also in chronically short supply) and many of the non-metropolitan areas of the Soviet Union. One of the world's leading exporters of grain before the First World War, Russia is no longer able to feed itself without outside support.

Only in satisfying the "right to work" has the Soviet type of socialism been able to maintain a statistical show of full employment; but, as Gorbachov and his economic advisers have frequently hinted, the price has been over-manning, fictitious employment and loss-making State enterprises,[1] the penalties of which are now coming home to roost. It was the view, in 1987, of one visiting group of West European industrialists that the Soviet Union was suffering from a *de facto* unemployment of about 30 per cent of the workforce. If "restructuring" is to have any meaning, full employment as the Soviet people have come to know it may soon have to be abandoned together with other features of the command economy. The rationalization of labour, the need to respond to the demands of the market, and the devolution of economic control from Moscow to the self-managing enterprises can, short of a miracle, have no other consequences. Mikhail Gorbachov is the last man to expect *perestroika* to be a painless affair, and pain, if he can stay the course, is what he is most likely to encounter. Nowhere will this be more keenly felt than in the sensitive area of job-security, for the Soviet Constitution guarantees, under Article 40, everyone's right to work. "Right" and "work" may well have to be re-defined in a manner that will agree with neither the corrupt life-style of Soviet Man nor Russia's engrained Oblomovism.[2]

BUT suppose the Soviet record in satisfying social and economic rights were better than it is—how much would that tell us about the worth of Soviet society as a civilized and peaceable partner we could share a globe with? The current Western debate about human rights, based as it partly is on Principle VII of the Helsinki Final Act, is flawed in at least one important respect. Paragraph 2 of Principle VII states:

> The [participating States] will promote and encourage the effective exercise of civil, political, economic, social, cultural and other rights and freedoms all of which derive from the inherent dignity of the human person and are essential for his free and full development.

The inclusion in this stipulation of "economic, social, cultural and other

[1] 13 per cent of the total, as Prime Minister Nikolai Ryzhkov told the Supreme Soviet on 29 June 1987.

[2] "So it is one thing to look at the problem while pretending that we have no unemployment and another thing altogether to do so when one calmly takes into account the fact that we do have unemployment and that it has to exist. . . . We should not close our eyes to the economic harm caused by our parasitic confidence in a guaranteed job. . . . The real danger of losing one's job and having to take, temporarily, unemployment benefit or work wherever one is sent is a very good cure for laziness, drunkenness or irresponsibility.

Many experts believe it would be cheaper to pay temporary unemployment benefit for a few months than keep masses of people in industry who do nothing and could break (and are breaking) any self-financing scheme and any attempt to raise the quality and efficiency of public labour." Nikolai Shmelev, leading Soviet economic commentator in *Novy Mir*, No. 6, June 1987.

Asked about Shmelev's article on 22 June 1987, Gorbachov said: "It is being suggested that unemployment is something suitable for us. That won't do; that won't do."

rights," along with those traditionally associated with the Rights of Man, has encouraged the European and American Left to act as though Soviet society and the liberal-democratic societies of the West were of comparable merit—Soviet society giving, for familiar reasons of its own, greater emphasis to certain social and economic rights such as the right to housing, health care and employment, and the Western societies to civil rights and freedoms; but in the fullness of time the two would converge and future denizens of a unified world would be in a position to enjoy the best from both systems. This is misleading and mischievous, for what it says in plain language is that the satisfaction of "social and economic rights" is somehow on a par with, or perhaps even superior to the satisfaction of the freedoms of thought, conscience, religion, assembly and public articulation. This is patently not so.

It is possible to imagine a successful and efficient despotism that would satisfy the "social and economic rights" of its citizens without ceasing to be a despotism. The National Socialist system of Adolf Hitler was one such despotism. Undeniably, it provided adequate housing, more than adequate health care, old-age pensions and full employment for the (non-Jewish) German citizen; it imposed no limitations on travel and subsidized cultural activities of the classical kind generously. Yet it was, apart from Stalin's, the modern world's worst tyranny because it failed to satisfy human rights in every other respect. It provided no freedom of thought, no freedom of conscience, no freedom of the press, no freedom of assembly, no freedom of belief without distinction as to race, sex, language or religion. In other words, its title to be accepted as "one of us" in the comity of civilized nations was nil. So should be that of the Soviet Union, even if it did satisfy every social and economic "right" it set itself to satisfy but remained the Soviet system. And let there be no mistake about it—it *could* remain the Soviet system. Lord Home's observation that a "fat Communist" should be less of a threat to us than an under-nourished Communist rings true enough as a piece of anecdotal evidence in the context of personal relations, but offers a misleading clue to the behaviour of Communist governments.

Much of the confusion in Western thinking about what is and is not a human right stems from the gradual abolition, under Jimmy Carter's Administration, of the demarcation line between the Anglo-American concept of the Rights of Man (political and civil liberties) and the Soviet-Third World concept of "social and economic rights."

"Social and economic rights" are not rights in the sense in which the freedom from arbitrary arrest or the freedom of opinion is. They are, rather, provisions or entitlements which may, but need not, lead to the enhancement of freedom and human dignity. Their satisfaction may, but need not, be relevant to a reasonable man's judgement whether a society is free or unfree, civilized or uncivilized, responsive or unresponsive to the sensibilities of culture. My reason for saying that our examination, in this volume, of the Soviet record applies the Soviet yardsticks without accepting them, springs from that distinction.

One would, of course, like to see every Soviet and East European citizen well-fed, well-housed, well-shod, fully employed, medically well attended to, and well cared for in his old age. That may or may not happen. It may or may not be in the Western interest that it should under existing Soviet auspices. Certainly, a fully efficient dictatorship, with a materially well-satisfied population to support it, is not what Western civilization is about, nor what Karl Marx foresaw as the consummation of the Communist revolution.

WITH Mikhail Gorbachov at the helm of the Soviet empire and the slow expiry of Ronald Reagan's presidency, the Post-War era seems to be drawing to a close. The future satisfaction of social and economic rights in the Soviet bloc will depend not only on the domestic fortunes of the Communist system, but also, and predominantly, on what sort of international order will come to replace the world as we have known it since 1945—whether future historians will have reason to record that in the late 1980s the Post-War period came to an end, and was followed by a gradual reconciliation of conflicting ideologies and interests . . . or a pre-War period.

In the last analysis, the debate about social and economic rights is the debate about living "by bread alone." Reason and experience tell us that a worth-while human life requires both bread and the freedom to wrestle with "every word that proceedeth out of the mouth of the Lord." Bread without liberty cannot endow us with a dignified existence, nor can liberty if our basic needs and creature comforts are left unsatisfied. Political organizations that hoist themselves to power with bread and liberty on their lips but can secure neither, have rendered themselves doubly irrelevant to the concerns of ordinary men and women. From the Sea of Japan to the Adriatic, the world Communist movement is in the grips of a profound crisis. The spectre haunting it is neither imperialism nor capitalism, but the nature of Man.

Social and Economic Rights in the Soviet Union

Aaron Trehub

Articles 40, 42, 43 and 44 of the Constitution of the USSR (1977) guarantee the right to work, the right to health care, the right to material security in old age, and the right to housing respectively.

The Right to Work

THE "right" to work is the most prominent item in the Soviet human rights' panoply. Work in the Soviet Union, however, is not so much a right as an obligation, enforceable by law. Article 40 of the Constitution is complemented by Article 60:

> Conscientious labour in one's chosen field of socially useful activity and observance of labour discipline is the duty and a matter of honour for every Soviet citizen who is able to work. Avoiding socially useful work is incompatible with the principles of a socialist society.[1]

Those who avoid "socially useful work" are liable to prosecution as "parasites" under Article 209 of the RSFSR Criminal Code or the corresponding articles of the criminal codes of the other Union republics. It would be wrong, nevertheless, to assume that the "right," or the obligation, to work is resented by the Soviet population. It is rather seen as protecting Soviet citizens from the threat of unemployment.

UNEMPLOYMENT was officially eliminated in the USSR on 9 October 1930, the day unemployment benefits were stopped. Since then, according to Soviet spokesmen, there has been no unemployment of any kind. Such statements ignore the existence of frictional unemployment (unemployment between jobs), the forced employment of men below their skill levels, and overmanning (or underemployment). No mass unemployment, however, seems to exist in the USSR.

But as J. L. Porket has pointed out, "the regime's ideological commitment to full employment" involves considerable economic sacrifice. The practice of overmanning is especially harmful:

> *Inter alia*, [overmanning] contributes to slow and undemanding work

[1] F. J. M. Feldbrugge, (ed.), *The Constitutions of the USSR and the Union Republics: Analysis, Texts, Reports* (Sijthoff & Nordhoff, Alphen aan den Rijn, 1979), p. 105.

> rhythms, slack work discipline, low productivity, high production costs, inefficiency, and a divorce of rewards from performance. It has an adverse impact on work habits and attitudes towards work, and enables moonlighting during working hours. And it negatively affects the standard of living of the population, helping to bring about low average wages, hidden and repressed inflation, and shortages of consumer goods and services.[2]

Although no exact figures are available, Porket quotes Soviet sources as claiming that overmanning typically accounts for between 10 and 20 per cent of the work force. This is probably a conservative figure. A survey conducted in 1978 among British and West German chemical-plant contractors who had worked in the Soviet Union found manning levels on the completed Soviet plants to be 1·5–1·7 times higher, on average, than would be considered normal for equivalent plants in Western Europe. In an article that appeared only a few months after Gorbachov's accession to power, the Soviet economic journalist Vasily Selyunin remarked: "We [in the USSR] have forgotten what the word unemployment means, but is it a good thing that we should only half-work?"[3]

This state of affairs is incompatible with Mikhail Gorbachov's emphasis on economic "acceleration" and higher labour productivity. The General Secretary seems to be determined to tackle the problem of overmanning, even at the cost of "freeing" (i.e. sacking) hundreds of thousands of workers. The axe has fallen in several areas. In November 1985, five Union republican ministries and a state committee were merged to form a single state agro-industrial committee, Gosagroprom.[4] As a result, at least 3,200 officials lost their jobs.[5] According to a spokesman for the State Committee for Labour and Social Problems (Goskomtrud), up to 70,000 scientific workers will lose their jobs as a result of a new incentive pay system introduced at the beginning of 1986.[6] Modernization displaced over 700,000 industrial workers in 1985, and an estimated 880,000 more jobs were expected to be lost by the end of 1986.[7]

The long-term prospect is even more unsettling. In an article that appeared in *Sovetskaya Kultura* early in 1986, Professor Vladimir

[2] J. L. Porket, "Unemployment in the Midst of Labour Waste," *Survey*, Spring 1985, p. 23.

[3] "Eksperiment," *Novy Mir*, No. 8, 1985, p. 173.

[4] "V Tsentralnom Komitete KPSS i Sovete Ministrov SSSR," *Pravda*, 23 Nov. 1985.

[5] "Agroprom segodnya i zavtra," *Selskaya Zhizn*, 20 Feb. 1986. This report went on to say that new jobs had been found for "practically all' of the sacked employees.

[6] "Ne za stepen, a za trud," *Literaturnaya Gazeta*, 15 Jan. 1986. The spokesman, V. D. Kharin, said that the new pay system will affect "more than half" of all scientific workers (*nauchnye rabotniki*) in the USSR. Since there were 1,491,300 scientific workers in the USSR at the end of 1985 (*Narkhoz 85*, p. 64), it can be assumed that over 700,000 people will be affected by the new system. Kharin predicted that between six and 10 per cent of these will "inevitably" lose their jobs. At a closed meeting with Moscow propaganda workers in April 1986, Boris Yeltsin, first secretary of the Moscow City Party Committee, said that 15 unproductive scientific research institutes had been shut down; as a result, 30,000 scientific workers would be transferred to production jobs (AS 5721, p. 6).

[7] *APN*, 27 Jan. 1986 and 5 Feb. 1986.

Kostakov predicted that between 13 and 19 million jobs in the manufacturing sector would be eliminated by the end of the century if labour productivity growth targets were to be met.[8] Although he assured readers that retirement and a shrinking work force would take care of most of these redundancies, he made it clear that the process would not be entirely painless:

> The need to look for a job, something that many people . . . will certainly face, may also be new and unaccustomed for us. After all, we are used to just the opposite—the job looking for the person . . . Considerable psychological restructuring will also be required, apparently. We consider it natural and necessary that, if for objective reasons a job slot becomes unnecessary, the employee should immediately be given another job. Very often that is precisely why staff reduction takes place more slowly that it could even now: the managers of enterprises and institutions . . . prefer not to burden themselves with the job placement of people who have been let go—especially since their possibilities for doing so are very limited. Now we will have to accustom ourselves to the thought that finding employment is, to a considerable extent, the individual's own concern, and that this search may require a certain amount of time—a sufficient, but not unlimited, amount of time.[9]

This raises the question of what "freed" workers are supposed to live on between jobs. The 3,200 or so officials sacked during the formation of Gosagroprom were entitled to receive full pay for up to three months after being made redundant, without harm to their social security and pension status (as a rule, full pension rights can only be retained if the time between jobs does not exceed one month[10]). In other words, they received what might be regarded as unemployment benefits.[11] In reality, however, some of the sacked officials were out of work for almost a year.[12] Whether these benefits were extended in their cases is not known.

Not surprisingly, Kostakov's article caused a stir in the West, provoking speculation whether the Soviet Union might be heading for mass unemployment. Soviet officials strongly deny that modernization will lead to unemployment. "In a planned economy," said Gorbachov in an interview with the French Communist Party newspaper *L'Humanité*, "the two things are not connected."[13]

[8] "Odin, kak semero," *Sovetskaya Kultura*, 4 Jan. 1986.

[9] Ibid. Translated in *Current Digest of the Soviet Press*, 19 Feb. 1986, pp. 1–4.

[10] "Sokrashchenie shtata," *Trud*, 7 Jan. 1986.

[11] According to Kostakov, this was an unprecedented measure. It may be pointed out that legislation containing a similar measure was enacted in 1970. The 1970 legislation, however, was applicable only to "workers transferred directly from administration to production and not possessing production qualifications," and the payment of three months' salary was made conditional on their attending a retraining course (*Sobranie Postanovlenii Pravitelstva SSSR*, No. 4, 1970, Article 30).

[12] *TASS*, 14 Nov. 1986.

[13] "Otvety M. S. Gorbacheva na voprosy gazety *Yumanite*," *Pravda*, 8 Feb. 1986. See also "The System Must Give Way" in this issue.

Perhaps not. It is clear, however, that the right to work is being modified in the direction of economic efficiency. In a recent article in the journal *Agitator*, L. A. Kostin, the First Deputy Chairman of Goskomtrud, reminded readers that the right to work and to choose one's profession is subject to certain limitations:

> The state-guaranteed right to work and to remuneration in accordance with the quantity and quality of that work, the ensuring of full employment for all able-bodied citizens, is one of the most important economic and social achievements of socialism. But this right should not be oversimplified. For all its humanitarianism, our society cannot guarantee that everybody, throughout their working life, will be able to work in the field they have chosen once and for all, or in the same location.[14]

Stanislav Shatalin, an economist and social scientist, went even further. In a recent article in the Party theoretical journal *Kommunist*, Shatalin argued for a shift away from full employment, which he called "a superseded stage of extensive development," to "socially and economically effective rational full employment."[15] He emphasised that the popular understanding of the right to work would have to change accordingly:

> The principles of socialism are not principles of charity that automatically guarantee everyone a job regardless of his ability to work. A person should have to fight every day to hold on to a job that is suited to his abilities.[16]

Shatalin's remarks echo those of Academician Tatyana Zaslavskaya. In an article that appeared just before Shatalin's, Zaslavskaya noted that "the change in the conditions of employment" now under way in the Soviet Union would force some workers to move to other branches of the economy or to other parts of the country, which would in turn stiffen labour discipline:

> There is no doubt that the need to transfer to other production branches which are short of labour and to move to other regions and towns will primarily be faced by workers who are the least valuable in the eyes of the labour collectives, who are distinguished by an indifferent attitude to work and product quality, and who are poor participators in social life, not to speak of idlers, drunkards, drifters, and so on. Such a situation will promote the growth of the social

[14] "Intensifikatsiya i problemy trudoustroistva," *Agitator*, No. 20 (October), 1986, p. 22. It is interesting to compare Kostin's remarks with those of Aleksandr Sukharev, chairman of the Association of Soviet Jurists, who at a press conference in December 1985 stated that "no intensification or reconstruction of production" can deprive a Soviet citizen of the right to a job "corresponding to his professional training and his interests" (*Moscow Television*, 1545 GMT, 9 Dec. 1985; see also "SSSR: realizatsiya prav i svobod cheloveka," *Pravda* 10 Dec. 1985).

[15] "Sotsialnoe razvitie i ekonomicheskii rost," *Kommunist*, No. 14 (September), 1986, p. 63.

[16] Ibid.

value of workplaces in social production, the strengthening of labour discipline and an increase in the quality of work.[17]

In short, the right to work is becoming increasingly conditional on job performance. This does not necessarily mean that slack workers will face the prospect of unemployment—at least not in the sense of having to spend months or even years on the dole, as is the case in some Western countries. It does mean, however, that they will risk demotion, perhaps to a minimum-wage job, or will have to resettle in parts of the country they do not consider congenial.

The shift to "rational full employment" is currently in progress at a number of Soviet enterprises. One of these is the Belorussian railway.

"THERE is no labour shortage" in the USSR, declared Gorbachov in his report to the 27th Party Congress of the CPSU in February 1986.[18] To prove his point, he cited the example of the Belorussian railway, where an experiment aimed at raising productivity by shedding staff succeeded in "freeing" 12,000 workers in little over a year. Gorbachov's endorsement thrust the Belorussian experiment into the limelight. Since the congress, the Soviet press has carried a number of articles describing the experiment in some detail.

According to A. G. Andreev, chief of the Belorussian railway, the need for reform became apparent about five years ago,[19] when falling productivity, and an accident involving a drunken switch operator, forced the administration to consider eliminating superfluous jobs.

Over a two-year period, the Belorussian railway observed the use made of the working day (*fotografii rabochego dnya*) in 1,500 cases; this revealed that at some work places up to 22 per cent of working time was wasted. The next step was to freeze outside hiring, thus taking advantage of natural labour turnover in order to create vacancies for some of the workers whose jobs were threatened. Between December 1984, when the freezes went into effect, and May 1985, just before personnel cuts began, 5,500 vacancies were created. Then the process of shedding workers began in earnest. An engineer from Mogilev proved that freight trains

[17] "Chelovecheskii faktor razvitiya ekonomiki i sotsialnaya spravedlivost," *Kommunist*, No. 13 (September), 1986, p. 70. In December 1980, Professor Gavriil Popov of Moscow State University suggested that workers who had been sacked because of poor job performance should be paid the legal minimum wage of 80 rubles a month (*sic* Popov; others give the minimum wage in the Soviet Union as 70 rubles a month) and be put to work repairing streets or working in vegetable markets or on farms until a "normal" job can be found for them: "And when after a little while they get a 'normal' job, it stands to reason that they will hold on to it and try not to fall in among the poorer workers. And doubtless those who remain at the factory will work much better. A stern measure? Perhaps. But, I think, an unavoidable one." ("Tvoe rabochee mesto," *Pravda*, 27 Dec. 1980).

[18] "Politicheskii doklad Tsentralnogo Komiteta KPSS XXVII Syezdu Kommunisticheskoi Partii Sovetskogo Soyuza," *Kommunist*, No. 4 (March), 1986, p. 36.

[19] "Doroga i lyudi," *Nedelya*, No. 20, 1986. For a detailed discussion of the railway situation in the late 1970s and early 1980s, see Vladimir Kontorovich, "Discipline and Growth in the Soviet Economy," *Problems of Communism*, Nov.–Dec. 1985, pp. 24–5.

could be driven by one person; this enabled the railway to sack 2,000 workers in a single move. Installation of automatic signal controls at level crossings meant the loss of 1,600 jobs, the merging of two inspection services resulted in several hundred more redundancies, and so on.

In just over a year, the railway dismissed 12,000 workers, or about 10 per cent of its total workforce. Of these, 4,000 retired on pensions, 500 were transferred to railway construction organizations, and the rest—7,500—were found jobs in other branches of the Belorussian economy.[20] Only 37 of those sacked took their cases to court; in eight cases they were judged to have been unfairly treated.[21]

The apparent ease with which sacked workers were found new jobs may have been due to the fact that Belorussia has an extensive network of employment bureaux. According to A. Fomich, chairman of the State Committee for Labour and Social Problems of the Belorussian SSR, there are now employment bureaux in 150 towns and districts throughout the republic; they have cut the average time spent looking for a job from 20–25 days to five–six.[22]

So far, the economic results of the experiment have been encouraging for administration and workers alike. Labour productivity rose by 24·1 per cent in the first four months of 1986 over figures for the first four months of 1985.[23] Wages have gone up by an average of 25 rubles a month.[24]

The Belorussian railway experiment, with its guiding principle of more work performed by fewer workers, closely resembles the Shchekino method.[25] Both are based on the simple idea of using a stable wage fund to induce enterprises to shed redundant labour. However, there is an important difference between them concerning the way in which savings in the wage fund are distributed to the remaining workers.

In the USSR, "wages consist of two parts—the tariff element (about 75 per cent of the total) and the bonus element."[26] The tariff element (the official term is "tariff rate," or *tarifnaya stavka*) is determined by the particular character of a given job and the qualifications needed to perform it; the more demanding the job, the higher the "tariff rate."[27] Under the Shchekino method, savings from the wage fund are handed out to workers in the form of bonuses. In the Belorussian experiment, savings are used to jack up the tariff rates of jobs that have become more

[20] "Na povorote," *Trud*, 3 Aug. 1986.

[21] "Na povorote," *Trud*, 5 Aug. 1986.

[22] "Chelovek i rabota," *Pravda*, 8 Aug. 1986.

[23] "Eksperiment na belorusskoi zheleznoi doroge," *Planovoe Khozyaistvo*, No. 8 (August), 1986, p. 27.

[24] "Na povorote," *Trud*, 3 Aug. 1986.

[25] Ibid. For recent Western analyses of Shchekino, see Peter Rutland, "The Shchekino Method and the Struggle to Raise Labour Productivity in the Soviet Union," *Soviet Studies*, July 1984; and Henry Norr, "Shchekino: Another Look," *Soviet Studies*, April 1986.

[26] Rutland, op. cit. p. 355.

[27] "Tarifnaya sistema," *Bolshaya Sovetskaya Entsiklopediya* (Moscow, 1976), Vol. 25, p. 277.

demanding as a result of rationalization.[28] In the words of one Soviet commentator, the latter method means that pay rises are "*guaranteed*, and this . . . is an important difference."[29] This refers to the fact that, under the Shchekino method, higher labour productivity has not always meant higher wages, primarily because ministries have repeatedly broken the stable wage fund rule.[30] The implication, therefore, is that "tariff rates" are less vulnerable than bonuses to ministerial meddling, although it is not clear why this should be so.

It is too early to assess the real significance of the Belorussian experiment. As one Western observer has remarked about other repercussions of the Shchekino method, the first results "may indicate more about the slow pace of work before the Shchekino-induced changes than about the intensity of labour afterwards."[31] In any case, the Belorussian experiment has the support of Gorbachov, whose hand can be detected in the decision to extend it to all Soviet railways by the end of the decade.[32] So far, it has been adopted by 10 other railways; one of these, the Odessa railway, had released 7,000 workers by late 1986.[33] In short, the Belorussian railway experiment is being touted as an example of how to raise labour productivity—and wages—through staff cuts while minimizing worker resentment, and avoiding unemployment.

If the fundamental change in employment conditions foreseen by Kostakov, Zaslavskaya and others actually occurs, hundreds of thousands, perhaps millions, of workers will lose their jobs. Many will have to switch to the "non-productive" sphere—i.e. to services and consumer industries. Others will have to move to Siberia, the Far North, or the Far East. Average wages in the non-productive sphere are considerably lower than in industry, and living conditions in Siberia, the Far North, and the Far East are poor.[34] Soviet officials recognize these problems, and claim that they are being solved. However, industrial workers who are made redundant and are forced to seek work in the

[28] "Na povorote," *Trud*, 3 Aug. 1986.

[29] Ibid. Emphasis in the original.

[30] Norr, op. cit. pp. 147, 160. *Pravda* is even more emphatic on this point, saying that the failure to observe the stable wage fund rule "buried" (*pokhoronilo*) the Shchekino method ("Zarplata," *Pravda*, 3 Nov. 1986).

[31] Ibid. p. 154.

[32] "Na povorote," *Trud*, 3 Aug. 1986.

[33] "Zarabotannyi rubl," *Izvestia*, 1 Nov. 1986. There are 32 railways in the Soviet Union.

[34] For example, in the northern port city of Murmansk (1985 population 426,000) it is "not unusual" to wait 15 years for a flat, there are shortages of everything from alcohol to hospital beds, and the rate of worker absenteeism due to sickness is high ("Kak zhivetsya cheloveku na severe," *Sovetskaya Rossiya*, 31 Jan. 1986). *Izvestia* recently admitted that "good living conditions have not yet been created" for inhabitants of the oil-producing Tyumen region of Western Siberia ("Sever sudit strogo," *Izvestia*, 27 Oct. 1986). Things are no better in the Far East: during the Eleventh Five-Year Plan (1981–1985) only 58 per cent of those who settled in state and collective farms in the Maritime Province remained there; the rest left the region altogether or switched to jobs in industry, mainly because of the critical housing shortage in the countryside ("Pereselentsy," *Sovetskaya Rossiya*, 25 Oct. 1986).

service sector or in inhospitable parts of the country will almost certainly experience an initial drop in their standard of living. As Zaslavskaya remarked, "the redistribution of workers between branches of industry, enterprises, professional and official groups, and regions and towns of the country is fraught with considerable complications."[35] It remains to be seen how well the Soviet authorities will deal with them.

The Right To Health Care

ONE of the proudest achievements of the Soviet state is its comprehensive system of "free" (government funded) health care for all Soviet citizens. In recent years there have been signs that the health of the Soviet population is deteriorating.[36] Soviet officials rigorously refuted articles by Western analysts who suggested this, pointing to the ever-growing number of hospitals, doctors, etc. as proof that all was well in Soviet medicine.[37] This approach is now being challenged in the Soviet press, probably as a result of Gorbachov's campaign for more "openness" (*glasnost*) in discussing sensitive subjects. Two of the most vulnerable points are life expectancy and infant mortality.

LIFE expectancy is perhaps the best indicator of a nation's health. It is significant, therefore, that The USSR Central Statistical Administration (TsSU) suspended the publication of life expectancy figures for the Soviet Union between 1971–1972 and 1985–1986. The reason for this 14-year gap can be deduced from the following table, which incorporates figures given in the latest edition of the statistical yearbook.

Average Life Expectancy, USSR (years)[38]

Year	*Entire Population*	*Men*	*Women*
1896–1897 (in 50 gubernii of European Russia)	32	31	33
1926–1927 (in the European USSR)	44	42	47
1938–1939	47	44	50
1955–1956	67	63	69

35 "Chelovecheskii faktor razvitiya ekonomiki i sotsialnaya spravedlivost," *Kommunist*, No. 13 (September), 1986, p. 70.

36 See, for example, David E. Powell, "The Emerging Health Crisis In The Soviet Union," *Current History*, October 1985.

37 In June, 1984, *The Blade* (Toledo, Ohio) published an uncomplimentary article on the Soviet health system, based on information collected by Murray Feshbach and other Western researchers. The day after the article appeared, an official from the Soviet embassy in Washington, D.C. delivered a 30-page rebuttal of the article's main points to *The Blade*'s Washington office. See *The Blade*, 10 and 11 June, 1984.

38 *Narkhoz 64*, p. 598; *Narkhoz 65*, p. 603; *Narkhoz 67*, p. 702; *Narkhoz 69*, p. 588; *Narkhoz 72*, p. 564; *Narkhoz 85*, p. 547.

Average Life Expectancy, USSR (years)—continued

Year	*Entire Population*	*Men*	*Women*
1958–1959	69	64	72
1963–1964	70	66	73
1964–1965	70	66	74
1966–1967	70	66	74
1968–1969	70	65	74
2nd Half 1970–1st Half 1971	70	65	74
1971–1972	70	64	74
1978–1979	68	62	73
1983–1984	68	63	73
1984–1985	68	63	73
2nd Half 1985–1st Half 1986	69	64	73

Average life expectancy for both men and women in the Soviet Union dropped from 70 years in 1971–1972 to 69 years in 1985–1986. Life expectancy for men dropped from a peak of 66 years in the mid-1960s to 62 years in 1978–1979; it has now regained its 1971–1972 level of 64 years. Life expectancy for women dropped from 74 years in the early 1970s to 73 years in 1985–1986.

One can hardly overstate the importance of these figures. The Soviet Union is the only country in the developed world to have experienced such a severe drop in life expectancy in the post-Second World War period.[39] Moreover, the drop in life expectancy has been accompanied by a rise in the crude death rate—from 8·2 deaths per 1,000 population in 1970 to 10·6 in 1985.[40] Soviet demographers attribute the rise in the crude death rate to the "ageing" of the Soviet population, the demographic after-effects of the Second World War and the stresses associated with urbanization.[41] Western analysts attribute it to alcoholism, smoking, poor diet and an outmoded health care system.[42]

IN October 1986, the USSR Central Statistical Administration published official infant mortality statistics for the first time in 12 years.[43] These confirmed what most Western analysts had long

[39] Male life expectancy in the United States has fallen on at least four occasions since 1955 (in 1958, 1963, 1966 and 1969), but never by more than 0·5 years (Murray Feshbach, "The Soviet Union: Population Trends and Dilemmas," *Population Bulletin*, Vol. 37, No. 3, August 1982, Table 1.3, p. 34).

[40] *Narkhoz 85*, p. 31. The crude death rate in the Soviet Union is said to have dropped to 9.7 in 1986 ("Diagnoz samomu sebe," *Pravda*, 15 Feb. 1987).

[41] See *Dinamika Naseleniya SSSR 1960–1980 gg.* (Moscow, 1985), pp. 14–16.

[42] See Christopher Davis in the *Wall Street Journal*, 31 Oct. 1986.

[43] "Naselenie SSSR," *Ekonomicheskaya Gazeta*, No. 43 (October), 1986, pp. 6–7. The Soviet Union suspended the publication of infant mortality figures after 1974, when the rate reached 27·9 deaths per 1,000 live births (*Narkhoz 75*, p. 40).

suspected; namely, that the infant mortality rate in the Soviet Union has risen considerably since 1971, when it reached its lowest ever figure of 22·9 deaths per 1,000 live births. The current infant mortality rate in the USSR is almost 2·5 times higher than the 1985 American rate of 11 deaths per 1,000 live births.[44] It is also the highest rate in the European Comecon member countries:

Infant Mortality in European Comecon Countries, 1950–85 (number of deaths per 1,000 live births)[45]

	1950	1960	1970	1980	1983	1984	1985
USSR	80·7	35·3	24·7	27·3	25·3	25·9	26·0
Bulgaria	94·5	45·1	27·3	20·2	16·5	16·1	18·0
Hungary	85·6	47·6	35·9	23·2	19·0	20·2	18·0
GDR	72·2	38·8	18·5	12·1	10·7	10·0	11·0
Poland	111·2	54·8	33·4	21·3	19·3	19·1	18·0
Romania	116·7	74·6	49·4	29·3	23·9	23·4	22·0
Czechoslovakia	77·7	23·5	22·1	18·4	15·7	15·2	14·0

It should be noted that the Central Statistical Administration has still not published infant mortality figures for the years 1975–1979. Western analysts estimate that the rate reached a peak of 31 deaths per 1,000 live births during this period.[46]

Why did infant mortality in the Soviet Union rise so sharply during the 1970s? According to Dr V. A. Tabolin of the USSR Academy of Medical Sciences, one reason for the rise was overconfidence.[47] By the 1970s Soviet medicine had progressed to a point where doctors felt able to allow women in poor health to conceive and give birth. As Dr Tabolin remarks, however, "sick mothers give birth to sick children," and Soviet medicine proved to be unequal to the task of keeping underweight and/or premature babies alive:

> Of course, we fought to save every new-born baby, but, excuse me for saying so, with the methods of our grandfathers. We have neither the equipment nor the special devices for taking care of such children.

The lack of specialized equipment (neo-natal resuscitators, incubators, etc.) is not the only problem. There are no doctors, only nurses, on duty in Soviet maternity homes at night, which is precisely the time when most

[44] *World Health Statistics Annual: 1985* (World Health Organization, Geneva, 1985), p. 25.

[45] *Narkhoz 75*, Moscow, 1976, p. 40; "Naselenie SSSR," *Ekonomicheskaya Gazeta*, No. 43 (October), 1986, pp. 6–7; *Statistichesky Ezhegodnik Stran-chlenov Soveta Ekonomicheskoi Vzaimopomoshchi: 1985*, Moscow, 1985, p. 17; *World Health Statistics Annual: 1985* (World Health Organization, Geneva, 1985), p. 25.

[46] *Wall Street Journal*, 31 Oct. 1986.

[47] "Vrach vstrechaet novorozhdennogo," *Sovetskaya Rossiya*, 31 Oct. 1986.

women give birth. The Ministry of Health recently issued a decree requiring doctors to provide night cover.

The main problem is a drop in the quality of the doctors themselves, the result of poor training. Dr Tabolin claims that paediatrics departments do not devote enough time to the study of paediatrics itself, presumably because the curriculum has been filled with other subjects. In addition, very little practical experience is provided—paediatrics' students encounter babies only in their penultimate year of study, and then only in groups of 10 or more. Dr Tabolin suggests following the example of Czechoslovakia, where groups are limited to five students. Adopting this practice in the Soviet Union would require special permission from the Ministry of Health because it would result in more groups, an increased burden on teachers. This would raise the difficult question of pay. It seems likely that Dr Tabolin's other suggestions—to extend the training period for paediatricians by at least one year, and to require professors to continue working as paediatricians while they teach—would encounter similar obstacles.

Another important problem concerns unsanitary conditions in maternity homes. In the summer of 1985, an infectious disease broke out at a maternity home at Rostov-on-the-Don.[48] Over 60 new-born babies were affected; an unspecified number died. The ensuing investigation revealed serious violations of sanitation rules. For example, because of a shortage of sterilized material, infants were wrapped in unsterilized swaddling clothes; they were also given unpasteurized milk. The outbreak was made worse by overcrowding. The maternity home was built to hold only 70 beds; in fact, it held 155. Although this outbreak seems to have been unusually severe, *Pravda* noted that there had been "similar cases" in the city before.

THE unsatisfactory state of public sanitation in the Soviet Union as a whole is reflected in tables showing sickness rates in the USSR for seven infectious diseases. These tables are published regularly in the main statistical yearbook, along with tables giving the numbers of hospital beds, doctors, etc. The USA has been chosen for purposes of comparison because it has a population of roughly the same size as the Soviet Union.

There has been a modest improvement in this area since 1983. At a recent meeting of the board of the Ministry of Health, First Deputy Chairman O. Shchepin claimed that between 1985 and 1986 the sickness rate (*zabolevaemost*) for whooping cough in the Soviet Union dropped by two thirds, while the rate for measles dropped by half.[49] He went on to say, however, that the Soviet population continues to suffer from

[48] "Gorky urok," *Pravda*, 19 Oct. 1985; see also "Pokrivili dushoi," *Pravda*, 31 Aug. 1986.

[49] "Diagnoz samomu sebe," *Pravda*, 15 Feb. 1987. The numbers of cases of whooping cough and measles in the USSR in 1985 were 53,900 and 272,800 respectively (*Narkhoz 85*, p. 545).

Infectious Diseases, USSR and USA, 1970–83:
Number of Cases (USA in Italics)[50]

	1970	1975	1980	1982	1983
Typhoid Fever, Paratyphoid A, B, C	22,500	26,000	16,900	17,200	18,600
	346	*375*	*510*	*425*	*507*
Scarlet Fever	469,900	361,100	230,100	324,700	293,100
	na	*na*	*na*	*na*	*na*
Diphtheria	1,100	200	350	920	1,410
	435	*307*	*3*	*2*	*5*
Whooping Cough (Pertussis)	39,500	14,900	13,900	27,500	19,300
	4,200	*1,700*	*1,700*	*1,900*	*2,500*
Tetanus	650	490	300	350	360
	148	*102*	*95*	*88*	*91*
Acute Poliomyelitis	270	130	170	260	180
	33	*8*	*9*	*8*	*15*
Measles	471,500	363,800	355,700	466,200	233,800
	47,400	*24,400*	*13,500*	*1,700*	*1,500*

Infectious Diseases, USSR and USA, 1970–83:
Number of Cases Per 100,000 Population
(USA in Italics)

	1970	1975	1980	1982	1983
Typhoid Fever, Paratyphoid A, B, C	9	10	6	6	7
	0·17	*0·17*	*0·23*	*0·18*	*0·22*
Scarlet Fever	194	142	87	120	108
	na	*na*	*na*	*na*	*na*
Diphtheria	0·45	0·08	0·13	0·34	0·52
	0·21	*0·14*	*0*	*0*	*0*
Whooping Cough (Pertussis)	16	6	5	10	7
	2·1	*0·79*	*0·75*	*0·82*	*1·1*
Tetanus	0·27	0·19	0·11	0·13	0·13
	0·07	*0·05*	*0·04*	*0·04*	*0·04*
Acute Poliomyelitis	0·11	0·05	0·06	0·10	0·07
	0·02	*0*	*0*	*0*	*0·01*
Measles	194	143	134	173	86
	23·3	*11·3*	*6*	*0·73*	*0·64*

50 *Narkhoz 84*, p. 559; taken or derived from *Statistical Abstract of the United States: 1986* (Washington, DC), 1985, pp. 5, 115. Figures for the USA after 1983 were not available at the time of writing.

"serious intestinal infections, infectious [*virusnyi*] and serum hepatitis, and diptheria." According to official statistics, the number of cases of diphtheria in the Soviet Union rose from 1,410 in 1983 to 1,610 in 1984, falling to 1,510 in 1985.[51]

DR Tabolin's article implies that the rise in infant mortality during the 1970s was at least in part a consequence of the growing bureaucratization of Soviet medicine, whereby administrative indicators take precedence over effective treatment. The Soviet approach to medical and population statistics reflects this tendency.

Despite the reappearance of figures for infant mortality and life expectancy, the lack of meaningful statistics is still a serious obstacle to any attempt to assess the effectiveness of the Soviet health system. In the words of one Western specialist, "we do not have . . . age and sex-specific death rates for any years since 1973/74 . . . cause-of-death data by age group since 1971/72, the number of doctors by speciality for any year since 1975 (let alone their urban-rural distribution), age data from the 1979 census, etc."[52] What we do have are tables showing for any given year the number of doctors, visits to doctors, hospital beds, medical establishments, etc. in the USSR.[53] Of course, these statistics reveal next to nothing about the quality of Soviet health care. For Western observers, the Soviet insistence on irrelevant numbers is a mere nuisance. For Soviet doctors, however, it is a serious problem. A series of articles in *Izvestia* suggests that the pressure to meet irrelevant statistical targets has resulted in a drop in the quality of Soviet health care.

In January 1986, *Izvestia* published a letter from Dr Yu. Tomashevsky of Lvov, under the title of "Paper Fever."[54] Dr Tomashevsky's letter claims that Soviet doctors spend too much time on paperwork and too little with their patients. The Soviet health-care system, like Soviet industry, operates in the *val*, or gross-output principle, with the emphasis on quantity, not quality. For example, a doctor at a Soviet polyclinic is expected to see eight patients an hour, which works out at 7·5 minutes per patient. Soviet studies have shown that, on average, five of these seven minutes are spent filling out forms.[55] Furthermore, the competence of Soviet doctors is judged first and foremost by the number of patients they see, not the quality of care they provide. In Dr Tomashevsky's words, "physicians' work is evaluated primarily according to statistical indicators . . . numbers determine our way of working." The results have not been uniformly encouraging:

[51] *Narkhoz 85*, p. 545.

[52] Murray Feshbach, "Issues In Soviet Health Problems," in *Soviet Economy in the 1980's: Problems and Prospects* (Part 2), (US Government Printing Office, Washington, DC, 1983), p. 205.

[53] E.g. *Narkhoz 85*, pp. 539–547.

[54] "Bumazhnaya likhoradka," *Izvestia*, 7 Jan. 1986.

[55] William A. Knaus, MD, *Inside Russian Medicine* (Beacon Press, Boston, 1981). pp. 219–220.

> As far as I know, not all health indicators have improved in recent years. In some areas we are standing still, in others there has even been a drop in previously achieved levels. Isn't it time [asks Dr Tomashevsky] to put quality ahead of quantity in our work?

"Paper Fever" inspired a flood of letters, mostly from fellow doctors. Some of the correspondents asked *Izvestia* not to reveal their names, presumably for fear of retaliation from their superiors. Others were bolder. Dr G. Ivanov of Leningrad wrote that paperwork takes up half his working day and that he has to make diagnoses and prescribe treatments as quickly as a jet pilot has to make decisions in aerial combat.[56] When he suggested to his superiors that precious time could be saved by pre-printing standard medical forms (it seems that Soviet doctors do their paperwork in longhand), he was told there was a paper shortage. Dr Ivanov was not convinced: "We don't write longhand on air, do we?" Dr A. Stolyarov from Mozyr had some rather critical suggestions to make about one of the most sacred statistical indicators of "progress," the number of doctors in the Soviet Union:

> We ought to stop relying on and pounding the drum about the enormous number of doctors. Produce another million doctors and put them to work scribbling too? No thank you!

Dr O. Grishchuk, an ophthalmologist from Ust-Ilimsk, challenged the eight-patients-an-hour norm, asking "is it not because of the pursuit of numbers, of 'volume,' that young doctors have started to conduct examinations any old way?" Whatever their particular complaint, all the doctors whose letters were published in *Izvestia* agreed that doctors should be freed from paperwork and allowed to concentrate on treating their patients.

In June, *Izvestia* published two letters which addressed the problem of medical statistics in more detail. V. Gubenko of Moscow repeated Dr Tomashevsky's call for quality to come before quantity in evaluations of a doctor's work. He admitted, however, that there are cases where even qualitative indicators can discourage initiative and risk-taking:

> Take, for example, the general mortality indicator, i.e. the percentage of people treated to die. It is clear that, if a doctor works well, this number should be as low as possible . . . But situations often arise in which the indicator "works against" the creative, questing doctor. This doctor takes risks more often, is not afraid to accept a "difficult" patient.[57]

As a result his mortality indicator goes up, "and they don't pat you on the head for that." But even this, concluded Gubenko, shows that it is high time for the medical bureaucracy to recognize that "many forms of statistical accounting used today do not help the doctor, but rather

[56] "Nachistotu," *Izvestia*, 7 Feb. 1986.
[57] "Za chastokolom svodok," *Izvestia*, 13 June, 1986.

prevent him from working normally." Dr A. Nemenov of Tula was equally emphatic:

> The need for a radical improvement in the organization of health care is obvious. Statistical information is also in need of improvement . . . Quantitative indicators (use of budget, capital construction, the growth of the network, equipment, the number of visits etc.) predominate in health-care accounting. It is practically impossible to extract information about the effectiveness of treatment from all these numbers. Has the patients' health improved? Stayed the same? Deteriorated? There is no way of knowing.[58]

The only solution to this problem, according to Dr Nemenov, would be universal computerization of the Soviet health service. The few moves that have been made in that direction have petered out into isolated "experiments," sometimes lasting years.

THE "railway-station hurly-burly" (to quote one Soviet doctor) that reigns in state polyclinics has driven many Soviet citizens into the waiting rooms of the sole (legal) competition—fee-paying polyclinics. There have been such polyclinics in the USSR since 1926.[59] Originally, they were designed to be an affordable alternative to private specialists. Now they serve as an affordable alternative to the state health-care system (a typical visit to a private polyclinic costs about 3 rubles 50 kopecks[60]). At present, there are 20 fee-paying polyclinics in Moscow; it is not known how many there are in the country as a whole (*Izvestia* claims that the number of "self-financing [medical] establishments in the country has almost tripled since 1975").[61] Whatever the number of such polyclinics in the USSR may be, it is supposed to grow by 60 per cent in the current Five-Year Plan period.[62]

The main reason why people turn to private polyclinics is the quality of treatment. As Dr M. Khutornenko, the head doctor of a Moscow fee-paying polyclinic, put it, "people come to us primarily because they can get an appointment with a highly qualified specialist without having to go through a lot of red tape."[63] Old people like private polyclinics because their complaints are taken seriously, instead of being ascribed simply to their age, which often happens at state polyclinics. This typifies the difference in attitude between the staff of state polyclinics, where, as one woman complained, "we seldom feel even a small part of the attention we have a right to expect from medical personnel,"[64] and

[58] "Na polozhenii padcheritsy," *Izvestia*, 13 June 1986.
[59] "Bednye millionery," *Izvestia*, 21 Jan. 1986.
[60] Ibid.
[61] Ibid. One source has estimated that there were 130 private polyclinics in the USSR in the mid-1970s: Michael Ryan, *The Organization of Soviet Medical Care* (Blackwell and Robertson, Oxford/London, 1978), pp. 30–31.
[62] "Platnaya poliklinika: za i protiv," *Izvestia*, 11 July, 1986.
[63] "Bednye millionery," *Izvestia*, 21 Jan. 1986.
[64] "Platnaya poliklinika: za i protov," *Izvestia*, 11 July, 1986.

fee-paying polyclinics, where "a sick person can see that they want to help him, not get rid of him."[65]

The status of fee-charging polyclinics is, however, still somewhat ill-defined. In theory, private polyclinics work on the principle of *khozraschet*, or self-financing. This means that they have the right to dispose of their earnings as they see fit after operating expenses have been met. In practice, their earnings are often appropriated by higher administrative organs, to be incorporated into a common fund. For example, even though the 20 Moscow fee-paying polyclinics regularly earn one million rubles in annual profit, the city's Main Health Care Administration appropriates four-fifths of this sum, leaving the polyclinics with only 200,000 rubles to spend on maintenance, equipment, repairs, etc.[66] The reason for this is that fee-paying polyclinics do not enjoy true administrative autonomy; their governing body, the Department for Self-Financing Medical Establishments, is subordinated to the various *glavki*, or chief departments, of the Ministry of Health—including the Moscow Main Health Care Administration.

Besides, some Soviet citizens fear that expanding the network of private polyclinics will undermine their constitutional right to state health care and, by extension, the "socialist system."[67] Although such fears are apparently groundless—self-financing medical establishments amount to only 0·4 per cent of the total Soviet health system[68]—they show that any amendment of the existing practice, however modest, must overcome strong resistance. However, other letters published in *Izvestia* suggest that dissatisfaction with the existing health system may be just as strong. One reader made the point that government health care in the Soviet Union is becoming more and more expensive:

> The practice of "thanking" doctors with a round sum of money has become so fashionable that the expansion of the self-financing health-care service could only be a blessing. . . . I would rather pay the state.[69]

Another argued that "it's not private polyclinics that are 'undermining the socialist system,' but disorder in the state ones! That is what is forcing people to find another way."

NO health system can operate effectively without medicines and medical supplies. Recent items in the Soviet press show that the Soviet health system suffers from chronic shortages of both. An article that appeared in late 1985 in *Izvestia* revealed that in 1985 the Ministry of Light Industry had met only 81 per cent of demand for plain bandages; its supplies of other items such as sterile napkins, dressing kits, cotton wool

65 "Bednye millionery," *Izvestia*, 21 Jan. 1986.

66 Ibid.

67 See the letter entitled "Ne soglasen!" in "'Bednye millionery'," *Izvestia*, 17 March, 1986; and "Platnaya poliklinika: za i protiv," *Izvestia*, 11 July, 1986.

68 "Platnaya poliklinika: za i protiv," *Izvestia*, 11 July, 1986.

69 Ibid.

and gauze pads, were considerably less.[70] Another problem is packaging. According to *Izvestia*, in 1985 only 18 per cent of bandages were delivered to pharmacies in pre-packaged form. The rest were delivered in bales weighing between 60 and 100 pounds. As a result, pharmacy workers wound 200 million bandages by hand that year.

Even more serious than the bandage shortage is the shortage of medicines. Between March and August 1986, the newspaper *Sovetskaya Rossiya* published a series of articles under the heading "How Are Things at the Pharmacy?"[71] More than one thousand readers wrote to the newspaper to complain about shortages of everything from medicines for hypertension to throat lozenges and mustard poultices. A pharmacist from Kalinin oblast complained about irregularity of supplies:

> I can't figure out how they plan deliveries . . . In our region, for example, there are over 700 diabetics, and we have only enough medicine on hand for half of them.[72]

According to *Sovetskaya Rossiya*, the reason for this and similar problems is that "there is no clear-cut system" for the production and delivery of medicines:

> Over 20 per cent of the medicines turned out by domestic industry are produced only once a year. Customers do not know precisely when this "once" will be. All they can do is hope that their suppliers won't let them down. But they do let them down, and pretty often too . . .[73]

Some readers alleged that pharmacy workers occasionally refuse to fill prescriptions for medicines that are in especially short supply. This complaint aroused the indignation of Aleksandr D. Apazov, head of the pharmaceutical department of the RSFSR Ministry of Health, who spoke of the need for more "explanatory work" among pharmacy workers.[74] Apazov pointed out, however, that the main problem was not impolite or uncooperative pharmacy staff, but the chronic shortage of medicines.

Ironically, the medicine shortage has been made worse by Gorbachov's anti-alcohol campaign. The weekly *Literaturnaya Gazeta* recently reported that desperate alcoholics have taken to buying up stocks of alcohol-based medicines, including soporifics and tranquillizers.[75] In order to discourage this practice, some pharmacies have started treating these medicines like vodka or wine, refusing to sell them before two

[70] "O vate, bintakh, protsentakh," *Izvestia*, 25 Oct. 1985. It will be recalled that a shortage of sterilized swaddling clothes was one of the causes of the tragedy in the maternity home in Rostov-on-the-Don.

[71] "Kak v apteke?" *Sovetskaya Rossiya*, 25 March, 1986. This was followed by: "Propavshie lekarstva," 14 May, 1986; "Kak v apteke?" 15 July, 1986; and "Kak v apteke?" 17 Aug. 1986.

[72] "Kak v apteke?" 25 March, 1986.

[73] Ibid.

[74] "Kak v apteke?" 15 June, 1986.

[75] "Otchego blagoukhayut muzhchiny, ili o Parfyumernom sposobe borby s alkogolizmom," *Literaturnaya Gazeta*, 12 Nov. 1986, p. 12.

o'clock in the afternoon. The newspaper did not say what happens to people who really need these medicines.

YEVGENII Ivanovich Chazov, the recently appointed Minister of Health, has remarked, "a rational diet is a necessary condition for a healthy life."[76] Despite the Food Programme, launched with great ceremony in May 1982, the diet of the average Soviet citizen has not yet reached acceptable levels of consumption established by Soviet scientists some time ago.

Per Capita Consumption of Staple Foodstuffs, USSR, 1985 (kilograms)[77]

	1985 (actual)	1990 (plan)	Rational Norms of Consumption
Meat and Meat Products	61·4	70·0	82·0
Milk and Dairy Products	323	330–340	405
Eggs, number	260	260–266	292
Fish and Fish Products	17·7	19·0	18·2
Sugar	42·0	45·5	40
Vegetable Oil	9·7	13·2	9·1
Potatoes	104	110	110
Vegetables and Melons	102	126–135	130
Fruits and Berries	46	66–70	91
Bread and Cereals	133	135	115

Poor diet, like alcoholism, drug abuse and smoking, is a problem whose causes go beyond the Soviet health system. It is principally the result of failures in Soviet agriculture, theft and mismanagement. According to some estimates, approximately 20 per cent of all production is lost in transit from the countryside to the consumers.[78] Whatever its causes, inadequate and ill-balanced diet has contributed to the generally poor health of the Soviet population, especially of children.[79]

The achievements of Soviet health are undeniable by Soviet standards. Nevertheless, as First Deputy Chairman O. Shchepin announced at the meeting referred to above, "the current level of health care [in the Soviet Union] cannot satisfy a Socialist society in its seventieth year of

76 "Zdorove–smolodu," *Trud*, 3 July, 1985. Chazov has headed the Fourth Department of the Ministry of Health—the department responsible for providing medical services to the Soviet administrative elite—since 1967. He replaced Sergei Petrovich Burenkov as minister of health in February 1987 (*Izvestia*, 18 Feb. 1987).

77 *SSSR v Tsifrakh v 1985 Godu* (Moscow, 1986), p. 217; *Narkhoz 84*, p. 459; G. S. Sarkisyan, *Narodnoe Blagosostoyanie v SSSR* (Moscow, 1983), p. 165.

78 "Sotsialnoe razvitie i ekonomicheskii rost," *Kommunist*, No. 14 (September), 1986, p. 60.

79 "Rastushchemu malyshu," *Sovetskaya Rossiya*, 13 Aug. 1986; "'Rastushchemu malyshu,'" *Sovetskaya Rossiya*, 4 Sept. 1986.

development."[80] Thanks to Gorbachov's policies, the shortcomings of the Soviet health system are increasingly coming out into the open. So far, however, willingness to discuss previously taboo problems has not been matched by concrete steps to correct them. Murray Feshbach recently estimated that the Soviet authorities will have to increase spending on health care at least five times over to bring the Soviet health system up to world standards.[81] They have not done so. Moreover, although in absolute terms the amount of money allocated to health care has been increasing (albeit modestly) in recent years, health care's share of the overall state budget has been shrinking: between 1975 and 1985, for example, it fell from 5·3 to 4·6 per cent.[82] In 1987, health care will receive 4·4 per cent of the state budget.[83] In short, talk about the need to improve Soviet health care has not yet been translated into meaningful action.

The Right To Material Security In Old Age

IN theory, the right to material security in old age in the Soviet Union is guaranteed by the pension system. Basically, there are three types of pension: old-age pensions; disability pensions; and pensions for the loss of a breadwinner. The latter two types of pension were introduced soon after the October Revolution; old-age pensions for blue-collar workers were introduced in 1928 and extended to white-collar workers in 1937. Collective-farm workers (*kolkhozniki*) were granted pension rights in 1964. The present-day pension system is based on legislation passed in 1956.[84]

Soviet spokesmen make much of the fact that the Soviet Union has the lowest retirement age for men in the developed world. Men can qualify for a full old-age pension at 60, provided they have 25 years of service behind them; women at 55, after 20 years of service. By way of comparison, the retirement age in the USA, UK, Canada, Netherlands, Spain and Finland is 65 years; in Denmark, 67.[85]

Old-age pensions represent a percentage of creditable pay—that is, the pay earned during the final year of service or the average pay of the best five years of the last 10 years of service. Old-age pension scales have been raised three times since 1956—in 1972, 1981 and 1985.[86] At present, the value of pension is 85 per cent for those earning up to 50 rubles a month; 75 per cent for those earning between 50 and 60 rubles a month; 65 per

[80] "Diagnoz samomu sebe," *Pravda*, 15 Feb. 1987.

[81] Murray Feshbach, "Recent Research on Soviet Health Conditions" (Paper presented to the National Association for Soviet and East European Studies, Cambridge University, UK, 23 March, 1986), p. 29.

[82] *Narkhoz 85*, p. 560.

[83] "O Gosudarstvennom byudzhete SSSR na 1987 god i ob ispolnenii byudzheta za 1985 god," *Pravda*, 18 Nov. 1986. p. 4.

[84] *Vedomosti Verkhovnogo Soveta SSSR*, No. 15, 1956, Article 313.

[85] "Sotsialnoe obespechenie i sotsialnoe strakhovanie v SSSR," *Vestnik Statistiki*, No. 9 (September), 1985, p. 68.

[86] "Sotsialno-ekonomicheskoe razvitie i sovershenstvovanie pensionnogo obespecheniya," *Sovetskoe Gosudarstvo i Pravo*, No. 11 (November), 1986, p. 22.

cent for those earning between 60 and 80 rubles a month; 55 per cent for those earning over 100 rubles a month.[87] The minimum old-age pension for blue- and white-collar workers is 50 rubles a month and the maximum is 120 rubles a month. The minimum old-age pension for collective-farm workers is 40 rubles a month.[88] There is no tax on pensions.

Pensioners now make up one-fifth of the total population of the Soviet Union. In 1985 there were 55,728,000 pensioners in the USSR; over 70 per cent of these were old-age pensioners.[89] The average pension in the Soviet Union in 1985 was just over 67 rubles a month.[90]

IN September 1986, the CPSU Politburo announced that it had decided to start drafting a new law on pensions, the aim being to improve living conditions for "veterans of labour" and to encourage "their more active participation in social production."[91] The drafting of the new legislation will take two years, during which time suggestions will be solicited from the public and discussed in the press.[92]

There are at least three problems involved in the current pension system. The first problem is that it does not take sufficient account of differences in length of service once the minimum has been met. It is not unusual for a worker with 45 years' service to receive the same pension as a worker with 25 years' service.[93] The second problem concerns calculation of pensions on the basis of pay during the final year of service. This leads to situations in which low-paid workers who manage to find a high-paying job in their last year before retirement end up receiving pensions that do not reflect their actual job performance.[94] The third problem has to do with pensioners who continue working:

> At present, some 10 million of a total of 56 million pensioners are employed in production but, for some of these, choosing to continue working entails major financial losses. The fact is that for certain categories of working pensioners there exists a so-called ceiling—a maximum income consisting of a combination of a pension and earnings—which, if exceeded, automatically leads to a reduction in the pension. Within the framework of this fairly complex ceiling system, employees of the government apparatus, for example, may not exceed a ceiling of 150 rubles a month, while for certain

[87] *Sobranie Postanovlenii Pravitelstva SSSR*, No. 17, 1972, Article 86, p. 337; *Sobranie Postanovlenii Pravitelstva SSSR*, No. 17, 1985, Article 81, p. 304.

[88] *Sobranie Postanovlenii Pravitelstva SSSR*, No. 17, 1985, Article 81, p. 303. The previous minimum pension for collective-farm workers was 28 rubles a month.

[89] *Narkhoz 85*, p. 452. By way of comparison: in 1949 there were four million pensioners in the Soviet Union; they accounted for two per cent of the total population ("Sotsialno-ekonomicheskoe razvitie i sovershenstvovanie pensionnogo obespecheniya," *Sovetskoe Gosudarstvo i Pravo*, No. 11 [November], 1986, p. 21).

[90] The state paid out 45 billion rubles in pensions in 1985 (*Narkhoz 85*, p. 412). Thus, (45,000,000,000/55,728,000)/12 = 67·29 rubles a month.

[91] "V Politburo TsK KPSS," *Pravda*, 12 Sept. 1986.

[92] *Argumenty i Fakty*, No. 39, 1986, p. 8.

[93] Ibid.

[94] Ibid.; "Sotsialno-ekonomicheskoe razvitie i sovershenstvovanie pensionnogo obespecheniya," *Sovetskoe Gosudarstvo i Pravo*, No. 11 (November), 1986, pp. 25–6.

categories of engineering and technical workers, who retain the right to 50 per cent of their pension if they continue working after retirement age, the ceiling is 300 rubles.[95]

Besides discouraging many able-bodied pensioners from continuing to work after retirement age, the pension ceiling has been criticized for violating the constitutional right to be paid in accordance with the quantity and quality of work.[96]

THE main problem with the current pension system, however, is that it does not guarantee material security in old age, for the simple reason that in many cases the pensions are too low to ensure a decent standard of living, even by Soviet standards. Consequently, many Soviet pensioners suffer from what official Soviet terminology calls 'underprovisioning" (*maloobespechennost*)—in other words, poverty.

The official "underprovisioning" level in the Soviet Union is 205·6 rubles a month for an urban family of four, or 51·4 rubles a month per person. This budget—its official name is "budget for minimum material security" (Russian abbreviation BMMO)—was worked out in the late 1950s and early 1960s by economists G. S. Sarkisyan and N. P. Kuznetsova.[97] It was written into law in 1974.[98]

Clearly the Sarkisyan–Kuznetsova budget is long out of date and needs upward revision, but by how much? One Soviet source argues that the "underprovisioning" threshold rises by approximately 25 per cent every five years.[99] Taking 1974 as a starting point, this would mean that the poverty level in the Soviet Union now stands at around 80 rubles a month per person. Another source studies the question in regional terms, claiming that the poverty level ranges from 50 rubles a month in the southern republics to 90 rubles a month on the island of Sakhalin.[100] The propaganda weekly *Argumenty i Fakty* states that "according to expert calculations, the budget for minimum material security now stands, on average, at around 75 rubles a month per person."[101] Professor Mervyn Matthews prefers the figure of 70 rubles a month, which he derives from the "prospective" poverty budget for the mid-1970s as forecast by

[95] RL 387/86, "New Law on Pensions Being Drafted in the Soviet Union," 10 Oct. 1986, p. 2.

[96] "Chto volnuyet veterana," *Trud*, 27 April, 1986; see also "Zarabotok bez potolka?" *Trud*, 23 March, 1986.

[97] G. S. Sarkisyan and N. P. Kuznetsova, *Potrebnosti i Dokhod Semi* (Moscow, 1967), pp. 56 and 66.

[98] *Sobranie Postanovlenii Pravitelstva SSSR*, No. 21, 1974, Article 121. This legislation concerns "underprovisioned" families.

[99] *Sotsialnye Problemy v Perspektivnom Planirovanii* (Moscow, 1982), p. 159; cited by V. Z. Rogovin in "Sotsialnaya spravedlivost i sotsialisticheskoe raspredelenie zhiznennykh blag," *Voprosy Filosofii*, No. 9 (September), 1986, pp. 16–17.

[100] "Sovremennyi podkhod k probleme maloobespechennosti," *Sotsialisticheskii Trud*, No. 10 (October), 1986, p. 22. I am indebted to my colleague Mr Sergei Voronitsyn for this reference.

[101] *Argumenty i Fakty*, No. 51, 1986, p. 8.

Sarkisyan and Kuznetsova in the mid-1960s.[102] This is a reasonable figure, especially since it is the same as the current (1987) minimum wage in the Soviet Union.

As the minimum old-age pension in the Soviet Union is 50 rubles a month (40 for collective-farm workers), and the average pension in 1985 was just over 67 rubles a month, it seems likely that many pensioners—it is impossible to say exactly how many, but the number certainly runs into the millions—live under, at or near Professor Matthews' poverty threshold of 70 rubles a month.

This assumption was indirectly confirmed by recent legislation on pensions. In May 1985, the CPSU Central Committee, USSR Council of Ministers, and All-Union Central Council of Trade Unions ordered that pensions of up to 60 rubles a month, assigned more than 10 years ago, were to be raised to the level of pensions currently paid to workers in similar fields and with similar qualifications.[103] The new law, which went into effect on 1 November 1985, raised the pensions of 6·2 million collective-farm workers and 7·5 million blue- and white-collar workers,[104] providing evidence that until quite recently there were at least 13·7 million pensioners in the Soviet Union living on pensions of considerably less than 70 rubles a month. Since the Soviet authorities do not publish information on income distribution, it is impossible to say how many pensioners still receive pensions of less than 70 rubles.

The May 1985 legislation was a step in the right direction, but it did not go far enough. Sarkisyan has written that, in order to prevent a sharp drop in living standards after retirement, pensions should amount to 75 per cent of a worker's pay.[105] According, however, to the pension scale given above only those workers earning between 50 and 60 rubles a month—i.e. less than the current minimum wage—are entitled to pensions amounting to 75 per cent of their pay. We can assume that the overwhelming majority of Soviet workers earn more than 80 rubles a month, and so fall automatically into the 55 and 50 per cent pension brackets.[106]

The problem of "underprovisioning" is aggravated by the lack of support services for elderly people, especially those who live alone. This is a substantial group; at present, approximately 15 million—i.e. around 27 per cent—of the almost 56 million pensioners in the Soviet Union live alone.[107] Soviet officials admit that there are not enough old-age homes

[102] Mervyn Matthews, *Poverty and Paterns of Deprivation in the Soviet Union*, Berkeley-Duke Occasional Papers on the Second Economy in the USSR, Paper No. 6, June 1986, pp. 3–4. See also Mervyn Matthews, "Poverty in the Soviet Union," *The Wilson Quarterly*, Autumn 1985, p. 76.

[103] *Sobranie Postanovlenii Pravitelstva SSSR*, No. 17, 1985, Article 80.

[104] "Povyshenie razmera pensii," *Trud*, 16 Oct. 1985.

[105] G. S. Sarkisyan, *Narodnoe Blagosostoyanie v SSSR* (Moscow, 1983), p. 134.

[106] The average cash wage in the Soviet Union in 1985 was 190 rubles a month (*Narkhoz 85*, p. 413).

[107] "Starost–v radost," *Sovetskaya Kultura*, 2 Sept. 1986.

to accommodate all these people.[108] In order to improve living conditions for single pensioners, some republics—most notably Estonia—have begun organizing systematic visits by nurses to provide a variety of home services.[109] So far, however, attempts to extend this system throughout the Soviet Union have been thwarted by bureaucratic indifference and inertia.[110]

In an interview that appeared in late 1985 in the youth newspaper *Komsomolskaya Pravda*, Vladimir Posner, a well-known Soviet radio and television commentator, said that "a society should be judged not by how it treats its most prosperous members but by how it cares for the weakest and most defenceless, and in this respect the United States cannot stand up to criticism."[111] Nor, it would appear, can the Soviet Union. The pension system, which is the main instrument for ensuring material security in old age in the USSR, is no longer capable of fulfilling this function, and needs to be overhauled. Shatalin emphasized the urgency of the task:

> Especially pressing is the implementation of a complex reform of the pension system. As is well known, the last reform was carried out in 1956, and the system it introduced has in many respects become obsolete. The economic situation of pensioners is constantly worsening in comparison to that of the working population. When one takes into account the real rise in retail prices over the last 25–30 years, then one can say that their [pensioners'] standard of living has declined even in absolute terms.[112]

The CPSU Politburo has decided to carry out a complex reform of the pension system. This reform, however, will take up to two years to implement. In the meantime, the standard of living of millions of Soviet pensioners, already low, will continue to decline.

The Right To Housing

THE Soviet Union spends considerable resources on housing construction. According to official statistics, approximately two million flats are built in the USSR every year, enabling 10 million Soviet citizens to "improve their living conditions" by moving into new flats or by expanding their living space in existing buildings.[113] Soviet flats have grown in size, from an average 42·3 square metres in 1960 to 56·4 square metres in 1985.[114] Average *per capita* living space for Soviet city dwellers rose from 8·9 to 14·4 square metres in the same period.[115] Rents

108 "Sluzhba miloserdiya," *Trud*, 31 Aug. 1986.
109 "Kak vashe samochuvstvie?" *Sovetskaya Kultura*, 30 Aug. 1986.
110 "Kto skrasit odinochestvo?" *Sovetskaya Rossiya*, 15 Aug. 1986.
111 As reported in the *New York Times*, 30 Dec. 1985.
112 "Sotsialnoe razvitie i ekonomichesky rost," *Kommunist*, No. 14 (September), 1986, p. 69.
113 *Narkhoz 85*, pp. 422, 424.
114 *SSSR v Tsifrakh v 1985 Godu*, p. 207.
115 Ibid. p. 209; 1960 average given in "Sotsialnaya programma Partii v deistvii," *Vestnik Statistiki*, No. 11, 1985, p. 5.

for state housing in the USSR have remained unchanged since 1928, accounting for an average three per cent of a Soviet family's budget in 1985, as opposed to 20–30 per cent in the United States and the United Kingdom.[116]

The Soviet Union continues to suffer, nevertheless, from an acute housing shortage. The Party Programme of 1961 promised, among other things, that within 20 years every Soviet family, "including newly-weds," would have a fully furnished flat of its own.[117] This promise was not kept. At present, about 20 per cent of the urban population in the USSR—approximately 36 million people—lives in communal flats (that is, flats with shared kitchens and bathroom facilities), dormitories, or rented rooms.[118] This figure includes an estimated 9·4 million families.

The social and economic consequences of the housing shortage in the Soviet Union are severe. It is largely responsible for the unacceptably high (by Soviet standards) rate of labour turnover, the lowering of the birth rate, and the rise in the number of divorces, especially among young families, for example.[119]

The leadership is well aware of these facts. The new Party Programme, adopted at the 27th Congress of the CPSU in February 1986, promises to provide "practically" every Soviet family with a flat or house of its own by the year 2000.[120]

If the Party is to keep this promise, it will have to deal with three serious problems. First, although capital investment in housing construction has risen steadily in absolute terms since the late 1950s, the share of all capital investment devoted to housing has declined—from 23·5 per cent in the Sixth Five-Year Plan (1956–1960) to 15·1 per cent in the Eleventh Five-Year Plan (1981–1985).[121] Second, the construction of new flats has been slowing down since the mid-1960s: during the Seventh Five-Year Plan (1961–1965), 11,551,000 flats were built in the USSR; during the Eleventh Five-Plan (1981–1985), 10,028,000.[122] Finally, the construction of new flats lags behind the rate at which couples marry and start families: between 1980 and 1985, the number of marriages in the Soviet Union exceeded the number of new flats by more than four million.

116 *SSSR v Tsifrakh v 1985 Godu*, p. 208.

117 *Pravda*, 30 July 1961, p. 7.

118 "At present, over 80 per cent of the urban population lives in separate flats" (*Narkhoz 85*, p. 425). This means that up to 20 per cent does not. In 1985, the urban population of the USSR was 180·1 million people. Thus, 180,100,000 × 0·2 = 36,020,000. According to Moscow Party chief Boris Yeltsin, there are 2·5 million people in need of better housing in Moscow; one million of these are living in communal flats, and 28,000 live in extremely dilapidated buildings (AS 5721, p. 1).

119 "Dom uzhe postroen . . .," *Sotsiologicheskie Issledovaniya*, No. 1, 1985, p. 50. In 1983, only 37·2 per cent of the marriages between "young" people lasted as long as four years, and only 29·4 per cent lasted as long as nine years ("Molodaya semya—neprostoe, no vazhneishee delo," *Moskovskaya Pravda*, 6 July, 1986).

120 "Programma Kommunisticheskoi Partii Sovetskogo Soyuza," *Kommunist*, No. 4 (March), 1986, p. 125.

121 "Vo imya cheloveka," *Pravda*, 22 July, 1986.

122 *Narkhoz 85*, p. 422.

Flats and Marriages, USSR, 1980–85[123]

Year	Flats	Marriages
1980	2,004,000	2,724,600
1981	1,997,000	2,788,100
1982	2,002,000	2,769,200
1983	2,030,000	2,834,800
1984	2,008,000	2,634,100
1985	1,991,000	2,717,800
Total	12,032,000	16,468,600

ONE way to bring about a swifter solution to the housing problem would be to expand the cooperative and individual sectors.[124] This approach seems to be favoured by Gorbachov, who, in his report to the 27th Congress of the CPSU in February 1986, stressed the need to "encourage in every way the construction of cooperative and individual housing."[125] Not only would this relieve pressure on the state, it would also soak up some of the Soviet population's excess purchasing power, which has almost nowhere to go except into the bank, under the mattress, or into the pockets of black marketeers.[126] A recent article in *Literaturnaya Gazeta* proclaimed that cooperative housing will account for over 30 per cent of all housing construction in the USSR by the Fourteenth Five-Year Plan (1995–2000).[127]

This will require a considerable reversal of current trends. Since the mid-1960s the cooperative and individual house-building sectors have been shrinking, not expanding. During the Eighth Five-Year Plan (1966–1970), cooperative housing construction accounted for a modest 6·5 per cent of all housing construction; in the first four years of the Eleventh Five-Year Plan (1981–1984), this share dropped to 5·7 per cent.[128] The drop in individual house-building in the same period was even more striking: from 29·7 per cent of all housing construction in 1966–1970 to 14·5 per cent in 1981–1984.[129]

As one Western specialist has remarked, "it is difficult to account for

[123] *Narkhoz 85*, p. 422; *Vestnik Statistiki*, No. 11, 1986, p. 73; *Vestnik Statistiki*, No. 11, 1985, p. 77; *Vestnik Statistiki*, No. 11, 1984, p. 78; *Vestnik Statistiki*, No. 12, 1983, p. 51; *Vestnik Statistiki*, No. 11, 1982, p. 66; *Vestnik Statistiki*, No. 11, 1981, p. 70.

[124] There are, roughly speaking, three housing sectors in the Soviet Union: state, cooperative, and individual (private). The state sector is by far the largest, accounting for over 79 per cent of all housing construction in the Eleventh Five-Year Plan (derived from *Narkhoz 85*, p. 420).

[125] "Politicheskii doklad Tsentralnogo Komiteta KPSS XXVII Sezdu Kommunisticheskoi Partii Sovetskogo Soiuza," *Kommunist*, No. 4 (March), 1986, p. 41.

[126] According to one Soviet estimate, involuntary savings accounted for 50 per cent of all savings bank deposits in 1980 (*EKO*, No. 2, 1982, p. 82).

[127] "Kazhdoi seme—otdelnuyu kvartiru," *Literaturnaya Gazeta*, 24 Sept. 1986, p. 10.

[128] "Tsena novoselya," *Sovetskaya Kultura*, 20 March, 1986.

[129] Ibid.

the singular lack of success in this sector [cooperative house-building] as a whole, for it is quite clear that cooperatives have not developed as rapidly as the state has intended."[130] The high cost of cooperative and private housing is an obstacle. A typical two- or three-room cooperative flat in the USSR costs between 10,000 and 15,000 rubles.[131] A downpayment of 30 per cent of this sum is required before construction can start (in certain regions—e.g. Siberia, the Far East, and the Far North—the downpayment need be only 20 per cent).[132] This means that a would-be cooperative member must find between 2,000 and 4,500 rubles in cash. This is simply out of the question for many people in a country where the average cash wage in 1985 was 190 rubles a month.[133] Private housing is even more expensive: according to the Soviet trade-union newspaper *Trud*, a three-room brick house in the city costs between 25,000 and 30,000 rubles.[134]

But the main obstacle is not the high cost of cooperative and individual construction, but bureaucratic foot-dragging. In September 1985, the supply of cooperative housing in the USSR was at least 10 years behind the demand for such housing.[135] Clearly, there are people who have the money to buy a cooperative flat. The problem is that not enough cooperative flats are being built, especially in the cities, for the simple reason that neither the city soviets nor the city building organizations are interested in building more cooperative housing. Municipal officials are concerned above all with making sure that those who have been waiting in the housing queue get flats as soon as possible, and, as *Pravda* pointed out,

> the construction of cooperative blocks of flats does nothing to satisfy this goal, because for obvious reasons [that is, the fact that cooperative housing belongs to the members of the cooperative, not to the city] the local soviet of people's deputies does not get a single flat.[136]

For their part, building organizations are entitled to 10 per cent of the living space in every state-financed block of flats they construct—a perk that enables them to attract and to retain workers. In the case of privately financed—i.e. cooperative—blocks of flats, however, they must forgo this privilege. So naturally builders build state housing first, and cooperative housing when they can get around to it. Finally, cooperative members

130 Gregory D. Andrusz, *Housing and Urban Development in the USSR* (Macmillan, London, 1984), p. 95.

131 "Kvartira po sberknizhke," *Sovetskaya Rossiya*, 29 June, 1986.

132 *Sobranie Postanovlenii Pravitelstva SSSR*, No. 23, 1982, Article 120.

133 *Narkhoz 85*, p. 413.

134 "Dom dlya gorozhanina," *Trud*, 17 Sept. 1985.

135 "Stroit kooperativ," *Pravda*, 30 Sept. 1985. At the time this article appeared, there were more than 1·3 million applications for cooperative flats on file in the USSR; at most, 130,000 cooperative flats were being built each year. According to a more recent article, there were 1·6 million applications on file at the beginning of 1986 ("Zavtrashnii den gorodov i sel," *Izvestia*, 12 Nov. 1986).

136 Ibid.

tend to be more demanding about quality than those who must take what the state provides, and this sometimes interferes with the payment of cash bonuses which builders receive for furnishing a building on time and in good shape. In short, municipal officials and builders regard cooperative housing as an additional burden.

Several suggestions for solving these problems have been put forward. The most interesting and, perhaps, the most promising is to wait until a large housing complex (*mikroraion*) is finished before selling individual blocks of flats to a cooperative.[137] Thus the builders, unable to discriminate between state and cooperative housing, will have only one goal—to finish the whole complex on time and without defects. This tactic was supposed to be introduced in 15 to 20 large cities in 1986, but whether it actually has been is not known.

Similarly, the decline of the individual housing sector has been due largely to the reluctance of enterprise and trade-union officials to help workers to take advantage of the few state credits available for that purpose.[138] Moreover, in May 1986 the state passed legislation aimed at stamping out "nonlabour incomes" (*netrudovye dokhody*), requiring all those building private homes or *dachas* worth more than 20,000 rubles to disclose their source of income to the authorities.[139] This will probably only hasten the decline of the individual housing sector.

THE housing shortage in the Soviet Union is especially severe among newly-wed couples and other young people, for two main reasons. First, as was noted above, the number of marriages each year in the USSR regularly exceeds the number of new flats built. This means that newly-weds must live for years with their parents or (sometimes illegally) in dormitories before they can get a flat of their own.[140] Second, housing is often allocated on the basis of job seniority, which puts young people at an automatic disadvantage. Housing is the most pressing social problem amongst young people in the Soviet Union.[141]

In response to this problem, the state has started to sponsor the construction of young people's residential complexes, or MZhKs (*molodezhnyi zhiloi kompleks*). These are cooperative-style housing complexes built by young people themselves, with material and financial assistance from the factories or enterprises where they work. There are three main differences between normal cooperatives and MZhKs. First, membership in an MZhK is limited to people between the ages of 18 and 30. Second, MZhK members must undergo a competitive selection process, in which such factors as job performance and participation in

[137] Ibid. See also "Kvartira po sberknizhke," *Sovetskaya Rossiya*, 29 June, 1986; and "Khochu kupit kvartiru," *Sovetskaya Rossiya*, 12 Oct. 1986.

[138] "Dom dlya gorozhanina," *Trud*, 17 Sept. 1985.

[139] "O merakh po usileniyu borby s netrudovymi dokhodami," *Pravda*, 28 May, 1986.

[140] See, for example, "Na svidanie . . . k zhene," *Trud*, 21 July, 1985; and "Vozrast lyubvi," *Komsomolskaya Pravda*, 6 Oct. 1985.

[141] "Chto zabotit i volnuyet molodezh," *Argumenty i Fakty*, No. 1, 1987, pp. 2–3.

"social work" are weighed in the overall assessment. Finally, MZhK members contribute labour, not money, to the construction of their flats. The first MZhK was built in Kaliningrad, a suburb of Moscow, in the mid-1970s; others were built soon after in Sverdlovsk, Perm, and Kazan. Thanks, perhaps, to pressure from influential supporters (among them the economist Abel Aganbegyan[142]), the MZhK achieved official recognition in July 1985, when the USSR Council of Ministers passed a resolution requiring ministries, enterprises, and councils of ministers at the Union republican level to allocate money and materials for the construction of MZhKs beginning in 1986.[143] The response was swift: by the time Gorbachov lent his support to the idea in his speech to the 27th CPSU Congress, there were 70 MZhKs under construction in 50 cities across the country.[144] At present, there are more than 150 MZhKs in various stages of construction.[145]

From the state's point of view, there are three main advantages to be derived from the MZhK programme. First, it will speed up the process of urban renewal in the USSR; an article in *Komsomolskaya Pravda* revealed that in 1985 over 20 per cent of the housing stock in the Soviet Union was in need of reconstruction and suggested following the example of East Germany, where young people are allowed to renovate dilapidated buildings for their own use.[146] Second, it will strengthen young families and encourage women to have more children.[147] Third, since admission to an MZhK is competitive, the programme will encourage young people to work harder, stay at the same job longer (the problem of labour turnover is especially severe among people under 30), and take a more active part in the collective. In short, the MZhK offers young people a tangible incentive to behave the way the state wants them to behave. Most young people, however, seem to view the MZhK primarily as a way to get a flat of their own without having to wait for years in the state housing queue.[148]

142 "Molodezhnyi zhiloi kompleks—segodnya i zavtra," *EKO*, No. 1, 1985, pp. 67–93.

143 *Sobranie Postanovlenii Pravitelstva SSSR*, No. 22, 1985, Article 111. This legislation was supplemented in June 1986; see *Sobranie Postanovlenii Pravitelstva SSSR*, No. 25, 1986, Article 142.

144 "Molodezhi—zabotu i vnimanie," *Trud*, 1 Feb. 1986.

145 "Zavtrashnii den gorodov i sel," *Izvestia*, 12 Nov. 1986.

146 "Dom, kotoryi postroish sam," *Komsomolskaya Pravda*, 7 July, 1985. The practice of letting young people renovate old buildings for their own use has caught on in Riga: see "Peremeny v sudbe starogo doma," *Izvestia*, 30 Sept. 1985; "Novyi vzglyad na starye steny," *Pravda*, 17 July 1986; and "Dom svoimi rukami," *Izvestia*, 12 Aug. 1986.

147 In the MZhK in Sverdlovsk, the coefficient of fertility—that is, the number of children per family—rose from 1·3 to 1·6 between 1982 and 1985 ("Dom uzhe postroen . . .," *Sotsiologicheskie Issledovaniya*, No. 1, 1985, p. 54). In general, however, the connection between housing conditions and the birthrate is ambiguous. See Andrusz, op. cit. pp. 141–2.

148 In a poll taken in Sverdlovsk, 62·5 per cent of the applicants to an MZhK said that the main reason for their entering the competition was the prospect of getting a flat ("Gruppovoi portret s domom," *Izvestia*, 9 July, 1985).

ANOTHER new approach to a faster solution to the housing problem was unveiled several months after the 27th Party Congress. On 5 July 1986, Stepan Alekseevich Shalaev, chairman of the All-Union Central Council of Trade Unions, announced that the workers of the Gorky Automobile Factory (GAZ) had pledged to provide every factory worker's family with a separate flat by 1995, five years before the deadline for the country as a whole.[149]

In some ways, the GAZ initiative resembles the Belorussian railway experiment. Both are based on the idea of increasing discretionary funds by rationalizing production and raising output. But whereas the railways spent the funds saved on higher wages, the GAZ workers are putting their extra money into building more housing. Between now and 1995, they plan to build 40,000 flats with an overall space of two million square metres. This means that they will have to build 200,000 square metres of housing each year. In the first six months of 1986, they built 70,000 square metres.[150]

According to Shalaev, the GAZ initiative has been adopted by scores of enterprises around the country.[151] It was formally approved by the CPSU Politburo in September 1986.[152]

THE shortage of housing in the Soviet Union is worsened by shoddy construction. In an early short story by Vladimir Voinovich, a Soviet housing official and his secretary are shown drafting the documentation for a newly built block of flats:

> "Ready yet?" he asked.
>
> "In a minute," answered Lyusya. "Should we type in the rating now or will you write it in after?"
>
> "Let's do it right now," said Drobotun. "So it won't have to be handwritten. Put 'Building accepted with the rating of good.'"
>
> "But what if the building was excellent?" asked Lyusya.
>
> "Impossible," said Drobotun. "Rastrelli or Rossi, they used to build excellent. Now the best they can do is good."[153]

That was in 1963. Today, Drobotun might add: "The best they can do is good—half the time." A conference of builders, planners and architects in Suzdal in July 1985 revealed that only 50 per cent of all new housing in the RSFSR receives the rating "good".[154]

[149] "Vazhnyi etap v zhizni profsoyuzov," *Trud*, 5 July, 1986.

[150] "Kvartiru kazhdoi seme," *Izvestia*, 21 Sept. 1986. Part of the housing is being built in the form of a young people's residential complex; see "Stroim doma i sebya," *Sovetskaya Rossiya*, 3 Oct. 1986.

[151] For example, at the Taganrog Metallurgical Factory ("Novoselya s garantiei," *Izvestia*, 13 Oct. 1986).

[152] "V Politburo TsK KPSS," *Pravda*, 12 Sept. 1986.

[153] "Khochu byt chestnym," *Novy Mir*, No. 2 (February), 1963, pp. 178–9. The quotation has been taken from Richard Lourie's translation of this story *In Plain Russian*, (Farrar, Strauss and Giroux, New York, 1979), pp. 60–61.

[154] *Radio Moscow-1* 18 July, 1985.

Alongside queues and drunkenness, shoddy housing construction is one of the most infamous aspects of Soviet life. Newspapers are filled with complaints about floors that ripple, walls that buckle, doors that refuse to shut, railings that come away in the hand, etc.[155] According to *Trud*, it costs the state 500 million rubles a year to correct these defects (*nedodelki*).[156] What it costs ordinary Soviet citizens nobody knows, although one worker in Ryazan estimated that it would cost him between 800 and 900 rubles to make his new flat habitable.[157]

What is known, however, is that a large proportion of all housing repairs in the Soviet Union is performed on the side, by moonlighters. According to *Izvestia*, moonlighters are responsible for 45 per cent of all flat repairs in the city and up to 80 per cent in the countryside.[158] The reason for this is simple: the state repair services are slow, inefficient, and likely to leave a flat in even worse shape than before. *Pravda* recently remarked that roof-patching brigades in Smolensk seem to work according to the motto "After us, the deluge."[159]

The shoddy quality of Soviet housing is the natural result of the endemic Soviet practice of rushing to reach targets laid down in the plan irrespective of quality. This point was made by Denis Chetyrkin, head of the technical division of Stroibank, which is responsible for overseeing the quality of housing construction:

> In my view, material incentives for high-quality work are poorly developed in our country. Just look at how builders get their bonus. Basically, they get it for turning over the building on time, regardless of what kind of rating the state commission gives it. The only difference is that you get a bigger bonus for a rating of "excellent" than for one of "satisfactory". That's why builders rush to turn the house over on time, whether it's ready or not.[160]

Chetyrkin suggested following the example of Bulgaria, where builders and inspecting officials are fined four times the amount needed to correct defects if the repairs are not completed within a strict time limit. Although such a drastic step does not seem to be in the offing for the Soviet Union, *Pravda* did report that the managers responsible for the poor work of the roofing teams in Smolensk were fined the equivalent of three months' pay.[161]

Besides adding to the miseries suffered by ordinary Soviet citizens, shoddy construction breeds corruption, sometimes in very high places. In July 1985, *Sovetskaya Rossiya* published the first of a series of articles describing how unfinished blocks of flats in Moscow were pronounced fit

155 For a frank discussion of this problem, see "Dom sdan i . . . dostraivaetsya," *Izvestia*, 29 June, 1985.
156 "Krivaya stena," *Trud*, 6 Aug. 1983.
157 Ibid.
158 "I drugie zainteresovannye litsa," *Izvestia*, 19 Aug. 1985.
159 "Dyrka na frake," *Pravda*, 11 Sept. 1986.
160 "Dom sdan i . . . dostraivaetsya," *Izvestia*, 29 June, 1985.
161 "'Dyrka na frake,'" *Pravda*, 23 Nov. 1986.

for habitation by local authorities anxious to fulfil the housing plan.[162] The ensuing scandal led to the retirement of Viktor Grishin, First Secretary of the Moscow City Party Committee, and Vladimir Promyslov, Chairman of the Executive Committee of the Moscow Soviet, in December 1985 and January 1986 respectively.[163]

ACCORDING to Soviet spokesmen, homelessness, like unemployment and (until recently) prostitution, does not exist in the USSR. TASS in English recently proclaimed, "there are no homeless people in this country."[164]

There *are* homeless people in the Soviet Union. They are called *bomzhi* (from the Russian term for "of no fixed residence") or, more simply, *brodyagi* ("tramps"). Most of them are alcoholics. They usually fall into the category of "parasites," or people who do not work. *Sovetskaya Rossiya* recently described the inmates of a detention centre for such people in Moscow:

> Bulygin still had something approaching a normal human appearance, but to look at his neighbour, N. A. Moiseev, was, frankly speaking, creepy: the man looked like a caveman. And no wonder, because it's hard to stay respectable-looking when you sleep in abandoned cellars and coal-bunkers.[165]

The problem is not confined to Moscow. In July 1986, an Estonian-language regional newspaper described derelicts living in "the cellars, courtyards, and nooks" of Tallinn.[166] Shortly before that, in May, *Literaturnaya Gazeta* published an article about *bomzhi* living in a run-down village in the Semirech'e region of Kazakhstan.[167] The author of the article, writer Anatolii Sterlikov, made it clear that this was not just a local phenomenon:

> It wouldn't be right to think that the village in the steppes where I grew up . . . is the only place that harbours people characterized by the militia abbreviation *bomzh*—person with no fixed residence. You can meet them in other towns and villages in my native Semireche. I've seen *bomzhi* in the northern port cities, and in the settlements of Tyumen oblast.

No official estimates of the number of homeless people in the Soviet

[162] "Net prava na isklyucheniya," *Sovetskaya Rossiya*, 21 July 1985. This was followed by: "'Net prava na isklyucheniya'" (Promyslov's reply), 18 Aug. 1985; "Po trebovaniyu kommunistov," 8 Sept. 1985; "Zakon odinakov dlya vsekh" and "'Net prava na isklyucheniya'" (Grishin's reply), 20 Oct. 1985.

[163] "Plenum MGK KPSS," *Pravda*, 25 Dec. 1985; "Sessiya Mossoveta," *Izvestia*, 5 Jan. 1986. Grishin was succeeded by Boris Yeltsin; Promyslov, by V. T. Saikin, whose previous position was general director of one of Moscow's largest enterprises, the I. A. Likhachev Automobile Factory.

[164] *TASS*, 12 Oct. 1986.

[165] "Skolko nyanek u tuneyadtsa?," *Sovetskaya Rossiya*, 7 May, 1986.

[166] Baltic Situation Report (SR) 6/86, Radio Free Europe Research (*RFER*), 25 Sept. 1986, item 2.

[167] "Bezhal brodyaga . . .," *Literaturnaya Gazeta*, 28 May, 1986, p. 12.

Union have been made public. All that can be said is that they exist and that they are beginning to be noticed. As Sterlikov put it, "they have already begun to stand out against the background of contemporary life."

Soviet spokesmen are fond of repeating Friedrich Engels' observation that the way in which a country meets its citizens' housing needs "can serve as a standard for judging how well other needs are being satisfied."[168] They would do well to ponder the implications of this remark for the Soviet Union. It cannot be denied that housing conditions in the Soviet Union have improved greatly since the mid-1950s. According to Yegor Ligachov, Secretary of the Central Committee of the CPSU, 240 million people—that is, over 85 per cent of the total Soviet population—live in housing built within the last 30 years.[169] Nevertheless, the housing problem remains severe, since the state has failed to allocate sufficient resources to solve it. Nor has it succeeded in enlisting the financial resources of the population by expanding the cooperative and individual housing sectors. In short, the housing situation continues to undermine official attempts to invoke the right to housing as proof of the material well-being of the Soviet people.

"The Human Factor"

GORBACHOV revealed the broad outlines of his social policy at the 27th CPSU Congress in February 1986. Speaker after speaker alluded to the promises contained in the new Party Programme: a flat or house for every Soviet family by the year 2000, better housing construction, higher wages and pensions, better food and medical care, more maternity homes and nursery schools, more paid maternity leave, and so on.

But none of the speakers tackled the underlying questions: Why, 40 years after the end of the "Great Patriotic War," is there still a housing shortage in the Soviet Union? Why aren't there enough maternity homes and nursery schools? Why is the health system so poor? Why is there a shortage of medicines and medical supplies? Why isn't there enough meat, milk, fruit and vegetables to ensure an adequate diet for every Soviet citizen? Why are there still areas of poverty? Why, in short, are living standards in the Soviet Union so low?

An indirect answer to these questions is given in the speech of Stepan Alekseevich Shalaev, Chairman of the All-Union Central Council of Trade Unions.[170] Shalaev began by discussing working conditions and safety at work. Since the Soviet Union, unlike the United States, the United Kingdom, East and West Germany, and other developed

[168] In *Die Lage der arbeitenden Klasse in England* (1845); Russian translation in K. Marx and F. Engels, *Sochineniya* (Moscow, 1955), Vol. 2, p. 302. See G. S. Sarkisyan, *Narodnoe blagosostoyanie v SSSR* (Moscow, 1983), p. 178; and "Vo imya cheloveka," *Pravda*, 22 July, 1986.

[169] "Kursom Oktyabrya, V Dukhe Revolyutsionnogo Tvorchestva," *Pravda*, 7 Nov. 1986, p. 2.

[170] *Trud*, 2 March 1986.

countries, does not publish statistics on work-related accidents and injuries, it is difficult for observers to determine how serious the problem is. Shalaev provided no hard data, but he made it clear that the problem is serious and that it is not being resolved. "Dissatisfaction with working conditions," he said,

> is now one of the main reasons for labour turnover. Many factories and work sites are slow in eliminating heavy manual labour, there is no effort to get rid of fumes and other health hazards, in many cases there is nowhere to change, take a shower or have lunch, there are no medical or general services on the premises, there are no recreational facilities.

Conditions are especially bad in the energy and chemical machine-building sector, where "tens of thousands of workers . . . continue to work amidst elevated fume levels, noise, vibration, and other unfavourable factors." The reason for this state of affairs, said Shalaev, is that "the question of providing all workers with normal, healthy working conditions does not receive the attention it deserves," even at the planning stage.

The situation is much the same in housing. Despite great progress, providing people with decent housing is still a severe problem, "especially in newly developed regions and industrial centres." Shalaev suggested that ministries and government departments should build more housing for their workers. He admitted, however, that for some ministries and departments "the interest in output, and the concern for people, for their working conditions and daily life, are not equally strong."

It is clear from such statements that the Communist Party of the Soviet Union, which constantly congratulates itself on its concern for working people, produces and promotes officials who simply cannot be bothered with trying to convert rhetoric into reality. To some extent, this is one of the legacies of Stalinism. As Alec Nove has remarked, the Stalinist system produced men who "were remarkably indifferent to the welfare of the masses":

> Petty officials, managers, army officers, disregarded the most elementary needs of their subordinates to a degree almost past belief, in a country supposedly under working-class dictatorship. The obverse of this is, of course, petty (and not so petty) privileges for the *nachalstvo* (bosses). One cannot document this, but no one who knows Russia, or reads the more realistic novels, can fail to know it is so.[171]

According to Valentin Tolstykh, a Doctor of Philosophical Sciences, the legacy of indifference is still strong:

[171] Alec Nove, *An Economic History of the USSR* (Pelican Books, 1982), p. 388. The existence of privileges for the administrative elite was officially acknowledged for the first time in February 1986, just before the 27th Congress of the CPSU ("Ochishchenie," *Pravda*, 13 Feb. 1986).

> As long as it's a matter of words, they [Soviet managers] are all for the slogan "everything for man," they're for it with all their heart, as we say. Alas, this formula has not become a *principle* for them, a guide to action in their daily economic policy and activity. Here is the root cause of the practice of fulfilling the plan at any price, of neglecting the living and working conditions of the people who represent the main productive force of society.[172]

It is reasonable to assume that the neglect of living and working conditions has exacerbated the problem of low labour productivity in the Soviet Union. According to official Soviet estimates, the productivity of industrial workers in the Soviet Union is only 55 per cent of that of industrial workers in the United States, while agricultural workers are only a quarter as productive.[173] Non-Soviet estimates tell an even less flattering tale.

Gorbachov appears to be determined to change all this. As part of his strategy for the "restructuring" of Soviet society, he has adopted a socio-economic concept that first became current in the Soviet Union in the late 1970s and early 1980s—the human factor.

THE essence of the human factor is the common-sensical recognition that economic performance depends on the morale, training and motivation of the workforce; that well fed, well housed, well trained and above all well motivated workers are more productive than poorly fed, poorly housed, poorly trained and poorly motivated workers. Academician Tatyana Zaslavskaya argued as early as 1980 that the importance of the human factor would grow as the scientific-technological revolution—that is, the modernization of Soviet industry—got under way:

> Today, production is more sharply aware of the importance and complexity of the human factor. To an unprecedented degree, it is dependent on the qualities of the worker, who, on the one hand, is capable of using to great effect the colossal industrial apparatus it has created, but who, on the other hand, because of negligence or low qualifications, is also capable of causing serious damage to the economy.[174]

Elaborating more recently on the last point, Zaslavskaya attributed the accident at the Chernobyl nuclear power station to neglect of the human factor during the Brezhnev years.[175]

The urgent calls to "activate the human factor" that are now appearing in the pages of the Soviet press are a not-so-tacit admission that for many years the Party's social policy has been seriously flawed. They also

[172] "Sut dela, ili chego ne nado uproshchat," *Sovetskaya Kultura*, 16 Sept. 1986.

[173] *Narkhoz 85*, p. 581.

[174] "Ekonomicheskoe povedenie i ekonomicheskoe razvitie," *EKO*, No. 3, 1980, p. 17.

[175] "Chelovecheskii faktor razvitiya ekonomiki i sotsialnaya spravedlivost," *Kommunist*, No. 13 (September), 1986, p. 61.

represent a surrender of sorts to a hitherto despised capitalist concept. Until quite recently, Western theories of human relations were a favourite target of Soviet ideologists. The 1983 edition of a standard Soviet political lexicon defined "the doctrine of 'human relations'" in the following way:

> The doctrine of "human relations" is an apologistic bourgeois theory, developed within the framework of so-called industrial sociology, or labour sociology, and having as its main goal higher labour productivity and bigger profits for the capitalists by perfecting the system of labour organization, above all by influencing the consciousness and psychology of the workers. The doctrine of "human relations" attempts to establish the possibility of attaining a psychological and moral community within the entire production collective of a capitalist enterprise, from the owner and director to the lowliest worker, and of creating a system of "human relations" in which the worker will regard the interests of the enterprise as his own, will care about its profitability, will strive to raise labour productivity, and so forth.[176]

Apparently, raising labour productivity by influencing the consciousness and psychology of the workers is precisely what is meant by "activating the human factor" in the Soviet Union too. Soviet workers are being increasingly encouraged, and in some cases forced, to regard the interests of the enterprise as their own, to care about its profitability, to strive to raise labour productivity, etc. As for "so-called industrial sociology," this seems to have found a convert in Gorbachov, who stressed the connection between sociology and the human factor in production[177] in his speech to the All-Union Conference of Social Science departments in October 1986.

THE belated discovery of the importance of the human factor, first by Soviet economists and sociologists and then by the leadership, is almost certainly a result of disturbing trends in "the correlation of forces" (*sootnoshenie sil*) between socialism and capitalism. David Holloway has provided a succinct definition of this important concept:

> The "correlation of forces" is the term used in the Soviet Union to describe the power relationship between capitalism and socialism. It is a broader concept than the "balance of power," for it embraces not only military, but also political, economic and moral elements: it is not always clear, however, what weight is being given to the different elements in the relationship . . . The object of Soviet policy is to further the movement of the correlation of forces towards socialism, not to maintain a balance of power between socialism and capitalism.[178]

[176] *Nauchnyi Kommunizm: Slovar* (Moscow, 1983), p. 336.
[177] "Rech tovarishcha Gorbacheva M. S.," *Pravda*, 2 Oct. 1986.
[178] David Holloway, *The Soviet Union and the Arms Race* (Yale University Press, New Haven and London, 1983), p. 82.

Clearly, tilting the balance in the correlation of forces in favour of socialism has been hindered by social and economic stagnation in the Soviet Union. Hence the emphasis on social and economic "acceleration." But, as the new Party Programme states, acceleration depends on "increasing the role of the human factor":

> Socialist society cannot function effectively if it does not find new ways of developing the creative activity of the masses in all spheres of life. The more immense the historical goals are, the more important for their attainment is the economically interested, responsible, conscious and active participation of millions of people.[179]

The words "economically interested" are especially important, since they raise the crucial question of motivation. The Soviet leadership is now having to confront the fact that, more than 30 years after Stalin's death, the state has failed to create an effective economic system for getting people to work harder. This failure was conceded by Shatalin, who called for its immediate correction:

> Socialism has reached the point of having to resolve a fundamental, global historical problem—namely, the creation of a powerful, comprehensive motivational mechanism for the economically effective use of production resources; a mechanism stronger than the capitalist West has been able to create in the hundreds of years of its existence. Only on this basis can socialism realize its chief ultimate goal—the creation of the highest standard of living in the world, the guaranteeing of the truly many-sided and harmonious development of the personality, and [the establishment] of the socialist way of life as the most attractive in the world, the goal of social, economic, moral and ethical progress everywhere.[180]

One recent step towards the creation of a powerful motivational mechanism is the reform of the wage system, in which increases must be taken from enterprise profits.[181] But the problem of motivation cannot be solved by higher wages alone; more money is useless if there is nothing to spend it on. The activation of the human factor, on which Gorbachov's programme for the acceleration of social and economic development depends, is impossible without more and better consumer goods, more and better food, and more and better housing. In other words, it is impossible without a radical reform of the Soviet economy. Despite the failure of past attempts at reform in the Soviet Union, this cannot be ruled out. The recent legalization of certain forms of individual labour activity and the contemplated legalization of privately owned cooperative

179 "Programma Kommunisticheskoi Partii Sovetskogo Soyuza," *Kommunist*, No. 4 (March), 1986, p. 144.

180 "Sotsialnoe razvitie i ekonomicheskii rost," *Kommunist*, No. 14 (September), 1986, p. 62.

181 For a comprehensive discussion of the new pay system, see "Perestroika sistemy zarabotnoi platy," *Ekonomicheskaya Gazeta*, No. 43 (October), 1986, pp. 6–7.

enterprises suggest that it may already have started.[182] For all their novelty, however, these are only the first steps in what is likely to be a long and difficult process. As Gorbachov reportedly told a group of Soviet writers at an informal meeting in June 1986, "generations will have to pass before we can really restructure."[183]

ON the whole, the Soviet Union's performance in fulfilling the rights contained in Articles 42, 43, and 44 of the 1977 Constitution has been poor. The right to free health care has not produced a decent health system; the right to material security in old age has failed to eliminate poverty among the elderly; and the right to housing has not eliminated the housing shortage or solved the problem of shoddy construction. Only the right and obligation to work has been scrupulously observed, but at the expense of economic efficiency, which the Soviet leadership is now trying to achieve through a disruptive shift to "rational full employment"—that is, a form of unemployment.

The need to face these facts and their implications for the Soviet Union's status as a superpower has led to certain ideological concessions on the part of the leadership. As an editorial in *The Times*[184] put it, the Politburo has apparently decided that "some degree of liberalization may be necessary for economic and social progress." But it warned against taking too optimistic a view of the changes going on in the Soviet Union:

> Soviet history gives scant comfort to those who believe that intellectual freedom is a necessary condition for economic and social progress. A regime that has taken its people from wooden shoes to spacecraft in 70 years, from backwardness to superpower status, will have difficulty believing that future progress depends on allowing its citizens freedoms it never allowed them before.

It is perhaps worth asking whether the Soviet leadership is as confident of its superpower status as *The Times* implies. Gorbachov has made it clear that the continuation of that status depends upon the fundamental reorganization of Soviet society, which in turn demands the cooperation of individual human beings. Now that the Soviet leadership has recognized the importance of the human factor for economic progress, it may well find itself compelled to see the importance of human rights too.

[182] "Zakon Soyuza Sovetskikh Sotsialisticheskikh Respublik ob individualnoi trudovoi deyatelnosti," *Pravda*, 21 Nov. 1986; *Financial Times*, 28 Nov. 1986.

[183] AS 5785. This *samizdat* document was first obtained by the *Forschungsstelle Osteuropa an der Universitaet Bremen*, which translated it into German and published it in the *Frankfurter Rundschau*, 18 Sept. 1986, p. 17.

[184] *The Times*, 28 Nov. 1986.

Doctor for All Seasons

A conversation with Dr Anatoly Koryagin soon after his release from detention; Bern, May 1987.

Urban: *As a medical practitioner and psychiatrist you must have had a lot of experience of what one might call "customer-satisfaction" in the Soviet health services. What does the man in the street think about the medical care he is given?*

Koryagin: *The man in the street believes that the service is plagued by many shortcomings. There is, first, the low standard of medical care itself, especially in the provinces. Then there aren't enough specialists; there is not enough good-quality specialized equipment and many medicines are just not available. The transportation of patients is bad because there aren't enough vehicles; so, in many places, is the ambulance system. Doctors in the provinces are overburdened and waste much of their time filling in forms. All this spells low-quality health care.*

Urban: *How, in practice, does the population react to this?*

Koryagin: *The medical authorities are inundated with complaints. People protest that they are not treated quickly enough or with sufficient tact, that the medicines they need are simply not available at the pharmacies. They write to the central establishment with various requests to be sent one or another medicine. About seven years ago a decree was issued ordering doctors and clinics to prescribe only those medicines that were in stock in their particular localities. None of this helps.*

Urban: *In Romania a semi-official practice has developed under the pressure of the Communist authorities whereby people over 70 are neither given certain medicines nor admitted to hospital. Scarce medical resources are said to be wasted on them. Does a parallel practice exist in the Soviet Union?*

Koryagin: *I am not aware that any official instructions exist to that effect, but the doctors' attitude to elderly and old people is frequently one of utter cynicism. They will tell old people: "Nothing will cure you at your age. You are ill because you are old; there is no need for you to go to hospital."*

This attitude is, of course, part of Soviet psychology and part of the Soviet definition of what a human being is for. Man, in the Soviet view, is valuable only to the extent that he is of advantage to society. He is a means, not an end.

Urban: *Being a means must land the Soviet citizen with a whole skein of problems. Andrei Amalrik once said to me that no one who had been born and brought up in Soviet society was quite normal. Would you agree with that?*

Koryagin: *No, as a doctor I would not. Man's psyche is dynamic. It is capable of adapting itself to the most adverse conditions. The laws of the psyche are universal—they are valid for people in the Soviet Union in exactly the same way as they are for people in the West. They spring from the nature of man.*

The difference is this: Soviet people have a specific interpretation of external phenomena foisted upon them by the state and state ideology. In that sense their opinions and judgements cannot be independent. Western man is much more objective. He does not experience the pressures of a centrally controlled set of interpretations of reality. He can choose for himself more or less freely (as freely, at any rate, as the general limitations of the human condition allow) and he has his own will. He can express his opinions as an individual and will insist on his dignity as an individual. Soviet man is a mass-produced being; his consciousness is that of the masses.

Urban: *As an old and not very witty dictum has it: "Christians look for their ancestors in heaven, Darwinists in the zoo," so, of course, do Marxists—*

Koryagin: *That is putting it rather crudely but it is basically true. But, as I say, from the purely medical point of view, it cannot be said that the run of the mill person in the Soviet Union is abnormal.*

Urban: *Amalrik was, of course, not talking medicine. Abnormality for him was a way of saying that no one who had to live with the make-believe of Soviet ideology could emerge from it unscathed. The pressures of having to profess one thing in public and believe another in private would destroy any human being's integrity.*

Koryagin: *That is a sociological interpretation and I entirely agree with it if we think of "abnormality" as a symbol. Machiavelli looked upon duplicity in a politician not only as a necessary tool of his craft but as a virtue. Indeed, politicians often need a treble and quadruple consciousness to do justice to their vocation. So do diplomats, yet we cannot say that these people are psychologically disordered. What we can say is that they are liars, that they "interpret" the truth in this or that way to please their masters or confound their enemies—and that is what Soviet people do under the pressures of ideology. They will consciously say things they don't believe. They don't believe the slogans, they don't believe the appeals, but they parrot them because that is what's expected of them.*

Urban: *And not parroting them would make them suspect—*

Koryagin: *It would. If you speak outside the framework of propaganda you exclude yourself from the whole mode of being and thinking of the population, and your fellow citizens—not just those in authority—start wondering what sort of man you are. They will keep a watch on you. You are different, and that exacts a price. But the average person conforms and will stick to the double-think and double-talk.*

Urban: *My own experience and readings as a student of politics tell me that you cannot keep up this duality indefinitely. Having told lies for a number of years, self-respect eventually induces you to believe that those lies were not lies at all. You want to justify yourself in your own eyes and the eyes of those close to you; you therefore stand the truth on its head.*

Koryagin: *Yes, this can and does happen. People who have lived all their lives in Soviet society acquire a vested interest in upholding the mendacity. Even if, after several decades, they are forced to admit that all the official promises came to nothing or indeed produced the opposite of what had been promised, they would still insist that, in the light of the conditions then prevailing, they had acted correctly. Otherwise they could not look themselves in the face and would have to admit that all their lives had been wasted and were a lie. No one likes to think of himself as a rascal.*

That kind of self-justification is well known to us from the lives of criminals. Having lived a double-life for a number of years they think up, after a time, an overall justification for what they had been doing and stop feeling guilty. They now accept, or are even proud of, their misdeeds. Soviet people are like that.

Urban: *But, in that case, isn't Amalrik right after all, for that kind of behaviour would certainly strike me as abnormal.*

Koryagin: *Not really. The psyche of a man who behaves like that can be completely healthy. If he chanced upon other conditions of life he would, after a time, come to* *terms with them and become a different person. To take an example: many of us now living in emigration undoubtedly carry the Soviet syndrome around with us. But after a number of months or years—it can be three years or 10 or 15, depending on individual characteristics—the syndrome ceases to operate and the former Soviet citizen becomes indistinguishable from Western man.*

Urban: *Robert Jay Lifton has shown in* Thought Reform and the Psychology of Totalism *that US prisoners of war who spent years in China during and after the Korean war and had been thoroughly brainwashed (they had been used as broadcasters to US troops and international propagandists), could nevertheless be won back to normality after a fairly brief period. Being back in their home surroundings and with their families was enough to restore their perspective.*

Koryagin: *Yes. Imprisonment does, of course, produce its own strains and neuroses. People in prison, any kind of prison, are much more vulnerable to psychological disorders than those leading a normal life. This stands to reason. But the effects of brainwashing wear off. Human beings are, fortunately, immune to it in the long run, whether brainwashing is of the Chinese or Soviet variety.*

Urban: *But while the system lasts, Soviet Man is something you would recognize as real?*

Koryagin: *Oh yes, there is undoubtedly a psychological type we can call Homo Sovieticus. When I was in the Gulag the camp commander said to me one day: "Come on, Koryagin, after all you and I are both people. You're a man and I'm a man; so come on, let's try and find some common ground, let's try to make some compromises." What he had in mind was that I should meet his demands half way. So I answered: "Yes, we are both human beings, but I am Homo Sapiens, while you are Homo Sovieticus. You and I can't possibly find a common language."*

Urban: *Have you an easy definition for Soviet Man?*

Koryagin: *He is a man who has inwardly accepted the stereotypes foisted upon him from above and is to various degrees (each according to his makeup) willingly controlled from above. He is a programmed being, a psychological robot, putty in the hands of Soviet ideologues.*

Urban: *So Zamyatin, Huxley and Orwell were, in most ways, right in their forecasts?*

Koryagin: *They were—with this important difference, that Homo Sovieticus is a passing disease.*

Urban: *If the Soviet system would vanish tomorrow, Soviet Man would vanish with it too—is that what you are saying?*

Koryagin: *He would not disappear at once; the change would be gradual. Some people would be lost to decent human intercourse, but the young in particular would bounce back and live normal lives.*

Urban: *How do you account for the fact that your son Ivan behaved with so much courage when ordered in school to denounce you in front of the school assembly? He refused, tore off his Pioneer scarf and was expelled. Later he was imprisoned for alleged hooliganism.*

Koryagin: *We were and are a close-knit family. We always spoke the truth among ourselves, we never allowed double-standards to prevail, we never deceived ourselves or others, we always said what we thought, there was no quarter given to hypocrisy. I should think Ivan was just remaining true to himself and his family.*

Urban: *One could hardly think of a more telling contrast with the once famous case of young Pavlik Morozov, a much acclaimed model under Stalin, who denounced his father for concealing grain. The father was shot but a group of enraged peasants, led by Pavlik's uncle, eventually killed Pavlik.*

Koryagin: *Pavlik Morozov and Ivan Koryagin grew up in totally different moral environments. That is the simple explanation.*

Urban: *How did you find the inner strength to resist the demands the state and your collective made on you as a psychiatrist? You were supposed to certify sane people as insane, and when you refused and told the world, you were yourself incarcerated. Having just heard from you how tempting it is for the Soviet citizen to allow himself to be wrapped around by the system, I have a special admiration for your courage.*

Koryagin: *It is difficult to talk about myself. But as you have asked: I always hated evil, injustice and cruelty. These were inborn characteristics, parts of my deepest being. I would not like to say where they'd come from because I wouldn't know.*

Urban: *Immanuel Kant ended his famous book* with the reflection that two things in the world filled him with awe and wonder: the starry skies above man and the moral law within him. I would have thought yours is a good example of the triumph of the latter.*

Koryagin: *That is not for me to say.*

Urban: *Was a sense of religion in any way responsible for your courage?*

Koryagin: *In camp I became a Christian. I had no religion before my arrest, but, as I say, I had it in me to oppose and undo suffering, wrong-doing and injustice. That is why I became a doctor; I wanted to be of some help to people. My life in the Gulag added to those instinctive convictions the realization that we are all particles of the Almighty.*

* Critique of Practical Reason

Social and Economic Rights in Eastern Europe*

Sophia M. Miskiewicz

1. The Right to Health Care

LONGER life expectancy, lower infant mortality and a declining death rate are generally accepted as measures of the well-being and health of a nation. The greater prosperity that usually accompanies the industrial and technological development of a modern state is expected to stabilize and then reduce death rates and to increase life expectancy. Yet in the Soviet Union and Eastern Europe these indicators of health conditions have run counter to expectation. As Nicholas Eberstadt of the Harvard Center for Population Studies recently reported:

> Progress in reducing mortality virtually ceased during the 1960s in most of these countries. By the early 1970s life expectancy at birth for men and women was unmistakably falling in some of them. . . . Like the Soviet Union, Eastern Europe enjoyed rapid improvements in health in the 1950s and early 1960s, when life expectancy at birth rose by nearly six years. By contrast, life expectancy in the 12 European NATO states rose less than 3·5 years. In the early 1950s life spans were nearly six years shorter in Warsaw Pact Europe than in NATO Europe. By the later 1960s the gap had been narrowed to 2·5 years. Since that time, however, the gap has once again widened; by the early 1980s life spans were nearly five years longer in NATO Europe than in Warsaw Pact Europe. In part this spoke to health improvements in the West, but the rapidly growing gap was also due to Eastern European trends. After rapid strides, health improvements had come to a halt, and for the region as a whole, life expectancy has actually dropped in recent years.[1]

Figures submitted to the World Health Organization show that in three countries in the world, Bulgaria, Hungary and Poland, the general age-standardized death rate for men has risen since 1970. In two other East European countries, Czechoslovakia and Romania, and five others elsewhere in the world, Cuba, Uruguay, Denmark, Ireland and Sweden, this rate has declined by less than 10 per cent since 1970, although in Denmark and Sweden it was already relatively low at the beginning of the 1970s. Countries in which the death rate has declined by 10–20 per cent

* The author has drawn extensively on papers by Radio Free Europe Research and would particularly like to thank the following: Stephen Ashley, Barbara Donovan, B. V. Flow, Anneli Ute Gabanyi, Rada Nikolaev, Karoly Okolicsanyi, Judith K. Pataki, Alfred Reisch, Vladimir Sobell and Roman Stefanowski for their contributions.

[1] Nicholas Eberstadt, "A Pattern of Soviet Bloc Health Reversals," *Wall Street Journal*, 30 April 1986 (to appear in the forthcoming book, Henry S. Rowan and Charles Wolf Jr. (eds.), *The Failure of the Soviet Empire*).

over the same period include Canada and the USA; similarly, death rates in Puerto Rico, Hong Kong and Japan have fallen by more than 30 per cent since 1970.[2]

Death rates among women have fallen universally since 1970. But in Bulgaria, Hungary, Poland and Cuba they have declined by less than 10 per cent. Alongside Canada, Denmark, France, Norway, Sweden, the UK and New Zealand, Czechoslovakia, Romania and Yugoslavia have registered falls of from 10–20 per cent since 1970. During the same period, Japan, Finland, Chile, Costa Rica and Puerto Rico have reduced their female death rates by over 30 per cent.[3]

SEVERAL factors are responsible for deteriorating health conditions in Eastern Europe in comparison with the West. The pressures that accompany modern industrialization, which was introduced at a faster pace in Eastern Europe than in the West, has undoubtedly contributed to an increase in heart and circulatory problems. Since concern for the environment was inadequate during this period, industrial pollution is likely to have added to the health hazards. The incidence of respiratory diseases in particular is likely to have been raised by pollution as well as by increased cigarette smoking. From 1965–85 cigarette consumption per adult rose nearly a third in Poland, over a third in Hungary, and over 50 per cent in East Germany. Alcohol consumption also rose sharply in Eastern Europe during the 1960s and 70s. In 1960 East Europeans already drank more distilled spirits on average than West Europeans; by 1980 their consumption was estimated to be more than 70 per cent higher.[4]

Thus, new health risks seem to have emerged in Eastern Europe; but as Eberstadt noted;

> Increased health risks . . . do not necessarily lead to deterioration in national health conditions. State social policies can prevent health deterioration when properly framed and implemented, even during periods of seriously increased health risks. The public health programs of the East European countries are, in varying degrees, replicas of the Soviet system. These are characterized by relatively high ratios of medical personnel and hospital beds to population, and provide extensive services that are nominally free of charge. However, the relationship between the availability of medical personnel and health level of the national population, in fact, appears to be negative; countries with the greater number of medical personnel per 10,000 people generally seem to have lower levels of adult life expectancy. This illustrates that in these countries' labor extensive health care programs priority is given to the quantity of "doctors" fielded rather than to the quality of training or equipment.[5]

[2] *World Health Statistics Annual* (WHO, Geneva, 1985), p. 467.
[3] Ibid.
[4] Eberstadt, op. cit.
[5] Ibid.

In terms of statistics, public health care in all the East European countries looks impressive. There have been steady increases in the numbers of doctors, nurses, pharmacies, hospitals, hospital beds, clinics, dentists, and specialized care centres. The mass media report official concern for public health, proclaim advances in medical research and technology and announce numerous national decisions to update, modernize and augment the country's medical facilities. But the promised new facilities are often slow to materialize and sometimes never appear at all because there are shortages of materials, funds and manpower, or simply because of poor planning.

SOVIET and East European medical care is financed directly and almost entirely by the state; as a result, the quantity and quality of these services are determined by the authorities in the light of political priorities. Given the centrally planned economies of Eastern Europe, in which supply and demand are not allowed to play a rational role, patterns of state expenditure do not give a reliable picture of the quality or quantity of care. It is, moreover, difficult to separate health-care expenditure from outlays on other social welfare programmes since the former is usually included with pensions, disability outlays, medical research and the cost of hospital construction.

As with other social services, East European governments do not give high priority to health care. When cutbacks are required, for example, in investment or modernization programmes, the health-care service is often among the first to be affected. Auxiliary medical institutions have also long been greatly neglected. More attention is paid to crude statistics and to presenting an image of ever-rising expenditure and uninterrupted technological advance than to the actual services provided. New housing projects with inadequate sewage-disposal systems or new factories that neither comply with proper safety standards nor possess the necessary waste-disposal facilities illustrate this preoccupation with a purely statistical picture of progress. To this day, Warsaw does not have a single sewage treatment plant; two are under construction, but work on the first has already been in progress for 11 years.[6]

Since shortages abound in all areas of health care from hospital beds and pills to doctors and nurses, those who have friends in the right places or are willing to pay a bribe or gratuity tend to get quicker and better treatment. Party functionaries and other members of the ruling elite enjoy priority in medical treatment; special facilities have been provided for Party and military personnel and sometimes also for fee-paying patients from abroad. Those who are not members of the elite or who are unwilling or unable to pay gratuities, which can often amount to several months' salary, simply go without treatment, join the long waiting lists, or are "processed" by medical personnel who are forced to worry about meeting quotas and filling out forms rather than diagnosing and treating

[6] Polish SR/13. *RFER*, 29 Aug. 1986, item 6.

illnesses. Since a patient may be treated by a different doctor every time he visits the same treatment centre, it is difficult to apportion blame for slackness to individuals.

MEDICAL services vary geographically. The difference between services provided in large urban centres compared with rural areas (where it is difficult to attract well-qualified medical personnel on account of poorer living conditions and inadequate technical support) is particularly marked. This uneven spread of medical treatment within each East European country is partly because the shortage of personnel leaves staff little time to update and improve their knowledge and skills. Given the shortage of doctors, those who fall behind are unlikely to be dismissed or demoted. The quality of treatment provided also depends on the amount of time and effort the doctor can afford to devote to a particular case; an overworked doctor is more likely to pass on the more difficult cases than to accept responsibility himself. Even the most dedicated and best qualified doctors will be discouraged when forced to work without essential supplies and equipment.

Patients in Poland and Romania have now been granted a limited freedom to choose their own doctor. They can also pay for certain optional treatments and services. But these reforms come dangerously near to transgressing the ideological concept of the right of all citizens to "free" health care, and further substantive reforms have so far been avoided even at the risk of the population's health.

While each of the East European regimes has repeatedly voiced its concern for the nation's welfare and has boasted of the benefits secured for the citizen by socialism, it is questionable whether the statistics and reports published in the state-controlled media within these one-party systems give a full and balanced picture. The information presented to the public on pollution, environmental damage (such as the Chernobyl accident) and current dangers to public health (such as AIDS and drug abuse) seems inadequate—a situation that will surely have serious and irreversible effects.

The fact that certain deficiencies and difficulties are common to all the East European health-care services suggests that these are not the result of the accidental shortcomings of one or two mismanaged health-care programmes, but of problems rooted in the very concept of "free" health care within a centralized, planned system. Indeed, these health services, which are in every respect subject to strict central planning, merely illustrate many of the weaknesses of the whole social and economic system that incorporates them. Much effort goes into compiling and presenting statistics to show the amount of money spent on health care. But no amount of statistics can hide frequent shortages of the most basic medical items resulting from the habitual failure of the centralized system to coordinate supply and demand. And when they are available, the equipment and medicines on offer are far below Western standards, since health care suffers from the same obsolescence, stagnation, excessive bureaucracy, widespread corruption and isolation from the rest of the world that afflict Eastern Europe as a whole.

Meanwhile, bacteria and viruses develop new strains, immune to older drugs, while medical research in the East is slow to develop new ways of combating them. Patients tend to lack confidence in their doctors and in domestically produced medicines. Doctors are often obliged, for lack of domestic equivalents, to prescribe Western medicines which are only available for hard currency. When the state budgets cannot or will not allocate funds for these drugs, the patient must pay up or do without.

Throughout Eastern Europe, central planning generally engenders excessive bureaucracy, inefficiency and constant shortages. Health facilities are no exception and fall seriously below the population's needs; and there is nothing to suggest that the gap can be closed without major changes in the entire system.

Bulgaria

Over 40 years of communism have brought impressive progress in health care in Bulgaria, it was claimed at a meeting of the Bulgarian Medical Academy held in Sofia in May 1984. Atanas Maleev, Chairman of the academy (and, incidentally, a relative of Bulgarian Communist Party Secretary-General Todor Zhivkov) said that the death rate in Bulgaria was now only one-eighth of what it had been in 1944, and life expectancy had increased over the same period by 20 years, currently standing at over 71 years; many previously common diseases, such as malaria, typhoid, rabies, poliomyelitis and diphtheria, had been eradicated, while the incidence of tuberculosis, tetanus, anthrax, scarlet fever and whooping cough was only a fraction of what it used to be. Deaths from infectious diseases such as tuberculosis are reportedly uncommon; in 1983 only three cases of measles and 38 of mumps were registered in the whole country.[7]

But whilst official statistics and proclamations present an impressive picture of health care in Bulgaria, closer examination reveals a considerably less satisfactory situation. The choice of the year 1944 as the basis for comparison for death rate and life expectancy statistics given above, for instance, tells us very little about recent conditions in Bulgaria and much more about the abnormally high number of deaths from injury and disease shortly before the end of the Second World War.

Efforts to reduce the high infant mortality rate in the early post-war years yielded good results in the 1950s and '60s, but the current rates are no longer considered satisfactory. According to official statistics, the mortality rate among infants under one fell from 20·2 per 1,000 live births in 1980 to 16·5 in 1983 and 16·5 in 1983 and 16·1 in 1984. At the 13th Bulgarian Communist Party (BCP) Congress a rate of 15·8 was given for

[7] Bulgarian Telegraph Agency (BTA) in English, 26 May 1984.

1985, but this was said to be "still far from the best achievement in the world."[8]

Maleev listed the main issues for Bulgarian doctors as the "preservation and maximum improvement of the living environment, rational feeding programmes and health protection for mothers and children, and the campaign against the diseases of the century: arteriosclerosis, hypertension, cancer, diabetes, and occupational diseases."[9] This indicates a particular concern with infant mortality and the rising incidence of illnesses associated with the stress imposed by modern industrial societies.

FREE medical care for Bulgaria's entire population has been statutory since 1951. The state pays for all essential in-patient and out-patient examinations, analyses and treatment. Medicines are provided free of charge or for a nominal fee. The state finances this service, the cost of which rose by 150 per cent between 1970 and 1980, accounting for six per cent of the 1980 state budget. The citizen, in fact, contributes to the cost of the "free" health service through taxation. Moreover, in practice the citizen finds that many medicines are simply unavailable; and only those with a legal entitlement to hold foreign currency (such as those who have worked abroad) have access to the Western medicines that are sometimes sold in special shops for hard currency.

Since 1980 health establishments and institutions have been permitted and encouraged to help to finance themselves by signing contracts with various organizations for "rendering additional services." The kinds of services for which fees can be charged, listed in the regulations accompanying the decree, are "medical activities not directly connected with meeting the health needs of the citizen," including abortions on request, cosmetic surgery, the provision of medical certificates to car drivers, and so on.[10] The system is designed to avoid breaching the socialist principle that medical services are free. In addition, individuals may pay directly for consultations at certain institutions and for all medical treatment at certain "specialized medical and dental institutes at the personal choice of the citizen." This kind of "first-class" medical care for direct payment was quietly introduced after the abolition of private medical practice in 1972 had created much popular dissatisfaction and had aroused demands for a choice of doctor.[11]

At the same time, the Medical Academy was transformed by

[8] *Statisticheski Godishnik 1985* (Statistical Yearbook 1985) (Committee on Social Information, Sofia, 1985), p. 64; and *Rabotnichesko Delo*, 6 April 1986, p. 6. Bulgaria reported a figure of 16·5 to WHO for the same period. According to the WHO statistics for 1983, Canada reported 8·5 per 1,000 live births, France 8·2, the FRG 10·3, Sweden 7·2 and Japan 5·9.

[9] BTA in English, 26 May 1984.

[10] BTA, 20 Jan. 1981.

[11] Concerning the decree on new economic mechanism in health care, see Bulgarian SR/4, *RFER*, 1 March 1982.

government decree into a "scientific-productive complex,"[12] with the aim of "expanding its activities, increasing its foreign currency income, and better meeting the needs of the health system through imports and the production of medicines, reagents, chemicals and medical equipment."[13] Instead of concentrating on its primary task of supervising medical science and teaching (the academy supervises four higher educational institutes and 24 scientific research institutes, which altogether employ 2,790 scientific and teaching personnel and are attended by 12,390 students), it acquired the characteristics of a business organization. For example, after reorganization the pharmaceutical faculty in Sofia became responsible for producing medicines as well as training personnel. Indeed, the entire pharmaceutical industry was transferred from the Ministry of Chemical Industry to the Ministry of Public Health.[14]

The Academy takes pride in its achievements in earning foreign currency; the Scientific Institute of Orthopaedics and Traumatology produces artificial limbs and orthopaedic appliances not only for domestic use but also for export. Various new medicines and other chemicals are also exported. The Bulgarian media and foreign press service are filled with laudatory reports of the country's excellent facilities, modern equipment (lasers, high-speed X-ray machines, etc.), the neurosurgical and orthopaedic operations that are carried out, new developments in artificial joints and prostheses, new strains of antibiotics, and a host of other developments of modern medical research that bring in money from the other CMEA countries and the West.[15] Many of these skills and facilities are used solely to treat fee-paying foreigners; indeed, a special hospital for foreign patients was set up in 1978. (Two years earlier the free medical care that Bulgaria used to offer its foreign visitors had been made subject to payment in hard currency.)[16]

As a result of this commercial success, in 1978 the Academy ceased to be allocated any foreign currency by the state. Moreover, it was forecast that by 1981 the entire Bulgarian health service would be self-sufficient in terms of hard-currency requirements, an objective that was probably not quite attained.[17] Nevertheless, these exports and services to foreigners have developed into a valuable source of foreign currency, in the interests of which great efforts are made to present the world with a favourable picture of medical and health conditions in Bulgaria.[18]

IN April 1982 the weekly *Pogled* published an article about the "two-tier system" of medical care introduced in 1980. The stated

[12] Decree No. 25, 7 July 1981.
[13] *Darzhaven Vestnik*, No. 57, 21 July 1981.
[14] *Rabotnichesko Delo*, 17 Oct. 1981.
[15] BTA, 21 Oct. 1981.
[16] Bulgarian SR/25, *RFER*, 8 Sept. 1976, item 3.
[17] Bulgarian SR/4 loc. cit.
[18] *Rabotnichesko Delo*, 28 Dec. 1978, 28 Dec. 1979 and 21 Feb. 1980.

purpose of this system was to improve the care of patients, but it was motivated by cuts in the state budget. What it did, in effect, was to phase out most lower-grade paramedical workers (doctors' assistants, orderlies, etc.), passing their duties on to doctors and nurses (a similar system exists in the GDR), and thus leaving them even less time to carry out their professional duties. Because of the lack of mechanization in Bulgarian hospitals, paramedical duties had been classified as hard, unskilled labour and were therefore poorly paid and usually performed by pensioners, some of whom were themselves in need of medical attention.[19] It was the steady increase in the number of professional personnel that had presumably led the authorities to consider this system practicable. In 1984 Bulgaria had 24,718 doctors and 49,643 nurses; and in terms of the ratio of doctors to population it claimed to be close behind the USSR and Czechoslovakia, and ahead of Hungary, the GDR, Poland and Romania.[20]

In practice, however, under the new system many jobs are simply left undone. Another *Pogled* article described conditions in hospitals where paramedical workers had been retained as cleaners, while their auxiliary medical duties had simply been abandoned. Patients frequently tipped or bribed such staff to perform what had once been their normal duties, and some hospitals even allowed relatives of seriously ill patients to help to care for them "on condition that they help other patients as well."[21]

Others too have expressed concern for the standards of the domestic health service. The former Minister of Public Health, Angel Todorov, and his successor, Radoy Popivanov, have officially criticized "the negligent or harsh treatment of patients." Todor Zhivkov himself has been quoted as saying that the standard of health care lags behind the needs of the population.[22]

The daily *Narodna Mladezh*, in an article on the country's chronically overworked paediatricians,[23] gave another example of the differences between the actual condition of the health service and the rosy official picture. Despite their relatively large number (second only to internists), paediatricians examine up to 70 children a day. They attend to out-patients, make home visits, visit kindergartens and day-care centres; they must also be available for emergency calls for which they receive no additional pay. For every 10 minutes they spend seeing a patient, at least five are taken up with paperwork. The article urged a reduction in their duties and an increase in their salaries.

Medical facilities and equipment are also generally considered highly inadequate. In spite of all the specialized clinics, spas, and treatment available for foreigners, in 1984 there was still no specialized children's

[19] *Pogled*, No. 15, 12 April 1982.
[20] *Bulgarian Statistical Yearbook 1985*, op. cit. pp. 444 and 680.
[21] *Pogled*, No. 12, 22 March 1982.
[22] *Rabotnichesko Delo*, 13 Jan. 1982.
[23] *Narodna Mladezh*, 29 Feb. 1984. See also Bulgarian SR/6, *RFER*, 11 April 1984, item 5.

hospital in Bulgaria, although work on one began in 1979, while the decree providing for its construction was issued as long ago as 1961.[24] Nor were there medicines available specially prepared for children, forcing doctors to treat them with adaptations of adult medicines and dosages, clearly a risky practice.

The number of articles in the Bulgarian domestic press about health problems and problems within the health service has been rising. In 1985 an article in *Zemedelsko Zname* described the deplorable state of health care in the villages and the great differences between the health services in urban and rural areas. A national conference on health care in rural areas was held on 22 November 1985, and *Rabotnichesko Delo*, the Party daily, devoted a series of articles to the issue.[25] The general inadequacy of dental care has also been a cause for concern, and it is questionable whether health care in the predominantly Turkish areas is on the same level as that in the rest of the country. The complaints of the Turkish population that they are being discriminated against (which they are) can lead to no other conclusion.

In 1986 several articles appeared about the generally poor health of Bulgarian schoolchildren, many of whom are reportedly overweight as their diet often contains too many carbohydrates and not enough proteins and vegetables.[26] Restricted public access to most of the country's sports facilities is unlikely to improve their health.[27]

In a speech at the BCP Congress in 1986, Dr Stefan Zhelyazkov of the Lovech District Hospital expressed concern over the growing medical needs of the aged in his district. This problem is likely to increase in the years ahead since the average age of the Bulgarian population is rising. Bulgaria's lack of specialized facilities and nursing homes is causing particular concern.[28]

Overall, therefore, while progress was undoubtedly made, especially in the earlier decades of communist rule, the situation is far from satisfactory. Problems with the standard of health care in rural areas, and for children and the old have been particularly noted. More generally, an emphasis on commercial considerations appears to have resulted in financial success to the detriment of the quality of care provided for most ordinary citizens. It is hard to see how this approach can be reconciled with the aims and principles of socialist society.

Czechoslovakia

In purely statistical terms it may be argued that the Czechoslovak health service works well enough. Official figures indicate sustained growth and

[24] Ibid.

[25] *Zemedelsko Zname*, 21 Sept. 1985. For reports on the conference, see *Rabotnichesko Delo*, 18, 20 and 23 Nov. 1985; 7 and 18 Dec. 1985; and 15 Jan. 1986.

[26] *Narodna Mladezh*, 10 May 1986.

[27] *Anteni*, No. 3, 15 Jan. 1986.

[28] *Rabotnichesko Delo*, 5 April 1986.

improvement. The number of hospital beds, for example, rose from 76,000 in 1950 to 156,000 in 1984, which works out at 101 beds per 1,000 inhabitants, placing Czechoslovakia second among East European countries, just behind the GDR, which has 102. (Bulgaria has 91·8, Romania 89·4, Hungary 88·2, and Poland 69·7 beds per 1,000 citizens.) Czechoslovakia scores even better in terms of the ratio of doctors (and dentists) 41·2 per every 10,000 heads of the population. (Bulgaria has 33·8, Hungary 31·2, the GDR 29·0, Poland 23·8 and Romania 20·4.) The absolute figure rose from 12,600 doctors (and dentists) in 1950 to 54,700 in 1984. The number of pharmacies in Czechoslovakia fell from 1,410 in 1960 to 1,284 in 1980, but rose to 1,298 in 1984.[29]

But the reality behind the glowing statistics is another matter. In August 1984 the Charter 77 human rights group issued a statement on the deplorable condition of the health service, exposing widespread corruption and inefficiency. It said that in many cases bribes were necessary to ensure proper care and that many urgently needed medicines were available only on the black market. Indeed, the chronic shortage of modern diagnostic equipment, hospital staff and medicine caused the black market to flourish in all sections of the health service.[30]

The Czechoslovak Party daily *Rude Pravo* also stated that the fall in morale in the health service "remains a serious problem," and singled out for criticism bribery, protectionism, and "a lack of feeling" on the part of physicians and health-service personnel. The same paper reported that health-service expenditure was rising continually, noting that this was not due solely to expansion. The constant increase in the cost of construction, medical equipment and other materials led to additional expense. Few construction projects were completed on time; indeed, "a delay of several years is considered almost a matter of course." It said that the country's electronics and other industries lagged behind their targets in supplying the health sector.[31] Czechoslovakia's health care was—and would remain for some time—dependent on imports, and even imported technology was not always properly utilized.[32]

In September 1984 the Czech Minister for Health, Jaroslav Prokopec, said on Radio Prague that the management system of Czechoslovakia's health service, designed for the 1950s, was too old to meet current needs. In addition, he said, the performance of health workers was often sub-standard. In June 1984 he had reported on the state of the country's health-care services at a session of the Czech National Council in Prague. He then warned that:

> . . . waste, inefficiency, and the misuse of the health services must be reduced. It makes no sense to conceal the fact that the country's medical technology gives little reason for satisfaction. . . . It is not in

[29] *CMEA* (Council for Mutual Economic Aid) *Statistical Yearbook 1985* (Finance and Statistics, Moscow, 1985), pp. 435–7.

[30] Reuter, 24 Aug. 1984; see also "The Czechoslovak Health-Labyrinth" in this issue.

[31] *Rude Pravo*, 17 Aug. 1984.

[32] Radio Prague, 17 Aug. 1984, 9.00 am.

> the country's power to come up to world standards of scientific and technical development in health care.[33]

Experts seem to agree with Prokopec: 40 per cent of all Czechoslovak medical equipment is apparently obsolete; most health-care buildings are more than 50 years old and almost one-third of the auxiliary buildings are 30 years old; 8·09 per cent of hospital beds are over 100 years old, while 21·1 per cent are over 75, and 21·9 per cent over 50 years old. It would take an enormous amount of money over many years to rebuild the infrastructure of the Czechoslovak health-care system.[34]

WHILST Czechoslovakia has reduced the incidence of several diseases and facilitated progress in the care of the elderly, other figures attest to the declining health of the population in general. In 1982 and 1983, for example, an average of 293,000 workers (or 4·18 per cent of the workforce) was absent from work each day on the grounds of illness or accident, despite the government's announcement that it is committed to programmes that include environmental protection, work safety and accident reduction. Excessive absenteeism is also blamed on "overprotective" health-care schemes, alcoholism and low morale.[35]

There is growing concern about the effects on health of industrial expansion, urbanization and the greater use of motorized transport. In 1984 between 750,000 and one million people in Czechoslovakia (out of a total population of 15·48 million) had symptoms of hypertension, which is currently one of the main causes of death in the country, alongside heart disease, cancer, strokes, respiratory diseases and general accidents. In Prague 40 per cent of the population suffer from diseases closely associated with the effects of rapid industrial expansion and the strains of modern living. The rate of cardiovascular disease in the city is 30 per cent higher than the national average. In Slovakia one sixth of the population lives in areas with dangerously high levels of industrial pollution. Virtually every part of the country has its own story about environmental dangers to health. Economists have come to realize that, in addition to direct medical costs, much more money would have to be allocated to indirect health care.[36]

Prokopec stated that because medical services and medicines were free, the number of people whose health had been damaged by the excessive use of medicines has increased in the past few years and now accounts for five per cent of all hospital patients. Other sources say that drug addiction is a growing medical and social problem, apparently affecting some 400,000 people, the majority of whom are said to be teenagers.[37]

Yet another problem is that the number of physicians is growing faster

[33] *Rude Pravo*, 27 June 1984.
[34] *Planovane Hospodarstvi*, No. 3, 1984, p. 57.
[35] Czechoslovak SR/15, *RFER*, 10 Aug. 1984, item 4.
[36] Ibid.
[37] *Socialisticka Zakonnost*, No. 7, 1983, p. 420.

than the number of paramedical workers. As a result, the number of health-care assistants per physician declined from 2·5 in 1970 to 2·1 in 1981. Prokopec blames this on mismanagement in the educational system. Others blame it on the poor pay and working conditions of the paramedical workers which also affects the quality of service provided by doctors. According to a survey conducted by the Research Institute on Living Standards, 30–35 per cent of those questioned blamed doctors for the long waits for medical care; 18–20 per cent criticized doctors for negligence; 14 per cent said their doctors gave preference to certain categories of patient; 18–20 per cent had little confidence in their doctors; and over 50 per cent said that they would prefer to have a "free choice" of physician instead of the present system whereby patients are assigned to doctors according to their [the patients'] places of residence.[38]

Given the lack of choice of physician and constant shortages of facilities, medicine and hospital beds it is perhaps not surprising that bribery has become widespread. The size of the bribe varies according to the treatment required. It sometimes amounts to several months' pay.[39] A poll conducted by the Party periodical *Tribuna* found that one in three Czechoslovak citizens is "not sure" whether he would receive adequate medical treatment without giving bribes. Indeed, the report spoke of doctors who would treat their patients conscientiously only when given such payments.[40] Czechoslovak television also commented that bribery, though found throughout Czechoslovak life, is probably most prevalent in the health service.[41]

BY 1985 the health service in Prague had deteriorated to such an extent that, in an interview with the Czech media, Jan Klima (head of the health department in the Prague National Committee) called the situation a "collapse."[42] In addition to the usual problems of obsolescence and long waiting periods for hospital beds and operations (there was said to be a shortage of 3,000 hospital beds, including some 1,100 in wards for patients awaiting operations), the city is increasingly unable to shoulder its special obligations to the rest of the country. Hospitals in Prague have a number of specialized wards; more than 14 per cent of their patients come from outside the city.[43]

Measures announced over the last decade to modernize facilities in Prague have not been properly implemented. Hospital reconstruction has not been undertaken; some units, e.g. those providing laundry and food services, have ceased to function.[44] Ambulances are dirty, in need of

[38] *Planovane Hospodarstvi*, loc. cit.

[39] *Tribuna*, 18 Jan. 1984.

[40] Ibid. 15 March 1985.

[41] Czechoslovak Television, 29 May 1985, 5.30 pm.

[42] *Vecerni Praha*, 4 May 1985, p. 5.

[43] See Czechoslovak SR/10 *RFER*, 27 June 1985, item 7.

[44] Jan Klima, "Prague's Health Service," *Zdravotnicke Noviny*, No. 16, 19 Nov. 1985, p. 3.

maintenance, technologically inadequate and too few in number since most were designed in the mid-60s.

A long-term programme for regenerating the city's health service was adopted by the government in January 1985, with a view to increasing the number of hospital beds in Prague to about 16,000 (from 12,500). Two new hospitals are planned to be finished by the year 2000. The programme also envisages an increase in the number of staff in the health service, with a total of 8,000 new employees by the year 2000. Although it may be relatively easy to find enough doctors (medical graduates are generally eager to work in Prague), there will still be problems recruiting enough graduates from nursing schools and finding technicians, manual and auxiliary workers.[45]

The Charter 77 report on the state of the health service, compiled by doctors and other health-service professionals, clearly indicated that these problems were not unique to the health-care programme, but were similar to those found in other sectors of the centralized economy. The health service (including medical research and equipment) is subject to strict central planning, with emphasis on reports and statistics to prove performance. There are frequent complaints about shortages of drugs, instruments, and such routine items as hypodermic needles and X-ray film. The technical standard of medical equipment in Czechoslovakia lags behind that of the advanced Western countries—a symptom of the technological stagnation of Czechoslovak industry. The same applies to pharmaceuticals. Many patients now lack faith in domestically produced drugs and demand to be treated with Western ones; but hard-currency constraints make it impossible to import enough of these. In addition, doctors are inundated with paperwork and other non-medical duties. For example, during the harvest in Slovakia doctors are expected to do "voluntary" work on the farms.[46]

The regime treats the health service as a gift extended to an often ungrateful population. Since everyone is entitled to free health care and resources are not adequate, the care that is provided is standardized—whereas people and their illnesses are not. As a result, patients are "processed" rather than treated. Doctors are "civil servants" whose limited time is absorbed by filling quotas, providing statistics and signing documents. The care of patients comes second or worse.[47]

The "German Democratic Republic"

Statistics for the GDR show consistent progress in the health-care sector since the 1950s. In the 1950s the number of doctors (and dentists) grew only slightly, from 20,500 in 1950 to 20,900 in 1960, but since 1960 it has steadily risen to 34,600 in 1970, 43,600 in 1980, 48,400 in 1984 and 49,500 in 1985. From 483 inhabitants per doctor in 1981, there were 433 in 1986

45 Czechoslovak SR/10, loc. cit.
46 Ibid.
47 Ibid.

(compared with 390 in West Germany) and from 1,658 inhabitants per dentist in 1981, there were 1,405 in 1986 (compared with 1,700 in West Germany).[48] This equals 29 doctors per 10,000 heads of the population. East Germany is now in fifth place among its East European neighbours, after the USSR, Czechoslovakia, Bulgaria and Hungary.

There has also been a steady growth from 1,694 pharmacies in 1950 to 1,990 in 1960, 1,932 in 1970 and 2,002 in 1984. The number of pharmacists increased from 2,002 in 1950 to 3,700 in 1984.[49]

A major reason for the lack of growth in the number of doctors in the GDR in the 1950s was emigration to the West, and despite the great need for their services in East Germany, numerous highly qualified medical professionals are still moving to West Germany because they feel restricted within their own centrally organized state health system.[50] Doctors are paid very little in East Germany: a staff doctor earns on average only 1,000 Ostmarks a month, and a supervisory doctor about 2,000 Ostmarks.

A public health-care service was introduced in 1945 modelled on the Soviet network of dispensaries, prophylactic programmes, diagnostics, therapy and treatments for various major illnesses; certain modifications have been made since 1971. There are no privately practising physicians; all doctors work through central polyclinics. Some effort is, however, being made to allow patients a choice of doctor, or at least to ensure that each course of treatment is carried out by a single physician.[51] In 1983 residents of East Berlin could in theory choose their physician from among the 381 general practitioners in the out-patient clinics.[52] In practice, however, such choice is only possible where general practitioners can fit in additional patients after what is, on average, a 12-hour day (six-day week). The choice of doctors is largely illusory.[53] It has been argued that matters might improve if doctors were assigned to the same hospital for a considerable length of time. This would ensure continuity of treatment and familiarity with patients.[54]

Because doctors are (despite their increasing numbers) overworked patients often endure long delays. Other common complaints concern delays in completing new buildings, great differences between conditions and services in urban and rural areas, and shortages of medicines.[55] Extra strain is being placed on the medical service in the GDR by the high incidence of alcoholism, generally poor nutrition, widespread obesity and heavy smoking.

[48] Deutsche Presseagentur, Berlin, 28 May 1986.
[49] *CMEA Statistical Yearbook 1985*, op. cit., p. 435.
[50] *Sueddeutsche Zeitung*, 19 June 1982.
[51] Ibid.
[52] *DDR Handbuch* (Verlag Wissenschaft und Politik, Cologne, 1985), pp. 557 and 560.
[53] *Zeitschrift fuer Klinische Medizin*, No. 15, July 1985, pp. 1, 114–7 and 145.
[54] *DDR Handbuch*, pp. 540–1.
[55] *Zeitschrift . . .* , loc. cit.

FOLLOWING the lead of Mikhail Gorbachov, East Germany is beginning to crack down on alcoholism by banning drink advertisements and imposing stiffer penalties for drunken driving. *Neues Deutschland* said that 45,800 road accidents recorded in 1985 were caused by drunken driving—one accident in every 12. The weekly paper, *Wochenpost*, reported that every East German drinks an average of 150 litres of beer per annum, making the nation the eighth largest beer consumer in the world. Another official newspaper, published by the Protestant Church, *Mecklenburgische Kirchenzeitung*, recently described widespread alcohol abuse among teenagers, stating that about half the country's youth between 14–18 years of age drink alcohol at the weekends.[56] Cigarette smoking is also increasing as a health problem, according to Ernest Strauzenberg, President of the Committee for Health and Nutrition, who stated that nearly 60 per cent of males and 50 per cent of females between the ages of 14–18 are more or less regular smokers.[57]

The unhealthy diet of many East Germans also contributes to the demands made on the country's health services; a survey of eating habits in various districts of the GDR showed that most East Germans eat too much in general, and too much of the wrong foods. Lothar Heinemann, a health expert, told the trade union daily *Tribuene* that East Germans hold "orgies of eating" at the weekend, devouring too many sweets and drinking too much alcohol. He said that although it was a great achievement that nobody suffered from hunger, the country faced a new social problem—obesity. An earlier survey showed that about 40 per cent of the population was overweight.[58] Public awareness of the links between diet and health is far less developed than it now is in many Western societies.

Life expectancy for 50-year-olds in the GDR in 1981 was 73·39 years for men (compared with 74·19 in the FRG), and 77·58 for women (79·36 in the FRG). The mortality rate per 10,000 inhabitants for all ages in 1981 was 132·7 for men (compared with 118·33 in the FRG) and 144·8 for women (115·94 in the FRG). The high mortality rate for women in East Germany is due to the fact that women in the 65–67 age group registered a mortality rate 32·3 per cent higher than their counterparts in West Germany.[59]

The infant mortality rate is widely regarded as a key indicator of the health of a nation, and according to the World Health Organization's statistics, compiled from figures submitted by member states, the GDR had by far the lowest infant mortality rate in Eastern Europe in 1983, the most recent year for which data are available, namely 10·7 deaths per 1,000 live births. (West Germany recorded 10·9 infant deaths per 1,000 live births in 1982.)

[56] Associated Press, 10 April 1986.
[57] *Agence France Presse*, 23 March 1985.
[58] Reuter, 25 April 1986.
[59] *DDR Handbuch*, op. cit. p. 567.

Eastern Europe as a whole, however, trails well behind the West European countries, among which the West German figure is comparatively high. The 1985 rate, as recorded by the WHO, was 15·7 in Czechoslovakia, 16·5 in Bulgaria, 19·0 in Hungary, 19·2 in Poland, and 23·9 in Romania. By comparison, the rate in Spain is 9·6, in France 9·0, in Denmark 8·2, in Norway 8·1 and in Sweden 7·0.[60] Whilst the Scandinavian countries' combination of high income and high public expenditure levels can explain their leading position here, the contrast between Spain and the East European countries is particularly striking. The relatively good showing of the GDR in respect of infant mortality, despite the weaknesses of the country's health services, is probably due to traditionally high standards of German hygiene and educational factors.

Hungary

Government statistics about the Hungarian health service are impressive. The number of medical practitioners (physicians and dentists) increased rapidly, from 9,600 in 1950 to 15,300 in 1960, 30,100 in 1980, and 33,300 in 1984. This corresponds to 10·3 doctors (including dentists) per 10,000 people in 1950 and 31·2 per 10,000 in 1984, and compares favourably with the other East European countries, among which only Czechoslovakia can boast a significantly higher rate. In terms of hospital beds too, Hungary appears to have done well; the 1950 total of 49,200 had risen to 94,000 by 1984. This figure represents 88·2 beds for every 10,000 people, compared with 52·5 in 1950. Although the number of pharmacies has not increased significantly (1,430 in 1984 compared with 1,427 in 1950), the number of pharmacists has, from 2,800 to 4,500. Beds in sanatoria increased from 1,200 in 1951 to 3,300 in 1984 and numbers of patients treated in sanatoria from 15,100 in 1952 to 51,000 in 1984.[61]

Statistics of health provision can, however, be misleading. In September 1986 Laszlo Medve, Minister of Health, told a meeting of the Government's Social and Health Commission that public health was, in fact, deteriorating. The death rate in Hungary in 1985, said Medve, was the highest in Europe, ahead of Czechoslovakia and Bulgaria, which rank second and third respectively. Hungary's rates for suicide, infant mortality and alcohol consumption are also very high. Medve blamed the deterioration in health on poor nutrition, smoking, alcoholism, lack of physical activity and long-term nervous strain. Combinations of these factors contributed to diseases that affected 90 per cent of the country's population.[62] The minister added, however, that these should not be considered merely as medical problems, since alcoholism and smoking are also social issues; solutions could not be provided by doctors alone.

More specific evidence of inadequate health standards was given in June 1986 by Ferenc Karpati, the Minister of Defence, who told a

[60] *World Health Statistics Annual*, op. cit.

[61] *Council for Mutual Economic Aid Statistical Yearbook 1985*, op. cit. pp. 435–7.

[62] Radio Budapest, 8 Sept. 1986, 12.00 noon. See also Hungarian SR/6, *RFER*, 27 May 1986, item 4.

National Assembly committee that 10–11 per cent of young Hungarians were "unfit for military service," and a further 4–5 per cent are only moderately fit and had therefore to be exempted from strenuous physical exercise.[63] Moreover, 3–4 per cent of conscripts had to be discharged before the end of their service mainly because of nervous or physical disorders, including cardiovascular, circulatory and digestive complaints. Of those suffering from the latter, 23 per cent were overweight. According to another report two-thirds of officers in the armed forces are heavy smokers.[64]

MORE serious and more general charges of inadequacy were made in an interview, broadcast by Radio Budapest in June 1986, with the Hungarian doctor and sociologist Eva Istvan, who said that the country's health system deserved to be described as "scandalous." Istvan claimed that this applied to the entire system, from dermatology to psychiatry, from the state of repair of hospitals to hospital equipment. The deluge of complaints from patients and medical staff alike confirmed the validity of her criticisms, she said. Employees in the health service felt that the situation in their particular field had reached a critical point. The allocation of hospital beds, the barbaric conditions in operating theatres and waiting rooms and the long waiting hours were sufficient testimony to the seriousness of the situation.[65]

The official aim of the health service in Hungary, Istvan reminded listeners, was to provide the public with a high standard of basic medical care, so that patients should not have to travel from one doctor to another, or resort to their personal connections or influence to get medical attention. Istvan maintained that it was practically impossible to control this "back-door" access to adequate—or what was considered to be adequate—medical care. Unless there was a major increase in investment, she said, there was no hope for improvement. The time had passed when radical changes might have been expected from improved management and mobilizing the "human factor."

On 25 June 1986 the leaders of the health workers' union met to discuss improvements in the management of the Hungarian health service and in social welfare. Lajos Juszt, the deputy Minister of Health, told the meeting that the government wanted patients to have more say in deciding in which hospital they wanted to be treated and hoped to improve care for the elderly.[66]

A report from the National Council for Medical Ethics shows that some 30 per cent of the patients in one of Hungary's 19 counties admitted giving extra money to doctors for medical treatment, while 52 per cent said they did not; 17·2 per cent of the doctors accepted the money offered. The chairman of the council, Dr Zoltan Szabo, said that the figures were

[63] Ibid.
[64] *Nephadsereg*, 22 Feb. 1986.
[65] Radio Budapest, 23 June 1986, 5.00 pm.
[66] Ibid. 25 June 1986, 6.30 pm.

based on reports and complaints sent to the council. There were no statistics for the country as a whole. 40 per cent of all complaints concerned the way in which doctors dealt with their patients. Most mentioned inappropriate conduct and lack of sympathy.[67]

GROWING evidence, and criticism, of the inadequacies of the Hungarian health service contrast with an official declaration of 1975 that free health care was the right of every Hungarian citizen. This evidently heightened the demands on medical services, but there was no increase in funds. Unable to finance itself adequately, the Hungarian health service has lowered its standards, resorting to often dubious practices.[68]

On average, hospital buildings in Budapest are 80 years old. Not enough hospitals have been built over the years and not enough equipment bought to meet the most elementary needs. There is a constant shortage of beds and an even worse lack of facilities for caring for the elderly. Many old people are simply sent home to die, according to articles in the Hungarian press. When the chief physician of a Budapest hospital was recently asked why he had refused to admit a patient dying of cancer, he said, "If we admitted all such patients, we would have no room left for those who can be cured." Hospitals in Budapest are particularly overcrowded, but the problem is not confined to the capital.[69]

The equipment used in most hospitals is outdated: 30 per cent of hospital facilities are more than 10 years old, and although Hungarian-made medical instruments have not changed over the last 10–15 years, their prices have risen by some 40 per cent. Other equipment is obsolete or not in use because of the lack of hard currency to buy spare parts. Even the kitchens and laundries are incapable of servicing the hospitals properly.[70] Patients' families bring in food and clean laundry for their relatives.

Apparently it takes two to three years for the more expensive items of equipment to reach hospitals because so many bureaucratic procedures have to be completed before delivery. During this time prices often rise enormously; an instrument ordered by one hospital, for example, cost 250,000 forints when the order was placed, but when it finally arrived, the hospital had to pay 500,000. Patients are often sent from one treatment centre to another for the right diagnostic equipment; only one-third of all the centres in Komarom county inspected by the People's Control Commission had the necessary diagnostic instruments. 13 out of 19 surgeries inspected did not have the necessary equipment or what they did have was too old to function. The intensive care unit of a hospital in Ajka, for example, had only one respirator, 14 years old. The state

[67] Ibid.

[68] Hungarian SR/7, *RFER*, 8 June 1985, item 5.

[69] *Nepszava*, 10 May 1986; and *Magyar Nemzet*, 1 Dec. 1984.

[70] Weekly Bulletin (MTI) 2 May 1986, p. 4; Radio Budapest, 26 June 1986, 12.00 noon; and Gyorgy Andai, "The Everyday Exam," *Budapest*, April 1985, pp. 6–7.

institutions responsible for repairing equipment take advantage of their monopoly and charge excessive fees. They, also, do not return the equipment for long periods. One county hospital sent dental surgical equipment to Budapest for repair and had not had it returned a year later.[71]

The lack or shortage of medicines is another severe problem. In 1984 some 150 basic medicines were not available in Hungary because the pharmaceutical industry lacked the hard currency to import raw materials.[72]

A medical member of the Hungarian National Assembly's Committee for Health and Social Affairs, Dr Gyorgy Bazso, complained that nobody bothered to ask doctors what kind of equipment they needed. Many of them had no time to use their electrocardiographs because they could spend only a few minutes with each patient. "I have to treat between 80–120 patients a day," he said, "and if I did even one electrocardiogram, I could treat no more than 50 people by 11 o'clock at night."[73]

THE training of physicians is inconsistent and some have to work under unsafe conditions. Many people are reluctant to work in the health service because of low pay and shift work. On average, doctors earn 10,000 forints less per annum than blue-collar workers. In an interview in *Magyar Nemzet*, a doctor claimed that the mental health of workers in the health sector was a cause for concern. He argued that the extraordinary demands of the profession and difficult working conditions were destroying both their family lives and their nerves. These problems had a visible effect on the quality of their work and their relations with colleagues and patients. He implied that many doctors and nurses themselves needed medical help.[74]

Criticism of the health service in the press has not been confined to cataloguing its technical failings; it is broad and substantive. For example, the economist Gyorgy Gosztonyi blamed its poor condition on the fact that health care is free and that patients cannot choose their doctor. The sociologist Lajos Csaszi called the free health service a "utopian propaganda measure" which raises the demand for medical services without increasing the number of doctors, hospital beds or equipment. The share of the domestic net material product spent on the health services has remained unchanged at about 3·3 per cent since 1950.[75] The official statistics, however, do not refer to medical services alone but to the combined figure for health and social services, which is

[71] Hungarian SR/8, *RFER*, 31 July 1986, item 7.

[72] *Nepszava*, 10 May 1986.

[73] Hungarian SR/8, loc. cit.

[74] *Magyar Nemzet*, 19 June 1986. See also, Hungarian SR/6, *RFER*, 27 May 1986, item 4, on the general state of mental health of the Hungarian people. (Reprinted in this issue as "Neurotic Disorders in Hungary.")

[75] *Magyar Nemzet*, 1 Dec. 1984.

about six per cent. The Hungarian media fail to mention that Western countries spend 6–10 per cent of their national product on public health care alone; and since private health care also exists in most Western countries, Hungarian provision for health care falls far below Western standards.[76]

Following the same line of argument, one well-known Hungarian doctor, Laszlo Levendel, went so far as to say that by declaring medical services free, Hungary had set a goal that even the wealthiest countries could not afford.[77] According to Levendel, Hungary's basic problem is that no one wants to admit that "communist propaganda about the health service—to each according to his needs—is unrealistic." Levendel claimed that the only way to solve the problem is to admit that a mistake had been made, just as mistakes in agriculture also had to be admitted.

Csaszi described some of the tragedies that result from the demand for "free" medical services. Since the medical sector cannot meet everybody's needs, it is often forced to provide services guided by questionable criteria. It has to decide, for example, who should be allowed to use the few, albeit free, kidney dialysis machines, or who should go abroad for a life-saving operation when there is only a meagre supply of hard currency available. In 1984 when Siamese twins born in Hungary had to be separated in West Germany, the German surgeon appealed for donations from Germans to cover the cost.[78] In most cases the money for an operation abroad has to come from sources other than the Hungarian government. Often the patient has to pay for the treatment himself. This means that if he does not have relatives or friends in the West who are willing to cover the hospital expenses, he must do without even a lifesaving operation. Limited funds at home sometimes force hospitals to be "inventive" in the worst sense of the word.

THE inadequacy of facilities and the work-load on doctors often lead Hungarians to resort to illegal gratuities and petty bribes in an effort to secure better treatment. *Heti Vilaggazdasag* estimated that every year about 4,000 million forints are given to doctors and health workers under the table. Thus, the communist motto "to each according to his needs," changed long ago into "from each according to his means." Elderly patients are worst hit because they usually have the lowest incomes and the greatest health problems. They give a much larger share of their income to doctors in the hope of treatment and a longer stay in hospital than do younger patients.[79]

The practice of giving gratuities causes tensions in the profession, because it raises the salaries of certain doctors. A substantial number of the medical personnel, those who have no direct contact with the public receive no extra payment (nurses, lab technicians, staff doctors and

[76] Hungarian SR/7, loc. cit.
[77] Radio Budapest, 10 Jan. 1985, 9.40 pm.
[78] Hungarian SR/7, loc. cit.
[79] Hungarian SR/2, *RFER*, 6 Feb. 1984, item 5.

surgeons). The public often mistrusts doctors, feeling that they care only about the money and not about the welfare of their patients.

Various solutions to these problems have been proposed, but most conflict with the regime's official ideological principles. Some would allow citizens to pay for their own private insurance on Western lines. There have also been suggestions to allow patients to choose their own doctor, and to pay doctors according to the number of patients they treat, or the type of service they provide.

Levendel has called for the legalization of gratuities. He wants their secrecy removed and the moneys more fairly distributed, indirectly admitting that the public is being asked to supplement doctors' salaries because the government is unable or unwilling to raise the necessary funds. The official income of doctors is low in relation to the number of hours worked. In 1983, on average, medical personnel (doctors, nurses and dentists) earned 51,125 forints per annum (compared with the national average wage of 64,820 forints). Undoubtedly, low wages are part of the reason why at least 6–7 per cent of jobs in the medical profession are unfilled.[80]

Levendel's proposal would increase the money flowing into the state service; it would be paid to the doctor and other professionals through the hospitals according to how much a patient is able to pay and the sort of service provided. Legalizing gratuities, however, would amount to a fee-paying system which would be at odds with the communist principle of "free" health care.

There will probably be changes in the Hungarian health service. The Social and Health Commission drafted a new national health programme and submitted it to parliament in 1986, hoping to improve health-care by the year 2000.[81] But the Health Minister recently reiterated: "We must stick to certain basic principles. One of the most important principles is a free health service."[82] Another obstacle to introducing real change is that those doctors who benefit most from the present system are often highly placed. Many of them are opposed to any change that would jeopardize their additional income. This obstacle, combined with the political insistence on a nominally free service, would appear to rule out the more radical proposals we have seen put forward, though the fact that they are publicly advocated in the way they are indicates both the seriousness of the crisis and the relative freedom and breadth of discussion in Hungary.

Poland

Following the Second World War, the most dramatic improvements in the Polish health service were made in the 1950s.[83] In those early years of

[80] *Nepszava*, 5 March 1985.

[81] Radio Budapest, 8 Sept. 1986, 12.00 noon.

[82] *Delmagyarorszag*, 2 March 1985.

[83] For a detailed study of the Polish health service in the 1950s see: *Health Services in Poland: the Statistics, the Realities, the Prospects* (Free Europe Press, 6 July 1954), trans. from *Zagadnienia Polskie*, Vol. I, No. 1–2, 1954.

"building socialism" it was (literally) essential to heal the nation's wounds and bring the health service up to an acceptable basic standard.

At the end of 1946 there were 7,732 physicians (including dentists) in Poland, or 3·2 per 10,000 people. By 1950 there were 11,600; there were 38,000 in 1960; 62,900 in 1970; 80,400 in 1980; and 88,300 in 1984, that is to say, 23·8 doctors per 10,000 heads of the population. Although Poland made a great improvement in those years, compared with its CMEA neighbours it still lagged behind all except Romania.

The number of hospital beds doubled between 1950 (128,000) and 1980 (256,000), yet grew slowly in the next three years to 258,000. In 1984, the last year for which statistical information is available, it did not grow at all. The number of pharmacies grew from 2,361 in 1960 to 4,177 in 1984; and pharmacists from 3,800 in 1950 to 16,000 in 1984.[84]

These figures, however, do not tell us whether the quality of the services offered meets the country's needs. They tell us nothing about the level of medical training, attitudes towards patients, or sanitary standards in hospitals and clinics. They do not describe the conditions under which doctors work, nor do they mention low wages, transport difficulties and shortages of medicines. They say nothing about the priorities that govern admission to hospital and access to specialized equipment.

Speaking on Radio Warsaw, Professor Marek Okolski, a demographer at Warsaw University, said that the Polish mortality rate had been rising, among some groups of the population, since the mid-60s.[85] At first, this affected middle-aged men, then the entire male population and a considerable part of the female population. In general, the ground which had been gained in terms of public health between the end of the Second World War and the mid-60s was subsequently lost again.

More recently, World Health Organization figures showed that life expectancy in Poland (male and female combined) fell from 67·3 years in 1982 to 67·1 in 1983 and 66·8 in 1984.[86] Deaths from diseases of the circulatory system have more than doubled; they are the main direct cause of death. But people also fall ill through the pressures of modern living, unbalanced diets, heavy smoking and drinking and environmental pollution. Okolski said that the standard of sanitation in Poland was on a nineteenth-century level; it was impossible to find a clean lavatory in Warsaw, and there was no toilet paper and no soap in schools or other public buildings. It was not a question of establishing courses in hygiene but of ensuring the necessary supply of materials and personnel.[87]

ALCOHOL consumption in the country is extremely high, so much so that Polish experts have described the drinking problem as an "alcoholic time-bomb." Recent official figures estimated that about

[84] *CMEA Statistical Yearbook 1985* op. cit., p. 435.
[85] 17 Sept. 1986, 7.00 am.
[86] *World Health Statistics Annual*, op. cit. p. 30.
[87] See Polish SR/13, *RFER*, 29 Aug. 1986, item 6, reprinted as "Sanitary Conditions in Poland" in this issue.

three million Poles get drunk daily out of a population of 38 million. Of these, 1·2 million absent themselves from their jobs. In 1984 32,000 people were drunk at work; in 1985 this figure jumped to 38,000. Deputy Interior Minister Lucjan Czubinski said that "alcohol is the number one plague." The Polish government has yet to follow the Soviet lead in declaring war on alcohol abuse beyond reducing the number of shops selling alcohol by 10 per cent in 1983 and raising prices twice in 1986 alone. Neither measure has apparently had much effect on consumption.[88] The Catholic church declared August a "month of sobriety"; it is the priests who are urging the state to institute tougher measures to combat alcoholism.[89]

At a time when health standards are improving worldwide and the incidence of various diseases is declining,[90] the latest Polish statistical yearbook lists several major illnesses as having become more common in recent years. The incidence of salmonella poisoning, for instance, has increased sharply, from 11·8 cases per 100,000 people in 1971 to 50·0 in 1984; other food poisoning decreased to 24·7 cases per 10,000 in 1976 from 30·4 in 1975, but increased again to 45·5 in 1984. This is consistent with a report criticizing the quality of a considerable proportion of the food on sale in Polish shops, including cheese and meat.[91] Cases of measles decreased from 431·1 per 100,000 in 1971 to 69·9 in 1980, but increased to 147·4 in 1984, probably because since the 1970s only 30 per cent of children have been vaccinated. Viral infections of the liver increased from 135·6 cases per 100,000 in 1980 to 141·6 in 1984. Cases of influenza almost doubled between 1980 (3,964 cases per 100,000) and 1984 (6,642·7). The incidence of chemical poisoning has been steadily increasing from an average of 29·1 per 100,000 in the early 1970s to 33·5 in 1984.[92]

An article in *Zycie Warszawy* analyzed the state of health of Warsaw residents. Over 50 per cent die of circulatory illnesses; cancer is on the increase, more so than in the rest of the country; psychiatric illnesses—usually connected with alcoholism, but also with the psychoses of the elderly—have increased; respiratory problems have been the leading cause of absence from work. Tuberculosis continues to be a serious problem. Although the number of cases has fallen in recent years, Warsaw still registers three times the international average recorded by the World Health Organization. According to the health authorities in Warsaw still registers three times the international average recorded by the World Health Organization. Accoding to the health authorities in Warsaw the main threats to public health stem from pollution, poor sanitary conditions (partly caused by a shortage of cleaning agents and

[88] UPI, 13 Aug. 1986; *Rzeczpospolita*, 17 June 1986. In March prices were raised by 10 per cent and in September by an average of 15 per cent; *Zycie Warszawy* 15 Sept. 1986.

[89] For a review of the drinking problem in Poland, see Polish SR/13, op. cit. item 8.

[90] *World Health Statistics Annual*, op. cit. pp. 214–370.

[91] *Zycie Warszawy*, 6 April 1986.

[92] *Rocznik Statystyczny* (Polish Statistical Yearbook) (GUS, Warsaw, 1985), p. 488.

disinfectants) and the general lack of certain medicines. The article criticized the generally poor performance of the city's health services.[93]

POLAND has generally the same staffing problems as the other Soviet bloc countries. Doctors are overworked, saddled with bureaucratic duties and badly paid. A skilled paediatrician may earn one-third of the income of a skilled mechanic.[94] A nurse with 20 years of experience earns 13,000 zlotys a month including overtime and weekend pay, while the average monthly wage in Poland was 22,700 zlotys (June 1986).

With such poor levels of pay it is no wonder that many medical professionals opt for contract work abroad. There were, in 1986, 950 Polish medical specialists (doctors, nurses and technicians) working on individual contracts abroad. Thousands more worked under collective contracts (medical teams farmed out as a group to staff an entire hospital or department). Over 1,400 professionals in this category are currently employed in Libya alone. Most contracts are signed with Arab countries: Algeria, Libya, Morocco, Tunisia, Kuwait and the United Arab Emirates, as well as Nigeria and Zambia. Both types of contract are arranged by the Foreign Trade Enterprise, Polservice, for two-year periods. Fees are paid to Polservice by the employee. Polservice reports that contract work brings in the equivalent of US$13–14 million a year in hard currency.[95] Sending medical professionals abroad is just one more way in which the country's overall economic plight works to the detriment of health provision and leads to declining standards of treatment and declining life expectancy.

Romania

Expenditures on public health in Romania increased yearly over the last 35 years in absolute terms and as a percentage of the national budget; from 664 million lei in 1950 (3·4 per cent of the national budget), to 4·79 billion lei in 1965 (5·1 per cent of the national budget), and to 17·26 billion lei in 1984 (6·6 per cent of the national budget).[96]

In numbers of hospital beds, physicians and dentists as well as numbers of pharmacies, there was a steady increase from 1938 to 1984 (the last year for which such statistics are available). Recently the number of auxiliary medical staff declined slightly, from 132,912 in 1980 to 132,645 in 1984.

Romania has also made steady progress in reducing infant mortality from 116·7 deaths per 1,000 live births in 1950 to 44·1 in 1965 and 23·4 in 1984. (The real number of deaths may be much higher, since the Romanian Statistical Office does not record a birth until the infant is one

[93] *Zycie Warszawy*, 11 June 1986.

[94] *Tygodnik Powszechny*, 27 March 1986; also *Chicago Tribune*, 26 May 1986.

[95] Polish SR/2, *RFER*, 5 Feb. 1985, item 4.

[96] *Anuarul Statistic al RSR 1985* (RSR Statistical Yearbook 1985) (Directia Centrala de Statistica, Bucharest, 1985), pp. 282–3 and 286.

month old.) Life expectancy has risen from 61·4 years for men and 64·9 for women in 1956 to 66·9 for men and 72·6 for women in 1984.[97]

Romania provides 'free' medical assistance for all "according to the provisions of the law."[98] All private practice was abolished in 1978. The man in the street is indeed offered free medical care to the extent that the regular services can provide it. He has no choice of doctor, and will not be treated either with Western medicines or with modern Western equipment. These can usually be obtained only at special health units serving the Party apparatus or the security police and leading army personnel. The state does not provide free medical care for some 500,000 private peasants, nor to the country's 40,500 private artisans. Recent reports indicate that citizens excluded from free health care now include the elderly as well who are refused treatment on the grounds that nothing can be done for them at their advanced age.[99]

Since 1983, to cut health costs, the state has officially established special medical units that treat patients for a fee. This service is normally limited to medical consultations but it is also known to have provided some surgery.[100] The regular 'free' service is not completely free of charges either as gratuities are an accepted tradition. Money and goods, especially foodstuffs, are acceptable forms of tipping and bribery, king-size cigarettes being an apparently favourite gift with many doctors and nurses. So much for the health-consciousness of the health-caring section of Romanian society.

THERE are significant differences between urban and rural standards of medical care. Of the country's total population of 22·6 million, just over 50 per cent live in the countryside. Yet only 7,000 of the 44,484 physicians in Romania work in rural areas (15·7 per cent).[101] Most medical units are located in the towns, forcing peasants to travel far to find medical help.

Physicians enjoy good social standing in Romanian society but are paid less than technicians and economists. A doctor earns from 2,560 to 5,590 lei a month (wages in Romania range from 1,425 to 6,430 lei).[102] They are not exempt from doing "patriotic work" such as cleaning hospitals and other "voluntary" labour.

Romanian health experts, prominent physicians and officials have been critical of the health service for some time.[103] The most severe criticisms concern the poor training of medical staff, the neglect of

[97] Ibid. pp. 22–3 and 40. Romania's peculiar way of recording births is described in "Balkan Socialism" in this issue.

[98] Law No. 3, Article 2, on public health (published in *Buletinul Oficial al RSR*, Vol. I-a, No. 54, 10 July 1978).

[99] See "Romanian Pensioners Barred from Moving to Population Centres," "Balkan Socialism" and "Worse than During the War," in this issue.

[100] Decree No. 279 (*Buletinul Oficial al RSR*, Vol. I-a, No. 60, 1 Aug. 1983).

[101] Agerpres, 10 May 1986.

[102] Law No. 57 (*Buletinul Oficial al RSR*, Vol. I-a, No. 59–60, 23 July 1980).

[103] Romanian SR/23, *RFER*, 22 Sept. 1978, item 9.

Romania's famous medical college, and the closure of certain medical schools. In 1986 the Party's Political Executive Committee again recommended that firm measures be taken to improve medical staff training. Other complaints concerned the arbitrary introduction of new drugs and treatments. While some new, safe and effective medicines are caught up in bureaucratic delays, others, less safe, have come into use.[104]

Romania has established national programmes to counter cardiovascular diseases, cancer, mental illnesses, contagious diseases (including tuberculosis) and rheumatism.[105] Official concern for public health education is demonstrated by mass sports activities. Romania does not allow birth control education; nor are contraceptives or abortions legal. The regime enforces a strict policy to promote the birthrate including monthly gynaecological examinations for all women to monitor pregnancies. Yet, to official dismay, the birthrate continues to stagnate. Abortion is punishable, earning prison sentences for doctor and patient alike.[106] No measures have been taken to counter drug abuse, but alcoholism and excessive smoking are officially recognized as serious medical problems. The Party's Political Executive Committee has demanded a campaign to combat them.[107]

The approach to preventive health education is also poor. For example, the first reference to AIDS in the press appeared in late 1985. It explained the name and classification of the disease and said that its causes were unknown and that it was fatal. But nothing was said about how AIDS is acquired, the incubation period, the symptoms and evolution of the disease or how it can be prevented. Nor was it stated that male homosexuals are particularly at risk. This omission is perhaps not surprising as homosexuality is not publicly acknowledged in Romania. Only AIDS cases in the West are reported, no mention being made of those reported in the USSR, Poland, Czechoslovakia, Hungary and Yugoslavia.[108]

The reaction to the Chernobyl accident also showed up the ineffectual nature of the Romanian public health services and public information policies. Despite high levels of radiation, the Romanian media did not discuss the health issues involved and no scientist or doctor is known to have explained to the public what exactly had happened. The Romanian media did not mention Bucharest's request to the US State Department for assistance to assess the risks, nor that the Department complied and sent a team of nuclear experts. It was also withheld from the public that the British National Radiological Protection Board had issued data on radioactivity levels in Bucharest and that these were found to be higher than in most parts of Eastern Europe. It was dubious comfort for Romanians that the food shortages may have been relieved by the West

[104] *Scinteia*, 7 July 1978.
[105] Ibid. 1 and 23 Sept. 1975.
[106] See "Abortions in Romania" and "Balkan Socialism" in this issue.
[107] *Scinteia*, 10 May 1986.
[108] Romanian SR/17, *RFER*, 17 Dec. 1985, item 10.

European ban on Romanian (and other East European) agricultural exports in the wake of the Chernobyl accident.

Whilst comparatively little detailed information on the health service and the state of health of the Romanian population is available, the general poverty, austerity and authoritarianism of the system clearly show up in the health sector. Romania is now almost certainly the least developed East European country, and both provision and achievements in health care are correspondingly low. In Bulgaria and Poland the health services have been made to earn hard currency in one form or another; in Romania the dominant conseqence of the lack of hard currency is the extreme shortage of imported medicines and equipment. This has resulted in parsimony and calculation to the point of callousness in the selection of those who receive treatment after the needs of the privileged elite have been met. Whilst elitism is a characteristic of all East European countries (and the Soviet Union), the economic "targeting" of health care has reached an exceptionally high level in Romania. It is best expressed in the refusal to treat the elderly "because they will soon die anyway."

2. The Right to Work

AT each follow-up meeting of the Helsinki process, as indeed in any discussion on human rights, representatives of the Soviet bloc restated their position that the fundamental human rights are social and economic: the right to work, health care, social security and housing, and that governments should guarantee those rights. Only when those basic economic and social rights are provided, they claim, can the political rights of individuals acquire significance.[1] In the United States:

> . . . there are millions, in some cases tens of millions of people who are permanently or temporarily out of a job, who are forced to live in slums or who have no roof over their heads at all, who are driven with increasing ruthlessness at work, who are discriminated against on account of the colour of their skin, sex or age, whose incomes stay below the official poverty level, who have been unable to receive even an elementary education or medical care they sorely need, who live under conditions of utter lawlessness, persecution of dissidents, racism, rampant organized crime, corruption and rising drug abuse . . . .[2]

Each of the countries of Eastern Europe includes in its constitution some variant of Article 40 of the Soviet Constitution which explicitly defines the Right to Work as a right belonging to every citizen, i.e. guaranteed employment and payment according to the quantity and quality of work

[1] Vojtech Mastny (ed.), *Helsinki, Human Rights and European Security* (Duke University Press, 1986), p. 290.

[2] N. Setunsky, "Verbiage around Human Rights," *International Affairs* (Moscow, March 1986).

performed.[3] With minor differences in style, each country also claims that this right is assured by the socialist economic system which, by its very nature, "does not recognize economic crises nor unemployment, and guarantees a continuous rise in the real value of remuneration." Further, "the state directs its policy so that, as production increases, a gradual reduction of working time without a reduction in wages can be achieved."[4]

Alongside the separate labour codes in each country, these constitutions invariably mirror the wording of Articles 23 and 24 of the Universal Declaration of Human Rights (1948), which does not carry the force of law but to which the USA is a signatory:[5]

Article 23: 1. Everyone has the right to work, to free choice of employment, to just and favourable conditions of work and to protection against unemployment.
2. Everyone, without any discrimination, has the right to equal pay for equal work.
3. Everyone has the right to just and favourable remuneration ensuring for himself and his family an existence worthy of human dignity, and supplemented, if necessary, by other means of social protection.
4. Everyone has the right to form and join trade unions for the protection of his interests.

Article 24: Everyone has the right to rest and leisure, including reasonable limitation of working hours and periodic holidays with pay.[6]

The USA, however, does not see it as the government's responsibility to guarantee those rights, but rather to create an economic climate in which the individual can pursue them.[7]

Rights always involve duties and obligations. The Soviet Constitution states that:

> . . . it is the duty of, and a matter of honour for, every able-bodied citizen of the USSR to work conscientiously in his chosen, socially useful occupation and strictly to observe labour discipline. Evasion of socially useful work is incompatible with the principles of socialist society. . . .[8]

There are similar paragraphs in the constitutions and Labour Codes of

[3] See the respective constitutions: Bulgaria, Articles 40 and 41; Czechoslovakia, Article 21; GDR, Article 24; Hungary, Article 55; Poland, Article 68; Romania, Article 18.

[4] Czechoslovak Constitution, Article 21, paragraphs 2 and 3.

[5] The Universal Declaration is supplemented by two covenants, the International Covenant on Civil and Political Rights and the International Covenant on Economic, Social and Cultural Rights. These covenants are binding, but only a minority of states has ratified them. The USA is not among the ratifiers of either. See Joshua Muravchik, *The Uncertain Crusade* (Lanham, New York, 1986), pp. 76–77.

[6] *Human Rights: International Documents* (The United Nations, New York, 1975), p. 11.

[7] Richard Schifter, Head of US Delegation. Address presented at Ottawa, 22 May 1985. Current Policy No. 713, Department of State.

[8] Constitution of the USSR, Article 60.

the other Soviet bloc countries. These cover compulsory labour, fines or even prison sentences for "parasites," as those who avoid whatever the authorities may consider to be socially acceptable work are described.

WHEN full employment is officially guaranteed, unemployment does not, and cannot, exist according to the Marxist vision of a transformed society. The USSR last officially recorded unemployment figures in 1930, and announced a ban on unemployment in 1931 abolishing, at the same time, unemployment benefits.[9]

No East European country (apart from Yugoslavia) records or publishes unemployment figures in its regular statistics, which tells us more about the uses of terminology than the actual state of employment in those countries. Clearly, there is hidden unemployment: workers between jobs, mothers on extended maternity or child care leave; there are individuals who are denied work because of political activity or as applicants for exit visas, and those accused of parasitism.

Throughout the Soviet bloc full employment is organically linked to economic planning. Full employment policies developed alongside the nationalization of the means of production and the transformation of largely agricultural societies into industrial ones. These policies transferred manpower from the countryside to the towns with the partial exception of Czechoslovakia and East Germany which were industrialized before the Communist takeover. Rapid industrialization created an immediate need for labour and demanded a massive accumulation of fixed capital. The collectivization of land turned farmers into farm workers (Poland and Yugoslavia were exceptions because private farms have been largely retained there.)

TABLE I

Percentage of agricultural land outside the State and Cooperative Sectors (Private Farms and Plots)[10]

	1955	1960	1970
Bulgaria	36·7	9·1	10·7
Czechoslovakia	57·4	19·1	13·7
GDR	72·7	17·6	14·9
Hungary	68·0	32·1	17·0
Poland	77·3	87·3	84·4
Romania	65·3	20·4	15·8
USSR	5·0	3·3	3·2
Yugoslavia	92·4	89·6	85·3

[9] *Trud* v *SSSR* (Moscow, 1986), p. 23.

[10] Source: Manouchehr Ganji, *The Realization of Economic, Social and Cultural Rights: Problems, Policies, Programs* (UN Commission on Human Rights, New York, 1975), p. 136.

Table II[11]

Growth of Employment

	Year	Population (in thousands)	Total employed (in thousands)	Employed as % of total	Approx. % of women employed
Bulgaria	1950	7520	No figures available		
	1960	7867	1780	23	14
	1970	8490	2761	32	28
Czechoslovakia	1950	13093	4300	33	24
	1960	13654	4972	36	28
	1970	14334	6182	43	38
East Germany	1950	18388	3231	18	10
	1960	17241	5438	32	26
	1970	17058	6025	35	32
Hungary	1950	9338	1510	16	8
	1960	9984	2822	28	8
	1970	10239	3558	34	29
Poland	1950	24824	4914	20	12
	1960	29561	7184	24	16
	1970	32473	9744	30	23
Romania	1950	15873	2123	—	—
	1960	18407	3229	18	9
	1970	20250	5037	25	15

[11] Ibid.

Statistics also show steady growth throughout Eastern Europe both in the total number of those employed and in the percentage of wage-earners, as well as consistent growth in the percentage of women in the work force.

The arrival of Marxism–Leninism in Eastern Europe brought with it the right to work and the obligation to do so. The citizen became a wage earner with little prospect of investing in the future through his private exertions (Hungary, since the late 1960s, has been a partial exception). He was guaranteed survival but little more.

TODAY the Soviet Union and the East European countries claim that they suffer, in various degrees, from shortages of labour. In some countries, however, labour resources remain untapped and people with certain qualifications have difficulty in finding jobs. There are areas where jobs are available but living conditions are inadequate or uninviting—where housing, access to transportation, food, consumer supplies and cultural and social amenities are poor.

Labour shortages obviously limit growth and are an obstacle to economic flexibility and technological progress. The latter is especially important for the small East European countries which depend on foreign trade and face strong competition from Western suppliers. A tight labour market has also punished the service sector and thus any attempt to improve the standard of living.[12]

At the same time, labour shortages are accompanied by a gross under-utilization of labour, overmanning and underemployment. These facts are well known. They are publicly admitted and likely to become some of the most sensitive issues under Gorbachov. Labour discipline is lax throughout Eastern Europe; alcoholism is responsible for a great deal of absenteeism, disruption of work schedules and accidents. Automation and the better utilization of existing plants and equipment have been suggested as obvious ways of overcoming the shortages of labour.[13]

If policies of this nature were effectively implemented there could be a danger of serious unemployment for the first time in Eastern Europe. Although labour is in short supply at present because it is inefficiently used, the labour force is also unevenly distributed. But there are difficulties of an even more intractable nature.

> . . . To cure the tight labor market effectively would require, among other things, the shutting down of enterprises which produce unsaleable goods, the transfer of labor from non-efficient to more efficient enterprises, the removal of redundant workers and, last but not least, the tightening of labor discipline in all respects. An attempt to solve any of these problems fast and consistently, even if

[12] Jan Adam (ed.), *Employment Policies in the Soviet Union and Eastern Europe* (Macmillan, London, 1982), p. xiii.

[13] Ibid.

> incentives are used, involves political risks which are greater than the politicians are willing to take. . . .
> . . . The commitment of Communist leaders to full employment (one of the trumps they hold—a trump which it would be very risky to give up) is one of the factors which make it difficult to enforce labour discipline.[14]

Demographic trends do not bode well for the future of the East European labour market. Birth rates in all Soviet bloc countries are decreasing and mortality rates rising. In East Germany and Hungary the population is declining.[15] Emigration and defections from East Germany and Poland have had a direct effect on the supply of labour because it is mainly young people who leave in search of better living conditions.

Also, the percentage of retired people, and thus the burden on the working sector of the population, is swiftly increasing. According to an International Labour Organization study, in 1950 economically inactive people aged 60 and over comprised 7·3 per cent of the population as a whole in the world's industrialized countries. By 1985 this figure rose to 13·3 per cent, and in the year 2025 it is expected to reach 20·7 per cent. The comparable percentages are not available for Eastern Europe, but over the same 75-year time span the number of people aged 60 and over, dependent on every 1,000 workers, is expected to rise from 56 to 345 in Romania, from 82 to 445 in Bulgaria, from 82 to 389 in Poland and from 119 to 463 in Yugoslavia. In the USSR the number will rise from 94 to 408, and in the USA from 184 to 428.[16] These figures suggest that the East European countries would experience the same trend as the rest of the industrialized world.

THE East European labour codes cover most of the points listed under the "right to work" of the Universal Declaration of Human Rights: the right to the free choice of employment, occupational training, protection against dismissal, the functions of the trade unions (some even deal with strikes and work stoppages), the definition of adequate wages, the right to equal pay for equal work, fair conditions of work and the right to leisure and rest. There are some additional rights and guarantees covering obligatory labour, the right to leave one's work, work discipline, the rights of farm labourers, rights to communal property and regulations for (or limitations on) self-employment. All these rights are determined according to Marxist–Leninist ideological principles which define what is to be considered socially useful or appropriate according to the conditions prevailing in each country.[17]

As signatories to international agreements and conventions, the Soviet

[14] Ibid. p. xiv.
[15] See RAD Background Report/179 *Radio Free Europe Research*, 8 Dec. 1986.
[16] *Estimates and Projections of the Economically Active Population, 1950–2025*, third edition (ILO, Geneva, 1987).
[17] For a detailed survey of the above rights and guarantees in the various Soviet bloc countries in 1975, see Manouchehr Ganji, op. cit. pp. 134–61.

bloc countries echo lofty ideals, rights, promises and guarantees in their legislation, but then fail to put them into practice, either by reinterpreting them to fit political specifications, or subordinating them to more urgent ideological priorities.

Official trade unions exist in all East European countries, but they are subordinated to the Communist Party and function primarily as the Party's agents implementing economic plans, stimulating increases in productivity and strengthening labour morale. Attempts by workers to organize themselves independently in defence of their interests parallel with the official unions have been rigorously suppressed.[18]

Bulgaria

New regulations for economic activity, embodying the latest version of the Bulgarian "New Economic Mechanism" (NEM), came into effect in January 1987. They seek to promote "self-management" down to the level of enterprises and even individual brigades.[19] Labour collectives now have the right to make management decisions. Wage funds and individual wages will depend on their economic achievements.

Earlier regulations introduced the piece-rate system, both for individual workers and brigades. The Prime Minister, Georgi Atanasov, presenting a draft of the new regulations for discussion at a BCP Central Committee Plenum in December 1986 said that "the principles guaranteeing wages have been restricted"; by this he meant that according to the new regulations any worker or group that produces little and/or of poor quality may be paid less than the basic wage.

In 1985 a long opposition leaflet on economic, social and political grievances, written by employees of the locomotive factory in Sofia, lifted the curtain on the workers' real feelings. One of the leaflet's basic demands was for a massive wage increase. It argued that instead of the current 200–300 leva, the monthly norm should be 1,000 leva. It covered working conditions at some length, and warned that over-zealous production records would become obligatory norms. It expressed a fear of unemployment, noting that in order to make up for low productivity the Bulgarian regime had already introduced 5,000 Vietnamese to perform low-paid, unskilled work, and that in the future more foreign workers would be brought in. It also reported on the use of labour brigades in the countryside to compensate for "passive resistance" on collective farms. School and university students, soldiers and pensioners were being forced to participate.[20]

Worker's unrest has not been widespread in Bulgaria. After several

[18] ICFTU (International Confederation of Free Trade Unions), *Annual Survey of Violations of Trade Union Rights 1985/86* (Brussels, June 1986), p. 11.

[19] *Rabotnichesko Delo*, 23 Dec. 1986; *Darzhaven Vestnik*, No. 3, 13 Jan. 1987; see also Bulgarian SR/1, *RFER*, 13 Feb. 1987, item 1.

[20] Bulgarian SR/5, *RFER*, 27 May 1986, item 1. See also "Our Work is Our Strength!" pp. below.

instances of serious opposition in the early 1950s (the most famous being a strike by Plovdiv tobacco workers in 1951), there were reports in 1982 of an independent trade union, "Solidarity of Work," which appeared to have some degree of support nationwide and sympathizers within the BCP, but nothing is known of its fate. Early in 1986 a three-day strike was said to have taken place among Polish guest workers at a site where a nuclear power station was under construction.[21]

A new labour code, first mooted in 1966, finally became law in March 1986.[22] A lengthy document, it sets out to align labour legislation with economic reorganization. Earlier, in November 1982, a BCP Central Committee Plenum adopted a guiding document, "The Party Concept on the New Labour Code," which laid down the broad principles of any future labour legislation. In March 1983 a Committee on Labour and Social Questions was established under the auspices of the Council of Ministers as a successor to the Committee on Labour and Wages. It was to be a "public-state agency" including representatives from district and municipal councils and was to play a major role in developing a "new system of labour," covering, for example, the reduction of heavy manual work, new ways of setting labour norms, improving working conditions, better use of leisure time and correct wage differentiation.[23]

Meanwhile, other changes in labour regulations have been put into effect by decree. In March 1985 workers at enterprises which had been lagging behind production quotas were required to work a six-day rather than a five-day week. This was one of a number of emergency economic measures intended to counteract delays in production. The extended working week is meant to stay in effect until the workers have made up for lost ground. Working hours on priority construction sites are being extended to two or even three shifts, and machinery is being used seven days a week instead of five. The press reported that labour productivity was not rising, and that construction enterprises were using their machinery to only 30 per cent of capacity.[24]

There are continual calls to work two or even three shifts in the national economy in general in order to make more rational use of production capacities. This has not happened, however, partly because workers, in particular women, are unwilling to work night shifts. The management supports them, admitting that besides being unpleasant, night work shows a higher accident rate and is less productive.

The struggle against "persons deviating from socially useful labour and living an anti-social, parasitic way of life" seems to be a continuing problem. The first decree designed to provide a solution was issued in 1962,[25] but in 1971 the number of young people neither studying nor

[21] Ibid.
[22] *Darzhaven Vestnik*, Nos. 26 and 27, 1 and 4 April 1986.
[23] Bulgarian SR/5, *RFER*, 18 April 1983, item 2.
[24] *Rabotnichesko Delo*, 27 March 1985, and Tanjug (Sofia), 31 July 1985.
[25] *Izvestia na Presidium*, No. 63, 7 Aug. 1962.

working stood at 51,643.[26] Decrees "securing work or professional training" for them were passed in 1975 and again in 1985. In March 1986 the prominent Bulgarian journalist Marko Semov wrote in *Narodna Mladezh*:

> . . . there are idlers, yes, there are. There have always been and I'm afraid there always will be. The point is that we, as a society with ambitious tasks, cannot afford their number to be larger than that which is simply inevitable in every human society. . . .[27]

Tighter discipline, control and financial stringency have been the Bulgarian authorities' attempted answers to this problem.

Czechoslovakia

With the experience of 1968 still in mind, the Czechoslovak authorities are evidently afraid that loosening central economic control could undermine political control. In an interview with Reuter's correspondent, government spokesman Frantisek Kouril said that Czechoslovakia was not interested in Hungarian-style market socialism and that its experience with private enterprise was not encouraging.[28] There seems, however, to be a lot of public interest in Gorbachov's reforms, and developments in the Soviet Union are closely followed. The leadership is apparently divided over their applicability to Czechoslovakia.[29]

Czechoslovak economists are talking about the need to "restructure" the economy. In order to reduce the consumption of fuel and raw materials and increase competitiveness on the international markets, a number of obsolete industries, such as metallurgy and heavy engineering, will have to be streamlined while more attention is to be paid to service industries. The authorities have been aware of this need for the past 20 years but they have done little about it, partly because they feared that restructuring might entail unemployment.[30]

Yet some Czechoslovak economists, such as Valtr Komarek, argue that while "socialism and full employment are indivisible" it is only "rational employment" that should be guaranteed by socialism. The protection of inefficient industries and slavish adherence to an unqualified and oversimplified conception of full employment impoverish society and ultimately weaken what Komarek calls the "real" security that people should get from a well-run economy (as distinct from enjoying risk-free employment but for low real wages).[31]

[26] *Literaturen Front*, No. 46, 16 Nov. 1972.
[27] *Narodna Mladezh*, 20 March 1986.
[28] Reuter, 18 Dec. 1986.
[29] See Czechoslovak SR/1, *RFER*, 7 Jan. 1986, item 11 for a Yugoslav evaluation of major changes to come in the Czechoslovak economy.
[30] Czechoslovak SR/11, *RFER*, 31 July 1986, item 5.
[31] Czechoslovak SR/5, *RFER*, 26 March 1986, item 4.

A wage reform is now being gradually introduced throughout the Czechoslovak economy. The new system of remuneration (known as ZEUMS) is intended to stimulate labour productivity by clearly rewarding individual effort. This would correct one of the most serious impediments of the centrally planned system: egalitarianism of reward regardless of individual commitment or merit. The reform is being implemented in two stages. The first, setting new production norms, was carried out in the early 1980s. The second began in January 1985 and is expected to take two or three years to take effect.[32] In December 1985 however, Kazimir Nagy, the Slovak Minister of Labour and Social Welfare, complained that ZEUMS was not creating a greater differentiation of income, nor increasing production, because few workers had been punished for shoddy work or rewarded for exceptional effort.

Meanwhile, Nasta Baumrukova, the Czech Minister of Labour, announced that the authorities were preparing to alter the Labour Code and planning to submit their amendments to the Czechoslovak Trade Union Congress in 1987. These changes are intended to "strengthen labour discipline in harmony with the interests of working collectives" and to enhance workers' interest in the quality of the goods they produced. Baumrukova stated that the government would "continue" to improve the cost-effectiveness of the wages system and do away with "the outdated methods of an extensive economy." It would concentrate instead on "technological modernization." She did not explain whether this would mean reducing work forces or indeed lead to unemployment,[33] but if the structural changes that modernization inevitably involves were, in fact, to occur on a substantial scale they would entail a considerable redeployment and retraining of labour or worse. Such changes are always resisted. Older workers find it hard to adjust. They fear losing income and status. So far, at least, Prague has not given much thought to these problems.

The "German Democratic Republic"

The 1986 Congress of the Socialist Unity Party of Germany (SED) confirmed the economic policies of the preceding 15 years. The GDR is unwilling to start a fresh round of reforms on the grounds that it already has an efficient centralized economy of the kind the USSR is now trying to develop.[34]

Among East German workers, however, job dissatisfaction is widespread resulting in a high rate of labour turnover. Workers complain of the same frustrations and discomforts as they do in the other

[32] For a complete description of the wage problem and reform, see "Friction over Reform of the Wage System in Czechoslovakia," RAD (Research and Analysis Department)/ Sobell, 14 April 1986.

[33] Radio Prague, 4 Aug. 1986, 18.30.

[34] Reuter, 18 Dec. 1986. See also RAD Background Report/32, 6 March 1987 and RAD Background Report/23, 20 Feb. 1987.

centrally-planned economies: lack of good quality machinery and equipment, shortages of materials and parts, low wages, systemic inadequacies in labour organization, long commuting times and arbitrary transfers from one work-place to another,[35] long queues and shortages of consumer goods (particularly when compared with lifestyles seen on West German television).

Despite dissatisfaction, there has been no major labour unrest since the workers' uprisings of 1953. Sympathy among East Germans with the demands of the Polish workers during the Solidarity period was hard to detect. The constitutional right to strike was abrogated in 1968.

The reduction of the working week to 40 hours has been under discussion for some years. The average working week was shortened from 45 to 43·75 hours in 1967, with a 42 hour week for shift workers. The line the Party is now taking is that this is not the right time for change. There are labour shortages[36]—and the economy is doing so well with the existing week that shortening it would be risky. Labour shortage is a fundamental problem. The population is declining and emigration to West Germany continues, although it has been greatly reduced since the building of the Berlin Wall. The number of East Germans of working age is expected to remain at the 1985 level until 1990. According to the estimates of both West and East German experts, the number of pensioners in employment will decline and the number of children grow. After 1990 some absolute growth in the labour force is expected[37] but the burden on that work force will increase because there will be a heavy rise in the number of pensioners.

Hungary

Since 1968 Hungary has led the way for all the other East European nations in economic reform. Although the economy has stagnated in recent years, personal living standards improved greatly during the 1960s and 1970s and are appreciably higher than elsewhere in Eastern Europe. A small but growing private sector has produced attractive shops and restaurants, joint ventures with Western firms have been encouraged and a fair supply of consumer goods, even though they are expensive, have brightened life for Hungarians. Labour laws and practices make it possible for those who are prepared to work hard to make additional incomes often by holding down more than one job.[38] Real wages, however, have been falling and may fall further as the government takes action to reduce a soaring budget deficit. This quadrupled in 1985, then tripled again in 1986 to total 35·7 billion forints (US$1·08 billion). After the expiry of a four-month wages' freeze in March 1987, firms now face

[35] M. Messing, *Industrie-Bauarbeiter in beiden Teilen Deutschlands* (Verlag Wissenschaft und Politik, Cologne, 1981), p. 318.

[36] RIAS, 11 Feb. 1987.

[37] Jiri Kosta, "Manpower Problems in the GDR," in Jan Adam (ed.), *Employment Policies in the Soviet Union and Eastern Europe* (Macmillan Press, 1982), p. 67.

[38] Hungarian SR/6, *RFER*, 27 May 1986, item 4.

severe tax penalties for awarding pay rises above a one or two per cent margin. This represents an appreciable cut in real terms because inflation is forecast to rise from 5·3 to seven per cent in 1987.[39]

In September 1986 Hungary passed Eastern Europe's first bankruptcy law since when the word "unemployment" began to be bandied about.[40] Some estimates for the number of workers likely to lose their jobs in inefficient industries are as high as 200,000. Redundant labour is to be "reallocated" by 1990. Although further reforms including the banking system are already in the pipeline, Janos Kadar, the General Secretary of the Hungarian Socialist Workers' Party, denies that the changes are capitalistic. In the words of a Western diplomat, however, "a lot of these reforms are designed to get companies to run as if they were in a market economy . . . they want all the things the market economy does."[41] The trade unions and politicians play down fears of unemployment, citing the shortages of labour in the service industries and other sectors of the economy.

So far, no major bankruptcy has been declared and no major "displacement of workers" has happened. It is unlikely that any enterprise considered vital to the economy will be allowed to go under; such firms will probably receive further subsidies from the central authorities. But the regime appears to have the political will to face the threat of unemployment and suffer the consequences. As Ivan Berend, Chairman of the Hungarian Academy, put it to the Spanish paper *Ya* on 1 June 1987:

> The idea of total unemployment used to be an untouchable principle, but the situation has now changed, and the government believes that structural unemployment is inevitable. . . . Such unemployment will not (however) exist as a permanent feature.

The 1987 budget allocates three billion forints (US$67 million) to "enterprise reorganization." This is designed to cover potential unemployment and retraining benefits.[42]

THE reduction of subsidies to the Hungarian railways led to a fall in operating profits from about 10 billion forints to 600 million in 1986; as a result 7,000 workers may be made redundant. Approximately 200 workers are to lose their jobs at a meat processing factory in the south, while several other meat processing plants are expected to announce redundancies in 1987. About 600 workers will be dismissed because of plant closure at a foundry near the Czechoslovak border, where a further 1,500 will be laid off before 1990.[43] The Rabatext textile company,

[39] Reuter (Budapest), 3 March 1987.
[40] Hungarian SR/10, *RFER*, 30 Sept. 1986.
[41] Reuter (Vienna), 18 Dec. 1986.
[42] Hungarian SR/2, *RFER*, 25 Feb. 1987, item 1.
[43] Roger Boyes, *The Times*, 30 Dec. 1986.

employing 2,540 workers, has announced plans to release 100 people within the first few months of 1987 in a bid to improve efficiency.[44] Arpad Voros, Deputy Minister of Industry, recently stated that over the next two years 10,000 iron and steel workers would lose their jobs in the most dramatic shake-up of its kind ever witnessed in communist Eastern Europe.[45]

So far no unemployment benefit is being paid. Redundant workers, it is said, will be retrained and offered new jobs. Officials say that the law is designed to make the economy more flexible by moving workers from inefficient enterprises to more successful ones. They insist that laid-off workers will not remain jobless for any length of time, and that mass unemployment of the Western kind will never occur in Hungary.

Low productivity remains a problem. Absenteeism wastes almost nine per cent of working time; alcoholism and overworking have caused the population's health to deteriorate and mortality to rise, particularly among men in the younger middle age group. This is widely attributed to the practice of holding a second and even third job, mostly to pay for a house or construction. The government is preparing a new taxation system designed to stimulate workers to increase their output to a point where they can actually live on a single income.[46] In his 1987 New Year message, Hungary's then President Pal Losonczi told the nation that it would have to work harder:

> . . . improving living conditions and fulfilling justified consumer demands will only be possible if every one of us works harder and more efficiently in his or her job . . . .[47]

The opportunity to exercise the right to work does not seem threatened, though the pressure on some workers to accept mobility and retraining will increase if the present reforms continue. If retraining is successful and new industries can provide new jobs, Hungarian real-wages should resume their increase in the long term.

Poland

In August 1980, Solidarity, the Independent Self-governing Trade Union (NSZZ Solidarnosc), focused the world's attention on the plight of workers in Communist countries in an unprecedented manner. Despite its subsequent suppression, Solidarity has made a permanent mark, and the struggle for workers' rights in Poland and elsewhere in Eastern Europe will continue to draw inspiration from that period.[48] This is true even though the emergency measures taken against the workers under martial law in 1981–82 have in many cases been incorporated in law in an

44 Reuter (Budapest), 14 Jan. 1987.
45 Misha Glenny, *The Guardian*, 5 March 1987.
46 Tanjug (Budapest), 21 Jan. 1987.
47 Reuter (Vienna), 1 Jan. 1987.
48 "Working in a Workers' State: Labour Law in Poland 1875–1985," *East European Reporter*, Vol. 2, No. 2 (London, 1986), pp. 28–33.

attempt to force the Polish working people to bear the main burden of the crisis produced by inefficient management of the national economy.

Over the past 10 years, with the exception of the period between August 1980 and the imposition of martial law in December 1981 when the activities of Solidarity were legal, the working conditions and legal position of the Polish workers have deteriorated. The Government, however, blamed the workers themselves for the consequences of bad management and planning.[49]

Since martial law was repealed, new laws, which further restrict the rights of workers, have included various provisions in criminal law, the law on tribunals,[50] the electoral law, the law on higher education and the trade union law. The latter firmly establishes the monopoly of the official trade unions set up by the authorities in 1982 by prohibiting more than one trade union per enterprise. A report on the violation of the rights of trade unions drawn up by the Brussels-based International Confederation of Free Trade Unions, observed:

> This whole legal arsenal is being used for a wide-ranging repression carried out against numerous Solidarity leaders and activists, resulting in physical harassment, denial of employment, discriminatory employment practices, arrests and re-arrests and severe prison sentences. In the course of 1985 and early 1986 several cases of brutality inflicted on Solidarity members by the security forces were reported, resulting in at least 15 deaths. Detentions of Solidarity activists have shown a further sharp increase since July 1985. While by the end of April 1985 some 100 trade union activists were in jail, this number rose to 239 in August 1985, according to figures published by the Polish authorities. However, the number given by Solidarity [underground] was 300, and this figure has steadily increased to over 500 at the end of 1985. Most of the detainees have been sentenced to prison terms between one and three and a half years for normal trade union activities, such as the printing, possession or distribution of trade union publications, participating in Solidarity demonstrations, the signing of petitions and protest letters and strike action. Trade union prisoners are held under particularly inhuman conditions and there are several reports of severe brutality inflicted on them by prison guards. This situation has forced several imprisoned Solidarity leaders to resort to hunger strikes in order to obtain better prison conditions, regular visits from family and lawyers and the status of political prisoner. . . .[51]

In September 1986 a general amnesty was declared and over 200 political prisoners, most of them connected with the Solidarity movement, were released. In January 1987 the Polish underground press claimed that there were 15 political prisoners still in jail.[52]

[49] See also Polish SR/13, *RFER*, 29 Aug. 1986, item 5.
[50] See also Polish SR/12, 13 Aug. 1986, item 3.
[51] *Annual Survey of Violations of Trade Union Rights 1985/86*, op. cit. p. 11.
[52] *Tygodnik Mazowsze*, No. 193, 7 Jan. 1987.

UNDER a new legislative procedure, introduced at the end of 1986, the tactics of repression have changed. Certain political offences, previously punishable by imprisonment, are now liable to fines and confiscations. The aim of this new policy is thought to be the destruction of the opposition's material base. Any illegal trade union activity is treated as political opposition. Within three months the authorities confiscated eight private cars, a microcomputer, two typewriters and three tape-recorders. They also imposed fines totalling 6·5 million zlotys. These included a sum of 974,000 zlotys in fines imposed on 19 people in Cracow in November. They had participated in a demonstration commemorating the recovery of Poland's independence on 11 November 1918.[53] Some individuals have been fined several months' salary and flats have been confiscated.

To alleviate the economic hardships suffered by those punished under the new legislation, Lech Walesa announced the establishment of a Fines' Fund. He appealed for support from home and abroad. The fund proposes to reimburse all fines and an amount of up to 400,000 zlotys for those whose cars have been confiscated. An Independent Publishers' Insurance Fund has been set up to cover losses resulting from fines and confiscations imposed on underground publishers.[54]

A typical form of repression, by no means new, is denial of employment:

> . . . A considerable number of those released under the terms of last year's amnesty have found it very difficult, if not impossible, to obtain work; others active in the opposition have been dismissed from their posts or are harassed by constant police surveillance. Despite official claims that staff shortages exist in major industries, these posts are not available to certain qualified applicants: Wladyslaw Frasyniuk, formerly a bus driver, was refused work despite vacancies for drivers in Wroclaw. Genowefa Pietrasz, a teacher with 20 years' experience, was dismissed on the grounds of having engaged in illegal activity and was refused a post as a teacher in Jaslo, although the region had taken on 56 unqualified teachers during the 1986–87 school year.[55] . . .

For over a year a special commission under the guidance of the Ministry of Labour, Wages and Social Affairs worked on preparing amendments to the Labour Code. Adopted by the Sejm, they went into force at the beginning of 1987. The changes include provisions for the role of the new (official) trade unions to which, according to government reports, only about 50 per cent of the work force belonged at the beginning of 1987; the abolition of arbitration boards and appeal commissions which formerly settled disagreements between employer and employee; the transfer of all labour disputes to Labour Tribunals; and the extension of the working

[53] Polish Press Review/2, *RFER*, 26 Feb. 1987, item 2.

[54] *Przeglad Wiadomosci Agencyjnych*, No. 1, 4 Jan. 1987.

[55] Polish Press Review, ibid.

week by four hours in certain factories deemed particularly important to the national economy.[56]

Other amendments put workers on a tighter leash. Sanctions against quitting one's job are harsher, it is more difficult to leave one job for another, and workers are prohibited from holding a second job without permission from their primary employer. A number of measures make it easier for the employer to dismiss workers. The subordination of the workers' interests to the success of the enterprise is emphasized. For example, a worker may be transferred against his will to perform work other than that specified in his labour contract. Under certain circumstances the employer may, "with the agreement of the majority of the staff," reduce wages for a period not exceeding six months.[57]

The amendments introduce a compulsory labour deployment system. Previously, job centres filled vacancies but did not have a monopoly of deciding who was to be given employment and where individual workers were to work. Compulsory deployment will drastically restrict the partial freedom of the labour market and make it more difficult to change one's place of work.[58] The threat of serious unemployment, which some economists thought, at the end of the 1970s, Poland would have to face, has not materialized. The right to a job does not appear to be in danger, but the right to choose that job freely, and the working conditions associated with it, are now severly restricted.

Romania

Nicolae Ceausescu's neo-Stalinist domestic policies have brought radical changes to Romania over the past 20 years and have impinged upon every aspect of human rights, political as well as social and economic. Increasingly restrictive and authoritarian political decrees have affected the Romanian citizens' lives in every way.

The innovation that caused most unrest was perhaps the reform of the wages' system. The relevant decree, known as the "Global Agreement," was initially promulgated in September 1983 and adopted, with minor changes, as law in 1986. It virtually eliminated the minimum wage in the major industrial, agricultural and research units. By depriving Romanian workers of a guaranteed minimum income that previously amounted to 80 per cent of their salaries, the government did away with a fundamental element of social legislation considered basic in most socialist countries. Under the new law workers sign a contract which amounts to a pledge of a certain level of productivity. If a worker does not fulfil this, his pledge is used as legal grounds for punishment. The law now makes wages dependent on a number of factors such as enterprise plan fulfilment, the economical use of raw materials and installations. These are factors over

[56] "What is New in the Labour Law?" *East European Reporter*, Vol. 2, No. 2 (London 1986), p. 33. See also Polish SR/5, *RFER*, 19 March 1986, item 5.

[57] Ibid.

[58] Ibid.

which even managers have often little or no control in centrally planned economies, much less the workers.[59]

A five-year training period was also instituted. While undergoing training, a worker is considered an "associate" employee with limited rights. He receives only half pay, the other half being deposited in a state savings' bank without interest. If he leaves the enterprise before the five-year period is up, he loses that money.[60]

The food crisis and the general austerity programme of the Ceausescu regime have led to repeated strikes, protest demonstrations and even acts of collective and individual violence. Strikes were reported in January and February 1981 at a steel mill and a chemical plant in Bucharest, as well as at petrochemical plants in Ploiesti and Pitesti. In October 1981 the first major miners' strike since the events of 1977 in the Jiu Valley erupted in three mines in the Motru area and at the Rogojelu heating plant. Acts of individual and collective violence were reported from the cities of Orsova and Giurgiu, and from the village of Matasari.[61]

AFTER the introduction of the new wages' system in 1984 more strikes were reported: first, in seven mines in the Maramuares area in the northwest; then 1,000 workers struck at the Brasov Steagul Rosu truck factory in November 1983 on hearing that their monthly pay had been cut from an average of 2,500 lei to around 700 lei. In February 1985 reports reached the West of discontent among workers in Timisoara; in August 1986 transport workers were said to have gone on strike in Arad, western Romania.[62] According to the samizdat news agency "Hungarian Press of Transylvania," an undisclosed number of workers at the heavy machinery plant in Cluj went on strike in the autumn of 1986 because their salaries had been reduced by 40 per cent for the non-fulfilment of production plans. Apparently, they were also protesting against the food rationing system which allots only 300 grammes of bread to each person per day. There were also protests at the Cluj Tehnofrig plant. The strikers went back to work only upon the delivery of additional food. Some strikers are said to have disappeared after these events; others apparently lost their jobs.[63] Another strike is reported to have occurred at the end of October 1986 in the Transylvanian town of Turda. Several thousand workers at the local glass factory staged a "Polish-style strike," standing in front of the machines with their arms folded. Their demands, too, included a better supply of food and the abolition of the "Global Agreement." After three days the strikers' demands were met.[64]

The only independent trade union to exist in Romania was SLOMR (the Free Trade Union of Workers in Romania) formed in 1979 by a

[59] Ibid.

[60] *Violations of the Helsinki Accords: Romania* (The International Federation for Human Rights, Vienna, Nov. 1986), p. 34.

[61] Ibid.

[62] See also Romanian SR/10, *RFER*, 26 June 1985, item 10.

[63] Romanian SR/1, ibid.

[64] Ibid.

group of intellectuals and workers. It succeeded in attracting about 2,000 supporters but was quickly suppressed by the authorities. Dr Ionel Cana, one of the founding members, was sentenced to five and a half years' imprisonment for "conspiracy and anti-government propaganda." He was eventually released under an amnesty. Carmen Popescu, another founder, was imprisoned and then released, but was rearrested in 1981. Sentenced to six years' imprisonment, she was released in August 1983.[65]

Romanian labour policy displays a distinctive combination of extreme illiberalism and financial stringency. Its key features are tight political control and economic austerity. Romania's position as the poorest and least developed country in Eastern Europe is aggravated by the brutally repressive character of the Ceausescu regime.

3. The Right to Housing

MORE than 40 years after the end of the Second World War basic housing needs have not been met in Eastern Europe. Some waiting lists are years long (in Poland, as many as 30); unrelated families often share kitchens and bathrooms; people spend years living in hostels and dormitories, and newly-weds with their parents or in-laws. Divorced couples often continue living under the same roof. Older buildings are often unsafe while the quality of new housing is poor. The urban infra-structure—roads, shops, transport—is frequently inadequate.

To control urban congestion and prevent towns and cities from growing beyond a planned maximum, state authorities have closed many major cities to new permanent residents. Young people leaving the countryside and university graduates from large cities often have no choice but to move to villages or satellite developments far from town centres. A young person's first criterion for choosing a job is to ask whether company housing goes with it.

Housing requirements involve not only the size and quality of accommodation but also the availability of public services such as shops, roads, schools, play-grounds and open spaces. These amenities are often not provided.

Although the housing problem has been raised at successive Party congresses with ambitious targets set in each new Five-Year Plan, the East European leaders have failed to fulfil these promises. In the 1960s, following the Soviet lead, they said that by the end of the 1970s "every family, including newly-weds, will have a comfortable flat."[1] The date for the fulfilment of this promise has since been rescheduled by most CMEA countries for 1990.[2]

While the East European governments repeatedly affirm the pressing importance of solving their countries' housing problems, they have

[65] *Violations . . .*, op. cit. p. 33.

[1] *Programme of the Communist Party of the Soviet Union* (Pravda Publishers, Moscow, 1961), p. 94.

[2] Henry W. Morton, "Housing Problems and Policies of Eastern Europe and the Soviet Union," *Studies in Comparative Communism*, Vol. XII, No. 4, 1979, pp. 300–21.

Table 1[3]

Apartments Completed (in thousands)

Country	1960	1970	1978	1980	1983	1984
Bulgaria	49·8	45·7	67·8	74·3	69·7	68·9
Czechoslovakia	73·8	112	129	129	95·9	91·7
East Germany	80·5	76·1	168	169	197	207
Hungary	58·1	80·3	88·2	89·1	74·2	70·4
Poland	142	195	292	217	196	196
Romania	253	159	167	198	147	132
USSR	2,591	2,266	2,080	2,004	2,030	2,008

consistently given priority to investment in other areas. Not only have they failed to meet the promise to provide every family with its own housing, but since 1980 the number of housing units built has been falling in all these countries with the sole exception of the German Democratic Republic (Table 1).

It is difficult to gauge the size of the housing deficit because comparable figures are not available for all countries under review. The true demand is hidden by the fact that most housing is allocated by the authorities; there is virtually no free housing market. One can determine the possible size of the deficit by comparing the number of marriages each year with the number of new housing units built. Table 2 shows the cumulative housing deficit measured in this way for the years 1971–75.

Table 2[4]

The Accumulated Deficit in Housing Units 1971–75

Bulgaria	Czechoslovakia	GDR	Hungary	Poland	Romania	USSR
−112,124	−71,904	−282,557	−53,651	−433,683	−64,015	−1,419,248

The way in which housing construction is financed in Eastern Europe varies widely from state to state. In the 1950s housing cooperatives and private construction were introduced to relieve the pressure on governments as the main source of housing investment. This move marked a departure from the principle of 'free' housing as of right. Not one Communist government in Eastern Europe proved able to meet its original objectives.[5] None has admitted, however, that private financing and private ownership represent a retreat from socialist aspirations. In Bulgaria, Czechoslovakia, Poland and Romania since the 1960s, the

[3] *Statistical Yearbook of Member Countries of the CMEA* (Statistika, Moscow, 1979), p. 212; and ibid. (1985), p. 172.

[4] Henry W. Morton, op. cit. p. 309.

[5] For a detailed description of the situation in the late 1950s, see *Housing in the Soviet Bloc* (Radio Free Europe Research and Information Department, New York, 9 April 1957).

public has been encouraged to own condominium housing and buy individual flats in state housing complexes.[6]

Housing is a vital if not *the* vital element in public welfare. It can spark off unrest if left unsatisfied. The East European governments, concerned that their failure to meet the housing demand and their own solemn commitments might stir up discontent, have made a habit of focussing public attention on the living conditions of the homeless, the unemployed and under-privileged in the 'capitalist' West. 'Free' housing as a right has been effectively abandoned. Private and cooperative-construction is encouraged either with government support or by the authorities turning a blind eye on illegal construction and the black market. For many in Eastern Europe this retreat from a basic principle of socialism has opened up a welcome, albeit financially onerous, alternative to overcrowding and long waiting periods.

Bulgaria

Housing has been a perennial problem in Bulgaria, particularly in Sofia and other large cities. Figures for the last Five-Year Plan (1981–85) show that of 400,000 planned units, only 343,000 were completed. Under the previous Five-Year Plan there was also a shortfall of 57,000 units.[7] The report of the Central Committee to the 13th Party Congress in April 1986 proposed that targets for the next Five-Year Plan (1986–90) should be lowered to 360,000, suggesting that 100,000 of these units should be in Sofia where 80,000 families are waiting for flats. The report also recommended that the number of three-room flats should be increased by 50 per cent. and special attention be paid to housing young families and improving quality and maintenance.[8] Housing space per head rose steadily from 13.3 square metres at the time of the 1975 census to 16.6 in the 1985 census despite these shortcomings.[9]

In March 1986 Georgi Atanasov, then a Central Committee secretary and now Prime Minister, in a speech to the pre-congressional conference of the Sofia City Party, revealed some of the problems afflicting the housing industry's work in the city. Part of the blame for these "extremely serious problems" lay in the poor organization of building and planning. There were more than 100 building organizations and enterprises in Sofia, Atanasov said, grouped under 25 economic bodies, which in turn were responsible to nine different government agencies. There was no coordination between these units. Chaos was rampant. Moreover, the

[6] See Bulgarian Situation Report, *Radio Free Europe Research*, 24 Jan. 1967, p. 1; RAD Background Report (Czechoslovakia), 16 Aug. 1966, p. 3; Hungarian SR/60, *RFER*, 7 Oct. 1969; Polish SR/21, *RFER*, 29 June 1976, item 3; Romanian SR/25, *RFER*, Aug. 1974, item 1.

[7] Bulgarian SR/10, *RFER*, 12 Sept. 1983, item 1. The fact that identical figures were given for the shortfall in these two years puts one in mind of BCP Secretary General Todor Zhivkov's complaint at the recent Party Congress that information on social issues was routinely "distorted" and statistics "falsified." (*Rabotnichesko Delo*, 3 April 1986.)

[8] *Rabotnichesko Delo*, 6 April 1986.

[9] Ibid. 14 Jan. 1986.

Sofia People's Council had not done its job as the central investor; nor had the ward councils carried out their functions. There was a serious shortage of construction materials, supplies of which had not been increased in accordance with targets. There was inadequate cooperation between the producers of such materials, a lack of specialization and no coherent distribution system. As Atanasov said:

> The time has come to tell the whole truth about the architectural policies followed in Sofia—there have been unforgiveable decisions that will have future consequences for the new housing estates. The appalling decisions have no equivalent anywhere in the country.

Although, he said, towns like Tolbuhin and Varna had provided superior examples of how planning ought to be carried out, the post-war districts of Sofia were unattractive clumps of identical buildings conforming to no overall plan, with no centres or an inadequate infrastructure. These districts could not "possibly serve as any sort of model for the development of socialism," Atanasov said, giving the suburban Lyulin Complex near Sofia as an example. Here the provision of transport facilities was based on the assumption that a subway was going to be built. It was not until after building work had begun that the ground was found to be unsuitable for subway-construction and the plans were dropped, leaving the complex without public transportation. Moreover, no shops or children's play-grounds had been provided. In other parts of the city the housing was in disrepair; maintenance and modernization work were not being carried out. Water supply and heating facilities were inadequate.[10]

Housing construction was also criticized at a session of the National Assembly's Permanent Commission on Social Policy. The People's Councils, it was said, had often failed to allocate sufficient space for housing construction which made it difficult to operate machinery used for prefabricated housing. In other cases construction organizations had not given construction collectives the necessary financial and technical support.[11]

AT the 13th Bulgarian Communist Party Congress Georgi Stoilov, Chairman of the Bulgarian Architects' Union, delivered a speech strongly criticizing the construction industry. Having praised the work of architects and builders but given no statistics or precise information to support his praise, Stoilov said:

> But there is another, negative side in the work of designers, investors and builders. Above all there are many defects and weaknesses in buildings because of the poor quality of the work, and this causes discontent amongst our working population. There are more than a few cases in which people moving into new homes have immediately had to undertake extensive repair to buildings that have only just been completed. . . . Even more worrying is the fact that the way in which new towns and residential districts are established does not

[10] Ibid. 13 March 1986.

[11] Radio Sofia, 11 March 1986, 11.00 pm.

> meet the desires of the present, let alone of the future, generation. In Bulgaria our building industry produces totally identical blocks of apartments that degrade the appearance of our towns. The products of this unilateral school of design swarm all over not just the large cities but also the most attractive of our mountain towns (Karlovo, Troyan, Sopot, and so on), wiping out their unique and irreplaceable architectural character.
>
> Where the high cranes of the builders appear, often both worthwhile and worthless buildings disappear indiscriminately; and with them goes every fragment of tree and every leaf as the land becomes a desert. This pillaging of the environment does not always result in facilities that confer benefits and well-being on the population. Despite clear Party decisions, industrial areas are created in chaotic fashion; transport and communications are not assured.

Stoilov went on to criticize the building industry for its uneconomical practices, its wasteful use of cement and metal and its disregard for energy conservation. He called for the complete reorganization of the industry and greater concern for quality rather than quantity alone.[12]

The present state of affairs in the housing sector causes much frustration and has led to widespread corruption. In November 1985 officials in Varna and Plovdiv were punished for violating rules that guarantee preferential treatment for newly-weds and large families.[13] Presumably bribery and nepotism were involved. One safety valve against possible popular unrest has been the official encouragement of private housing construction and the introduction of "do-it-yourself" maintenance and construction work, notably the involvement of prospective owners in finishing work. In 1983, to alleviate the crisis, socialist organizations and enterprises were given the task of building housing for their own workers and employees, using their own financial resources and work forces.[14] Little is known about how this decree was implemented but it is very unlikely that enterprises, already burdened by the obligation to look after their auxiliary agricultural plots, would have readily diverted funds and manpower to housing construction.

Private building by people united in a cooperative has been an important factor in Bulgarian housing construction. In 1978 a special law on cooperative housing construction was adopted,[15] but its rigorous regulations are unlikely to have improved the cooperative housing stock. Nevertheless, together with private construction, these cooperatives seem to have relieved the state of some of its housing burden. According to official statistics, between 1980 and 1984 state construction decreased steadily while cooperative and private (individual) building increased.[16]

One of the major social concerns which is attributed to the inadequacy

[12] *Rabotnichesko Delo*, 10 April 1986.

[13] Radio Sofia, 26 Nov. 1985, 7.30 pm.

[14] Bulgarian SR/10, *RFER*, 12 Sept. 1983, item 1.

[15] Ibid. No. 15, *RFER*, 18 Aug. 1978, item 2.

[16] *Statisticheski Godishnik* (Komitet za Sotsialna Informatsiya pri Ministerskiya Savet, Sofia, 1985), p. 247.

of housing in Bulgaria is the falling birthrate. In April 1986 Siyka Neykova, secretary of the National Council of the Fatherland Front, made a speech highlighting the problems of young families. She stressed that the decree on the allocation of accommodation to young families was not being observed. (25 per cent of all housing financed by the People's Council was supposed to go to newly-weds and large families.) Because of this, young families were not having second and third children, especially in Sofia, Plovdiv and Varna.[17] The national birthrate had fallen from 21·9 per thousand inhabitants in 1944 to 13·6 per thousand in 1984.[18] This trend is especially alarming for Bulgarians in view of the sensitive Turkish nationality problem. Cities of primarily Turkish population, such as Kardzhali, Shumen and Razgrad, have much higher birthrates. The large Moslem families exacerbate the problem of overcrowded housing.

In short, the housing shortage in Bulgaria is severe and has many damaging social implications. Year after year the plans for housing construction have remained unfulfilled. The criticisms of the housing industry and the officials responsible for it have been excedingly harsh; yet, apart from the removal of a few corrupt or incompetent local officials, very little has changed for the better.

Czechoslovakia

Official figures show a continued neglect of housing in Czechoslovakia. Capital investment in housing for rental as a percentage of total capital investment declined from 18·3 per cent in 1982 to 17·2 per cent in 1984. The government has continued to invest heavily in industry at the expense of housing.[19] The construction of new housing for rental is slow. Costs are on the increase because of the rising prices of fuel, energy and building materials. Construction reached a peak of 144,678 homes in 1975, but there was a sharp drop in the 1980s; in 1981 the figure was only 95,387, and by 1984 it had fallen to 91,863.[20] 17,320 housing units were lost through demolition or decay over the same period. The construction of sufficient new housing and the necessary modernization of old buildings would require a large injection of capital, manpower and materials.

Out of a total of more than 5·25 million housing units in Czechoslovakia today, 220,000 are uninhabitable or destined for demolition for other reasons. Although the housing stock has been streadily improving, a quarter of it is still seriously sub-standard. In 1980, for example, 1·172 million flats had no lavatories and 945,000 no bathrooms. Some 40 per cent of families live in homes with less than eight square metres of living space per person. The modernization of old homes is proceeding slowly. There were plans to modernize 20,000

[17] *Otechestven Front*, 30 April 1986.
[18] *Statisticheski Godishnik*, op. cit.
[19] *Investicni Vystavba*, No. 1, 1984, p. 12.
[20] *Statisticka Rocenka CSSR* (SNTL, Prague, 1985), p. 227.

flats in the Czech lands between 1981 and 1983, but only 4,400 were actually done.

Another reason for the downward trend in housing construction is that a large number of workers has been leaving the construction sector for higher wages elsewhere in the economy. Every year, about 13 per cent of the work force in Czech housing cooperatives leaves for other employment, and in Slovak cooperatives the figure has reached 18 per cent.

Building one's own house privately does not offer a solution for more than a small proportion of the population. In 1978 37,982 privately owned houses were built; this figure fell in 1982 to 30,000 and in 1984 to 28,981. To build one's own house takes considerable motivation and courage, especially in a country where labour and construction materials are often in extremely short supply or unavailable to private persons by legal means. It is also becoming more and more risky to 'borrow' construction machinery illegally or pay bribes for building materials.

In September 1984 580,000 families had no homes of their own and had to live with relatives or friends, according to a government report.[21] Demographic statistics show that the situation could only worsen in the following years (Czechoslovak Statistical Yearbook 1986, Prague, pp. 216 and 103). In 1984 there were 121,340 marriages and 37,422 divorces; both will have added to the number of homes needed. Meanwhile, relatively few units will have been vacated and only 91,863 new units were built that year (down from 94,200 in 1983 and 101,829 in 1982). 1985 did not seem to show any improvement. At the time of writing (August 1987) only statistics for the first half of 1985 are available: 55,000 marriages and 19,000 divorces (*Rude Pravo*, 26 July 1985). A rough estimate for the entire year would be 110,000 marriages and 38,000 divorces to be served by 104,524 flats completed in 1985. The next Five-Year Plan (1985–90) calls for only 400,000 units to be completed.

Despite promises made in successive Five-Year Plans, and the fact that the average floor space of flats built in 1984 was 46.3 square metres,[22] housing conditions in general appear to be getting worse. The current waiting period for state and cooperative housing is five years or more.[23] There is nothing to indicate that this can be reduced in the foreseeable future.

The "German Democratic Republic"

The German Democratic Republic has accomplished much in the housing sector in recent years, and if the construction programme continues at its current pace the GDR may be the only East European country to reach its stated goal and to have "solved the housing problem as a social issue" by 1990. In 1970, shortly after taking office, Erich

[21] CTK as reported by AFP (Prague), 13 Sept. 1984.
[22] Czechoslovak SR/21, *RFER*, 7 Dec. 1984, item 3.
[23] Ibid.

Honecker declared to the Eighth Congress of the Socialist Unity Party of Germany that three million housing units were to be built or modernized (reconstructed) so that all citizens of the GDR would have "housing that, in keeping with the size of the family, provides decent quarters." Housing construction was to be the "core of our social policy."[24] In 1980 expenditure on housing construction accounted for no less than 10 per cent of the total national income. The new Five-Year Plan (1986–90) allocated 230 billion Ostmarks to this programme,[25] a 15 per cent increase compared with the previous Five-Year Plan. These figures include the cost of new construction, renovation, maintenance and rent subsidies. Between 1986 and 1990, 1·064 million flats are to be built at the rate of over 200,000 per annum.

In 1984 the GDR built 120,728 new flats (fewer than in any year since 1981) and renovated 85,380 (the highest number ever), while in the same year there were 133,898 marriages and 50,320 divorces. The loss of living space through demolition and decay cannot be calculated from the official statistics; nor can the number of habitable units vacated for other reasons. But a comparison between the number of marriages and divorces on the one hand (184,218) and the number of completed units on the other (206,108) gives some rough indication of the progress being made. The GDR seems to be well set to meet a growing demand. The contrast with Czechoslovakia is marked.

To meet the acute shortage that existed in 1971 when the current housing programme began, absolute priority was assigned to new prefabricated mass housing. The monotonous and depressing blocks of flats with few amenities and little contact with nature evoked the same sort of complaints as did housing complexes in other East European countries. They did, nevertheless, represent quantitative progress. Since the beginning of the 1980s there has been a limited shift in policy towards the renovation and modernization of older buildings, and more attention is being paid to inner city areas.[26] The process has not always gone smoothly. Although promises have been made to cause minimum disruption and move as few people as possible, rebuilding and repairs that were scheduled to take four weeks dragged on in some cases for six months.

A new or renovated flat in the GDR is on average small, about 35 square metres in size;[27] but East Germans pay very low rents even by East European standards (about five per cent of the average family income). A one-room, stove-heated unit costs about 40 Ostmarks per month, and a centrally heated three-room flat 110 Ostmarks. It was announced in January 1986 that existing rents were not to be raised.[28]

24 *Neue Zurcher Zeitung*, 7 April 1984.
25 Speech by Minister of Construction Wolfgang Junker, as quoted by dpa, 13 June 1985.
26 *Neue Zurcher Zeitung*, 7 April 1984.
27 *Statistical Yearbook of the GDR* (State Publishing House of the GDR, Berlin, 1985).
28 *Financial Times*, 7 Jan. 1986.

The quality of housing, however, leaves a lot to be desired. According to East German statistics, in 1985 about 28 per cent of GDR homes did not have "either a bath or a shower" (in 1971 the figure was almost 66 per cent) and lavatories in 35 per cent of homes were still outside the housing unit. By comparison, in 1978 only six per cent of West German homes had no bath or shower, and four per cent had no inside lavatory.[29]

In January 1986 new laws were passed to tighten existing regulations on living space and the allocation of housing. This was designed primarily to eliminate squatting (a widespread practice tacitly tolerated) but has done little to solve the problem. A state agency is responsible for the allocations and people are also encouraged to swap. This is done legally through local exchange offices or newspaper advertisements. In 1985 the central computer which registers such swaps in East Berlin processed 10,000 exchanges out of a total of 90,000 listings. Nationally, it is estimated that 100,000 swaps take place per annum. Homes can also change hands through private transactions without the authorities being told.

Hungary

Official Hungarian statistics show a steady annual decline in housing construction from a high point of 99,600 units in 1975 to 89,100 units in 1980 and 70,400 in 1984. The proportion of new flats built by the state has also steadily declined, from 41 per cent in 1970 to 38·1 per cent in 1975, 34 per cent in 1980 and 14·3 per cent in 1984.[30] This lack of government investment in such an important social and economic sector reveals the truth about government priorities despite the concern expressed in official statements. In 1985 Zsolt Oszlanyi, deputy head of the housing department at the National Planning Bureau wrote: "The housing situation is worse than before, indeed, it is hopeless. Nothing has essentially changed, nothing has improved."[31]

In 1983 the Hungarian Socialist Workers' Party and the Council of Ministers had passed a resolution about the renovation and maintenance of apartment buildings as well as problems of allocation and management. One of the most pressing problems, however, according to Oszlanyi, was to provide housing for young couples and families with low incomes.

In April 1986 it was announced that the maximum monthly incomes up to which Hungarian families could claim state-housing was to be raised. The limit for families with one child is now 2,500 forints (the previous limit was 2,200), for families with two or more children 3,000 forints, and for old-age pensioners 3,500.[32] The average monthly income in 1986

[29] *L'Humanité*, 23 Jan. 1985.

[30] *Statistical Yearbook of Member Countries of the CMEA* (1979) p. 212; and ibid. (1985), p. 172.

[31] Zsolt Oszlanyi, "The Housing Situation in Hungary Today," *Tarsadalmi Szemle*, June 1985, pp. 142–7.

[32] Radio Budapest, 22 April 1986, 12.00 noon and 6.00 pm.

was 6,660 forints. This explains the large proportion of apartments built with private funds.

In effect, the Hungarian government no longer promises state-supplied ('free') housing for its citizens. Constitutionally it only guarantees the creation of conditions for appropriate housing for all. Private construction is legal. Nevertheless, the private sector thus created bears no comparison to the private building industry in a market economy. The construction companies are still state-run and state-regulated. Official statistics list all housing units, whether state-allocated or privately built, under a single rubric.

In Budapest municipal officials have criticised high prices and long waiting periods. Over the next five years 56,000 new flats are to be made available, yet these will not be enough to house the 66,000 families on the current waiting list, not to mention 35,000 new applicants who are expected to join the queue by 1990. In 1986 the City Council announced that families with three or more children who filed applications in 1985 would be able to move into new homes by the end of 1986. The waiting period for families with two children, however, may be as long as four years. Childless couples and single people who applied before 1981 cannot expect to get housing before 1990. This would mean a 10-year wait.

Since 1984, the government has been trying to make a special effort to cope with the shortage of building materials, rising building costs (a rise of 10–13 per cent from 1982–84), the dearth of state-built housing and the poor protection of the interests of those who build privately. The housing recommendations of the seventh Five-Year Plan (1986–90) provide for special credits for private builders and new forms of advance savings' plans for young couples who want to build or buy their homes.[33]

An additional concern is that the state-built stock is deteriorating because of inadequate or non-existent maintenance. As Oszlanyi commented: "It is enough to compare any of the state-built housing estates with those built by private initiative; the difference in maintenance and cleanliness is tremendous."[34]

According to an article in *Magyar Nemzet* in June 1985, while the old type of flat-sharing no longer exists in Hungary, the high divorce rate and the dire housing situation have created a new type of co-tenancy.[35] In 1970 there were 16,673 homes with co-tenants. The new housing regulations introduced the following year were intended to put an end to this practice, but in 1985 the figure was still as high as 9,642. After a divorce the two parties have often no choice but to remain in the same flat with their new spouses and children.

In the absence of more government investment and with the downward trend in construction of both state and private housing, it is difficult to

[33] See Hungarian SR/9, *RFER*, 7 Aug. 1985, item 2.
[34] Zsolt Oszlanyi, op. cit.
[35] *Magyar Nemzet*, 28 June 1985.

foresee any marked improvement in the housing deficit. A home for every family by 1990 will probably remain a wish and a slogan.

Poland

The waiting periods for state-built housing in Poland are probably the longest in Eastern Europe. The programme prepared for the 10th Congress of the Polish United Workers' Party acknowledged the need to build four million housing units before the year 2000. Other official estimates of the minimum number required are as high as seven million.[36] A government report completed in 1984 set the number of homes needed by 1990 at 4·5 million.[37] This represents the 1980 deficit (1·7 million), new housing needed to match population growth (1·5 million) and housing to replace homes no longer suitable for habitation (1·3 million).

At least three million Poles are on waiting lists for cooperative flats, which is the predominant form of residential construction in urban areas. In Lodz, for example, a city of 850,000 inhabitants, the cooperatives have about 110,000 members on their waiting lists but the current rate of construction there is a mere 5,000 units per annum. It will take 22 years simply to satisfy existing needs. Unless the rate improves dramatically, the annual increase of an estimated 8,500 in the city's population and the abandonment of old buildings will make the situation even worse.[38]

The national picture is no better. Annual construction for all sectors (cooperative, communal, individual and factory-funded housing) seems to be static, at less than 200,000 units per annum. While this is more than in the worst year, 1980, it still falls 150,000 short of the number required each year to prevent the deficit from growing. Construction rates have fallen by a third since 1978, when 283,600 new units were built, and there was no sign of improvement in 1986. According to the Central Statistical Office, in January and February 1986 the state-sponsored construction sector had finished 5,200 units, a mere four per cent of the 130,000 targeted for the year.[39]

The Party's response to the housing crisis has been to raise rents. The amount has varied according to the type of housing, but increases have been reported as high as 600 per cent. Although one of the strongest arguments for Soviet-style socialism has been its promise of inexpensive housing for all, one local Polish Party secretary said bluntly that the time has passed for "the view that someone deserves a flat simply because he was born in a socialist country."[40]

Cooperative ownership has been the primary means of financing housing construction by individual families. At the end of 1984 almost three-quarters of urban housing was in the form of cooperatives. These

[36] "Housing Emotions," *Zycie Literackie*, 11 Aug. 1985.
[37] "Repairs Under Repair," *Perspektywy*, 31 Jan. 1986.
[38] Radio Warsaw, 21 Feb. 1986.
[39] "Without Euphoria," *Trybuna Ludu*, 17 Feb. 1986.
[40] Polish SR/6, 4 April 1986, item 2.

require a substantial down-payment from members but offer favourable credit terms for the repayment of the balance, often spread over 60 years. In 1986 cooperative payments were increased along with normal rents on state-owned buildings.[41]

Apart from tapping private funds to cover rising construction costs, the government expects help from an eventual general economic recovery. It hopes to reduce waste and increase productivity. For example, current plans call for cuts of 12 per cent in the building industry's consumption of materials and rises of 16 per cent in productivity.[42] The severity of the housing problem is such that the inefficient performance of construction workers, who now enjoy wages second only to those of miners, has led one frustrated commentator to propose the militarization of building sites.[43]

Criticism of all aspects of the housing industry is profound and reform proposals are correspondingly radical. More than a third of the 64,000 complaints received by the Party's Central Committee concerns housing. State investment has increasingly neglected housing which has led to a shortage of building land, building materials and trained personnel. Official policy has taxed small independent building and repair firms out of existence. Proposals to reorganize the construction sector including its funding have come from the official unions as well as from economists. Credit should be decentralized, they demand, investment allocated in a "professional" manner; housing should be self-financing; individual construction encouraged and small private firms given a free field of manoeuvre. These proposals do not differ radically from those suggested by Solidarity in its recent report, *Poland: Five Years After August.* Such measures, however, would require the restructuring of the entire economy.[44]

Both the public and the authorities face serious predicaments. The current rate of building is too slow to assuage social discontent. The national economic crisis shows no signs of abating. Fresh funds are most unlikely to be made available on a sufficient scale to turn the tables. In any case, the authorities are reluctant to launch radical reforms. There is, therefore, little relief in sight for millions of Poles, some of whom have been in the housing queue for two decades and may have to stay there even longer.[45]

Romania

Although the Romanian government's long-standing concern to improve housing conditions was re-emphasized at the 13th Party Congress in

41 "Why Cooperative Housing Rates Are Going Up," *Trybuna Ludu*, 28–29 Dec. 1985.
42 Central Committee Secretary M. Wozniak at the 25th Plenum of the PUWP CC, as quoted by Radio Warsaw, 13 March 1986, 9.10 am.
43 Polish SR/6, op. cit.
44 *Zycie Gospodarcze*, 2 March 1986.
45 Polish SR/6, op. cit.; PAP in English, 5 June 1986.

November 1984, the directives issued for the 1986–90 Five-Year Plan cut the housing construction programme from the 900,000 units planned under the previous Five-Year Plan to only 725,000 units, a reduction of 20 per cent.[46] The Romanian Communist Party's long-term guidelines envisage the "complete solution" of the housing deficit by the year 2000; but this had already been promised as long ago as the Third Party Congress in 1960, only then the government's pledge said that the shortage would end by 1975.[47] The 1972 National Conference postponed the date, without explanation, to 1990.[48] The 13th Party Congress again offered no explanation for the latest postponement.

Of the 900,000 units planned for the 1981–85 period, only 706,000 were completed. Even if one adds the total number of units planned for the current 1986–90 period (725,000), the actual construction figure still falls short by almost 40 per cent of the target set at the 12th Party Congress in 1979; the promise then was to construct between 2·35 million and 2·45 million units by 1990.[49]

The average size of a Romanian dwelling has increased steadily from 26·49 square metres in 1951–55 to 31·89 square metres in 1966–70 and 35·17 square metres by 1984. The guidelines for the 1991–2000 period foresee an increase of the average living space per person from 10 square metres in 1986 to 14 square metres by the year 2000.[50] Efforts to fulfil the promise to solve the housing shortage do indeed seem to have been stepped up; in order to do so by the year 2000, one dwelling will have to be built every three minutes, a rate the authorities claim to be achieving.[51]

Little seems to have been done, however, to eliminate the basic problems that led to poor results in the past. Deficiencies in housing construction result mainly from a lack of skilled labour, poor work organization, not enough spare parts and the inadequate utilization of both equipment and working time.[52] These are fundamental systemic problems which are not being tackled. The shortfall in construction will probably persist.

Romania is in the throes of an exceptionally ambitious programme of large-scale reconstruction of cities, towns and villages. It is one of those gigantic reorganizations of the human environment that dictatorships have always taken great pride in. This is Ceausescu's pet programme and it has appalled observers. More than 40,000 inhabitants have had to be displaced from the historic town centre of Bucharest to make way for the major demolition work that started there in April 1984; numerous exemplars of historic urban architecture have been destroyed. These include famous monuments as well as nineteenth and twentieth-century

[46] *Scinteia*, 2 July 1981 and 5 Sept. 1984.
[47] Ibid. 12 June 1960.
[48] Ibid. 23 July 1972.
[48] Ibid. 12 July 1979.
[50] Ibid. 5 Sept. 1984.
[51] Agerpres (Bucharest), 28 April 1986.
[52] Romanian SR/19, *RFER*, 1 Aug. 1978, item 7.

buildings that were in perfectly good order. It is estimated that by 1990–92 approximately 443,000 houses built between 1800 and 1920 will have disappeared and some 90 per cent of the inhabitants of Bucharest will live in new housing.[53]

It is not only Bucharest that is at risk. Other old towns are also being destroyed and rebuilt according to completely new plans. At least 27 town centres have already been transformed, and at least 20 smaller towns are also threatened. In the next 15 years, all Romanian villages, too, are scheduled to be reconstructed. The first phase, to 1990, will include the construction of 20,000 units per annum in rural areas.[54] Many Romanians are concerned that traditional Romanian architecture, especially in the countryside, will disappear and give way to a "universe of apartment blocks replacing individual houses," and that "Romanian native architecture will be reduced to a few examples preserved in folk art museums." Ceausescu's reconstruction programme has grave social implications, as the following Romanian comment from an anonymous letter signed by "a group of intellectuals" indicates:

> Life in blocks of flats is helping to implant in the people's mind a collective consciousness. It means living under the close scrutiny of your neighbours. It represents a new way of life in which the behaviour and the requirements of the collective body are present at every moment. It is a new social environment in which priority is given to collectivity over the individual.[55]

Another serious social consequence of the housing shortage is that over half a million (560,969 in 1984) young workers now live in workers' hostels for single people. The number of these hostels rose rapidly in the 1970s to 2,344 by the end of the decade. (There are also shacks and mobile cabins in which construction, oil and forestry workers are housed.[56]) Although the hostels are designed to be temporary quarters for those large segments of the rural population that are being settled in industrial centres, the housing shortage in the cities has often made these hostels the single person's permanent residence. He or she is frequently forced to spend more than 10 years in a dormitory. Many young people continue to live there even after marriage, although these hostels are without basic facilities such as individual kitchens. They are also cramped and provide little privacy. Each accommodates about 300 people. They are notorious for dirty floors and bathrooms, broken windows, burst pipes, litter and empty cans and bottles as well as heavy drinking and violent behaviour. For both single and married workers, male and female, an extended stay in a hostel makes the transition from rural to urban life much more difficult.[57]

There are other alarming social aspects of Romania's housing policies.

[53] Romanian SR/2, *RFER*, 3 Feb. 1986, item 2.
[54] *Scinteia*, 12 Sept. 1985.
[55] Romanian SR/2, *RFER*, 3 Feb. 1986, item 2.
[56] Romanian SR/5, *RFER*, 18 April 1986, item 3.
[57] Ibid.

In his closing speech to the Third Congress of the People's Councils in Bucharest on 11 September 1985, Nicolae Ceausescu announced a "special programme to support the moving of some pensioners from big cities to the countryside." Although such moves have not yet been made, Bucharest city officials have been withholding permission from pensioners wanting to move to the capital to live with their children or other close relatives. Clamping down on the mobility of the old either by preventing them from moving to major centres or, worse, ejecting them from the towns and cities of Romania is an inhuman policy of the first order. It would, however, if consistently applied, not be out of line with Ceausescu's Balkan despotism.

Postscript

Vladimir V. Kusin

Neither the free-market nor the centrally-planned economies meet every one of the stipulations of the Universal Declaration of Human Rights relating to employment, wages, and the organization of labor. In both, deficiencies exist. Nevertheless, Karl Marx's prediction that the working class would become poorer and poorer as capitalism develops has been belied by events. The working class is doing incomparably better under capitalism than under Communism. Its influence on both its own standard of living (which is surely the purpose of the right to work) and on conditions of employment exceeds the influence of workers in Communist societies. Moreover, workers and employees in liberal-democratic societies enjoy a whole gamut of additional rights and freedoms that emphasize their status as citizens, not just as wage earners. It is through their political rights that they can and do influence their standing as producers.

At the end of the penultimate decade of our century all West European countries are welfare states, making social services available to virtually everyone, and guaranteeing that no-one falls below the poverty level. While the state's safety-net is not fool-proof, it goes a long way toward ensuring that unforeseeable changes in the market economy do not cause avoidable hardship to individuals.

The Communist regimes have generally provided employment and basic social security to everyone except the "class enemy", a group of people that tended to be large—in the Communist definition—in the first stages of Communist rule and whose suffering and elimination were the first sacrifices exacted by the new system.

During the initial "extensive" phase of Communist industrialization, full employment was of economic benefit to the population. An element of compulsion however, has always been present: work under Communism is not only a right but also a duty. "Duty" distorts "right," because it eliminates choice: the right to act in a certain way entails the right not to act in that way; a right that is at the same time a duty denies that freedom. The Communist "right to work" means that everyone has to work as told and where assigned. Even so, the right/duty to work removes the anxiety of unemployment; and when social requirements are basic—as for example, in poor countries after a momentous experience such as war—the advantages of the right/duty prevail over the disadvantages arising from absence of choice.

It is, however, abundantly clear by now that the Communist economic systems cannot sustain a progressive improvement in wages. As Communist societies become more responsive to popular expectations, and as the workers begin to compare their situation not with their former conditions, but with what can be achieved in a market economy, job-security loses some of its appeal.

Of course, workers still prefer secure jobs to insecure ones; but they increasingly recognize that much of the work they and others do is useless, that mismanagement degrades the fruits of their labor, and that the reluctance and inability to shrink the labor force stand in the way of much overdue reorganization. What seemed, in an earlier phase, a purposefully organized society in which everybody pulled his weight to reach the age of plenty, has changed into a system in which a tenured work force produces low-quality goods and is stifled in all its rights except that of guaranteed employment. Workers and economists alike have come to recognize that job security alone does not create wealth and does not encourage innovation. It frequently does the opposite.

There is one advantage for the tenured wage-earner under Communism: he is not required to work as hard and as well as his counterpart in capitalist societies. Many people found and still find this preferable to the climate of a market in which labor is also a commodity. Under "extensive" industrialization, the "social contract" (as it has been ironically called) between an inadequate state and an inadequate work force—the "right to employment without exertion"—was the linchpin of political peace. But now that the economy needs to be modernized and made more efficient, the Communist regimes are unable to honor their part of the contract. To go on granting material improvement in exchange for political abdication has become difficult. In some parts of the Communist bloc industrialization is over; post-industrial society rests on different premises. Workers can presumably still be held down by force, as they are in Poland, but coercion cannot generate scientific and technical progress or make the products and marketing of the Communist economies internationally more competitive. Hence today's reform plans which cast doubt on so many of the earlier Communist tenets, including the one that holds that the right/duty to work is essential to the advancement of Communist society.

Unemployment, however, is not a serious threat to the command economies, even if a few thousand workers here and there experience the effects of bankruptcies and planned factory closures. They can be looked after by the Communist state easily enough through social benefits, retraining and relocation. What is and always has been a threat is unnecessary and unproductive work, overmanning, the mistaken allocation of labor and inadequate education in skills and expertise.

The Western economies are dynamic and technically superior not because they can shed unwanted parts of their workforce if necessary, but because they offer freedom of research and freedom of enterprise while cushioning the workers against the risks of free enterprise through social legislation. Conversely, the Communist economies are inferior not because they offer job-tenure for life, but because they are not free. They will not, one may safely predict, automatically improve by making workers redundant; in fact, they face the danger of creating some unemployment *and* remaining backward. The solution lies in freedom and has little to do with unemployment or full employment.

By the same token, in the context of Communist reform, the rights and freedoms relating to employment acquire a political significance over and above the social and economic ones. The focus shifts to the workers' participation in decision-making both at the factory level and, through free trade unions, on a national scale. The reformist leaderships in the USSR and East/Central Europe would be well advised to start treating the working class as responsible citizens rather than just a wage-earning mass, tenured for life, whose alleged interests are ritually invoked to justify one-party rule.

Short Notes on Health and Health Care in Eastern Europe

Sanitary Conditions in Poland

Linda Valentine

DURING a televised discussion of the impact of the Chernobyl nuclear accident on public health, the director of Poland's Mother and Child Institute praised frequent bathing, not as a measure to protect Poles against the effects of radiation but, as she put it, because "maybe this will lead to our being a nation that loves soap, [maybe] we will begin to wash ourselves."[1] Laments such as this, or the more direct "we are up to our ears in filth,"[2] have become daily fare in the Polish media. "Filth" has come to be used as shorthand for Poland's catastrophic sanitary situation.

In April 1986 Jerzy Bonczak, Poland's Chief Sanitary Inspector, announced that the entire country was in need of a general clean-up. Only nine voivodships had received "good" ratings from the sanitary inspectors and 22 were "acceptable," while "filth and slovenliness reigned" in the remaining 18. Conditions were unsanitary in 20 per cent of the factories and 10 per cent of the schools inspected. More alarming, more than a third of the hospitals and clinics fell below acceptable sanitary standards, as did over 40 per cent of the firms involved in food supply or production. The city of Warsaw was found to be "scandalously dirty,"[3] suffering from great quantities of uncollected garbage and infestations of rats and bugs. Most of the city's garbage dumps reportedly qualified for immediate closure, mainly because they were too close to residential areas; yet no new sites are planned for construction in the coming four years. Only 24 of the 97 public lavatories inspected in Warsaw were found to be clean, 28 were unsanitary, and 39 had to be shut down. Lublin, a city of more than 400,000, has only 11 public lavatories, of which seven are currently in operation. Up to 30 per cent of the public lavatories throughout the country have been closed because of a lack of workers to man them.[4]

CLOSELY associated with these conditions are high levels of infectious diseases, what the Polish media call "dirty-hands diseases." The incidence of food poisoning has risen dramatically since

[1] Polish Television/B, 30 April 1986, 7.30 p.m.

[2] Quoted in *Zycie Warszawy*, 5–6 April 1986.

[3] *Slowo Powszechne*, 20 March 1986.

[4] Danuta Wielunska, "Time for a Sanitary Terror," *Tygodnik Demokratyczny*, 25 May 1986; *Trybuna Ludu*, 14 Feb. 1986 and 26–27 April 1986; *Veto*, 6 April 1986 and Radio Warsaw, 20 Aug. 1986, 6.45 a.m.

1980, and data from 1986 suggest that the situation is deteriorating. In 1985, 22,000 cases were registered, a 35 per cent increase over 1984 and an increase of nearly 300 per cent over the rates in the 1970s. In the first half of 1986, officials registered 338 outbreaks of food poisoning affecting a total of 8,500 victims, a third of whom had to be hospitalized at a cost to the state of 100,000 zlotys per person.[5] The 1986 figures led one sanitation official to remark that while summer was once "the food poisoning season," now "the food poisoning season lasts the whole year."[6]

Other infectious diseases remain a potential threat to Poland, although they have been virtually eliminated in Western Europe. The incidence of tuberculosis, for example, has been rising since 1977: in 1984 Poland recorded 61 cases per 100,000 members of the population, compared with seven for Denmark and 26 for France. Hepatitis, which declined in the 1970s, is also on the rise, with Poland reporting approximately 260 cases per 100,000 (only in Romania are the figures worse), while hepatitis strikes only 1–3 per 100,000 in Western Europe. Poland's inability to produce an adequate supply of disposable syringes is largely responsible for the spread of hepatitis B. Hence the country's first report on AIDS commented that "Poland could become . . . the one country where this virus will spread in a non-sexual manner." Severe overcrowding means that up to eight per cent of patients contract infections in Polish hospitals; in other countries the rate is 1–2 per cent. This gives credence to the Polish saying, repeated by official publications, that "here one must be very healthy to afford to get sick."[7]

Officials are quick to point out that half of all cases of food poisoning are caused by practices in the home, but in many cases the public has no control over health-threatening sanitary conditions. For example, one journalist reported that "one-fifth of the food produced in Poland is hazardous to health."[8] There are special problems with milk; 40 per cent of the milk on sale is said to be unfit for consumption. "The milk arrives at the collecting points dirty, spoiled, sour, only to reach our tables as a high-quality product in theory alone."[9]

POLLUTION has made many sources of drinking water unsafe. Water from half of the country's wells is not fit to drink. Warsaw is the only European capital other than Tirana without a single sewage treatment plant, and only 11 per cent of sewage is treated in the entire capital voivodship. The construction of two plants is underway; but work on the

[5] Radio Warsaw, 1 Aug. 1986, 12.05 p.m.

[6] Ibid. 28 May 1986, 7.00 p.m.

[7] *Polska Piec Lat Po Sierpniu* (Poland: Five Years After August), (Aneks, London, 1986), pp. 225–8; *Glos Medyka*, No. 19, Sept. 1985; *Polityka*, No. 3, 1986, cited in *Nasz Czas*, No. 52, 28 Jan. 1986 and Barbara Harasimowicz, "Simply Shameful," *Tygodnik Demokratyczny*, 20 April 1986.

[8] Harasimowicz, loc. cit.

[9] Janusz Rowicki, "To Eat or Not to Eat," *Slowo Powszechne*, 27 March 1986 and Radio Warsaw, 16 July 1986, 5.05 a.m.

first, for Warsaw's right bank, has dragged on for 11 years. Although parts of Warsaw can expect service by 1988 or 1989, the building of treatment plants nationwide has been called "unending"; the construction tempo is extremely slow because investments are made in miserly doses in a gesture of what *Slowo Powszechne* called "pseudo-thrift."[10]

Responsibility for the unhygenic environment lies in the failure of Polish industry to produce sufficient sanitary supplies. Toilet paper production has failed to meet demand for years, and concern runs so deep that a government spokesman was forced to comment on the subject in 1986. Production in 1985 amounted to only about 260 million rolls, or approximately 5–6 rolls per person for the year. This is, officials admit, up to 200 million rolls below demand. No improvement is expected in the near future; a government spokesman predicted that supply would meet demand only at the end of the current Five-Year-Plan. Supplementary imports would have to come from the West and would cost more than US$8 million; remedying the shortage through domestic production would require an estimated 4·5 billion zlotys and costly imported machinery. Both solutions are unlikely given Poland's shortage of hard currency and credit opportunities.[11]

The entire market in cleaning supplies seems to work in what one economist described in 1984 as a "seesaw" pattern:

> We bought detergent for over a year on ration cards, and then this shortage turned into overproduction. A year ago shampoo filled the shelves . . . only to disappear without a trace. . . . Toothpaste occupies a prominent place on this seesaw . . . now one must again search high and low for it.[12]

In spite of government assurances in April that problems with the supply of laundry detergents would not recur in 1986, Radio Warsaw announced in July that domestically produced detergents were unavailable and that a box of imported detergent could be had only for the steep price of 300 zlotys.[13] Brooms were reported to be unavailable in June. Quality is often as much of a problem as availability; domestically produced disinfectant, for example, goes unused because it contains no artificial scent to mask its unpleasant odour.

GOVERNMENT measures to fight filth combine exhortation with intimidation. Press campaigns urge the adoption of healthier habits, starting with the frequent washing of hands by food service employees. Radio broadcasts in the summer of 1986 warned the public against the consumption of steak tartare and recommended refrigerating eggs and

[10] *Slowo Powszechne*, 29 July 1986; Ewa Dobrowolska, "When Will We Stop Poisoning Ourselves?" *Stolica*, 30 March 1986.

[11] *Rzeczpospolita*, 9 July 1986; Radio Warsaw, 17 Feb. 1986, 7.25 a.m. and 27 March 1986, 10.05 p.m.

[12] *Zycie Gospodarcze*, 11 Sept. 1984.

[13] Radio Warsaw, 30 July 1986, 7.00 a.m.

washing vegetables. The State Sanitary Office was given increased powers to punish violators and mounted an intensive inspection campaign. In April 1986 alone (declared the "Month of Cleanliness") inspectors made over 2·6 billion checks, revealed 400,000 violations, and issued fines amounting to 110 million zlotys to almost 270,000 people. Individual fines for filth ran as high as 50,000 zlotys;[14] but the official press has openly admitted that the campaigns have had "paltry results" and that recidivism runs high. Chief Sanitary Inspector Bonczak has nonetheless expressed his agency's determination to apply "harsh repression" against sanitary transgressors and, if necessary, to resort to a "sanitary terror."[15]

Commenting on the establishment in April 1986 of a Sanitary–Epidemiological Council to advise the State Sanitary Office, one journalist observed:

> So we have yet another council, yet another group of specialists . . . but I have my doubts about whether the mere existence of this council, the holding of successive meetings and discussions, [or] the presentation of expertise and proposals will affect Poland's sanitary situation in any way. Will there be equipment for cleaning our cities and towns, will we eliminate lice from kindergartens, will we at last be able to call public toilets public toilets and not squalid four-letter words, will disposable needles be available in health service establishments?
>
> The country's sanitary state is solely a reflection of the economy. . . . What council could possibly have any effect on this?
>
> The council's findings will say what has been repeated for many years in the reports of the sanitary inspectors, in doctors' findings, and finally in hundreds of articles in the press. It boils down to a single sentence: we are drowning in filth.[16]

The Supply of Medicines in Poland

Linda Valentine

IN 1985–86 the Polish health service was shaken by a number of scandals. In February a heart attack victim in Warsaw waited more than seven hours for an ambulance to take him to the hospital only to find on arrival that the gates were locked, the three orderlies and the porter on duty were drunk and had passed out, and the internal communications system was out of order. The patient died before a doctor or proper equipment could be summoned. In August 1985 eight newborn babies died after being administered contaminated medicines at a hospital in

[14] Ibid. 19 June 1986, 7.00 p.m. and *Zolnierz Wolnosci*, 20 June 1986.
[15] *Zycie Warszawy*, 2 April 1986.
[16] Ibid. 25 April 1986, quoting Jerzy Walawski in *Dziennik Polski*, April 1986.

Wloclawek. Between 4 December and 16 January five babies died and 44 became seriously ill when a bacterial infection swept a hospital in Koszalin. In another unidentified hospital, a 16-day-old baby burned to death after being left under a therapeutic heat lamp for 10 hours over two days.

Under the pressure of extensive press coverage, the ambulance system in Warsaw was reorganized, the children's wards in Wloclawek and Koszalin were closed and many staff members were dismissed or reprimanded. Some were brought to trial. In Wloclawek, the ward director and her assistant were found guilty of negligence and were sentenced respectively to one year and six months of "restricted freedom." This means they are not allowed to leave town, are banned from medical work for four years, and 10 per cent of their salaries is docked for the benefit of a hospital fund. In the Warsaw case—the "Barska Street Affair"—the four drunken hospital workers received prison terms ranging from 10 to 15 months.[1]

It has been suggested, however, that individuals are less to blame for these incidents than the catastrophic conditions in Polish hospitals. The judge in the Wloclawek trial stressed that "organizational factors" had contributed to the deaths, and Radio Warsaw commented that "something of this sort could happen at any time and anywhere in our hospital system."[2] Reporters covering the Warsaw case noted that while guilt was obvious in the case of the drunken orderlies, most of those involved were "entangled in situations limiting their potential for effective action." The underground press has been unanimous in finding that "the system is responsible."[3]

THE Wloclawek case resulted from a combination of all the maladies afflicting Polish health care: inadequate equipment, overcrowded and dilapidated buildings, improper sanitation, and an overworked and underpaid staff. In fact, medical experts testified at the trial that the misuse of medicines—the babies were given medicine that should have been discarded if not used immediately—was not directly responsible for the fatal infection, but that the hospital's lamentable sanitary situation had made contamination virtually unavoidable.

The hospital in Wloclawek was designed to accommodate 427 beds, but at the time of the deaths it had 749 beds, although no work on the facilities has been undertaken since the hospital opened in 1963. Yet even this number failed to meet existing needs. In the obstetrics ward,

[1] For the "Barska Street Affair," see "The Final Hours of Jozef S." in this issue. On Wloclawek and Koszalin, see Dobrochna Kedzierska, "Murkiness," and "Window on the People in White," *Polityka*, 24 Aug. 1985 and 14 June 1986, respectively; Stefan Krynski, "First of All—More Soap," *Polityka*, 3 May 1986 and "From Tragedy to Tragedy," *Nasz Czas*, No. 52, 28 Jan. 1986. Information on the burning is quoted from the official weekly *Sluzba Zdrowia* (1/1986) by the underground journal *Zwiazek*, No. 13, 21 April 1986.

[2] Radio Warsaw, 6 June 1986, 4.05 p.m.

[3] See the special issue of *Zeszyty Niezaleznej Mysli Lekarskiej*, No. 5, Sept. 1985, devoted to the Wloclawek affair.

overcrowding meant that it was not unusual to see women in labour on chairs or giving birth on hospital trolleys; the ward head even reported that sometimes 80 beds had to make do for 103 babies. On the night of the deaths, she and four nurses had 50 babies in their care, 15 of them premature, and six mothers in labour. The monthly pay for such duty, including overtime and weekend wages, for a nurse with 20 years of service amounted to a meagre 13,000 zlotys; the average wage in Poland was at this time approximately 20,000 zlotys a month. Almost everything required to ensure sterile conditions was in short supply: the laundry, for example, often had to do without disinfectant. Parents leaving the hospital with their babies had to follow a route that passed the hospital kitchen, the laundry, and the crematorium, and led through hallways filled with patients awaiting attention. In short, as the head of the panel of medical experts testified in the Wloclawek trial, "conditions here are only for hardy babies."

Poland's inability to produce or procure sufficient stocks of medicine was particularly evident in this case. The cause of the fatal infection was an albumin–glucose solution administered to babies suffering from jaundice (almost half of the 700,000 babies born every year in Poland have jaundice). Poland does not produce enough albumin solution to meet its needs and is therefore forced to import it from the West. Because it is expensive and requires hard currency, it is imported only in large containers, suitable for dosages administered to adults. The amounts needed for young infants, on the other hand, is very small. The Wloclawek hospital had long been able to procure only about 10–20 per cent of the albumin it needed. Hospital personnel were constantly urged to use medicines sparingly, and the Minister of Health had issued a directive linking pay bonuses to the conservation of medicines. Refrigerating containers of albumin for multiple use had become standard practice in the hospital, in spite of labels indicating the peril of this practice. As the official press asked, "Who would allow the wastage of medicine that is in short supply?"

OF the 2,314 varieties on the official list of medicines that should be available, if only in theory, in the Polish health care system, at least 1,000 are either completely unavailable or in very short supply. The most critical shortages are those of drugs used for treating cancer and heart disease—which are imported from the West—but even such common medicines as vitamin C and aspirin are frequently unobtainable. In the first quarter of 1986, pharmacies were supplied with less than half the penicillin they required. Operations had to be curtailed because of a shortage of anaesthetics, and in 1985 nurses were even instructed to limit their use of rubbing alcohol. The lack of intravenous fluids at one clinic had lengthened the waiting time for gastrointestinal surgery to more than two months, and doctors thought that they might soon have to suspend all but emergency operations. One director noted that because his factory had received no packing foil, it would have to send medicines to pharmacies in barrels.[4]

These perilous conditions stem from Poland's heavy dependence on the West for finished medical supplies and pharmaceutical raw materials and technology. The dependence arose during the period of easy credit in the 1970s; now that hard currency is unavailable or tied up in servicing the nation's US$31 billion debt, purchases from the West can no longer be made. Yet Poland is unable to produce sufficient stocks to replace Western supplies. Domestic industry covers only about 40 per cent of the health service's needs; moreover, 70 per cent of the medicines produced within the country require "hard-currency components." Consistent underinvestment in the chemical industry has meant that only one pharmaceutical factory has been built in the past decade and this, the Tarchomin Antibiotic Plant, although scheduled to go into operation several years ago, has not yet begun production.[5]

Although the health service has set its minimum requirements for 1987 at 54·5 billion zlotys, the 1986 plan for the chemical industry envisaged the production of medicine worth only 41·6 billion zlotys, thus assuming a 25 per cent deficit in medical supplies from the outset. Medicines worth some US$167 million had to be purchased abroad, but the 1986 plan mandated an expenditure of only US$104 million.

Faced with similar prospects in May 1986, the Council of Ministers adopted an ambitious plan to double medicine production by 1990; this assumes a yearly increase in output of 18 per cent. Yet the 1986 plan foresaw an increase of a mere one per cent. Output is measured by value rather than quantity, thus allowing the pharmaceutical industry to concentrate on a few "profitable" varieties and ignore the full range of drugs required by the health service. This method of costing production enabled the Deputy Minister for the Chemical and Light Industry, Marian Skowerski, to report a 44 per cent increase in medicine production in 1985 over 1984, while supplies of many medicines to pharmacies and hospitals in fact declined. To make matters worse, Polish pharmacology is 15 years behind that in the West, producing medicines that are only partly effective against new strains of bacteria.

The government recently spent US$200,000 on petri dishes for diagnostic purposes, hoping to try out antibiotics in this way rather than the more wasteful method now employed of injecting a patient with an antibiotic and hoping it is the right one. Yet the country lacks the microbiological capacity to put them to use; there are simply too few bacteriologists and bacteriological laboratories.[6]

4 Maria Zera, "Medicine by the Thimbleful," *Slowo Powszechne*, 17 June 1986; Grazyna Wroblewska, "The Bitter Pill," *Odrodzenie*, 23 March 1986; *Zycie Warszawy*, 14 March 1986.

5 Barbara Seidler, "To Get Sick or Not," *Zycie Literackie*, 18 May 1986; Radio Warsaw, 16 April 1986, 7.15 a.m.

6 "Ineffective Antibiotics and Useless Culturing Dishes," *Slowo Powszechne*, 14 July 1986.

THE steady worsening of the supply of medicines has drawn sharp and repeated criticism from the Sejm. In March 1986, the Sejm's Commission on Social Policy, Health, and Physical Culture rejected the report of the Ministry for the Chemical and Light Industry (responsible for medicine production) and demanded more concrete information and correctives. But given the obstacles to a significant jump in production the Sejm's unusual outburst is likely to have little effect. In the words of the Director of the Pharmaceutical Department of the Ministry of Health:

> The industry will crumble in the end. The funds we have on hand insure only that we can realize a programme of exploiting [our existing plant]. They are not sufficient for rebuilding. Moreover, factories do not have the time to do repairs—they have no product reserves.

Indeed, it is estimated that the creation of a viable domestic industry would require the construction of 17 new factories and cost more than US$1·1 billion in the next five years (one journalist admitted that "zloty alone will not cure the pharmaceutical industry").[7]

Such investments are out of the question. But Poland's failure to develop its own capacity to produce medicines will in the long run require far greater expenditures of hard currency. Shortfalls in production are currently cured by emergency supplies from Western sources. Surprisingly simple components are imported—pasteboard for medicine boxes, glue for labels, vials, aluminium foil; and there are many basic medical supplies Poland does not produce at all. Poland produces no adhesive bandages; and judging from supplies in Warsaw, Bulgarian imports last year met less than 25 per cent of demand.[8] Importing the equipment to manufacture such supplies would soon pay for itself, but the government departments involved have been too disorganized and too absorbed in meeting a myriad of immediate shortfalls to do so.

There seems to be no relief in sight: the public will have to continue "to hunt from pharmacy to pharmacy." And, as with the laboratory technicians who reported in December 1985 that they would have to discontinue sterilizing test tubes because their hospital had run out of toilet paper—which they had been using as a substitute for aluminium foil, also unavailable—the health service will have to prolong its desperate improvisations, often at the risk of patients, as in Wloclawek in 1985.[9]

[7] Grazyna Wroblewska, "The Bitter Pill," *Odrodzenie*, 23 March 1986.
[8] *Slowo Powszechne*, 5 June 1986.
[9] *Trybuna Ludu*, 18 Dec. 1985.

Abortions in Romania

Dan Ionescu

CEAUSESCU'S Romania has some of the most draconian regulations on abortion, with an eye to homogeneity and great-nationhood, in Eastern Europe. Together with a virtual ban on contraceptives, they are part of an official attempt to raise the birthrate. Despite mandatory monthly gynaecological examinations, fines for childless couples, certain financial allowances to encourage child-bearing, and a nationwide campaign to promote the birthrate, Romanian couples are still reluctant to have offspring. Deteriorating living standards, shortages of everything from food, baby products, adequate housing and medical care, as well as severe restrictions on civil liberties are said to have strengthened their reluctance.

Since contraceptives are virtually unobtainable, abortion remains the principal means of birth control. Despite harsh anti-abortion legislation, women still find ways of circumventing the restrictions.

According to a 1985 amendment to the anti-abortion law of 1966, pregnancies may be terminated only under the following conditions: if the mother's life is endangered; if the foetus is malformed; if the mother suffers from a serious physical or mental infirmity; if the woman is over 45; if the woman has already given birth to five children; or in the case of rape or incest.[1] Despite such rigorous restrictions a large number of abortions is still legally performed in Romania; in 1983 (the last year for which there are official figures) there were 421,386, compared with 321,489 live births.[2] Abortion has been officially condemned as "an anti-national and anti-social practice that hampers the [Romanian] people's development."

Commenting on the 1983 abortion figures, Ceausescu said that only nine per cent of the legally performed abortions had been medically justified.[3] Yet evidence we have of the generally poor health of Romanian women puts a question-mark against Ceausescu's assertion.[4]

POLITICAL interference is a source of worry for doctors, especially gynaecologists. They realize that a criminal case can easily be built up against them. One such case was reported by a medical weekly in 1986.[5] Carmen Rosca, a doctor with an excellent professional record, was put on

[1] *Buletinul Oficial*, No. 76, 26 Dec. 1985, p. 7.

[2] *Scinteia*, 3 March 1984, p. 3.

[3] Ibid. 8 March 1984, p. 1.

[4] According to a women's magazine, for example, cancer screening in Bucharest revealed that only five per cent of the 200,000 women examined had a healthy uterus. *Femeia*, Jan. 1985, p. 21.

[5] *Muncitorul Sanitar*, 16 Sept. 1986, p. 6.

trial together with four nurses for having performed three "unjustified" abortions. Although she had performed them on purely medical grounds and received no compensation, the court found her guilty of wrongful termination. As for the patients, one of the few grounds that can be invoked to support an application for legal abortion is rape or incest. In one case, a mother was said to have persuaded her 17-year-old son to claim that he had had an incestuous relationship with his 15-year-old sister so that the girl would receive permission for an abortion.[6]

It is difficult to estimate the number of illegally performed abortions. The figure was presumably high enough several years ago to have moved the authorities to impose mandatory monthly gynaecological examinations for women of child-bearing age in order to detect and register pregnancies in their early stages. It seems, however, that the system does not work as efficiently as the authorities hoped, mainly because there is not enough staff to undertake the large-scale monitoring required.

Illegal abortions continue to be reported by the media, often including the grisly details of what can go wrong, to act as a deterrent.[7] It was reported, for example, that a doctor from Covasna killed one of his patients while using his garage to perform an illegal abortion. He charged up to 5,000 lei.[8] A Communist youth daily reported the chilling story of a 27-year-old mother of two who lost consciousness during an abortion and was thrown into a dustbin while still alive, where she died later.[9] Another report suggested that many women, particularly those who cannot afford to support another child, know where they can get an illegal abortion and are quick to pass on the abortionists' names to others.[10]

Romanian Pensioners Barred from Moving to Population Centres

Anneli Ute Gabanyi

It was in his closing speech to the Third Congress of the People's Councils held in Bucharest on 11 September 1985 that Nicolae Ceausescu disclosed the regime's intention of adopting "a special programme to support the moving of some pensioners from big cities to the countryside." The purported motive for the programme was to provide conditions in which

[6] *Cronica* (Iasi), 28 Nov. and 5 Dec. 1986, p. 7 in both cases.

[7] *Femeia*, Feb. and March 1986, pp. 21 and 20, respectively; *Scinteia Tineretului*, 24 Feb., 3 and 10 March 1986, pp. 2, 2 and 3, respectively; *Muncitorul Sanitar*, 23 Dec. 1986, p. 6.

[8] *Muncitorul Sanitar*, 23 Dec. 1986, p. 6.

[9] *Scinteia Tineretului*, 23 June 1986, p. 2.

[10] Ibid. 3 March 1986, p. 2.

the pensioners could maintain their physical and spiritual health and "develop a certain useful activity."

On 21 March 1986, the weekly *Flacara* published the following note in response to a complaint by a Bucharest resident who had asked the magazine to intercede on behalf of his parents who wished to join him in the capital:

> With reference to our appeal No. 1018/1985 concerning the memorandum written by Ion Anghelina asking for approval for his parents to settle in the Bucharest municipality, the Executive Committee of the Bucharest People's Council has stated: "Taking into account the great number of pensioners residing in the country's capital city, as well as the great number of demands emanating from this category of people [to settle in Bucharest], the municipal commission is no longer giving its approval for old-age people who want to live with their children or close relatives to move to Bucharest."

This brief note discloses that the denial of permission for the elderly to resettle began in 1985. *Flacara* interceded on behalf of Anghelina that year; it took the Bucharest city officials more than three months to answer the inquiry. Their response reflects concern about the high number of pensioners residing in Bucharest. Their policy seems to be to stop the influx of elderly citizens. No laws have been passed in this matter; the government appears to have resorted to issuing direct "guidance" to local Party and state institutions.

This practice is not uncommon in Eastern Europe. In Romania it has been used extensively to put into effect particularly unpopular measures that discriminate against certain sections of the population. They include: a decision taken by the CC Political Executive Committee in 1983 to force schoolchildren living in rural areas to attend school in their own villages; the coercion of intellectuals and Party and state activists who live in the cities but work outside them to take up residence where they work; the barring of villagers from buying bread in the cities, and the obligation for city dwellers to buy food in their neighbourhood shops only.

There are several reasons why Ceausescu has decided to shift the burden of supporting old-age pensioners away from the cities to the countryside. First, he wants to reduce the state budget's allocations for supporting pensioners (in the 1986 budget payments to pensioners were reduced by 1·2 per cent as compared with 1985, while the number of pensioners rose[1]). Keeping elderly people in the rural areas would bring their care in line with the principle of local "self-financing." Second, the move would bring relief to the overburdened health system in the large urban areas and provide extra housing space. The housing problem in Bucharest is particularly acute, not only because construction lags behind schedule, but also because over 40,000 residents (many of them old[2])

[1] *Anuarul Statistic al RSR 1985* (Statistical Yearbook) (Directia Centrala de Statistica, Bucharest, 1985), pp. 288–9.

[2] See *Liberation*, 8 Nov. 1985.

have been forcibly evacuated to make room for Ceausescu's grandiose new civic centre.

A third reason has probably to do with a practice that has arisen in shortage-ridden Romania whereby the elderly supplement their meagre pensions by standing in line for other people for a tip.[3]

Despite Ceausescu's frequent protestations[4] that urbanization does not mean the migration of the rural population to urban areas, but, rather, the upgrading of rural areas to urban standards, the actual discrepancy in living conditions between the two is so great that only draconian measures are likely to stop rural people from trying to settle in Bucharest in search of a more tolerable life.

Neurotic Disorders in Hungary

Judith K. Pataki

EIGHT articles in *Otlet*,[1] the political and economic weekly of the Hungarian Communist Youth League, claim that a substantial number of Hungarians, perhaps as many as 50 per cent, suffers from some form of neurosis. *Otlet* placed most of the blame on the fact that Hungarians have to work excessive hours to earn the basic necessities of life. A prominent sociologist, Elemer Hankiss, writing in *Valosag*,[2] disagrees. He points to problems among the very young and very old and attributes much to the neurosis to factors such as the disruption of traditional values and rapidly changing life-styles.

Debates of this kind are relatively new because Hungary, like its Communist neighbours, officially rejected the teachings of Freud and discontinued psychoanalysis in the early 1950s. The Hungarian Psychiatric Association was not founded until 1980, and its psychotherapy section held its first meeting only in January 1984.[3] It was only after that that articles on psychlogy began to appear regularly in the press and Freud was rehabilitated.

Otlet said that many workers put in 16-hour days to make ends meet, labelling this phenomenon "self-exploitation." It quoted a psychiatrist as saying that some workers exceed the maximum number of overtime hours permitted by using the names of co-workers and paying them a share of the earnings for the use of their names. *Otlet* said this was possible in part because some enterprises permit the use of company equipment after hours on a semi-private basis.

[3] *Die Welt*, 16 Nov. 1985.
[4] *Scinteia*, 11 Sept. 1985, p. 2.

[1] *Otlet*, 24 April 1986.
[2] Elemer Hankiss, "Sloppy Society?," *Valosag*, Feb. 1986, pp. 37–47.
[3] *Magyar Nemzet*, 20 Jan. 1984.

The increasing number of work-related accidents suggests that Hungarian workers are tired and insufficiently alert on the job. Although the number of days of sick leave taken fell when the new semi-private production system was introduced, it is now rapidly increasing. Many people have apparently reached the limit of their capacity. *Otlet* suggests that the way to deal with the problem is to increase wages so that workers will not be forced to destroy their health by working extra shifts or doing second jobs.

Because patients' disorders are rarely explicitly diagnosed as neuroses, it is difficult to assess the number of Hungarians suffering from neurotic illnesses. Often the presence of neurosis can be inferred, however, from physical symptoms such as insomnia, headaches or stomach problems. *Otlet* conducted a survey of 300 persons between 21 March and 6 April 1986; the results suggest that about 15 per cent of the population takes sedatives on the job to cope with stress. About 50 per cent of workers have trouble falling asleep at night because of difficulties at work; the same proportion have jittery stomachs from nervous tension, and about 30 per cent regularly have migraines. 45 per cent of those questioned had two or more of these symptoms. If these findings are correct, roughly one in two Hungarians suffers from some form of neurotic disorder.

Otlet's findings were confirmed independently by a survey in the monthly journal of the Ministry of Health, *Nepegeszsegugy*[4] which said that in 1980 3·71 times as many persons took sedatives as in 1960. The number of suicides increased by a factor of 3·31 over the same period. In 1982 11·1 per cent of the disabled in Hungary were registered as such because of psychological problems; the figure for 1975 was 7·5 per cent. In 1960 only 16·4 per cent of young men reporting for military service were rejected because of neuroses, but by 1980 this figure almost doubled to 31·9 per cent.

THE pressures of having two jobs are also blamed for the increasing mortality rate of Hungary's middle-aged men. A World Health Organization survey of mortality rates in 27 countries shows that Hungarian men aged 35–44 have the world's highest mortality rate. 45–54-year-old Hungarian men have the world's second shortest life expectancy. Fifty per cent suffer no serious disease before their sudden death in middle age. The Hungarian authorities and press blame this drop in life expectancy on long working hours. Middle-aged Hungarian women are showing the same tendency, probably due not only to longer working hours, but also to the destruction of family life as a result of excessive overtime. Over the past 15 years, the average life span of all Hungarian men has fallen from 66·8 years to 65·6.

The recent drive to increase labour efficiency is likely to put even more pressure on workers. Reports in the Hungarian media tell us that

[4] Oct. 1985.

policemen are stopping pedestrians on the streets to check why they are not at their places of work during working hours. City councils and some shops have already adjusted their hours of business to ensure that workers do not have to take paid working time off to shop or take care of their personal affairs.

A further worry for workers is the steady increase in prices which, in 1987, will result in an estimated 8–10 per cent inflation rate. The average worker will try to put in even longer overtime hours to compensate for the loss of purchasing power.

The average Hungarian teenager costs a family an estimated 4,000 forints or more per month, while the average monthly salary ranges from 6–7,000 forints. The desire to provide a better life for their children is one of the main reasons why parents accept the burdens of an extra job. Others simply refuse to have a second child. The population is steadily decreasing despite generous maternity benefits. Hungary's traditional fear about a shrinking population has been given a powerful stimulus.

Folk Medicine in Bulgaria

Stephen Ashley

THE long-standing problem of formulating a consistent and rational policy towards the rich tradition of folk medicine in Bulgaria has resurfaced recently because of an attempt by journalists to defend one of the more celebrated practitioners from persecution by the medical authorities and the criminal courts. Dimitar Krastev from Varna achieved fame by inventing a herbal medicine that allegedly acts on a range of afflictions, including hypertension, epilepsy, varicose veins, Buerger's disease, and rheumatoid arthritis. With the assistance of a friend in Sofia, he manufactured and sold his solution at the modest price of four leva per 100 grammes.[1] (The average monthly wage in Bulgaria is approximately 230 leva.)

Krastev's problems began when, unlike many other folk healers, he offered his medicine for professional analysis. Dr Snezhina Kostova, an employee of the Varna Public Health Department, who was entrusted with the investigation, rapidly came to the decision that the solution was medically worthless and that Krastev was a charlatan. On the basis of this report, Krastev was forbidden in 1984 from practising herbal medicine and was prosecuted in 1985 by the Varna City Court for infringing the public health laws. He was sentenced to eight months' imprisonment for dispensing medicaments without having any medical qualification. Although the prosecution had apparently been ordered by the legal authorities in Sofia, the Varna District Court, on examining the verdict,

[1] *Zemedelsko Zname*, 4 April 1984.

commuted the sentence into a provisional discharge; the ban on Krastev's herbal practice nonetheless remained in force.[2]

Earlier in 1986 a group of journalists made a video film in Krastev's defence. This revealed that Kostova had not examined any of the people who had been treated with the herbal remedy. Nevertheless, she had dismissed all the letters of thanks produced by the folk healer as either having been written by Krastev himself or exacted from lying patients by means of bribes. The video film emphasized that there was no evidence to show that anyone had been harmed by Krastev's treatment; on the contrary, a number of people who had been diagnosed as incurable by the medical profession had apparently received relief and some had even been cured by his medication. *Otechestven Front*, commenting on the affair on 18 April, appealed to the government to pardon Krastev and to order that his herbal medicines be more thoroughly tested. On 26 April the story was reported in Yugoslav Macedonia by the Skopje newspaper *Nova Makedonija* under the characteristically disputatious headline "No Amnesty for the Folk Doctor."

A SECOND recent case has further illustrated the difficulty of establishing a rational policy towards traditional healers. After retiring, two brothers, Kiril and Georgi Desov from the Pernik district west of Sofia, began to work as healers of hepatitis and jaundice, prescribing a remedy that had been handed down in their family.[3] They, too, were eventually prosecuted and banned from tending patients. They continued to practise, however, with the tacit agreement of the militia, for it seemed accepted that their medicines were at worst harmless. As in the Krastev case, the scientific profession refused to investigate the brothers' cures. The newspaper *Kooperativno Selo* in reporting the story concluded that a new organization should be established under the auspices of the State Institute for the Control of Medicines to collaborate with traditional therapists in the perfection of new medicines from herbs.

The two cases demonstrate the difficulties facing a regime that would prefer to treat folk healers indulgently but is committed to upholding laws that ban all private and uncertified practice of medicine. Confronted with the implacable hostility of the medical and scientific professions to traditional therapies, the government has been obliged to take occasional action. It has, however, attempted to single out obvious frauds and tricksters for prosecution, thereby hoping to avoid censure from a public that overwhelmingly believes in and supports folk healing.

In 1981, for instance, a charlatan from Sofia, Aleksandr Zarev, a miner with no medical education, was fined 300 leva for prescribing potions that were discovered to be dangerous by the State Institute for the Control of Medicines.[4] In 1976 a driver, Lyubomir Kovachev, was imprisoned for three months for having operated as a quack; and in 1973 Lyubomir

[2] *Otechestven Front*, 18 April 1986.
[3] *Kooperativno Selo*, 30 May 1986.
[4] *Otechestven Front*, 6 Feb. 1981.

Georgiev was prosecuted and required to pay substantial tax arrears in connection with his dealings in herbal cures.[5] As the examples of Krastev and Desov showed, however, the refusal of the medical profession to conduct thorough analyses of herbal preparations has made it difficult to distinguish the genuine from the phony. There have been few cases as clear-cut as that of the "tortoise healers" who in 1982 poisoned two people by prescribing the blood and entrails of tortoises as a remedy for leukaemia.[6]

THERE is no doubt that in the course of the past 20 years the Bulgarian Communist Party revised its attitude to folk medicine. In the 1960s it dismissed traditional healing as a superstitious relic of the peasant past that would disappear with the advance of science. In 1974, however, a new approach was outlined in a letter sent by Todor Zhivkov to the Ministry of Public Health. It called for the opening of a hospital for herbal medicine and for the republication of a well-known pre-war work of reference, *Bulgarska Narodna Meditsina* (Bulgarian Folk Medicine) by Petar Dimkov.

In 1977 an examination of the conservation and cultivation of medicinal plants in Bulgaria was made by both the Ministerial Council and the State Council. The latter issued a special order in 1980 to encourage production levels and to expedite the scientific assessment of herbal cures. Some teaching of plant therapy was introduced into medical courses, and a postgraduate qualification was inaugurated to allow the opening of more herbal pharmacies. It was decided that a publicity campaign should be started to publicize the new policy and to encourage foreign tourists to come to Bulgaria for cures as well as to visit such attractions as the Museum of Folk Medicine, opened in Sopot in 1980.[7] An Association of Herbalists was also founded in Gabrovo in 1982.[8]

One can only speculate as to how much this change of approach was brought about by Lyudmila Zhivkova, the late daughter of Todor Zhivkov, who had a strong personal interest in herbal therapies.[9] It was, however, another Politburo member, General Ivan Mihaylov, who wrote on the subject for the press, boasting in 1981 that "the Party and the state have a correct attitude towards the use of herbs and the experience of folk medicine."[10] But, as is often the case with Bulgarian plans for reform, many of the decisions to promote and to institutionalize traditional healing have not been implemented.

In 1977 Dimkov's collection of folk cures was republished in three volumes by the Bulgarian Academy of Sciences. The first impression was,

[5] *Rabotnichesko Delo*, 14 June 1976 and *Literaturen Front*, No. 37, 13 Sept. 1973.
[6] *Rabotnichesko Delo*, 26 July 1982.
[7] BTA (Sofia), 25 Feb. 1980.
[8] *Zemedelsko Zname*, 2 July 1982.
[9] She was known to have consulted healers in the 1970s when recovering from head injuries sustained in a car accident. It was widely believed that the turbans she wore were stuffed with medicinal herbs.
[10] *Otechestven Front*, 9 Jan. 1981.

however, limited to 10,000 copies, which sold out straight away at the low price of 2·72 leva per volume. According to rumour, demand was such that on the black market a single volume might fetch 60 leva and a comparable price was to be obtained even after a second impression of 30,000 copies had been issued.[11]

THE Bulgarian government has enjoyed only partial success in its efforts to institutionalize traditional medicine. The herbal hospital that Todor Zhivkov called for in his letter to the Ministry of Public Health in 1974 was never established; instead, a 60-bed clinic was opened in 1976 under the auspices of the Medical Academy at the Dr Racho Angelov District Hospital in Sofia.[12] It was opposed from the outset by the majority of doctors who challenged the qualifications of its staff, even though its head, Dr Dimitar Pamukov, had published several books on herbal medicine. In 1984 the clinic was closed. Its functions were subsequently allotted to the Clinic for Clinical Pharmacology (at the Scientific Institute of Pharmacology) and the Scientific Institute for Internal Diseases; it is unlikely, however, that these institutes will earnestly commit themselves to the preservation of traditional healing.[13]

In 1980, in response to the order issued by the State Council to encourage the cultivation and use of medicinal plants, the Ministry of Public Health instructed every district hospital to open a department for herbal medicine. *Otechestven Front*, reviewing this decision in an article entitled "Anxiety About the State of Herbal Medicine," concluded that little had been put into effect. In six districts no such departments had been opened; in three districts departments had been opened but existed in name only, having no staff; in four districts departments had been set up and allocated staff but had seen no patients; and in four other districts departments had been set up and staffed but did not practice herbal medicine. The best departments (in Varna and Tolbuhin) saw five or six patients every day, but others (in Lovech, Mihaylovgrad, and Veliko Tarnovo) received fewer than 500 patients in a year. A decision to open six departments in Sofia to work in support of Dr Pamukov's clinic had been ignored.[14] A small herbal centre was, however, opened in the remote village of Tetovo near Kubrat in the Razgrad District, but it was to receive fewer than 100 patients a year.[15]

The resulting pressure on facilities was reported to be intolerable. It had been planned that 25,500 patients should receive herbal treatment each year in Bulgaria, but in 1984 40,074 people had in fact approached the functioning clinics and departments for treatment. They had included thousands of foreigners, from the USSR, the GDR, Czechoslovakia, Poland, Austria, India, and elsewhere; all had been attracted to Bulgaria

[11] *Pogled*, No. 33, 15 June 1977.
[12] *Anteni*, 7 July 1977.
[13] *Otechestven Front*, 5 July 1985.
[14] Ibid.
[15] *Zemedelsko Zname*, 30 Sept. 1984.

by the publicity given to Petar Dimkov and other healers. The problem had become particularly grave in Sofia, as people from the provinces had come in numbers to seek treatment in the capital, often oblivious of the existence of more convenient local facilities.

THE main obstacles that have prevented the health authorities from fulfilling the ambitious plans of the Party and the Ministerial and State Councils have been a lack of funds and trained personnel and an obvious absence of purpose on the part of planners. The scientific and medical professions have also posed serious difficulties by refusing to come to terms with herbal medicine and by often opposing the use of traditional therapies, even in the treatment of ailments such as cancer and leukaemia that cannot as yet be cured by orthodox medicine. On 19 October 1979 the daily *Zemedelsko Zname* complained that many conventional doctors aimed to reduce folk medicine to nothing.

The opposition of the scientific establishment presumably lay behind an extraordinary occurrence in 1979 when it took the media more than six weeks to report on the First National Conference on Folk Medicine in Sopot. It is revealing that the 120 participants included no fewer than 69 ethnographers and museum curators, which gave the event a historical rather than a medical air.[16] Although it was stated that the conference would be held biennially, the third (in Kyustendil in 1984), at which 95 papers were read, convened three years after the second.[17]

A further problem has been the extinction of valuable plant species, often because of injudicious picking by amateurs.[18] It has also proved difficult to cultivate on a commercial basis a sufficient range of plants to satisfy the demands of therapists and pharmacies. BTA reported on 15 October 1982 that of the 600 species of medicinal plants found in Bulgaria only 300 are commonly grown and used. There are plans to invest two million leva in new processing centres and to double exports by 1990, but it remains to be seen whether this will improve the domestic supply.[19] It seems certain, however, that popular interest in herbal therapy will not wane and that the demand will remain sufficient to force the government into another re-examination of its policy. This might result in what *Kooperativno Selo* and *Otechestven Front* have urged, namely, the full legalization of scrupulous and honest healers such as Dimitar Krastev and Georgi and Kiril Desov.

[16] Ibid. 13 Jan. 1980. The conference was held in Nov. 1979.
[17] *Rabotnichesko Delo*, 10 Nov. 1984.
[18] Ibid. 26 May 1981.
[19] BTA in English (Sofia), 15 Oct. 1982.

Documents

The purpose of this documentation is to provide an accurate and vivid picture of the state of social and economic rights in the Soviet Union and East-Central Europe. "Openness" and "restructuring" in the USSR have made our task easier. Since Mikhail Gorbachov's stewardship of the CPSU, official Soviet accounts and reportage are, in most areas, seldom radically different in substance, though they are in language, from those given by Western journalists and dissidents. Nevertheless, the eye-witness accounts assembled in section four surpass in their frankness anything official sources have so far made public and cover areas that are still out of bounds for the media.

Although these documents concern themselves predominantly with social and economic rights, they are not confined to them. They also contain a selection of official and semi-official articulations that should help the reader to obtain a better understanding of how "openness" (*glasnost*) and "restructuring" (*perestroika*) affect, and may affect in the future, the exercise of human rights in the Soviet bloc.

1. Why "Restructuring"?

Change and Resistance to Change in the Soviet System

Social Corrosion

Extracts from Mikhail Gorbachov's speech to the plenary meeting of the CPSU Central Committee, 27 January 1987. Pravda, *28 January 1987.*

Negative processes had a serious effect on the social sphere. The 27th Party Congress has already given an appraisal of its condition. In the past few Five-Year Plan periods the social goals of the economy were clearly diluted, and there was a lack of response to social issues. We can see today what all this has led to.

Having successfully solved the problem of employment and provided basic social guarantees, at the same time we failed to realize the full potential of socialism to improve housing conditions, food supply, transport, health care and education, and to solve a number of other vital problems.

The most important principle of socialism, distribution according to work, was violated. Efforts to control unearned income were indecisive. The policy of material and moral incentive to work efficiently was inconsistent. Large, unjustified bonuses and various additional incentives were paid; figure-padding for profit was allowed to happen. Parasitic tendencies grew stronger and the mentality of "wage levelling" began to take hold. All this rebounded on those workers who could and wanted to work better, while making life easier for the idle.

This violation of the basic relationship between the rate of work and the rate of consumption not only distorts attitudes to work, obstructing the growth of productivity, but leads to distortion of the principle of social justice—and that is a question of great political importance.

Elements of social corrosion emerging in the last few years had a negative effect on society's morale and subconsciously eroded the lofty moral values which have always been characteristic of our people and of which we are proud, namely, ideological dedication, labour enthusiasm and Soviet patriotism.

As an inevitable consequence of all this, interest in the affairs of society slackened, callousness and scepticism appeared, and the role of the moral incentive to work declined. The social stratum of people, some of them young people, whose ultimate goal in life was material well-being and gain by any means, grew wider. Their cynical attitude was becoming more and more aggressive, poisoning the mentality of those around them and triggering a wave of consumerism. The spread of alcohol and drug abuse and a rise in crime were indicative of the decline of social mores.

Disregard for the law, report-padding, bribe-taking and encouragement of sycophancy and adulation had a deleterious effect on the moral atmosphere within society.

Real concern for people, for the conditions of their life and work and for social well-being were often replaced with political flirtation—the mass distribution of awards, titles and prizes. An atmosphere of permissiveness was taking shape, and precision, discipline and responsibility were in decline.

Will It Fly?

Excerpts from Mikhail Gorbachov's speech at the CPSU Central Committee plenum, 25 June 1987. Pravda, *26 June 1987.*

The revolutionary transformations in society have brought to the fore the contradictions between the demands of renewal, creativity and creative initiative on the one hand and conservatism, inertia and selfish interests on the other. One manifestation of this real contradiction is the disparity between the masses' growing activeness on the one hand and the bureaucratic style of activity which is still alive in various spheres and the attempts to freeze restructuring on the other. Swift and resolute measures are needed to overcome this contradiction—both in cadre policy and in the assertion of new approaches and norms of party, state and public life.

What does the Politburo see as the most effective means of resolving this contradiction? The answer is unambiguous and definite—the extensive development of democracy. Today—and this has been proved by life yet again—it is the running of society in the form of administrative directives which is retarding our progress. Democratic, and only democratic, forms are capable of imparting powerful acceleration to our progress.

Experience of restructuring and its initial stage also prompts us to take a close look at the really existing conflicts of interests between various groups of the population, collectives, departments and organizations. Undoubtedly, socialism eradicates antagonistic interests. This thesis is well-known and true, but in no way does it mean that eliminating antagonistic interests is the same as unifying them or levelling them out.

Take the attitude to restructuring. On the whole there is a general realization of the impossibility of living and working in the old way and of the objective need for restructuring and profound transformations. But as soon as restructuring started to turn sharply towards work, to imbue all strata of society and to reach individuals, we saw how a contradiction surfaces between immediate, narrow interests and even the egotistical motives of certain individuals and groups on the one hand, and the interests of all society and working people's long-term interests, on the other.

We can clearly see the difficulties restructuring is encountering in party, Soviet and economic organs. And can we fail to sense how reluctantly it is received in certain central departments? The complexities of restructuring are attested by the experience of the state acceptance system, the struggle against drunkenness and alcoholism and the efforts to instill order and discipline. They are also attested by the first steps in introducing financially autonomous initiatives and asserting principles whereby pay is wholly linked with end results. All these, comrades, are real processes and actual contradictions. And we must be aware of them and take them into account. . . .

The behaviour of those who for their own selfish ends are hampering social transformations and standing in the way of restructuring looks particularly unseemly against the back-drop of the genuinely civic-minded position of the working class. I think that labour collectives and party and social organizations should be firm in their attitude to such people and not tolerate them. That is the demand of life. That is our understanding of the matter in the Politburo. . . .

Take, for example, letters of the CPSU Central Committee, the Presidium of the USSR Supreme Soviet, the USSR Council of Ministers, the editorial offices of central newspapers, journals, radio and television. Their content is the same. People write that they support restructuring but see no changes around them. Restructuring has not affected the work collectives, towns and villages where they live and work. Many people conclusively confirm this with facts. Thus despite tremendous efforts, restructuring has not really reached many places. This, comrades, is a very serious symptom. . . .

Our people have also noticed that in some areas not only is progress not being made but that the advances made at an earlier stage are even being lost. Take the campaign for discipline and order, for instance. It is a fact, after all, that in many places the momentum has been lost and work is proceeding extremely sluggishly. The incidence of drunkenness has increased again and idlers, parasites and pilferers—people who live at the expense of others—again feel at liberty. This worries working people. And that is a justified concern, comrades.

The fact that discipline is lax and the proper order is lacking is indicated by the periodic recurrence of major accidents. As a rule, the causes are the same: indiscipline, slipshod work, negligence and irresponsibility. That fact is shown by the violation of Soviet air space and the landing in Moscow by a West German light aircraft. The incident was unprecedented, whichever way you look at it. It is a reminder yet again of just how strong and tenacious are the negative phenomena exposed by the April plenum of the Central Committee and the 27th Party Congress in our society, even in the Army. This emphasises the need to increase vigilance, act even more resolutely and enhance discipline, organization, responsibility and efficiency at all levels and everywhere. On behalf of the

Politburo and the Defence Council, I firmly state that there must be no doubt, either in the party or among the people, of the USSR Armed Forces' ability to defend the country.

Comrades, You Must not Panic

Excerpts from 'Mikhail Gorbachov talking to the people' in Murmansk Moscow Home Service, *30 September 1987.*

Gorbachov Good day! (crowd answers: "Good Day!"—applause) How are you? (Crowd answers: "Fine".) When I ask that question I know absolutely how you are, but I want to know what you will say. I'm checking on how you are getting along here. You are informing us, as before, that everything's fine, everthing's fine—but in actual fact—not at all.

Man Tolystoy used to say: Thank goodness, there's never a dull moment. (laughter)

Gorbachov In general, we do have reason to be agitated. But there is no reason to be bewildered or uncertain, to panic. Not at all. We stand on firm ground, hard ground. The potential is enormous—but we have to change direction. . . .

I think that we really have a critical 12 or 18 months [ahead]. The whole economy is now going to go onto financial autonomy and self-financing. The processes of democratisation are already present in the laws, in elections. The state acceptance service, that again is a new experience. In general everything, now, the whole of society, is going to be affected. At the top it's all been a question of how? where? which choice? which decision to take? The options have been thought through. Now all of this has already entered society. . . .

I tell you, honestly, it's now going to be difficult. But if we get our fly-wheel turning, a great deal will be added in the country, a very great deal. But of course we would like restructuring to become a whole new stage; tremendous changes are going to have to take place. But it is essential for the present generation of people, too, to feel now not just the political atmoshpere—that is important in itself—but the housing situation has to be solved, problems have to be solved which concern a more or less regular provision of basic products, this has to be done. . . .

People must feel well in their own socialist home. That is our approach. There's the October Revolution, and there's restructuring—it's a revolution, without shooting, but it's a deep and serious one. You have to keep yourselves in check, comrades, and you must not panic. Never. It may be difficult. Sometimes it may be unpleasant. . . . I tell you—it's going to work, it's going to work.

Changes in the "Ownership of the Means of Production"

From an interview by Boris Simonov with L. I. Abalkin, correspondent member of the USSR Academy of Sciences and Director of the Economics Institute of the USSR Academy of Sciences, Moscow Radio home service, 24 March 1987.

Simonov: Leonid Ivanovich, all the questions you have replied to in *Kommunist* concern in one way or another restructuring and the revolutionary changes now taking place in economics, but, it seems to me, the most important of these concerns production relations. What is the current state of affairs, and what are the prospects for development of these production relations?

Abalkin: At present the situation is such that we find ourselves faced with the need for radical changes in this sphere; such profound ones, moreover, that they touch the very foundations of the system of production relations, including that of ownership of the means of production. So where exactly does the need for change arise? This is not, of course, a denial of the advantages of social ownership or a repudiation of socialist principles in the organization of society. To a large extent, it means giving back to ownership its inner meaning and content, that is, making these relations such that every person—not only in a formal, but in a real sense, in his everyday life—should feel himself to be an owner, within the work collective, an owner showing his concern for the preservation and multiplication of his property, an owner who is not indifferent about how it is used, whether carefully or extravagantly, and about whether it yields fruit. These economic relations need to be restructured in such a way as to interlock individual and common interests; in other words the property relationship needs to be filled with real economic meaning, to have returned to it its inherent meaning. One cannot limit oneself in this to partial amendments; everything needs to be restructured, starting with centralized planning and the prices system, and including the way pay is organized. It seems to me that this is the logical way ahead, to a large extent coincidental with the logic of the reform of the economic mechanism.

Simonov: You speak of ownership but let us take, say, land. Land comes into the category of belonging to no one individually, but to the people as a whole; in other words it has no specific owner, isn't that the case?

Abalkin: Indeed, this is an area where change is needed, so that land might have its specific owner. What exactly am I thinking of? Well, one could say, for instance, that this is being achieved in many places today where financially autonomous contracting teams have been set up. In such cases a parcel of land is assigned for a lengthy period to a particular team, perhaps even just a family team consisting of two, three or four people. So the land is assigned for a long period, and how well it is looked after, fertilized, and tended with loving human care, will determine the fruits it bears; via payments and incentive the owner should feel the benefit of those fruits for himself. Under these conditions he will not feel as though that land belonged to someone else about whom he is indifferent, as though it were a case of "Today I'm working here, but tomorrow I'll be somewhere else. . . ."

There is a concept—although it has not been cited in recent times in economic writings; at least, I cannot name a single serious major work that mentions it—the concept of leasing arrangements. I think it is legitimate to use the concept of socialist leasing with regard to land, machinery and so forth; this would be connected with the establishment of small, financially autonomous teams. Today in the example of the new small cooperatives one can see instances of state premises being handed over to those cooperatives as they are formed. I see this as one of the economic ways of arranging such a [production] relationship.

Simonov: On the subject of cooperative arrangements, which are now being introduced—what about cooperative associations, these comrades' cooperatives [*kooperativnye tovarishchestva*] which are being set up? Where do they fit into the scheme of production relationships? Aren't they a very serious infringement of [economic] forms which have already been established?

Abalkin: General development and progress as a whole is moving not towards unifying [economic] forms, but towards a legitimate process of sophistication and a growth in variety of forms for organizing economic life. In other words, progress is coincidental not with standardizing and simplification or the creation of synonymous forms; on the contrary, a growth in variety, a process of sophistication of structures and relationships is in fact a law of progress. This, naturally, enriches our ideas about ownership and makes them more flexible, more modern, brings them closer to real life.

Resistance to Change

Extracts from an interview with Academician Abel Aganbegyan, chief editor of the journal EKO, *by* Izvestia *scientific observer Boris Konovalov.* Nedelya, *No. 1, 8 January 1987.*

Aganbegyan: Why is restructuring necessary? It is necessary because the old structure of the economy, the old economic policy, the old system of management, the old development trends—that is, everything which determines the economy's progress—failed to fit in with the new conditions and new tasks which the times had sent us. All this can be seen particularly clearly from that general indicator of the national economy's development, the national income, because it is essentially the sum total of benefits, the "kitty" from which society takes funds for consumption and accumulation. It is well known that in the past 15 years the growth rates of this basic economic and social indicator have declined by a factor of approximately 2·5, with all the ensuing consequences. This downward trend had to be stopped at once, and reversed into acceleration. Unfortunately, we were unable to make an immediate assessment of the new conditions in which our economy had to exist, and we continued to act with inertia . . . .

Serious changes (well-known to everyone) have taken place externally—in the world situation. Serious changes have taken place in our domestic conditions. There has been a sharp reduction in the growth of all types of production resources—manpower, raw materials, capital investments and funds. After all, formerly we developed primarily by expansion, by allocating a larger and larger share of resources to production. Now we can no longer develop in this way. The old extensive development trends are leading us into an *impasse.* While the scientific and technical revolution has entered a new stage, we have been continuing to pursue our old scientific and technical policy. The role of the human factor has altered radically; yet we have continued to cling to the so-called residual principle of distribution, whereby only those budget funds left over after distribution for building up production are assigned to the needs of social development and the social sphere.

In the 1970s and early 1980s there was a marked drop in production and labour productivity growth rates, several indicators of efficiency deteriorated, and scientific and technical progress slowed down.

It became clear that the situation was such that we could not limit ourselves to mere adjustments to the structure of the economy. New, radical, measures were needed.

. . . There has been no large-scale restructuring so far, and there is still room for the old administrative methods of management to function.

Konovalov: Does that mean that the lower echelons of the national economy and the upper levels of management are actively advocating restructuring while the "middle echelon" seems to be opposing it?

Aganbegyan: Why "seems to be"? As we can see, it actually is opposing it. To give an idea of the present state of restructuring, I would cite the analogy of a man who is learning to swim. Even if no one obstructs him it is no simple matter. So, too, must our economic system now find its way in the sea of economic methods and learn to use new levers and stimuli. This is a difficult task in itself, for after all we have had virtually no experience. But it is even harder if people grab hold of the "swimmer's" arms and legs and try to push his head further under water to put him off learning to "swim" for a long time. Undoubtedly such "methods" greatly complicate the process of restructuring, all the more so since every economic leader has an alternative: he can stand calmly on the shore and wait. Let's see whether my bold neighbour busy restructuring his economy will sink or swim . . . .

Inertia in the Soul

Extracts from an interview with Academician Tatyana Zaslavskaya, Izvestia, *21 December 1986.*

Interviewer: Tatyana Ivanovna, our first question is what they call a contradiction in terms. Intellectually, we understand that reconstruction is bound to be a complex and lengthy process, but we would like everything to be moving more quickly. The ice has been broken, but has the ice-breaker started to move? Reconstruction is proceeding slowly and painfully. Why?

Zaslavskaya: What do you mean by "slowly"? Only nine months have passed since the 27th CPSU Congress, and the April plenum was little more than 18 months ago. Where historic processes are concerned, that is no time at all. They are extraordinarily inertial, but they do gather speed, drawing the generations into their movement, frequently over several decades.

What you call the painfulness of reconstruction is equally understandable. Whatever problem is concerned, sooner or later it all comes down to the "human factor." The cracks which it has produced in the present structure of our life at all events run through man, who is simultaneously both the object and the subject of all the changes taking place in the country.

Interviewer: In that case it makes sense, clearly, to switch from questions concerning the economy, production and economic mechanisms to a discussion of the present state of the "human factor."

Zaslavskaya: Do you want to comprehend the incomprehensible? It can't be done. It is not just reconstruction that is complex—man himself, participating in it and creating it is complex, contradictory and extraordinarily diverse. As M. S.

Gorbachov said in his speech at Krasnodar, at first many people thought the new situation concerned only the upper strata, as if they had to change their activities in some way. Now it is becoming clearer—if not to everyone, then at least to the majority—that all members of society, every single citizen must reorganize himself. But has everyone of us, regardless of whether he belongs to the "upper" or "lower" echelon, the ability, is he able, does he know how to revise his position, his views, attitudes and evaluations? And, most importantly, is he willing to? For example, some people are accustomed to acting solely in accordance with instructions handed down from above and are prepared to answer only to this "upper stratum." Others, in a situation which demands of them unquestioning assiduity and obedience, literally dry up.

Interviewer: But mindless obedience is incompatible with active, assertive participation in the process of reconstruction presently under way in the country. And in just the same way adminstration by decree was long ago proven to be defective as a method of management. Consequently, the main thing now is to increase people's independence. In making decisions and in determining means and methods of working. That's right, isn't it?

Zaslavskaya: That's as may be, but then again it's not everything. There is, after all, psychological inertia as well. People who are unused to displaying initiative and who do not know how to determine their aims, nor how to balance out personal, group and social interests are afraid of independence. There are quite a lot of people like that.

Recently an acquaintance of mine, a man with a university education, who although young has already shown himself to be a capable programmer, asked me: "Tatyana Ivanovna, you write about stimulating the human factor, and on the radio and on the television they're always talking about the need to start reconstruction with ourselves. But please could you explain this with a specific example? Let us suppose I have been inspired by the idea of reconstruction and am ready to activate myself. What should I do, what can I do? Me personally, in my position? As you know, in my institute nothing has stirred, everything remains exactly as it was; we have the same director and department heads, and the same self-financing with fictitious or semi-fictitious contracts. Does this mean that from now on, whenever I receive an assignment to develop a computer programme, knowing that almost exactly the same programme has already been produced by my neighbour, I, as an honest person, a man of principles, should announce this for all to hear and enter into battle with my superiors?"

Interviewer: And why not? Is it that after an announcement like that he wouldn't remain at the institute?

Zaslavskaya: Such a distressing prospect should not altogether be excluded. . . . although times are different now, and he would remain there. . . . You should note that the man asking the question is not looking for an answer in himself but he's expecting to get one from me, thereby shifting responsibility for the solution onto someone else, relieving himself of the choice.

"Justified Inequality"

Excerpts from an interview with Academician Tatyana Zaslavskaya, Moscow Radio, 6 June 1987.

Correspondent: Social justice is central to the process of restructuring under way in this country and, as it is now clear, mistakes have been made in that area both in theory and in practice. For instance, social policy was very often understood as something that improves the living standards of all social groups evenly. The view was current that it is necessary to level out pay regardless of the amount and quality of work done and that led to signs of stagnation and made life easier for lovers of easy living and dealers of all kinds. Some officials enjoyed benefits that they didn't deserve. In other words, the basic principle of socialism—from each according to his ability, to each according to his work—was violated. . . .

Zaslavskaya: . . . We're trying to move towards justified inequality arising from the quantity of work. That is a necessary process if economic efficiency is to be raised. In other words, the policy of social justice provides not only for improving the situation of certain categories but also for making others worse off. I mean the kind of people you mentioned—the social strata of profiteers, corrupt officials and other wheeler-dealers as well as a bureaucratic layer that has formed in the past two decades. . . .

Correspondent: And what is being done to overcome the trend towards the levelling of pay?

Zaslavskaya: . . . Our society must get rid of the tendency to level wages because it amounts to a dead end and what you may call an infantile social disorder. . . .

Correspondent: And how does individual enterprise fit in here?

Zaslavskaya: Individual enterprise will of course increase the differentiation of incomes . . . . It must be said, though, that social groups engaged in individual enterprise should be controlled in order to prevent them from developing into a social group of petty bourgeoisie accustomed to easy living. In my opinion, the incomes of those engaged in individual enterprise per a norm of work can be two to three times higher than those drawn from the publicly owned sector of the economy, but it would appear to me that a ratio of 10 to one would be too much and hard to justify.

Concealing the Facts

Extracted from "Questions of Theory: Restructuring and Sociology," an article by Academician Tatyana Zaslavskaya, Pravda, *6 February 1987.*

Of the socialist states, Hungary probably has the most developed system of social statistics. Regular sociological and statistical studies based on nationwide sampling and covering a wide range of problems are supplemented there by nearly 20 "panels" which ensure prolonged monitoring of the fate of particular population groups (for instance, young families, graduates from specific VUZs [Institutes of Higher Education] and so forth). On the completion of processing of the data, the statistical bodies pass them over to scientists for use in relation to the topics studied.

In the USSR, the picture is quite different. Of the developed countries, we have one of the lowest standards of social statistics. Let me stipulate that in my view social statistics are not what is kept in the storerooms of the Central Statistical Administration but the end result of data processing, published openly in the press and available to a wide range of people. Their development has been curtailed since the second half of the 1970s. Thus, for instance, the publication of data from All-Union Population Censuses has become increasingly meagre since 1959. More and more sections of social information have been "concealed" from social scientists.

Data are not published on the prevalence of crime, the frequency of suicide, the level of alcohol and drug abuse, or the ecological situation in various cities and regions, although these phenomena are traditional subjects of statistics in economically developed countries. Data on population migration between regions and between the city and the countryside have disappeared from the press.

And why are data on disease distribution amongst the population concealed? Why is such meagre information published on the differentiation of the level and structure of incomes and the population's prosperity? Even if negative trends have appeared in these areas, wouldn't it be better to draw the public's attention to them and together discuss ways of tackling the problems? The course of restructuring the system of social relations put forward by the 27th CPSU Congress requires precisely this approach.

For the sake of objectivity one must note that in recent years the collection and analysis of social information has been widening systematically. However, scientific organizations receive even fewer data from the USSR Central Statistical Administration than before, since the acquisition of such data is obstructed by a multitude of bureaucratic barriers.

At the same time the availability of social statistical data not only to scientists, but to broad strata of the population is linked in the most direct way to openness in public life. If you conceal from people summarized information about the conditions of their own life (for instance, the degree of environmental pollution, the level of accidents in production, the prevalence of crime, and so forth), you cannot expect them to become more active in either the production or the political sphere. People's trust and support can be obtained only by response to trust placed in them.

Although a large proportion of sociological research is oriented towards "assistance for the practical area," the sociologists' real participation in management is not great. Frankly, it is rather difficult to name a single administrative decision affecting the vital interests of many social strata and groups that has been based on a reliable sociological study carried out beforehand. Yet examples of the reverse are not hard to find. Remember, for instance, the unjustified course of eliminating personal plots in the early 1960s; the mass transformation of *kolkhozes* [collective farms] into *sovkhozes* [state farms], which undermined financial autonomy in agriculture; the division of rural settlements into those with and those without a future, which led to the degeneration of the network of settlements in many rural areas; the mass construction in rural localities of multi-storey blocks of flats whose inhabitants dream of returning to their own houses; the elimination of small rural schools which speeded up the population exodus to the cities, and so on, and so forth.

"The Shadow-Boxing is Over"

Paul Quinn-Judge in Christian Science Monitor, *20 February 1987.**

Since Vitaly Korotich took over as editor of *Ogonyok* seven months ago, the magazine has published an article on young right-wing toughs in the suburbs of Moscow, an *exposé* of police torture, and a major contribution to the rehabilitation of the the poet Nikolai Gumilyov, shot in 1921.

Such features have led many to regard *Ogonyok* as the most interesting example of the new outburst of aggressive Soviet journalism. A weekly magazine that used to be famous solely for its crossword puzzle, it now throws out ideas "like a hooligan," Mr Korotich says. It has a circulation of 1·5 million and is so popular that it is practically impossible to buy on the news-stands.

Korotich says his aim is simple: "To say everything that one can, while we can." Asked if there are any taboos left for the Soviet mass media, he said: "Right now I don't perceive any censorship. The old censor's organization, the Directorate for the Protection of State Secrets, still exists. But now they're actually protecting state secrets—rockets and things—and nothing else . . . The only feeling I'm aware of at the moment is a sense of personal caution." This does not appear to be very highly developed in Vitaly Korotich, however. *Ogonyok*'s previous editor, though, was not very adventurous: he had a little calendar showing whose photograph should be published in which edition of the magazine, and whether the person's picture should be in black-and-white or colour. Korotich's style is new.

> We've got to make people think. A lot of them don't want to think. People are complacent and afraid of change. We have to try to change the moral atmosphere.

Last week Soviet leader Mikhail Gorbachov talked to senior Soviet editors. The thrust of the conversation, Korotich says, was that if you end the policy of *glasnost*, you end the whole reform process that Mr Gorbachov is championing.

Much of that battle for reform is being waged by the media, with *Ogonyok* in the forefront. But even some major editors are lukewarm to the new ideas, Korotich feels.

> Up to now we've been shadow-boxing over reforms. Now it's a real fight. There are real threats. Real phone calls. People call and say: "Things will go back to the way they were, and then you'll shut up." I don't think there is any alternative to what Gorbachov's doing. I know I don't want to live the old way.

In the long run, he says, he is an optimist. But there is a real struggle going on. The meeting with Gorbachov showed that the leadership's support for *glasnost* was strong, but that "a lot of people were still opposed to it." The opposition came from some of the editors.

"Of course they didn't say, 'We're against *glasnost*.' They said 'Do we really need to touch on all the painful points in our history?' They wondered about the consequences of constant criticism of the system." Gorbachov took the opposite line, Korotich says. "He told the meeting, if we have real democratization, that means that everyone can be criticized, including himself."

For example, major discussion is going on about the painful points in Soviet history, Korotich says.

> Is it necessary or not to talk about 1937 (the high pont of the Stalinist purges)? I think so. Until we resolve the question of [the behaviour of Joseph] Stalin we'll never move forward. Other people object. They say: "Do we want to create the impression that the achievements of socialism were based on a crime?" and others—very sober people—feel that, well, Stalin may have been a bandit, but he got things done.

In fact, Korotich says, the current climate in the Soviet Union and the United States has roused Soviet conservatives. "It's interesting; conservatives here and in the US really need each other these days. Their interests are growing together," he says.

> Take [the ABC television mini-series] "Amerika." Conservatives here love it. They say: "Here is proof that the US is developing a war-like mentality." And every time they hear of a speech by [Defence Secretary Caspar] Weinberger, they say: "See, we have to be strong to face up to the US threat."

Science shows how to deal with conservatives, Korotich says. "We are now taught that dinosaurs died out because the climate changed. So we have to change the climate."

"They Are Afraid of Independence"

Extracts from an interview by Peter Horvath with Academician Abel Aganbegyan, Hungarian Television, 5 March 1987.

Horvath: What guarantees are there, in your opinion, that radical reform will not slow down in the Soviet Union?

Aganbegyan: I could list several guarantees. The first of these is clarification of our relationship to the past. If one wants to advance, then the path must be cleared; we must analyze the mistakes of the past objectively. This is not a pleasant task, of course, since we have to rummage in the dirty linen of the past. At such times the fact that it is easy to be wise after the event always comes up; it is easy to ascribe everything to one's predecessors, and so on. This is uncomfortable work. But necessary. The objective appreciation of the past is an unpleasant task especially when it concerns negative tendencies, and economic stagnation, such as our country has experienced in the past 10–15 years. The present leadership is now carrying out this objective, I might even say ruthless, analysis of the past. And moreover, very purposefully. For, with an eye to the future, by doing this it wants to draw certain lessons. In my opinion that is the first guarantee.

The second guarantee of reform is ideology itself, and the whole of intellectual life. If we really want to carry out the transformation seriously then we must do it by involving the widest public. For this reason we must develop criticism, self-criticism. There is a need for creative debates; we must not accept decisions in a slavish manner. We must debate the proposals on a wide scale. We must learn to listen to one another and not shut one another up. You no doubt know what changes are to be seen in the sphere of ideology. I do not know if this is apparent or not. New films, new literary works are appearing in our country. Newspapers and periodicals have changed radically. Wide-ranging critical rethinking of what has happened so far has begun. The whole of public opinion has made a move. The intelligentsia has become very active. Creative associations have been renewed. This is very important.

The third phenomenon, which is relevant here, is the development of democracy. We consider the January plenum, and the resolutions it adopted to be significant from this point of view, as the turning point that set the programme. Important decisions were made there about greater economic democracy, political democracy, the election of leaders, and their eligibility. One of the important findings of the plenum was that we may seek the cause of past mistakes first and foremost in the strangulation of the democratic initiatives affecting our lives. If we really want to continue the transformation, if we really want to, then the basic condition is to widen democracy. But the best guarantee is life itself. We have no other choice. Do you understand? We have no other alternative for the acceleration of social and economic development. And if we have no choice, then we must carry this transformation through to the end. Finally, the recognition of the fact that, as Comrade Gorbachov put it, there is no going back—well, in my opinion, that is an important guarantee as well.

Horvath: Can you tell us specifically who, what forces, are obstructing the realization of reform?

Aganbegyan: Such forces exist on nearly every level: within the Party, the council, the organs of economic management, in a significant area of the central authorities, including ministries, the State Planning Committee, the Ministry of Finance, the banks, and the union industrial associations. It is not possible to determine specifically where these forces are. There are some people who, as a consequence of the transformation, are losing some of their rights. Why are they losing them? Because the basic concept of the economic mechanism is the large-scale growth of enterprise independence. Areas of authority are being divided up anew to the benefit of the enterprises.

At the same time, interference in the work of the enterprises, petty tutelage over the work of the enterprises, must be eliminated. Well, those people who until now felt themselves to be masters of the situation, who distributed the raw materials, and gave instructions, can no longer do so. It is not only their sphere of authority, a part of their sphere of authority, that they are losing, but, along with it, their privileges as well. Many links in the chain of the management apparatus have simply become superfluous.

The middle level consists here of the all-union industrial associations, the trusts. The majority of them will probably be disbanded. Now, in the new situation, many central organs and ministries which until now carried out merely operative tasks will also become unnecessary. There is no need for them any longer. The tasks of the middle-level leaders, another significant section of the central apparatus, will change. Many are protesting against this.

. . . This is the root of their active resistance. Publicly, they say they are in favour of the transformation; they appreciate intellectually that it is necessary. But whenever some resolution is announced, concerning the expansion of enterprise independence, then they issue instructions which in essence revert matters to the old channels. They do not want to hand over real authority. . . .

A second group comprises conservative-thinking managers, directors, and co-operative chairmen. Now, when it appears that there will be no instructions, that they will have to manage the resources independently, and will have to take responsibility for their management, they do not feel strong enough to do so. They are afraid of independence, yes, they are afraid of being independent. What is more, if they are given independence, they fail to make use of it. They continue to ask permission to do this or that, even though they do not need permission any more. . . .

This second group has in general become isolated from the workers. In general, these people have been appointed as managers by superior bodies. They are afraid of elections. Some of these people are very concerned about the fact that managers will now be elected. They see it as wrong, as the undermining of management. They have always regarded themselves as representatives of the higher organs and now, suddenly, they can only remain managers if they are elected.

A third group comes from the ranks of enterprise workers, including some low-level office-holders. These are people who earn more money or gain a larger income that is proportional to their work. They work badly, but still get their salaries. These are the factory magpies. There are also those who make use of their official positions, generally to their own advantage, or who moonlight. The conditions are already becoming stricter; now it is demanded that they should do the equivalent amount of work for that money. Of course, now they are dissatisfied, because they have got used to receiving their wages even if they only work at half speed. Now, when better work is required from them, they are demanding more wages.

"The Ship Itself Must Be Reconstructed"

From an interview with Nikolai Shishlin, Deputy Head of a department of the CPSU Central Committee, Budapest Television programme, "The Week," 10 May 1987.

Questioner: Let us look at the issue from the standpoint of an ordinary Soviet person, let us say a Russian or a Ukrainian. What has the policy of restructuring given him during these past two years? What changes has it brought in his everyday life?

Shishlin: I understand, I understand the question. In my opinion, I must say in this connection that man does not live by bread alone. We should speak not only about material things, but also about intellectual things because, to put it mildly, our results in the material sphere are modest. Certain forms of meeting social requirements have been enlivened somewhat, they have become more palpable. For example, restructuring is taking place in health work. As a consequence of this, the wages of health staff and other categories of employees are increasing. Supplies of certain types of goods are increasing. At the same time, there has been less vodka everywhere.

Questioner: Well, that is something.

Shishlin: Yes, that is some kind of gain. And here, allow me to use a strong expression: society has woken up from its "Sleeping Beauty" sleep. It has moved out of a state of stagnation. It is debating every essential issue in lively fashion. It devotes its energy not to perpetual applause but to more useful things, to self-knowledge and seeking solutions. Many, many set targets are already being carried out. We are restructuring party work. We are preparing to introduce a new election system. We are vesting enterprises and production associations with wide-ranging rights. Therefore, people can feel the cause to be their own and they can feel that they are masters of the country. The results cannot sweep us away. We consider our situation soberly. . . .

Questioner: Many people draw parallels between the current changes and the 20th Congress in 1956, or the activity of Khrushchev. At that time, similar, enormous changes got under way in the policy of the Soviet Union, but economic reform somehow came to a standstill, and things developed in the known manner. What is your opinion about this parallel? What chance is there that what happened then might be repeated?

Shishlin: It is always easier to seek analogies than to draw independent, logical conclusions. On the Party's 20th Congress and Khrushchev's activity, I can say that, from many standpoints, doing away with the Stalinist personality cult was a difficult but nevertheless simple task, in a certain sense. The ballast had to be discharged from the ship, the ship had to be cleaned. The task now is much more complex. The ship itself must be reconstructed. It must be supplied with a new heart, a new mechanism. Its operational characteristics must be improved. That is a much more difficult task.

The System Must Give Way

Excerpts from an article by Nikolai Shmelev, Novy Mir, *No. 6, June 1987*

The state of the economy satisfies no one. Its two chief defects are clear: the monopoly enjoyed by the producers, given a general shortage of goods, and the lack of interest on the part of manufacturers in scientific and technical progress.

Persistent, long-term efforts to overturn the objective laws of economic life and crush the age-old natural incentives to work have brought results directly opposite to those we had anticipated. We now have an economy which is out of order and plagued with shortages, an economy which rejects scientific and technical progress and is unplanned and—if we want to be totally honest—unplannable.

Massive apathy, indifference, theft, disrespect for honest labour, together with aggressive envy toward those who earn more (even by honest methods) have led to signs of virtual physical degradation of a significant part of the people as a result of alcoholism and idleness. There is a disbelief in the goals and intentions which have been declared, disbelief in the possibility of a rational organization of economic and social life.

For a long time agricultural growth rates have been less than one per cent per year. In some years we had to use a minus sign to indicate our progress—even though the government has been making mind-boggling investments in this area. We must ask: Why are we paying these enormous sums? Can it actually be a fear of market relations? Or perhaps a very thin layer of our leading agricultural cadres need somehow to justify their existence?

The degradation of the countryside has progressed so far that it is unlikely that any measures conceived within the framework of the existing system will do any good. We must finally decide what is most important to us: to have enough of our own agricultural commodities, or eternally pacify the loudmouths who would see us all equal in our poverty.

We must call things by their proper names: foolishness as foolishness, incompetence as incompetence, Stalinism in action as Stalinism in action. Perhaps we will lose our ideological virginity, but it now exists only in the fairytale editorials of the newspaper.

The present system of material incentives for conscientious work is ineffective not only because it is worthless. Salaries and bonuses don't work because there is nothing for the people to buy with their money.

We need to permit companies and organizations to sell freely, to buy and borrow from their reserves so as to create a powerful and vibrant goods market. In place of fruitless efforts at central planning of our entire industrial production (some 24 million items), we should introduce contracts between supplier and consumer.

We need to realize that there is such a thing as natural unemployment among people who are looking for work or changing their places of employment. The real danger of losing one's job and having to take, temporarily, unemployment benefit or work wherever one is sent is a very good cure for laziness, drunkenness or irresponsibility. Many experts believe it would be cheaper to pay temporary unemployment benefit for a few months than keep masses of people in industry who do nothing and could break (and are breaking) any self-financing scheme and any attempt to raise the quality and efficiency of public labour.

The new economic policy of the 1980s must not sidestep the industrial ministries. There is such a disgusting proliferation of them and they are so top-heavy with administrators that they often have to invent something to do, and actually end up interfering with the work of the enterprises.

The hardest problem in organizing the economy on a totally cost-effective basis is readjusting prices. This is an exceptionally delicate question—partly because it will involve significantly raising prices of food and housing. Consumers are now receiving a subsidy of more than 50 billion rubles from the treasury. Why should they not receive this money in the form of a pay rise instead? Why underpay for meat while overpaying for yard goods and shoes? We will have to talk to people honestly, as was done in Hungary, where a major public relations effort was launched in 1976 to help introduce new prices painlessly.

The economic situation of enterprises and cooperatives will have to depend directly on profit, and profit cannot fulfil its function until wholesale prices are liberated from subsidies. Over the centuries, humankind has found no more effective measure of work than profit. Our suspicious attitude toward profit is a sort of historical misunderstanding, the cost of the economic illiteracy of people who thought that socialism would eliminate profit and loss. In point of fact, the criterion of profit under socialism is in no way tainted; it simply tells whether you are working well or not.

We have resolved to create undertakings using foreign capital. It is even possible that we should consider creating free economic zones.

Another prejudice is the rejection of the stock company. Why should the savings of our citizens and enterprises not be used to create new undertakings or expand old ones? Can it really be that the country is better off hoarding this money in a stocking?

I am convinced that our economy is in need of a financial reform of no less depth and scope than in the early 1920s. Money, prices, incomes, credit, budget, government borrowings and the resulting government debt are all questions which we have not even begun to discuss on a serious basis. In the meantime the defects of our current financial system are obvious: the magnitude of deferred consumer demand, a budget full of tax loopholes, inflationary methods of financing, loans which are never to be repaid.

Finally, we have the problem of quality. Good quality is not so much a problem of conscientious work as of production and management—areas which are the responsibility of the leadership, not the worker. According to our more "patriotic" assessments, only 17 or 18 per cent of the production of our manufacturing industry meets world standards. More cautious and pessimistic assessments run to 7 or 8 per cent.

Only a gradual weakening and, ultimately, a total elimination of the manufacturers' monopoly will result in anything really new. Consumers need to have both rights and opportunities to take what is offered or turn it down. That means they have to have a real choice. And the producer must be faced with the real possibility of loss and even total bankruptcy if the goods he produces cannot be sold.

It is time to stop deceiving ourselves, stop believing the office ignoramuses and calmly admit that the problem of "consumer selection," the problem of competition, is not rooted in any social or class relationships. There is no room here for even a whiff of ideology. This is a purely economic problem. In the final analysis, market stimuli must extend to all stages of the research, development, investment, production, marketing and service process. Only the market-place, not mere administrative innovations, can subordinate this entire chain to the consumer's demands.

Who is going to drum into the heads of our managers that the time of administrative methods is passing and that economics has laws that are just as terrible to violate as the laws of the atomic reactor in Chernobyl?

Who will break our managers, especially the high-level ones, of their feudal ideology, caste-like haughtiness, confidence in their own invulnerability and "God-given" right to command? Why should they think that they are above the law and immune to all criticism? What we need here is *glasnost* and democracy.

Perestroika Must not Lead to Pluralism

Extracts from a speech by V.M. Chebrikov, Chairman of the KGB, to commemorate the 110th anniversary of the birth of Felix Dzerzhinskiy, 10 September 1987 Pravda, *11 September 1987.*

. . . . The CPSU policy of accelerating socio-economic development and broadening democracy and glasnost has provoked a negative reaction from militant anti-communists. They are particularly concerned at the real prospects of a stronger Soviet state and at the growing attractiveness of the ideas of socialism as a whole. Therefore, the reactionary circles of imperialist countries are focusing their efforts on attempts to wreck or at least slow down the process of the socio-economic renewal of Soviet society.

The West has always assigned a particular role to its special services in the struggle against socialism. Their efforts are now shifting increasingly in the direction of undermining the concrete measures to restructure our economy and the system of management of the national economy. The special services are stepping up their attempts to obtain information on the Soviet Union's planned foreign policy acts, on fundamental research in the sphere of science and technology and on important national economic plans.

One of the main targets of the subversive activity of the imperialist states' special services is still our society's moral and political potential and the Soviet person's philosophy. That is only natural. After all, the implementation of the party's large-scale plans and the fulfillment of tasks in accelerating socio-economic development demand active, committed work by all the working people—that is, the kind of attitude that is only possible on the basis of profound ideological commitment. That is why the subversive centres spare no effort to carry out acts of ideological subversion, step up their attempts to discredit Marxist—Leninist theory and CPSU policy, and seek in every way to discredit the Soviet state's historical path and the practice of socialist building. To this end bourgeois ideologists are reworking their threadbare baggage, and they not infrequently draw arguments for their insinuations from the arsenal of Trotskiyism and other opportunist currents. Western reaction is now trying to use for subversive purposes the process of improving Soviet democracy which is developing consistently in the USSR.

Imperialism's special services are trying to find new loopholes through which to penetrate our society and are exerting targeted, differentiated influence on various population groups in the USSR with the aim of instilling in Soviet people a bourgeois understanding of democracy, removing the process of increasing the working people's socio-political activeness from the party's influence, splitting the monolithic unity of party and people, and installing political and ideological pluralism.

Naturally, in the Soviet Union there is not and cannot be any class base which socialism's opponents could regard as a stronghold for their subversive activity. At the same time, and this must be said frankly, we have people who hold ideas and views which are alien and even frankly hostile to socialism. Some of them embark on the path of committing anti-state and anti-social actions. Among them there are people who pursue selfish interests and hope to gain political capital through demogogic talk and by flirting with Western reactionary circles. There are also those who are prepared to enter into direct co-operation with the imperialist states' special services and betray the homeland.

The broad glasnost in publicising the topical problems of our country's development largely robs bourgeois propaganda of the opportunity to speculate with the shortcomings and unresolved issues which exist in the country. However, our opponents do not intend to renounce their favourite method speculating with the subject of human rights. In particular, in order to revive this propaganda fuss the Western subversive centres try to make more active use of the former Soviet citizens who have left for foreign parts at various times. One cannot fail to see that among this category of people there are many who, having thrown off the mask of "fighters" for human rights, have exposed themselves fully as implacable enemies of socialism and communist ideology.

As is well known, this year the Presidium of the USSR Supreme Soviet, guided by humanitarian considerations, has pardoned a group of people sentenced in the past for anti-Soviet agitation and propaganda and also for spreading knowingly false fabrications discrediting the Soviet state and social system. These people were released from continuing to serve their sentences. All of them were granted the opportunity to engage in socially useful work. How did the Western special services react to this patiently humanitarian act? They persistently incite Soviet citizens who have been released from punishment to perpetuate new illegal actions. The provocateurs' aim is clear: to inspire ostentatious anti-social acts which will require the intervention of law-enforcement organs, and then to fan yet more ballyhoo about the "human rights violations" supposedly taking place in the USSR, thus trying to cast aspersions on the democratisation process. . . .

. . . . All strata of our country's population are the targets of the imperialist special services. The Soviet creative intelligentsia is no exception. The works of writers, film-makers, artists, musicians, theatrical figures—in short, all creative workers—have a tremendous power of emotional influence on people. Realising this, our opponents are trying to push idividual representatives of the artistic intelligentsia into positions of carping, demagogy, nihilism, the blackening of certain stages of our society's historical development and the abandonment of the main purpose of socialist culture—the spiritual elevation of the working man. . . .

. . . . Clear awareness is needed that the restructuring is taking place in our state and society under the leadership of the Communist Party, within the framework of socialism and in the interests of socialism. And this revolutionary process will be reliably protected against any subversive intrigues!

"Openness" an Insult to Soviet Values?

The letter from G. N. Bochevarov and the reply by A. Bovin appeared in Izvestia, *14 March 1987.*

Esteemed editorial office!

Your 7 February 1987 issue published a dialogue between Phil Donahue and Vladimir Pozner, the leaders of the US–Soviet television link-ups, and the *Izvestia* editorial office. You reported that the editorial office had received numerous letters (V. Pozner: "tons of letters") from Soviet television viewers who had seen the latest television link-up with the participation of the Lokshin family. You declined to reply to these letters, merely saying that "it is difficult to reply to them." Why was it difficult for you to answer letters in which Soviet people expressed their anger and indignation at the dirty anti-Soviet show organised by Donahue and Pozner? But you let Pozner give his opinion of this show and these letters, having agreed in advance with what he was to tell your readers. And here is what he said:

> I was shocked inasmuch as it was the first time I had encountered veritable anti-Americanism expressed by Soviet people. I have encountered feelings directed against the US government, but I have never encountered real anti-Americanism. And now I have found it in these letters. . . . I was shocked and far from satisfied.

Esteemed editorial office, let's call a spade a spade. After all, you and Pozner are the ones who were shocked, that is, offended and distressed, by Soviet people's patriotic anti-American feelings and you are the ones who were dissatisfied with these feelings! How long have you nurtured a lingering, not even concealed, sympathy for an imperialist country enmeshed and nurtured by the power of darkness which rules it—a spirit of shameless anti-Sovietism and inhumanity, in a spirit of blind hatred for everything Russian? "Kill a Russian!"—only recently we could hear and read this during preparation for the Olympics in San Francisco [as published]. That is that country's real attitude towards us, towards Russia and no *détente*, no attempts to prove that we are not a "nation of monsters" or an "empire of evil," will ever change that attitude towards us.

Should we love America for its attitude towards us? Why should we nurture sympathy for a country which, like a latter-day troglodyte, crucified tiny, defenceless Grenada and which is cold-bloodedly trying to wear us down in Afghanistan, Poland, Angola, Mozambique, Cambodia and Vietnam?

This is not the first time you have promoted in your newspaper the idea that Phil Donahue is "a very popular commentator." In this issue (7 February 1987) also you assert that Donahue "enjoys the broadest popularity and respect." Among whom? Not among Soviet people at least. Among Soviet television viewers he has earned a reputation as a political provocateur and ideological saboteur and he attracts the burning hatred of all Soviet patriots. Just like Pozner, who acts in tandem with him but is more cautious. They have both admitted that they work together in selecting the US and Soviet audiences for television link-ups. It is thanks to their best efforts and endeavours that the Soviet audience invariably looks like a herd of wet-nosed calves beneath the attacking gang of anti-Soviet and anti-Russian "denouncers." We do not need television link-ups harmful to our country and our people.

One matter interests me and all my acquaintances who watch television: whose was the hand which made Pozner a political observer for the USSR State Committee for Television and Radio Broadcasting? Elections of leaders locally are now under way in our country and will be continued. We television viewers are also fully entitled to choose the observers and commentators who express our viewpoint.

G. N. Bochevarov, Leningrad

Bovin's Reply

Emotions, "burning hatred," predominate in G. N. Bochevarov's letter. But, in answering Bochevarov, I shall keep closer to logic, to avoid being abusive and to be considerate.

Why are Soviet–US (and indeed any other) television link-ups necessary? Obviously for Americans and Soviet people to learn more about each other, learn mutual understanding, tolerance, the ability to exchange arguments and not epithets. Every television link-up is just a small particle of, one of the elements of, our common course aimed at improving the international psychological atmosphere, and therefore the political atmosphere, and at forming public opinion favourable to the relaxation of international tension and disarmament. In building television bridges we increase the chances of mutual survival and reduce the risk of mutual death. That is the crux of the matter.

The first television link-ups between the USSR and the USA showed that Soviet people are better prepared—both intellectually and morally—for constructive dialogue than their partners. Our partners, including, incidentally, their television spokesmen, have proved far more biased and tendentious. And the letters which surprised V. Pozner by their "veritable anti-Americanism" have come flooding in as a perfectly understandable reaction to this tendentiousness on the part of some television viewers.

So what is to be done now? In Bochevarov's opinion, we must evidently re-educate the "herd of wet-nosed calves" and turn them into a "gang" of anti-American denouncers and we must cultivate anti-Americanism ("Soviet people's patriotic anti-American feelings"). I emphatically disagree with this programme.

Yes, we must know America and see clearly its plus and minus points, its weak and strong sides. And features of the American way of life like racism, militarism, lack of spirituality, the cult of violence, greed and so on and so forth can generate nothing but revulsion in any normal person.

Napalm-scorched Vietnam, crucified Grenada, money and weapons for the gangs of counter-revolutionaries. . . . Washington is tying America to the pillory of history. So what should we do—"kill an American?" No, we will not defile ourselves with such words. Nurturing hatred for the Americans means putting ourselves on a par with the most double-dyed chauvinism, with those whose "patriotism" and love for their own are unfailingly linked with hatred for "the other"—for the American, Chinese or German, it is of no importance.

I think Bochevarov is not alone. There are probably people who share his position. And this is further proof of how vitally necessary are restructuring, the struggle against stagnation and narrow views and people's education in a spirit of genuine internationalism.

Chernobyl: "One of the Best Accidents"

Excerpt from a phone-in conference of the readers of Druzhba Narodov *magazine, Soviet Television, 31 May 1987.*

Vladimir Yavorivskii is a Ukrainian poet and writer.

Yavorivskii: . . . I would say that it is a sad and perhaps dramatic paradox—I trust you will understand me correctly—that what happened at Chernobyl did not happen, say, five or six years ago. If it had, we would almost certainly have heard about the Chernobyl tragedy, but at that stage of our national openness we would probably only have heard that it was one of the best accidents in the world and on our planet [laughter]. It is a bad thing that this happened right at the start of the restructuring. Unfortunately, we lost a very great deal through this . . . I am asked: what is the situation now in Chernobyl? There is a dead slice of land in the centre of Europe, a dead slice of Ukrainian and Belorussian land, which the people have left. The most alarming thing—on which I should like to dwell for a moment or so—is the affected cheerfulness with regard to Chernobyl. These mistakes were committed by our press in the first articles, but the saddest thing is that this is also happening now. Take the Ukrainian Health Minister—a very respected person who incidentally, spoke only on the ninth day after the accident—informing us of the need to wash our hands and feet well with soap. That was the first information given, when people were waiting to know what to do after finding themselves in this situation for the first time. The minister has again been appearing on television and has, so to speak, been calming us cheerfully. He brought along a diagram—you will not believe this—from which it emerges that before Chernobyl things were worse than they are now. The thought simply struck me that perhaps another reactor needs to blow up for everything to be absolutely fine in this situation [laughter]. Chernobyl means pain and Chernobyl will not recede into the past.

A Case of Free Elections

Extract from a speech given by Viktor Mironenko, First Secretary of the Komsomol Central Committee, at the 20th Congress of the All-Union Leninist Communist Youth League, 15 April 1987.

Comrade delegates: 4,833 delegates have been elected to the 20th Congress of the All-Union Leninist Communist Youth League; 21 delegates are absent for valid reasons. On behalf of the Komsomol Central Committee, I declare the 20th Congress of the All-Union Leninist Communist Youth League open [applause].

Comrades, taking part in the work of our congress are leaders of the CPSU and the Soviet government who have unanimously been elected delegates to the 20th Komsomol Congress [applause]. We cordially greet Mikhail Sergeyevich Gorbachov, General Secretary of the CPSU Central Committee . . . [applause] . . . members of the Politburo and Secretaries of the Central Committee of the CPSU [applause]. . . .

Permit me, comrades, on your behalf and on behalf of all the young people of our country, sincerely and cordially to greet the representatives of the young generation of our planet who favour peace, democracy and social progress. I wish you successes and happiness [applause].

Comrade delegates, permit me to move on to forming the executive bodies for the 20th Komsomol Congress. We are to elect a presidium, a secretariat, a drafting commission and a credentials commission for the congress. At a conference of representatives of delegations of Komsomol organizations from republics, krais and oblasts, proposals were formulated for the composition of the executive bodies of the congress. You have these proposals there with you. Is there any need to read them out? [Mumbling from auditorium.] There is no need.

Let us first of all examine the matter of the presidium of the congress. It is proposed that it should be elected with a membership of 153 people. Do the delegates have other proposals on the numerical and personal composition of the presidium? No. How shall we vote—individually or collectively? Collectively. All those in favour of electing the presidium of the congress with the proposed composition please raise your provisional credentials. Please drop them. Who is against the motion? Any abstentions?

The Presidium of the 20th Komsomol Congress is elected. Let me ask those comrades who have been elected to take their places in the presidium [applause].

Comrades, we are proceeding now to electing the secretariat of the congress. A proposal is being put forward to elect 37 people to the secretariat of the

Freedom Indispensable

Fedor Burlatskii in a human rights' discussion, Moscow Radio, 6 June 1987.

"Information is democracy and liberty. Absence of information, or limitation of information, is limitation of democracy and limitation of liberty . . . . Legal and institutional guarantees are needed in addition to the ones which already exist."

Critical Letter-Writers Summonsed

From Rostislav Andreyev's interview with O. V. Soroka, USSR Deputy Procurator General, Soviet Television, 14 May 1987.

Andreyev: *Oleg Vasilyevich, we have recently heard of some examples of the activities of procuracy officials which surprised us, to say the least. In Krasnoyarsk kray, the kray procuracy started summonsing citizens who had sent complaints to the central press. They started calling them in to explain the circumstances of their complaint, and so on. In our opinion this is not in accord with the spirit of restructuring or of reinforcement of citizens' rights because, as you know, no summons to the procuracy is a source of great pleasure, nor is it a very pleasant invitation. We asked our correspondent [Yurii Sosnoy] to investigate and to interview the Krasnoyarsk kray procuracy officials. He has sent us his interview. Let us have a look at it and then you can give us your opinion.*

A. N. Trifokov, First Deputy Procurator of Krasnoyarsk kray: *The procuracy officials here did not show any lack of tact or any rudeness.*

Sosnoy: *Did you issue a summons for people to come forward?*

Trifokov: *Not at all. The procuracy officials invited, for example, the Krasnoyarsk inhabitants [Sashko, Udelin and Yefimova] by telephone. It was explained to them over the telephone why they were being invited, and what explanations were required of them; it was also explained to them that if they were unwilling or unable to come in person to the procuracy, then we would not insist that they should. These people came voluntarily. They also gave their explanations voluntarily.*

Soroka: *I think it is totally impermissible to summons the authors of critical letters and statements to the press. In this case, judging from what we have seen, the rayon procurator and the officials of the kray procuracy should have carried out a careful investigation of all the violations of legality pointed out by the authors in their letters to the press. Then the necessary measures should have been taken, and the authors informed of them.*

congress. Are there any remarks concerning the numerical and qualitative composition of the secretariat? None. Those in favour of electing the secretariat of the congress composed as proposed, please raise your provisional credentials. Please lower them again. Against? Abstained? None. The secretariat of the congress has been elected.

We have to elect the drafting commission of the congress. A proposal is being put forward to elect 39 people to it. Are there any remarks concerning the numerical and personal composition of the drafting commission? None. Those in favour of electing the drafting commission of the congress composed as proposed, please raise your provisional credentials. Please lower them again. Who is against? Abstained? None. The drafting commission of the congress has been elected.

We are proceeding to elect the credentials commission. A proposal is being put forward to elect 69 people to the credentials commission. Are there any remarks, comrades, concerning the numerical and personal composition of the credentials commission? None. Those in favour of electing the credentials commission of the congress composed as proposed, please raise your provisional credentials. Please lower them. Who is against? Abstained? The credentials commission of the congress has been elected. Delegates elected to the secretariat and the drafting and credentials commissions of the congress, please assume your duties.

Comrade delegates, we have to pass the agenda and procedures of the 20th Komsomol Congress. You have the proposals on the agenda and procedures of the congress. Shall I read them? No. A proposal is being made to allot two hours 45 minutes from the report-back of the Komsomol Central Committee. For the report-back of the central auditing commission—20 minutes. Whoever is in favour of adopting the proposed agenda and procedures of the 20th Komsomol Congress, please raise your provisional credentials. Please lower them. Who is against? Abstained? The agenda and the order of work of the congress have been adopted.

Comrades, we have thus completed forming the leading bodies of the 20th Komsomol Congress and have adopted the agenda and the procedures.

Glasnost and the KGB

From an interview with General Genii Ageyev, a Deputy Chairman of the KGB, Trud, *19 April 1987.*

Reporter: What are the traditions and principles of the work of state security under present-day conditions?

Ageyev: . . . These days the Chekists share the same thoughts, deeds, and concerns as all Soviet people. They fervently approve of the revolutionary resolutions of the Party on the acceleration of socio-economic development, and on the restructuring and renovation of all spheres of Soviet society. At the CPSU Central Committee plenum, a fundamental directive was given to the state security organs: detect promptly, and decisively nip in the bud hostile intrigues directed against our country. Following from this very important Party demand are our more specific tasks—in accordance with all the distinctive features of the present situation, where the chief danger threatening our state comes from outside, we must improve the professional standard of the KGB organs' and forces' activity, and aim for the unswerving perfection of forms and methods of combating the adversary's subversive intrigues . . .

Reporter: What role is played in the activity of state security organs by educational, preventive work aimed at keeping people from dangerous, illegal misdemeanours? What is the role of labour collectives in this sphere? How do Chekists co-operate with the public?

Ageyev: . . . Multi-faceted work to inculcate political vigilance is carried out in collectives under the leadership of party organizations; measures are taken to protect state and military secrets; and the constitutional duty of each person to strengthen the country's security is implemented in practice. Chekists are active participants in this work. Conversations, lectures, and reports, photographic exhibitions about the subversive activities of enemy secret services, patronage links with enterprises, institutions, and educational establishments, and other forms of work all serve the common cause. There is also the practical implementation of the Leninist principle of links with the masses and reliance on the masses of the working people. In the spirit of the glorious Chekist traditions, we maintain our consideration for children raised in children's homes. For instance, in 1968 a complex of new buildings at the Molodaya Gvardiya children's home outside Moscow was constructed on the initiative, and with the most active participation, of sub-divisions of the KGB central apparatus.

In turn, Soviet people help Chekist organs to reveal cunning ruses of espionage, sabotage, smuggling, anti-Soviet actions, and so forth.

The People Approve

The following exchange during Gorbachov's walk-about in Khabarovsk was reported in *Pravda*, 30 July 1986 and *Izvestia*, 31 July 1986.

Gorbachov: *I'm sure you heard me yesterday asking the same question everywhere: "Are our plans clear to you all?"*
Voices: *They're clear to us all!*
Gorbachov: *Are you in the mood for work?*
Voices: *Yes, we are! We're in the mood for even better work!*
Gorbachov: *What else do you want?*
Voices: *Peace! Peace!*
Gorbachov: *Did you notice that yesterday in Vladivostok I devoted half my speech to peace? . . . Did you listen to my speech in Vladivostok yesterday?*
Voices: *We listened to you! We saw you! We read your words!*
Gorbachov: *And that's how we're going to act! And over there they can take that into account in their policies. No one is going to force us to our knees!*
Voices: *We'll never allow it!*
Gorbachov: *Never! Not this nation. Sabre rattling is not our policy. But we are going to strengthen our defences, and the main thing is that we'll improve our economy, so that our people will feel good and secure.*

As you know, all sorts of radio stations—and they are not the only ones—are now trying to malign our plans and policies, hoping that they can create a confrontation between the people and the leadership. They want to destabilize our country. . . . The main obstacle to imperialism is the Soviet Union, our strength, and our organized, strong-willed people!
Voices: *We're not going to let ourselves be insulted!*
Gorbachov: *No, we're not. I agree. If we can preserve this mutual understanding . . . the understanding between the working class and the leadership of our country, the understanding within each collective, between the leaders and the working people, we can have everything, Comrades. You must feel that you are in charge of this country. Hold your heads up high!*
Voices: *We have been holding them high ever since the Party Congress!*
Gorbachov: *And don't let them drop again! . . . You must hold your heads high and bow to no one, especially not to boors and louts, no matter what their official position may be.*
A Voice: *Right, that's the most important thing.*

2. Rights—Views from the West

Some Western Accounts of the State of Social and Economic Rights in the Soviet Union and Eastern Europe

The Critical Condition of Soviet Health Care

Kenneth M. Prager in the Wall Street Journal, *29 January 1987. Prager is a specialist in pulmonary medicine at Columbia College of Physicians and Surgeons, New York.*

As a physician on a private visit to Moscow and Leningrad last spring, I had a unique opportunity to learn about the current state of Soviet medical care. As soon as my Soviet acquaintances learned that I was an American doctor, they organized makeshift clinics in various blocks of flats so that I could examine patients and dispense medical advice. Even though I expected Soviet medicine to be below American standards, I was appalled by what I saw.

The Soviet medical-care system is decades behind the West in technology, and stresses little more than keeping the mass of Soviet workers happy and on the job. It is a system that can adequately care for simple and self-limited health problems of its ordinary citizens, and it offers the privileged among them such amenities as resort-like sanitoriums where they can bathe in mineral waters, and rest. But the level of sophistication necessary to attend properly to such chronic and complex ailments of modern society as cancer and cardiovascular disease is what one would expect of a developing nation, and not one of the world's great powers.

My impressions of Soviet medicine were reinforced by my care of *refusenik* David Goldfarb, who arrived in the US aboard Armand Hammer's jet last October. After languishing for four months in several Soviet hospitals, Professor Goldfarb finally received definitive treatment for his multiple medical and surgical problems in New York. He is currently learning to walk on a modern prosthesis. The fact that he did not use his heavy and crudely made Soviet prosthesis since losing his leg at Stalingrad in 1942 speaks volumes about Soviet care for the disabled. Long waiting lists for wheelchairs further testify to Soviet disregard for the needs of the handicapped.

One of my first patients on my visit was an 80-year-old man in severe pain because he was unable to urinate. His bladder was markedly distended and he obviously needed to be catheterized immediately. The urologist who had been summoned to his home complied with my request for a rubber glove to examine the patient's prostate gland. After examining him, I was startled when the physician requested that I wash the glove so that it could be reused. She then relieved the patient of his distress by passing her only, reusable catheter into his bladder after lubricating it with butter. She had sterilized the catheter by boiling it in a pot of water in the patient's kitchen.

There is a virtual absence of such disposable items as syringes, needles, catheters, and intravenous tubing in hospitals and clinics. Patients pay a considerable price: reused items increase rates of infection, while intravenous needles, and scalpels that have become dull as a result of wear and tear increase pain and discomfort.

That this elderly man adamantly refused hospitalization pointed to another feature of Soviet medicine: the aged are afraid of being hospitalized. In a medical system that is chronically short of the most basic supplies, the elderly are considered expendable and will be the first to feel the brunt of such shortages.

Another patient I met was a 28-year-old man with a well documented heart attack two years earlier who was still experiencing chest pain when he exerted himself. His entire evaluation by Soviet physicians consisted of an ECG stress test, and his only medication was nitroglycerin to be taken as needed for chest pain. A coronary angiogram, which might have disclosed a surgically correctable reason for his premature heart attack and persisting angina, was never suggested and he was not treated with any of the potent cardiac medications that might lessen his pain, and possibly increase his longevity.

The case of this unfortunate young man discloses the unavailability of coronary angiography and surgery to all but a select few in the USSR. On a much more fundamental level, however, it reveals how few modern medicines are available to patients with serious problems. The tremendous strides made in the past two decades in development of potent and effective medicines in all areas of internal medicine seem to have made little impact in the USSR. New medicines are either totally unavailable from pharmacies or are in such short supply as to make them ineffective in treating chronic illness.

Such staples of modern medical treatment as Tagamet for ulcer disease, Sinemet for Parkinsonism, Beta Blockers and Calcium Channel Blockers for angina and hypertension, and anti-histamine-decongestant preparations for the relief of common cold symptoms are extremely hard to come by. Other useful medicines, such as anti-asthma drugs and multi-vitamins, are of such poor quality as to discourage their use. Liquid anti-acids are completely unpalatable. While I was in Moscow, I was told that a drug such as Tagamet could sell for a small fortune on the black market.

A major health problem facing Soviet women is the absence of reliable measures for birth control. Birth-control pills are impure and produce intolerable side effects, and diaphragms are poorly fitting and of low quality; condoms are crudely made. The result is that abortion is the major method of birth control used by non-Moslem Soviet women. A conservative estimate based on Soviet statistics is that the average Soviet woman undergoes six abortions in her lifetime. It is not uncommon to meet women who have had 10 or even 15 abortions.

And this primitive health system is far from free. Hospitalized Soviet patients frequently bring a roll of rubles with them if they want to make sure that they obtain such basic nursing care as linen changes and reliable delivery of medicines. Their families must bring them means from home. Payments to physicians in the form of cash, goods or services are often necessary to ensure proper treatment or a skilled surgeon. Even more money is needed to obtain scarce medicines.

Faced with a medical system that is too often ineffective in treating disease, Soviet citizens turn with desperation to a variety of quack medical practitioners. Starvation diets are commonly resorted to in treating chronic illness, with the unintended result of weakening an already debilitated patient. Psychic healers with a variety of potions abound, and amulets and other magical devices are frequently used.

Not everyone in the USSR must put up with these gross deficiencies of the medical system. The "classless" Communist utopia has a very rigid hierarchy of medical care facilities. The fourth department of the Ministry of Health consists of hospitals, sanitoriums and clinics that are available only to the Communist Party elite and other notables. These hospitals are stocked with the most advanced medical technology—all of it made abroad. It is to these flagships of the

Soviet hospital fleet that groups of visiting foreign physicians are taken when the occasion arises. The unsuspecting doctors leave the country with a totally distorted impression of the true state of Soviet medicine.

Why does one of the world's two great superpowers tolerate such primitive conditions in so much of its health-care sector? The answer is that modern medicine is very expensive. The Soviets have chosen to spend their limited resources on missiles, heavy industry, and space technology rather than on disposable medical equipment, modern drugs, and costly life-saving devices. Excellence in medical care is simply not a high priority in the Soviet system. The best estimates available indicate that the Soviet Union allocated 9·8 per cent of the gross national product to medical care in 1955, but only 7·5 per cent in 1977. The trend is clear.

Whether Mikhail Gorbachov's attempts to modernize Soviet society will include an overhaul of the medical-care system remains to be seen. Unremitting Western publicity about human rights' abuses in the USSR has sensitized the Soviets to this issue, and there seems to be some movement on Mr Gorbachov's part to try to mollify his Western detractors with conciliatory moves, however few. If the sorry state of Soviet medicine becomes a focus of concern in the West, perhaps the Soviets will be similarly instigated into carrying out some badly needed reforms to bring their medical system into the second half of the 20th century.

Illness and Mortality

Christopher Davis in the Wall Street Journal *31 October 1986.*

INFANT mortality in the Soviet Union rose during the 1970s and again in the 1980s, according to recently published Soviet statistics. Furthermore, both the number of babies dying per year and the mortality rate for the whole population were about one-third higher in 1985 than in 1970. This new information evidently is a byproduct of Mikhail Gorbachov's policy of *glasnost*, or openness. The data are the first provided by the Soviet authorities on infant mortality since age-specific death rate statistics stopped appearing in the mid-1970s. Although the Soviets still have not provided infant mortality data for the late 1970s, we now have statistics for the 1980s to supplement an official series, which provides information up to 1974. The emerging picture shows the existence of major health problems in the Soviet Union.

The new data show the infant mortality rate rising to 27·3 deaths per 1,000 live births in 1980 from 24·7 deaths in 1970. The pattern for the 1970s appears to be one of infant mortality dropping to a historic low of 22·9 deaths per 1,000 births in 1971 before climbing to 27·9 in 1974. Demographer Murray Feshbach and I have estimated that there was a further increase to 31 in 1976. The rate evidently then fell from that, or a later peak, to 25·3 in 1983. It rose again to 26 by 1985. The newly published 1985 figure is lower than some Western analysts had predicted, but it sill is higher than that of 1970. The larger point remains: Soviet infant mortality has been going up, a trend that stands in striking contrast with the experience of most industrialized countries. In the case of the US, infant mortality decreased uninterruptedly to 10·6 in 1984 from 20 in 1970.

The Soviets also have revealed that the total number of infant deaths per year climbed to 140,000 in 1985, from 103,000 in 1970. One arithmetical explanation for this is that the birth rate rose as well, to a peak of 19·8 births per 1,000 in population in 1983 from 17·4 births per 1,000 in 1970. This, of course, means that there were more babies at risk. However, rising birth numbers are no excuse for increased deaths, since modern medicine can cope with challenges of this sort. In the United States, for instance, the birth rate rose to 15·9 in 1982 from 14·6 in 1975. Yet the number of infant deaths fell to 42,000 from 51,000. Over the 1970–84 period the US reduced infant deaths to 39,000 from 75,000.

Rising Mortality

The crude mortality rate of the Soviet Union has risen by a massive 32 per cent. This measure of the total number of deaths per 1,000 people went up to a peak of 10·8 in 1984 from 8·2 deaths per 1,000 population in 1970. The new Soviet report—it appeared in an October issue of the authoritative economic newspaper, *Ekonomicheskaya Gazeta*—suggests that this is an inexorable consequence of the aging of the population. US experience indicates that such is not the case. The United States has a more elderly population than the Soviet Union, but has managed to reduce its crude death rate to 8·7 in 1984 from 9·5 in 1970.

The primary significance of the newly released statistics is that they call attention to the continuing health problems the Soviet Union is facing. Of secondary importance is the fact that they help to resolve a heated debate among American analysts of Soviet affairs about the health situation in the Soviet Union.

In 1978, the *Wall Street Journal* published an article co-authored by me and demographer Murray Feshbach that estimated Soviet infant mortality had risen to an estimated 31·1 in 1976 from a low of 22·9 deaths per 1,000 live births in 1971. Virtually all adult age-specific death rates had gone up substantially from the mid-1960s and life expectancy had fallen.

In 1980, the US Bureau of the Census published a report, again co-authored by me and Mr Feshbach, on rising infant mortality in the Soviet Union during the 1970s. It attracted considerable attention due to the unusual upward nature of the Soviet mortality trends, the international importance of the infant mortality indicator, and the related evidence of significant deficiencies in the Soviet system of socialized medicine. A number of analysts subsequently amplified our knowledge of health problems in the Soviet Union.

Some of our colleagues, however, disagreed with our conclusion and presentation. They responded with a series of articles with titles such as "Infant Mortality in the Soviet Union: Anti-Sovietism in the United States" and "On the Uses of Disinformation to Legitimize the Revival of the Cold War: Health in the USSR". These charges of "anti-Sovietism" have continued to the present day. For example, in a recent newspaper article a political scientist listed US press reports of infant mortality increases in the Soviet Union as an example of inaccurate and biased coverage.

The Davis-Feshbach report also has been subjected to criticism by various health and demographic analysts. This is an expected part of the research process. Some critics, however, have made exaggerated claims that the increase in Soviet infant mortality in the 1970s was primarily due to improved statistical reporting as the result of better registration procedures.

The recently published official statistics undermine the "improved statistical reporting" interpretation. First, they indicate that a substantial infant mortality rise occurred between 1970 and 1980 (with an implied peak in the late 1970s). Second, the Soviets make no claim that this growth was merely a statistical phenomenon. In fact, the possibility should be considered that the new figures incorporate a redefinition of the pre-1974 infant mortality measure and that both the level and trend are now biased downward.

Third, there were increases in both infant deaths and the mortality rate in the 1980s. It would not be credible to argue that procedural changes fully explained not only the rises in 1972–76 but also in 1984–85. Furthermore, the recent rise is consistent with figures presented in an April speech by Moscow party leader Boris Yeltsin, which showed life expectancy in the capital falling to 68 in 1985 from 70 in 1983. Mr Yeltsin gave this information to party workers as an example of how conditions had deteriorated under the previous administration, not as a prelude to awarding an efficiency medal to city statisticians.

In order to reduce mortality rates the Gorbachov regime must confront a complex array of problems related to health conditions, the illness pattern and medical system performance. With respect to health conditions the challenges are to correct deficiencies in consumption and the environment. In the consumption area these include the rising dietary cholesterol intake, inadequacies in the total quantity and nutritional composition of baby foods, insufficient supply of vitamins, and until recently, increasing *per capita* consumption of alcohol and tobacco.

Among the environmental factors that undermine health are inadequate housing and poor public sanitation. Others are rapid mechanization of industry and growth in road traffic without adequate safety programmes and rising air and water pollution.

The Soviet Union has an unusual illness pattern that reflects these health conditions and contains high rates of both infectious and degenerative diseases. Mr Feshbach has shown that infectious illnesses are still widespread in the Soviet Union and the incidence of many has risen in recent years. For example, the number of cases of typhoid and paratyphoid rose to 18,900 in 1984 from 16,900 in 1980. In contrast, the US had 300 cases in 1984. Vitamin deficiencies and inadequate nutrition adversely affect breast-feeding mothers, infants and other vulnerable groups. The Soviet Union also suffers from many alcohol-related accidents and poisonings. In the degenerative disease category the incidence of both cardiovascular illness and cancer has risen rapidly.

The growing complexity of the disease pattern has posed challenges for the Soviet medical system. In response, the system has increased the output of most services on the basis of the traditional extensive growth strategy of expanding the quantities of personnel, hospital beds and outpatients clinics. But the medical system has been unable to make the required transition to intensive development which involves raising the quality of its output. As a result it has been relatively ineffective in preventing the growth in illness or in curing cases presented. These failures have allowed mortality rates to rise.

One reason for these performance problems is that the medical system has been operating subject to tight resource constraints. Although total health spending in the Soviet Union has risen since 1970 its share of the state budget has fallen to 4·6 per cent from 6 per cent. Its share of national income—the Soviet measure of aggregate economic output—fell to 3·9 per cent from 4·1 per cent. In contrast, the US health share of gross national product rose to 10·8 per cent in 1983 from 7·6 per cent in 1970. This generated a 1983 *per capita* US expenditure on health of $1,459. In that year the Soviets spent 77 rubles per citizen on health, or about $93 at the official exchange rate. Although pricing and exchange rate differences make a direct comparison of these figures inappropriate, the magnitude of the disparity gives some sense of relative resource commitments.

Financial stringencies also have had adverse effects on the institutions which support the medical system and supply it with crucial inputs such as medicine. Pharmacies, pharmaceutical factories, and biomedical research institutes all have been performing in a substandard manner. Furthermore, insufficient amounts of medicines are imported, so widespread shortages are not eliminated.

Gorbachov's Efforts

The Soviet government under Mr Gorbachov is taking some steps to correct these problems. It is trying to develop more effective preventive medical programs and wants to reduce alcohol and tobacco consumption, improve sanitation, reduce pollution, and encourage its citizens to look after their own health. Unfortunately, it is difficult to have a health-maximizing yuppie life style in a shortage economy.

The regime is making an effort to improve curative medicine as well, but there is not yet evidence that substantial additional resources are being allocated to help. The 1986 planned state budget expenditures on the medical system are slightly higher than 1985s, but their share of total budget spending is down.

It is difficult to anticipate substantial progress in the health field until the Gorbachov regime takes decisive action to improve the health conditions of the population and significantly raises the amount of resources allocated to the medical system and supporting institutions. As in other areas of life, it is deeds, not words, that will have the greatest effects.

Soviet Faith Healer

Edmund Stevens in The Sunday Times, *29 August 1982.*

Grateful patients call her a miracle-worker—even those atheists in the Soviet Communist Party hierarchy who profess disbelief in miracles. Djuna Davitashvili is a Christian "extra-sensory healer" whose Moscow clinic today presents one of the most extraordinary examples of private enterprise operating successfully alongside strictly state-controlled medicine.

Miss Davitashvili, a 40-year-old brunette, was widely credited with causing the remarkable rejuvenation of an ailing President Brezhnev last year, and although this was officially discounted, it remains a fact that she has treated senior establishment figures, as well as humbler folk, for a variety of problems and has been applauded by the Soviet Academy of Science.

She has even treated Western journalists like myself (bad back, swollen legs: relieved but not cured) and the British photographer, Tom Blau: "Vastly improved and, I think, cured my vascular complaints. My feet, which used to be so swollen that I had to wear woollen bed socks, are no longer swollen."

Miss Davitashvili says she first became aware of her gift when as a young girl she worked as a waitress in a restaurant in the Georgian capital, Tbilisi. Customers spoke of feeling her extra-sensory influence. It was much later when she discovered its curative properties and only quite recently has she acquired a national reputation.

In reception hours, her second-floor flat is clogged with humanity of all ages and nationalities. There is standing room only in the hallway leading to a spacious hexagonal living room overlooking Leningrad Prospect. Paintings and photographs which highlight her piercing, hypnotic eyes are displayed throughout the flat.

From the waiting patients, Miss Davitashvili selects a six-year-old whimpering girl and coaxes her into the middle of the living room. The child gradually relaxes and becomes quiet as the healer makes several passes with her hand near the patient's head. This goes on for 10 minutes before the child, bright and apparently cured, leaves. Her ailment is diagnosed as acute cholic.

My turn comes and I am ordered to remove my shoes and lie on my stomach. One of Miss Davitashvili's understudys, a young Assyrian girl, goes through the motions above my afflicted back and legs. I seem to feel a faint tingling. After 15 minutes, Miss Davitashvili takes over and the tingling feels much stronger, almost like a mild electric shock. I then turn over on to my back and the treatment goes on for another 10 minutes. When I leave, there is much improvement though not yet a complete cure.

The healer's credentials include testimonials from high Soviet officials, stage and literary celebrities and numerous distinguished foreigners who have written thanking her for curing stomach ulcers, hernias, double pneumonia, kidney ailments and malignancies.

Her popularity is attributable not only to such written testimonials but to the widespread disenchantment with official medical facilities.

But some private healers who have tried to cash in on Miss Davitashvili's success have run into trouble. One pretender in the city of Voronezh, with a university degree in "radio-physics," added voltage to his own bio-magnetic field with an electrical contrivance of his own design. He prospered until several of his patients died.

Brains for Dollars

Roger Boyes in The Times, *10 October 1986.*

Thousands of human brains have been smuggled out of Hungary for use by Western pharmaceutical companies in a macabre East–West corruption scandal, according to an investigation by the Hungarian authorities.

The big fraud, a bizarre variant of the brain drain, has come to light in the trial this week of the deputy head of Szeged Medical Academy, Professor Ferenc Laszlo.

In many Western Countries the approval of relatives is needed before organs are removed from corpses, but in Hungary doctors can take what they need for diagnostic or scientific purposes. That was the basis of the brains-for-dollars business transacted between Professor Laszlo and an Italian company, Serono, according to the Hungarian state prosecutor.

It started 10 years ago. Professor Laszlo, head of the endocrinology department, allegedly dropped in on the dissection room of his academy—one of the best in Eastern Europe—and suggested that the workers deliver about four extra brains a week to his laboratory. For every pituitary gland (hypophysis)—the part of the brain that produces the growth hormone—he would tip them three forints (now about five British pence).

The pay-off eventually rose to about 40 forints a brain when the assistants in the dissection room realized that Professor Laszlo was making many thousands of pounds from the Italians. Until his recent arrest the Professor had allegedly disposed of almost 5,000 brains.

Altogether, according to the prosecutor, Professor Laszlo made about four million forints (£60,000).

The investigators seem to have suspected him when he asked the Italian company to cover the cost of his participation in a scientific congress in Utrecht in the Netherlands. US$1,000 (£700) was paid into an account—illegal under

Hungarian law—administered by a Hungarian who emigrated to the Netherlands after the 1956 uprising.

The pituitary gland is a valuable part of the body for Western researchers and companies experimenting with growth hormones.

The trial continues. It is sparsely reported in Hungary, but the fragments leaking from the courtroom have shocked the country, where the highest ambition of many mothers is that their son becomes a doctor or dentist.

Balkan Socialism

Extracts from "Birth and Death in Romania," New York Review of Books, *23 October 1986. The writer remained anonymous.**

It was May in Transylvania. The days had been mild, the evenings cold, and the Romanian people, as much obsessed with their situation as anxious to forget it, were watching for Halley's Comet with childlike anticipation. Their gaze was suddenly, brutally brought back to earth by the events in Chernobyl (a name somewhat avoided by the local press). Faced as they were with a danger unknown, inexorable, and impossible to defend against, the special quality of imagination that seems endemic to the Romanian people was less an asset than a liability. Stores of tinned goods that had lain about unsold for years disappeared overnight and when the crop of spring vegetables that had been dreamed of through a worse than austere winter was finally harvested, few were willing to eat it. Everyone had his own theory about the effects of radiation, a subject on which official discretion served only to make the panic more acute. Then the public mood shifted. Late into the night everyone stayed up, neighbours from time to time relaying this or that impression from one window to the next, until finally an excited group of people converged in Bucharest, shouting at the top of their lungs. Fallout was forgotten (at least for a night), and there was a positively Mediterranean sense of joy: for the first time a Romanian soccer team had won a game in a competition for the European cup!

Two old friends of mine stayed on the sidelines. After three years I had found them visibly changed, each in his own way. The more unbending of the two was becoming more rigid in his views, the more flexible seemed at times incoherent. Romania itself had changed considerably, it too in its own way: the three years seemed to have been the culmination of a much longer social ordeal that had left its mark on the country. One of my friends said that to understand the recent developments I must first consult a decree by the Council of State of the Romanian Socialist Republic issued on 10 October 1981. The exact text ran as follows:

> It shall constitute illegal trading activities and, in accordance with the terms set down in the Penal Code, shall be punishable by six months to five years in prison, to purchase from any state commercial centre or cooperative store, either with a view to hoarding or in any quantity that exceeds the requirements of a family for a period of a month, oil, sugar, wheat corn flour, rice, coffee and all other foodstuffs the hoarding of which might affect the interests of other consumers and proper provisioning of the population.

Since then, he said, the situation has changed drastically. Coffee can no longer be

* Reprinted with permission from the *New York Review of Books*. Copyright © 1986 Nyrev, Inc.

bought by private citizens and has been replaced by an *ersatz* substance disapproved of by physicians, which the public, guessing at the ingredients, has nicknamed "henna." Meat, buttermilk, and bread are rationed in most districts, sugar and cooking oil throughout the country—and the ration is much more generous than the shops charged with distributing them can supply.

Since 1968, it should be explained, Romania has been divided into more than 40 districts, each with a Party secretary, who is its supreme head. He is responsible for delivering a quota of food from his district to the central government—a task that must give him bad dreams. For it poses an insoluble problem: if he distributes locally less food than is called for by the plan—as he is virtually obliged to do—he will be popular with the authorities but held in contempt by the people of the district; and if he tries to help the population get more food, he will be unpopular with the authorities. Everyone has a different approach to the same dilemma—for even in the CP no district secretary is quite like another—and this psychological diversity makes for diversity in the distribution of food shortages throughout the country. In Cluj or Pitesti the situation, I was told, is frankly horrible; in Sibiu or Vilcea it is merely wretched. Thousands go from district to district on shopping excursions from which they often return empty-handed.

Romania seems unique in many ways. It is the only European country in which one can be sentenced to five years in prison for buying excessive quantities of food that is generally unavailable to the public. It is also, in my experience, the only such country in which the legal work week is 46 hours and the urban population often spends three to four hours a day shopping for groceries. In Romania President Ceausescu takes it upon himself to compose lyrics for a new national anthem, rather than entrusting the task to a poet. And in spite of a republican form of government of which he is the constitutional head, the president carries a sceptre and is grooming his son as his successor.

Workers often spend entire days waiting for raw materials that their factory cannot obtain. If they leave the premises without permission or bring alcoholic beverages, or cigarettes, or lighters, or matches onto the shop floor, they are regarded as having broken the law and can receive prison sentences from three months up to two years (Decree 400 of 29 December 1981, Article 18.)

The average wage, according to experts I talked to, is less than one fifth of the average Common Market wage, while the minimum wage is ignored. The state each month withholds a percentage of wages that can be returned at the end of the year only if the government's economic goals have been met—something that rarely happens.

Virtually every business establishment has (in addition to spies) a member of the Secret Police with a permanent desk, who reports to his superiors on the proper running of the business. All typewriters must be registered and presented for inspection at the police station every year to show that the keys have not been tampered with.

Perhaps this list is enough to suggest that the special quality of daily life in Romania bears little resemblance to Western perceptions of it. When Americans think of Romania they think of the 1984 Summer Olympics and the gymnastics team—even the US Secretary of State on the occasion of his visit this spring mentioned this; about less heroic activities he said nothing. . . .

* * *

Today, young people are no longer being allowed to leave their villages—following historic practice—and the adults transplanted to urban areas are being urged to return to the villages from which they were in many cases forcibly evicted. But the new measures being taken seem aimed not at alleviating but at worsening the situation of the rural population. The decree of 24 January 1982, which contains 89 articles and which is purported to represent "a new agricultural revolution," provided *inter alia* for the compulsory participation of the entire rural population, independent of profession, in agricultural labour, special mention being made of old people, invalids, and children from the age of 10 (Articles 10 and 11), and there are penal and economic sanctions—including the confiscation of individual land allotments—against those who do not put in the minimum number of work days, etc.

To supplement their meagre rations, farmers have turned *en masse* to stealing corn, wheat and potatoes out of the fields. A number have been tried and found guilty. I heard of a female farmer in the Prahova district who was caught carrying a sack of stolen corn by the rural militia. At her trial her lawyer read out the statement issued by the district Party committee announcing the end of the harvest. Since the offence had been committed a week after the date on which the statement was issued, it was obvious that the woman could not have been stealing corn; officially there was no longer any corn left in the fields to be stolen. She was acquitted.

Others were not so lucky—which has led the farmers to change their tactics: now they send their children to steal for them, since it is much more difficult for the authorities to take legal action against them. Teaching children to steal in order to obtain food is an act of desperation on the part of a farmer class that has traditionally adored children and prided itself on an exalted sense of personal honour. This entire battle over food can only serve to stabilize the weird state of affairs in which responsibility for agricultural production, now removed from the farmer class, has become the burdensome monopoly of those in power. . . .

* * *

When it comes to political independence, the Romanians find out about it through rumours. They can judge the country's energy independence from what they see. When darkness falls, the cities are plunged into shadows—paradise for burglars—and in the daytime, in some cities, buses run only between six and eight a.m. and three p.m. Electric energy and water services are interrupted daily, at irregular intervals and for periods that can exceed four hours. As a result, refrigerators defrost in the summer and in every season residents of Bucharest avoid using elevators so they won't be caught between floors: elderly people laden with packages and grandmothers carrying babies prepare for the return to their homes on the tenth or eleventh floors as though for a mountain climb. The strongest light bulb sold is 40 watts, and it is illegal to use more than one lamp per room; television programming has been cut back to two hours during the working day; each official organization is allowed to use only a limited number of the cars assigned to it (of course, there are exceptions, but not in favour of emergency hospital ambulances).

The private use of cars is now banned for the winter months and during the remaining nine months the lines to buy limited amounts of gasoline can last from 24 to 48 hours. The procession that crosses the city four times a day as the president moves between the residential palace and the one in which he works is made up of nine cars, not to mention the unknown number of automobiles not officially part of the retinue but assigned to protect it. (A doctor I talked to said that if the presidential *cortège* were to be cut back to four automobiles and the gasoline thereby saved turned over to ambulances, dozens of people might be spared death each week.)

Some bolder citizens, I was told, began to complain and to say that the vaunted energy independence had gone far enough. They were wrong. The proof came with the polar temperatures of the winter of 1984–85, when heat was virtually cut off in every city. At 20° below zero people were freezing at home and in theatres, and, most of all, in hospitals. Schools were closed; women who had to go to work in the morning learned to do their cooking after midnight, when the power would occasionally be turned back on for one or two hours, on forbidden electric plates: the fine for doing so is 5,000 lei, equivalent to the average salary for two months. . . .

* * *

When one speaks of civil rights in the West, one is usually thinking of freedom of speech or freedom of assembly, and not the right to keep oneself warm. Nevertheless, particularly during the winter, the right to keep warm becomes the obsession of most Romanians—the point where all the other rights invoked during the rest of the year tend to become forgotten. Thousands of people deprived of the right of free expression seem utterly indifferent to the fact. Very few remain indifferent about losing their right to keep warm.

Romania has a longstanding tradition of urban landscaping and Romanians have always taken pride in their public spaces. On winter nights, however, under the cover of darkness, people have taken to attacking the large trees that line the cities' streets, cutting off huge branches, and dragging them back to their homes on their children's sleds. Such behaviour suggests they actually have some means for burning the wood—a stove or furnace—which is more than most people have.

The story I was told about Grigore Hagiu, a prominent poet, and his wife Gabriela Cressin, a well-known statistician, is illuminating here. Both were in their forties. They were at home on one of the unbearable January days in the winter of 1985 when the temperature sank to minus 30° centigrade by the window thermometers and minus 20° by the radio. After midnight a thin stream of gas appeared in the kitchen. The couple sat down by the stove and tried to get warm. They fell asleep. Some time in the night the gas went off and came back on again. The couple went on sleeping. They never woke up.

The director of the Museum of Romanian literature, Alexandru Oprea, also died in this way—and so, I am told, did many others. "No *Gulag*, no death squads, no torture or arrests," one of my friends said. "They died in a state of liberty and in peace, dreaming of a summer they would never see. The human rights' organizations remain frozen on the issue of warmth: it isn't the right itself but its suppression that turns death into a political act." . . .

* * *

More than anything else my friends wanted me to write about birth and death. In 1966 the new regime in Romania adopted somewhat draconian methods for bringing about a sharp and sudden increase in a birthrate that, by European standards, was already reasonably high. Before long virtually all measures for birth control were banned. At their workplace many women have to submit to a monthly examination to see if they are pregnant or not. If they are, they know they must have a baby within nine months or risk prosecution. Such measures were the first sign that the scope of Romania's new policies for preserving its independence and standing up to the USSR had widened so as to include the most intimate experiences of private life. The clear and persuasive rhetoric of the new programme did its job; equally effective was the minute description of the heavy penalties reserved for those who refused to take part in it. According to the statistics, the number of infants rose from 273,687 in 1966 to 527,764 in 1967. (Under Romanian law, incidentally, no abortion can be performed unless an official from the Ministry of Justice is present to certify that the abortion was spontaneous and not induced. The word of the doctor is not enough. But the official, not trusting his own competence, may not show up. Even if the woman is having a haemorrhage the doctor may not act alone and in some cases the woman may die. This even happened, I was told, to the assistant of the man responsible for the law, the Minister of Health.)

That such policies were not a response to any demographic crisis in Romania is suggested by the available statistics. In 1965, the natural rate of increase in population per one thousand people was six in Romania, as opposed to 2·4 in Hungary, for example, and three in East Germany. It took nine months to double the number of newborn babies: but more than six years to double the number of gynaecologists, obstetricians, paediatricians, and wet-nurses to care for them (leaving aside the availability of maternity wards, day-care centres, and paediatric hospitals, housing and schools; or the production of powdered milk, baby clothes, and medical supplies). In the 10 years before the programme was started the number of babies born each year rarely rose above 250,000. Some people I talked to believe—and of course there is no way of confirming their view—that of the 500,000 women who became mothers in 1967, over half did so against their will. But beyond such statistical questions, it seems that a kind of underground battle between the regime and the female population has been going on.

The government recently opened a new offensive in this battle. In order to prevent statistics on the subject from being used to stir up trouble, such data are no longer being released. It is understandable that Romania should designate as state secrets the number of women who have died, been made invalids for life, or been thrown into prison because they have had abortions, usually performed by quacks. The following poem, however, which may be puzzling to Westerners, has been widely circulated:

The Children's Crusade

An entire people not yet on earth
Condemned to march along from birth
Foetuses from left to right
Devoid of hearing and of sight,
Foetuses on every hand
Who cannot even understand.
All march towards the tomb
Torn from some suffering mother's womb
Condemned to bear, condemned to die,
And not allowed to question why.

Published in the student magazine *Amfiteatru* in December 1984, along with two other poems in a similar vein, this depressing verse was signed by Ana Blandiana, a highly admired female poet. Within a very short time, thousands of copies of the poems, either Xeroxed or copied out by hand, were available everywhere—the work of a curious and widespread popular *samizdat*, according to the official press—and were in the hands of a good many families.

They could have been expected to understand what was being said. The offices that issue birth certificates, for example, ask parents of newborn children to return in a month. One might say that the infants find themselves face to face with a state that, after having forced them to be born, now refuses to accept them. Notwithstanding the fact that the child cries or behave well, clamours for food or rejects it, gains weight rapidly or too slowly—despite, that is, the fact that it becomes the centre of its family's life—for the state, it continues to be non-existent for a month. Why does the state confine the infant population to oblivion, creating a clandestine army of perhaps 400,000 newborn babies every year?

The answer, so I was told, is to be found in the officially published statistics for 1966 and 1967, which show unequivocally that the explosive rise in the number of births (up 92·8 per cent) was surpassed by the infant mortality rate (145·6 per cent). One can force women to bring unwanted children into the world; one cannot force those children to stay there. Too many of the new arrivals depart: hence the secrecy. Without a birth certificate, no birth has officially taken place. And where no birth has officially taken place, technically there can be no death. Thus, by not issuing the certificate for the period of a month, the state avoids recognizing any deaths that have occurred in that month. The infant who was never born in the sight of the law cannot die.

Still, while the official infant mortality rate continues to increase, the mortality rate among old people continues to become lower, as it does throughout the rest of Europe. The authorities see this as putting a heavy burden on the economy, since most old people receive pensions from the state. To relieve this burden (without modifying the law) certain adjustments have been made: the value of the average pension, for instance, was substantially reduced. That helped a bit, since it reduced the overall amount of money paid out, in pensions each month. It did not, however, lessen the number of months those reduced pensions had to be paid out, and from a budgetary standpoint, the average number of monthly cheques cashed by pensioners was far too high. The only solution was to try to curtail the average period of a person's retirement—by either delaying its start or hastening its end.

The amount allocated as pensions to each district was greatly reduced. But there was no suggestion of changing or breaking the law. Someone who had attained the specified age was legally eligible to retire, and this remained true: at 60 he could apply for permission to retire. Within five years' time he might well have obtained it. That shortened the length of time a pension had to be paid for those beginning retirement; but there was still something to be done about those who were coming to the end of it. Medical assistance, for instance. Let's say some member of the family suffers a heart attack. At once a call is put through to the local health centre or to a hospital. Either way, one of the questions on the other end of the phone will invariably concern the patient's age. For someone over 70, an ambulance or a doctor will seldom be available. Physicians, I was told, have strict instructions to cut down on prescription drugs in general but especially among the aged. In each health centre, doctors are watched closely to see that in prescribing a treatment they take due account of a patient's age.

Another suggestion for how to deal with the problem of older people recently came from the President himself. In his 1985 speech to the Congress of Popular Counsels he showed himself willing to offer whatever assistance might be necessary to enable older members of the urban population to move to the country with a view to taking up "some form of work conducive to physically and spiritual health." To my friends, this seemed a project designed to tear families apart and they feared it would amount to deportation and forced labour.

Before we parted, the tougher-minded of my two companions (who has a tendency to dramatize) said to me by way of farewell: "The bitter fact is that you have no need of us while we have need of you. When you are back in your own country, keep us in mind. Don't just screen out the hideous reality of the women and children we have been talking about, and the old and infirm who every day are peaceably being done away with. Repression isn't what you think it is. It's not the *Gulag* now, and it's not people being thrown into prison: it is the condition of ordinary life. So much for the lesson of present-day Romania."

"Worse Than During the War"

C. Silverstein from Bucharest, Die Welt, *16 November 1986.*

In the streets of Bucharest once again the cars are being covered over with nylon sheets in preparation for their winter hibernation. From the end of December until March the Romanians must do without their wheels—a symptom of the steadily growing energy crisis in the country that was once the richest in the Balkans.

The declaration of a state of emergency and the transfer of management of power plants to the army are only the tip of the iceberg; last winter, the supply crisis, cold, and hunger took on catastrophic proportions. "It's worse than during the war. If only we had something to eat, it would be just like then—at least we were not starving during the war." This is the frequently expressed opinion of the older generations.

Bitterness about the economic situation can only increase in the coming winter. The room temperature allowed by the state, set last year at 16 degrees Celsius (although in reality it never went above seven degrees), has been lowered for this year to 11 degrees. This is little consolation for families living in centrally heated blocks of flats who have to spend the cold months wearing their overcoats indoors, where temperatures remain at about three degrees. Nor do the black humour and jokes circulated to provide warmth do much to prevent their embitterment: "Don't open the window—the people on the street will catch cold!"

"We had no water, because freezing temperatures caused the water pipes in our building to burst," said one Bucharest family who are planning to spend the coming winter at their parents' house in the country. "There we have gas ovens, so no one can simply cut off our heating." It is above all mothers with small children who leave the city if they have the chance. The official infant mortality rate rose by 28 per cent in the winter months, but the actual rate is much higher. Because so many new-born babies die from the cold and from insufficient nourishment shortly after release from hospital, they are not registered in the first few weeks after birth. Often weeks go by without any milk products appearing in the shops.

Thus, it comes as no surprise that Ceausescu's population policies fall on deaf ears. There is a popular saying that a birth in Romania is the same as a death sentence. In a country where birth control is strictly forbidden, and where traditionally the birth rate has been high, the rate is now falling drastically, while the abortion rate stands at almost 60 per cent—despite the threat of a prison sentence for doctors and women who abort. The danger to which women who decide to abort, rather than see their children die, expose themselves would be inconceivable under Western conceptions of medical care. A German visiting her sick mother in Romania told of women in a Bucharest hospital bleeding to death as a result of having been denied medical care after unsuccessful private abortions; they would first have to name the "doctor" responsible, or admit their own guilt.

Reports of elderly people who, after reaching the age of 70, are no longer admitted to hospitals, and who have no right to a doctor on emergency call after turning 60, are spreading fear among senior citizens. One report tells of an elderly woman who was denied a tetanus shot because of her age. When she eventually died of tetanus, members of her family had to sign a certificate stating that unsuccessful treatment for tetanus had been carried out.

The official story is that most Romanians suffer from obesity and gluttony. Is there a more apt form of mockery for the people of a country whose shops are constantly empty of cooking oil, sugar, meat and cheese? As the guest of a Bucharest family one can see what it means to provide for a family under these circumstances. Simply to make soup from vegetables and chicken one must expect to spend six hours shopping. In Bucharest, unlike other cities, food is not rationed, which means that when a supply of butter or meat arrives, the competition for a place in the queue is fierce and merciless. Elderly people start standing in line during the night; in the morning they earn a supplement to their pensions by selling their place. While such practice is feasible during the summer months, in the winter, when temperatures fall to 40 degrees below zero Celsius, it becomes highly dangerous.

3. Rights—Views from the Bridge

Soviet and East European Accounts (Including *Samizdat*) of the State of Social and Economic Rights in the Soviet Bloc

Unhealthy Health Service

The Minister on Soviet Health Care

Extracts from a television interview with Academician Dr Yevgenii Chazov, controversial joint-winner of the 1985 Nobel Peace Prize for his work with the "International Physicians for the Prevention of Nuclear War" organization, and now USSR Minister of Health. Soviet Television, 12 April 1987.

Announcer: Top officials of the USSR Ministry of Health recently held a press conference at the Academy of Medical Sciences for journalists from the central press, television and radio. The discussion was about ways of restructuring Soviet health care, a problem which directly concerns and interests every one of us. In his address, Academician Yevgenii Ivanovich Chazov, USSR Minister of Health, said in part:

Chazov: The residual principle of planning, condemned by the 27th Party Congress, had a negative effect on the development of our society in general and also damaged the Soviet health services. Another thing that should be stressed is that all our planning work was guided by principles of extensive development and the value of quantitative indicators, which led to serious negative results. I have already said before—and there's probably no need to remind this audience—that we were trying to procure a large number of hospital beds, but in any case our hospital beds are not up to modern requirements, as you know. The average space for each bed in our hospitals for example, is, 4·2 square metres in contrast to the public health norm of seven square metres. Moreover, as I pointed out at the collegium, our hospital beds are not suitable for industrial production, and expenditure on medical production engineering amounts to only 15 per cent, while in the other socialist countries this figure is as high as 40 per cent.

Quantitative indicators have also done damage to primary levels of health care, particularly service at outpatients' clinics. Why do outpatients' clinics operate badly? Apparently because, like GPs, they are dominated by quantitative indicators. After all, how are our outpatients' clinics financed? They are financed according to the number of people treated. Logically, the more patients there are, the more people are treated, the more money the outpatients' clinic gets. If in the future we are going to assess a doctor's work according to figures, one of the figures would be the number of people he treats. Naturally, under conditions where there were no qualitative indicators of a doctor's work, it was simply impossible to get an outpatients' clinic to function properly.

That is one example. Then there is the health-care management system, of course. The quotas for everything were set, as it were, in Moscow. The number of nurses and medical technicians, not to mention the various specialist doctors, were all laid down by the planning and finance department, perhaps with the participation of the Semashko Institute, which we have greatly criticized for its poor work. Naturally, it was simply impossible to create a good health-care service within such a cumbersome and sluggish system of management. There was no independence, not only for the head doctor of an outpatients' clinic or a hospital, but even for the minister of a republic.

The second important part of our work involves personnel. Unfortunately the system of cadre training that has evolved in recent years, or in the past decade, let us say, has led to a reduction in the level of knowledge of the Soviet doctor, in particular his practical skills. So the training of personnel is the second important problem.

Hospitals Without Running Water

The third question involves the material and technical foundations. I have already spoken about hospitals. In their efforts to come up with enough hospital beds, I shall speak frankly and say that some people went in for a certain amount of figure inflation. Included in the calculation of numbers of hospital beds were beds sited in residential buildings and even those in wooden huts and hostels. All this was included in the total number of hospital beds. In Central Asia, many hospitals in our country today do not have sewerage systems or running water, let alone a hot water supply. Rural health services are in a bad way, too. Only 21 per cent of the outpatients' clinics and doctor's surgeries in rural areas, for example, are in purpose-built buildings.

There is also the matter of equipment. Unfortunately the equipment produced by Soviet industry—the medical industry and industries producing goods for the health service—has not been up to requirements. For example, when a surgeon operates, he has to sharpen his scalpel after only two operations because it would be good for only two operations; for the third the blade would need sharpening. I am not speaking of sophisticated equipment like computer tomographs, angiographic equipment and so on. But do you know what the new Minister of Health had to busy himself with when he first took up his post? He had to procure teats for babies' bottles. That problem had to be solved by the Ministry of Health, because of the 250 million teats required only 130 million had been supplied. There was a shortage of the simplest things in our country. And incidentally, no one spoke up about it. Not one single newspaper found out and printed the fact that the demand for medicines in our country is satisfied only 85 per cent. This means that 15 per cent of our sick people have no medicines. What talk of health care can there be when the demand for certain cardiovascular preparations and antibiotics was satisfied to only 40–60 per cent of the requirements? These are vital preparations on which lives depend. So the third part of our work concerns material and technical supplies.

Fourth, and finally, comes science. I find it embarrassing to speak about the problems of science within the walls of this Academy, where we are meeting, but I must tell you that today to a large degree it does not correspond to modern standards. To put it frankly, out of the—I think—333 institutes in the health-care system, perhaps 50 or 60 are actively providing practical results for the medical services. Another 100 perhaps are working on the solution of practical, but run-of-the-mill problems. But 80–100 or so could be closed down today with absolutely no problem, and neither the health-care services nor the population would be hurt by the fact that they had been shut down . . . .

"Very Grave State"

What I have spoken about, of course, are the shortcomings. What, though, do we intend to do? What I must say—and probably there are people from the

Moscow newspapers here—is that the Moscow health service is in a very grave state, a *very* grave state. It is, perhaps, one of the most backward health-care systems in our country today, or, let us say, it is at a substandard level. I won't just say that without giving any proof. For example, of the 33 maternity homes in Moscow city, only 12 are up to modern requirements and public health standards. Although we have specialists in virology and infectious diseases sitting here who are at work on this problem, I must say that over the past 10 years in Moscow not one extra hospital bed for infectious diseases, for example, has been provided, and meanwhile one major hospital has been closed down. Many other examples of shortcomings could also be cited concerning stomatology and other medical services in Moscow city.

So what do we plan to do? You are probably saying that this is all very well and good, but what are the reasons for these shortcomings? Well, I would say that it would be a good idea to remember what Mikhail Sergeyevich said at the January plenum of the Central Committee. "You know," he said, "in the past decade we have been deaf to the needs of the social sphere." I think that the fault here lies with the USSR Ministry of Health, which was not very active in raising issues: there was no headquarters, no health-care headquarters, to define the organization, the policy or the management. The fault, of course, lies with the State Planning Committee, the Finance Ministry and other departments and organizations which did not respond at the proper time and failed to notice the needs of the health service . . . .

Then there is management. We regard qualitative indicators as of paramount importance. What do we mean by qualitative indicators? The mortality index, the infant mortality index, the sickness rate, the temporary inability to work index, the complex illness index, the number of severe cases in the regions, severe cases of illness, the number of complaints received from the population. These qualitative indicators will determine the work of our medical establishments. We are going to try to create conditions for the public to have a free choice of a doctor. At first, of course, this is going to be done on an experimental footing, but we believe that this is something we must strive for. Incidentally, in some socialist countries, indeed, in many of them, this principle already exists. And naturally a doctor who gets extra new patients should receive more pay.

We consider it essential to reinforce pre-hospital medical care. It is wrong for a patient to have to go to hospital for a diagnosis to be established. Quite frankly, it is uneconomic. Another thing we have forgotten in health care is economics. Somehow or other we have not been counting the money . . . .

And, of course, we must have renovation. For example, we are raising the issue of trying, during the current Five-Year Plan period, to ensure that there are no hospitals in our country which do not have running water and sewerage systems. How, you may ask. Well, for example, a programme is now being projected in conjunction with the Ministry of Geology to provide water supplies for all the country's hospital establishments in various regions. We believe that up to about the year 2000 we are going to have to reconstruct old hospitals to provide one million and 1·5 million beds . . . .

Transfusion by Anaesthetist

There are many problems concerning education. We are now considering not awarding doctors' diplomas to all those who complete their studies, but of giving paramedical assistants' diplomas to those who do badly and who are incapable of mastering the practical skills. The prestige of the doctor is of course an important area of work. We have bad doctors and good doctors, bad polyclinics and good polyclinics. We have bad hospitals and good hospitals. I have given many examples. But a doctor's work isn't easy either; as no doubt you know, it is difficult work. All the same, I've been going on and on the whole time about operating theatres, hospitals and so on. I will never forget that recently there was a case where an essential operation was being carried out, a serious and complicated one, on the aorta, when fibrinolysis started, the blood ceased to clot, and the patient was bleeding to death. A direct transfusion was urgently needed. He had to be given blood. There was no time to run off and find a donor. There were about eight people in the operating theatre, so they asked—there was nothing else to do—who has No. 3 or No. 4, or whatever it was, blood group? All doctors know their own blood group. The anaesthetist, in the process of giving the anaesthetic, said: "That's my blood group." And as he stood beside his anaesthetic equipment—at that very moment they brought the transfusion system up to him. He held out his arm and his blood was transfused to the patient, while with the other hand he controlled the anaesthetic. These are not isolated examples. This is a fact of our life, you understand, a fact of our life.

"We Are Lagging Behind"

Excerpts from a "Health" programme talk by Academician Dr Yevgenii Chazov, USSR Minister of Health, Moscow Radio, 21 June 1987.

Let us be frank. What have the Institutes of Biochemistry, Enzymology, Morphology, Reflex Therapy and a whole range of others given to our science and practical health care over the past 10 years that is fundamentally new? We are lagging behind disastrously in the sphere of transplantology.

The shortcomings and lagging-behind of Soviet health care also depend on the lagging of medical science. And if we still have a high level of child mortality in our country then this is the fault of the Institute of Paediatrics, the Institute of Obstetrics and Gynaecology, and the Centre for Protecting the Health of Mothers and Children. We have an Institute of Antibiotics, but the health system today does not have highly effective antibiotics of, for example, the cephalosporin variety, so that the Soviet Union was obliged to purchase a licence for them. The Institute of Gerontology has lost its front-ranking status. Many people find it amusing that the Central Institute of Spa Treatment functions not in the Mineralnyye Vody area or even Yalta, but on Kalinin Prospekt in the middle of Moscow.

Soviet medical science has always been famed for its fundamental research and the development of new theoretical concepts. But today, to a considerable extent, these do not originate with us, but come to us from abroad. And the main reason for this is the low methodological level of research. Are there many of our laboratories working today at the cell and molecular level? Do many of our institutes have immunology or genetics laboratories, which today largely determine the level of scientific research?

It's surprising that when you study the reports on our work it seems, at first glance, that our medical science achieved brilliant successes during the 11th Five-Year Plan period, for example. Judge for yourselves: according to the data in the reports 14 scientific discoveries were registered; around 8,000 certificates were issued on new inventions; about 250 new kinds of medicine were devised—250 new medical preparations—as well as 700 items of medical equipment. It would naturally seem that there is every reason to rejoice. And perhaps it was these figures which created an atmosphere of complacency and euphoria. But the astonishing thing is that despite the fact that dozens—I repeat, dozens—of discoveries have been registered, not one single project by Soviet medical researchers has been awarded a Nobel Prize. Evidently the level of our fundamental research is still not sufficient. And indeed the significance of discoveries for developing medicine and solving practical tasks is not so great.

One could also mention the science of medical preparations. Of the more than 373 preparations permitted for clinical use during the 11th Five-Year-Plan period, there are only 15 or 20 which have entered the broad day-to-day practice of our treatment centres. But for many years the health service has been posing the question of the creation of Soviet beta-blockers, cephalosporin antibiotics, and a whole number of other agents. But apart from promises so far nothing has been received.

Today the development of preventive medicine in our country, the devising of criteria for health and principles for a healthy way of life and creation of methods for a health-centre system are urgent matters. But in practice we have found ourselves without a solid, scientific, experiment-tested foundation for working out these problems. It should be frankly stated that in embarking on the restructuring of the health service we are working in the dark, working sometimes by intuition and sometimes improvising experiments.

"Complacency Reigns in the Collective"

Excerpts from an article by A. Chernyak, Pravda, *15 September 1986.*

. . . Let's take a look at how the Communists [of the USSR Ministry of Public Health] are helping the branch's personnel to carry out restructuring.

"A lot has been done," says Party Committee Secretary E. Potekhin. "We sometimes even work on Saturdays and Sundays and much energy has been put into defining and working out central guidelines and important measures for the 12th Five-Year Plan." . . .

But one cannot close one's eyes to shortcomings in the work of the public health agencies either. The flow of complaints about the medical service has increased sharply. Last year alone the Ministry received over 66,000 letters, substantially more than in the year before.

The complaints go to regulatory agencies and newspaper editors. People write that many hospitals are overcrowded, patients lie in corridors, there is a shortage of medical staff, and many medicines are in short supply. There are queues at clinics, and it is difficult to get to see specialists or give samples for analysis. Serious claims have been made concerning emergency departments. The letters talk about the inadequate qualifications of some of the doctors, their lack of tact, and cases of profiteering and bribe taking.

But look in at the reception room of the Ministry of Public Health. It is besieged with patients from all ends of the country. . . . Unable to obtain the care they need locally, people take their cases to the last resort—the Ministry of Public Health. . . .

While reading reports in the Party committee, I ran across the following figure: the reception room received over 44,000 people in the first six months of the year. That is an increase of 18 per cent over the same period last year. . . .

The problems of the shortage of nurses and orderlies, and of the need to improve specialists' training in institutions of higher education are acute. On average, a person studies for seven years, but when he arrives at a hospital he sometimes cannot even perform a simple operation. The shortage of medicines and essential equipment makes itself felt. . . .

Unfortunately, the moral health of the branch's workers is getting too little attention at the moment. . . . For instance, A. Mayorov, the former head of the department of institutions of higher learning, was caught taking bribes. In expelling him from the ranks of the CPSU, the Party committee made the decision that all Party organizations were to hold meetings, with the principle item on the agenda to be entitled "The Campaign to Affirm Communist Morality is the Duty of Every Communist." I asked V. Dulnev, Party Bureau Secretary for administrative affairs, whether such a meeting had been held.

"No," he answered. Communists of the Ministry's Chief Administration for Treatment and Preventive Care and of other divisions did not hold meetings either. . . .

An atmosphere of tolerance and complacency reigns in the collective and initiative is not developing. Thus, in the past two years, 165 executives in the branch have been relieved of their duties. Only one, however, lost his portfolio at the initiative of the personnel department, whose duties include the selection and education of executives.

What is the problem? I asked this question of many Communists—the Minister of Public Health, directors of chief administrations, members of Party committees, secretaries of shop-floor Party organizations, and rank-and-file workers. And although they gave different answers, they all amounted to the same thing: it is an old ailment—lack of discipline in following actions through, and lack of sufficiently exacting standards. . . .

This failure to fulfil duties does not flourish in just any soil, but only in one that is well-fertilized with liberalism and an all-forgiving attitude. Such soil is in many ways cultivated by the Party committee. If you familiarize yourself with the minutes of Party meetings and of Party committee and bureau sessions, you will become convinced of this. . . .

For instance, First Deputy Minister E. Vorobyev, who was accused of abusing his official position, got off with a mild fright. He took materials and made use of his subordinates when building and repairing his dacha. At a meeting of the Party committee, he was given a strict reprimand, which was not entered in his permanent record.

Or another example. To this day, a dog-eared copy of one of the central newspapers in which Deputy Minister P. Bugasov was subjected to harsh criticism for improper actions is making the rounds of the Ministry. I asked the Party Committee Secretary:

"What sort of assessment has been made of his actions?"

"None."

"So the article is wrong?"

"No, all the facts are correct." . . .

At the entrance to the Party committee there hangs a slogan:

"Work daily to achieve unity of word and deed." The Communists of the Ministry of Public Health must embody these words in practical deeds as quickly as possible.

Nursery School Children Poisoned

F. Ivanov in Trud, *21 November 1987.*

The news of what had happened on that beautiful autumn day at Child-Care Facility No. 252 swept through the city [of Kharkov] instantaneously. Now that the investigation has been completed and the court has punished those responsible, we can reliably reconstruct the events.

Nanny L. Yagodkina was preparing soup in the kitchen for the children's dinner. When she couldn't find the salt, someone passing by told her to look in the corner. There she saw a whole pailful. Without a second thought, she tossed a handful into the pot. Soon the soup was served. Within minutes the children were vomiting and their faces were turning blue.

Before long some 16 ambulances and first-aid teams had descended on the scene. Their diagnosis: severe poisoning. With no time to lose, the doctors began pumping out the children's stomachs right then and there. Then the children were rushed to five local hospitals.

By evening a government commission, headed by M. Orlik, Vice-Chairman of the Ukraine Republic Council of Ministers, had been set up to investigate the accident and to help the victims.

Thanks to the highly skilled doctors, by evening most of the 60 youngsters affected were no longer in a critical condition, but not all of them could be saved: three died at the child-care centre, one died on the way to hospital, and a fifth died in the emergency room. Chemists soon identified the toxic substance as sodium nitrate. That is what the pail in the day-care facility's kitchen had contained. Those responsible were arrested.

When I visited Kharkov, more than half the children had already been discharged from the hospital. A special child-care facility has been set aside for them where they will undergo special treatment for nearly a year. Next summer they and their parents will receive free admission to sanatoria.

The events that led up to the tragedy present a striking picture of negligence and mismanagement.

Child-Care Facility No. 252 is a departmental facility attached to Kharkov State Bearing Plant No. 8. The plant utilizes sodium nitrate which is stored in a chemical warehouse, and from that same warehouse the plant dispenses cleaning soda to its day-care centre. According to regulations, all poisonous substances are to be kept apart from other chemicals. But as a result of poor discipline, that regulation was frequently ignored. And the last time the centre was issued with cleaning soda, warehouse personnel mixed up the sacks.

The warehouse employees have now been punished: the deputy head of the supply department and the supervisor in charge of chemicals have been dismissed from their posts and severely punished by the Party.

At the same time, at the child-care facility itself there was no-one on duty who might have noticed the warehouse's mistake. On that ill-fated day just 13 of the 43 employees were on the job. The director was absent, as were the cook and even the assistant cook. That is why a nanny was in the kitchen that day. And for two months no effort had been made to fill the vacant position of senior nurse.

The supervision of child-care centres, especially the departmental facilities, is poorly organized in the republic. The problem is that the statute which the USSR Ministry of Education and the USSR Ministry of Public Health adopted last year on pre-school child-care centres in effect codified a situation in which such facilities have two masters. Economically, Centre No. 252 is dependent on the Plant, but supervision of its operation rests with public-health agencies, many of whose recommendations the plant simply ignores. Last year alone, the Bearing Plant's management received 18 warnings about unsatisfactory conditions at the centre. Not a single one was heeded. And yet the last warning was received only three days before the accident!

A court has sentenced nanny L. Yagodkina, facility director A. Nezhurina and assistant director Z. Sklyarenko to varying terms of deprivation of freedom. Party and administrative punishments have been meted out to many officials of the plant and of local Party and Soviet agencies.

In the wake of the incident, inspections were conducted at all the province's pre-school child-care facilities. Five were temporarily closed because of unsatisfactory conditions. Decisive action is being taken to improve supervision.

Where Bad Doctors Come From

From an article by Professor Y. Shteingardt, head of a department of the Tomsk Medical Institute, Izvestia, *20 January 1987.*

. . . Why is it and how can it be that state examinations in medical schools . . . [have turned into] a *pro forma* act of self-deception? . . .

In several schools, sixth-form students are registered for receipt of diplomas before they have even completed their state examinations. But isn't it a manifestation of that same *pro forma* attitude that the state test of knowledge in two, three or four basic medical subjects is a single examination, in the form of one question on each of them, and the oral exam between student and examiner lasts five to 10 minutes? . . . Such exams merely sanction professional self-assurance on the part of half-educated people, detract from the prestige of the medical profession and its diploma, and serve as fertile soil for irresponsibility and indifference. . . .

70 years ago, my father had to pass about 10 state medical examinations in order to become a doctor. 40 years ago, during the war, I had to pass five; by 1973, my daughter had to pass four, and now two are enough! If this goes on, my grand-daughter will get her doctor's without any state test of the quality of her training. I don't know what Ministry of Public Health officials will do then, but as for me, I will seek treatment only from palm-readers. . . .

It's no wonder that when 242 graduates of seven institutes—general practitioners, surgeons, obstetricians and gynaecologists, paediatricians and dentists with two or three years' experience—were tested for knowledge by personnel of the Russian Republic Ministry of Public Health, . . . not one of them knew what every doctor should know about the diagnosis and treatment of fractured arms, rheumatism, ulcers, hypertension and tooth ailments. Nor is it surprising that six months after presentation of doctor's diplomas, 21 per cent of medical interns received unsatisfactory grades on a test on treatment set by the Ministry of Public Health. I believe that this is the end result of doing things for appearance's sake in the training of doctors. . . .

Pay Clinics

Editorial comment [condensed] by L. Ivchenko, Izvestia, *11 July 1986.*

The article "'Poor' Millionaires" (*Izvestia*, No. 21, 1986) provoked a lively correspondence. . . . [But] the most abundant flow of letters—a real torrent—followed the publication of responses to "'Poor' Millionaires."

Readers have engaged in verbal duels with other readers. Many who had paid no attention to the article itself, and had read only the positive comments about fee-charging medical services, have jumped to conclusions—that there is treatment available that is superior to state treatment, but that you have to pay for it! This has been taken as advice: if you want to receive good treatment, you have to pay for it. Isn't this a threat, these readers ask, to our valuable social right—the right to free health care?

"An attempt to revive fee-charging treatment would be nothing other than a violation of the working people's rights as stipulated in the Constitution," writes A. Bondarenko (Chernovtsy). Other readers express the same fear. . . . "To write that the time has come for a change-over to fee-charging medical services is sheer madness," says I. Barbal (Ocher, Perm oblast). We didn't write that, alarmed readers, we didn't write that! No such "change-over" was called for. . . .

"Fee-charging medical services make up just 0·4 per cent of the overall public health-care structure," explains V. Treskunov, Deputy Director of the USSR Ministry of Public Health's Chief Administration for Therapeutic and Preventive Aid. "And while the number of fee-charging services will increase by 60 per cent during the current Five-Year Plan, the overall public health network will grow too. So the percentage—or, more accurately, the fraction of a percentage point—will stay the same. Moreover, we are developing economic accountability firstly in those areas of medical care where fees are charged at the moment anyway—for example, dentures, cosmetic surgery and certain physical-therapy procedures. The basic principle of socialist health care—free medical assistance—is not being violated, and in no way is one form being pitted against the other. Self-financing polyclinics provide an additional service through which people can, for a moderate fee, receive additional consultations or treatment.

Thus, the question concerns the coexistence of the two forms. It must be remembered that fee-charging physicians provide a purely voluntary service. After all, in our country state-owned housing exists side by side with housing cooperatives. It would never occur to anyone to call cooperative construction unconstitutional or to say that it "undermines the foundation of socialism."

"In my view, it is a strange debate—whether fee-charging polyclinics are necessary or not," writes M. Gostev (Voronezh). "Of course they are necessary! Both kinds are—state ones, and ones that charge fees. The more of them there are, the better it is for the public. Then people are given another option, should the need arise. Supposing a patient can't get to see the specialist in his locality, has doubts about the diagnosis, or wants things to move faster—the reason is unimportant. . . . The point is that people have an opportunity to choose the type of consultation they want, and to choose a physician they trust. In an ordinary polyclinic, they don't always have this option. Fee-charging consultations also help to publicize the latest scientific achievements in medicine." . . .

Unfortunately, the letters contain many—very many—complaints about the poor organization of medical services at the local level. . . .

Readers from Rostov-on-Don, Riga, Petropavlovsk-Kamchatsky, Taganrog, Karaganda oblast and elsewhere ask: "Why should a bad doctor receive the same salary as a good one? The patient should be given the right to switch to another doctor if his 'own' doesn't suit him; in the process, a proportion of the latter's salary should be transferred to the preferred doctor. This will make it clear at once how well any particular physician does his job." . . .

M. Indman, a resident of Gomel, writes: "It's not fee-charging polyclinics that 'undermine the socialist system,' but disorder in the state ones! This is what makes people look for alternatives. It has long been time to impose order there." In this connection, I remember a conversation overheard among patients at a fee-charging polyclinic: "Treatment at a state clinic will cost you even more," a woman in the waiting room argued. "There they will look at your mouth and your hands, and if you came with nothing, that's what you leave with." . . .

A. Kopy (Baku) writes: "Often we don't feel that we're getting even a small portion of the attention that we have a right to expect from medical personnel. Moreover, it's become so fashionable here to 'thank' doctors with tidy sums of money, that expanding fee-charging medical care would only be a blessing." . . .

I showed these letters to officials of the USSR Ministry of Public Health. They told me that the matter of material incentives for medical personnel is under discussion. Steps are also being taken to improve the quality of consultation and diagnostic care. By the end of 1987, 317 consultation-and-diagnostic polyclinics will be in operation in all republics; about 200 of them are already functioning. The current Five-Year Plan calls for the establishment of 400 municipal institutions of this type; in contrast to the existing regional polyclinics, the very latest diagnostic equipment will be used in the new clinics. During their working hours, highly skilled specialists will see the public—free of charge, needless to say. On the other hand, how they spend their time off duty is each specialist's personal affair. Some may use their free time for fishing, others for reading, and still others may want to put in some time at a fee-charging polyclinic. This can only be welcomed: the overall level of health care will be raised. As the Moscow psychiatrist T. Belyavskaya writes: "All of us, the health of each of us, will benefit."

Incidentally, there are also many letters from doctors amongst the editorial mail prompted by the article "'Poor' Millionaires." The Leningrad surgeon A. Kharakh expressed a quite "seditious" thought—fee-charging hospitals. "I have worked as a cancer specialist for about 30 years," he writes. "How many unfortunate patients and their relatives have passed before my eyes! Many have offered to pay any amount of money to get the sick person admitted to a hospital, because it was not possible to provide care at home. But there are still no such hospitals in our country."

Such institutions are needed not just for cancer patients but also for other chronically ill patients who have long been bedridden. It's very difficult for a working family to organize care for such a patient. Relatives are deprived of vacations and normal recreation for years, and able-bodied members of society are sometimes forced to quit work and to withdraw from public life in their prime. In short, relatives find themselves in a real bind. "Wouldn't such fee-charging hospitals provide a way out?" asks B. Bessonova, also of Leningrad, supporting the surgeon.

Private Dentist

From "Man and the Law," a studio discussion broadcast on Soviet Television, 12 March 1987. A panel of officials discussed interviews shown with workers and representatives of enterprises in Dzherzhinsky rayon, Moscow. The dentist interviewed was in private practice.

Correspondent: So when we came to see you, you weren't surprised to see us, were you?
Dentist: No, I wasn't surprised, because I had been told you were coming. But what I don't understand is the purpose of your visit. Because . . ., you see, I am used to being visited by rather unfriendly people; either OBKhSS [Department for the Struggle against Embezzlement of Socialist Property] checks up on us, or the financial department comes to inspect us, or other such organizations. But before you no one has ever come to help us.
Correspondent: But your patients are probably well-disposed towards you, and they probably still feel the same way when they leave here.
Dentist: But of course, I do have some permanent clients who have been coming to me for treatment over a period of up to 20 or even 30 years—I have no [advertising] board on my door; my work is my advertisement. We help people, and we help them greatly; just as in agriculture shortages of foodstuffs can't be solved by private plots alone, but all the same the private plots do play a part.
Correspondent: A very large part.
Dentist: . . . In the same way the physician comes back home from his main job, and if after a rest he is able to receive a patient, or two or three, if he can work for an hour or two extra, it can only be beneficial . . .
Correspondent: And also to the state—I see you have your tax receipt here—the state, as I understand, also benefits from your earnings and gets considerable profits from them.
Dentist: You see, taxation in its present form is frightening; the financial inspector comes along and makes people wonder what sort of taxes they will have to pay, what sums they will have to pay—all that is frightening. Under the present system of taxation we send in statements. The statements—especially the new kind which came in with the law on non-labour incomes—had an effect on us too. They include an item about deliberately making false statements. But no matter what kind of statements we send in . . .
Correspondent: You are suspected of stating . . .
Dentist: . . . the inspector will still come up with larger sums through his activities. And so it looks as if I concealed something, and then I have to be charged under the law—that's what's frightening. Moreover, I have to pay extras to the plumber, the electrician . . .
Correspondent: Quite so, but what is your . . .
Dentist: . . . and the financial department cannot take that money into account, simply because I can't produce any receipts for it. They account for all expenditures on materials and medicines, just as they do in our [state] clinics, but I don't only use domestic [Soviet-made] products here. Furthermore, I give a statement of my working hours to the financial department, stating, for example, whenever I work for two hours, and whether or not I work at weekends. But what if the appointment time does not suit the patient after all, and he calls to tell me that he is tied up at work? If I see him at a different time, or on a different day, the financial department will tax me for that day every week throughout the year. And so I cannot see him. I have to refuse him.

Moreover, the financial inspector's visit is in itself unethical. He comes and asks [the patient] "what's wrong with you, what treatment have you had and what have you actually paid for it"—next thing he'll be looking into his mouth! And what if it's not a dentist but a urologist [laughter in the audience], or a gynaecologist, or a psychiatrist—cases where the patient isn't keen to go into detail?! After all, there have been some incidents; for instance, there was one time when a woman patient was rude to the financial inspector and even burst into tears because she did not want to answer his questions. And this very process is inappropriate—after all, a physician is not a craftsman in whose case it's possible to count the number of trousers or heels he makes or mends. After all, when the patient sits down in the [dentist's] chair, he has to be relaxed, and so too does the dentist so that nothing will distract him. And whenever we need to buy equipment they always put obstacles in our way, restrictions, etc. Why can't a physician earn some money; why is it that the only thing allowed him is lofty responsibility?

Well, in truth, being a physician is something special, and there should be some special rules for admission to medical institutes, because it's not just a case of [knowing] mathematics or whatever; what is involved here is the inner being—the physician himself . . . and the life and health of the patient is his responsibility. And we too are workers just like any other, we too are involved in production—our product is health. So why are we treated like this?

Why They Die Younger and Unreported

Extract from an article by A. Vishnevskii, doctor of economic sciences, entitled "The Human Factor in its Demographic Dimension." Kommunist, *No. 17, November 1986, pp. 69–80.*

It is the unity of the economic and social logic of development, as well as the humanist orientation of this development, which give the demographic revolution the nature of a historically progressive process which fits organically into Soviet society's progressive advance. The improvement in the utilization of the human factor is also connected with the successful development of this process. After all, every premature death is, apart from everything else, an irrevocable loss of unused potential. The demographic revolution makes it possible to wage a successful struggle against premature mortality.

Unfortunately, at the moment we cannot be satisfied with our successes in this struggle. It is precisely here that we come up against one of the most acute socio-demographic problems of today. After several decades of a rapid reduction in mortality and rise in longevity, a long period of "marking time" began, starting approximately in the mid-60s. Mortality, which was relatively high in any case, and particularly among men of working age, continued and in some cases even rose, and the USSR's lag behind the majority of economically developed countries of the world in terms of mortality and average longevity indexes became greater.

It stands to reason that the consequences of the present unfavourable trends in the sphere of mortality are in no way comparable in scale and significance with the enormous gains in a person's average longevity and life expectancy which have been achieved in the years of Soviet power. The evaluation of these trends must be objective but balanced, without excessively dramatizing the situation. However, it is equally indisputable that one must not reconcile oneself to them at all. In our country the mortality of children up to one year is considerably higher than in major capitalist countries. Average longevity is not even 70 years, whereas in the United States it is 75, and in Japan 77 years. There are calculations which show that simply as a result of such a lag in average longevity (that is, discounting differences in labour productivity), the volume of wealth which a generation produces in its lifetime is reduced by a minimum of 7–8 per cent, which is, after all, tens of billions of rubles. Can we be so rich as to bear such losses? What is involved, after all, is not just economic losses; above all, it is human lives. It is necessary to gain an understanding of the causes of the situation which has arisen, to put it right as soon as possible, and to restore the previous stable trend of decreasing mortality and rising average longevity.

It will be necessary to make up for an omission here. In our time we have become so accustomed to victorious communiqués from the front of the struggle against mortality that the change in the situation has caught us unawares. Instead of mobilizing all forces for the struggle to change the negative trends at that time, in the 1960s and '70s, we displayed unjustified complacency and were unable to resist them with anything. Statistical indexes which showed the unfavourable situation simply ceased to be published. Reliable information is in itelf a most important instrument for controlling social processes. Lack of information about the real state of affairs does not contribute to recognition of the gravity of the situation, to concentration of the necessary efforts in one of the most important sectors of the social sphere, or to the search for effective paths leading to the desired turning-point.

The Czechoslovak Health-Labyrinth

Extracts from Charter 77 Document No. 14/1984, addressed to the Ministry of Health of the Czechoslovak Socialist Republic and the Czechoslovak National Council.

Any citizen who has been through, or rather, has been dragged and processed through our health-service system feels as if he has fought his way through a labyrinth whose sense and organization are incomprehensible, where he has no choices, and where at every stage he has been registered, documented, added to a statistic or mechanically processed, several times over. Throughout this, the object of this admirable, if somewhat suspect manipulation has been his body, his life, himself, i.e. something he has every right to decide about for himself; without this right all other rights become pure fiction. . . .

The patients are bitter and angry as they cough in crowded waiting rooms, try to get medicines in various pharmacies, or die in public on emergency beds, while the physicians are overworked and overwhelmed by formalities. The nurses are downgraded to manual labour workers, unable to cope mentally in the face of such suffering, physically exhausted by work which elsewhere women would be forbidden to perform.

HEALTH-service workers are employees of the state. Access to health-service jobs is regulated by the interests of state control. Entrance to secondary schools is restricted by certain criteria, such as class origin and the political profile of a candidate's parents. It is the same for university entrance, where a candidate's political activities are again evaluated. After graduation from university the same criteria are used to assess those applying for post-graduate studies, for specialized professions and for top posts. Qualification for top posts in the health service is approved by the district committees of the CPCS [Czechoslovak Communist Party], and although there is no law saying so, physicians wanting to work at top levels are usually asked to sign an application for CPCS membership. Constant political education, which is a compulsory part of all professional training, only adds to the senseless overburdening of physicians. Marxism–Leninism, "scientific communism" and the history of the CPSU merely take up the time allotted to complex professional training.

Doctors are constantly made aware that subordination to the state is more important than the Hippocratic oath. The organs of State Security automatically assume that doctors know nothing more than *they* do, and that *their* decisions on whether someone is ill or not are bound to be better than an objective medical judgement. The same feudal system applies to prison and army doctors, and to a somewhat lesser extent, to enterprise physicians. Only those doctors who are prepared to obey instructions are called in for lucrative work as forensic experts. Any doctor who does this, even if he is violating the basic ethical principles of his profession, perhaps with fatal consequences, is guaranteed state protection and runs no risk, either from public opinion or from his fellow physicians.

MEDICAL research is carried out according to the State Plan. It is conducted in institutes belonging to the Czechoslovak Academy of Sciences, Ministry of Health research institutes and at faculties of medicine. Tasks for research are set by the Plan, coordinators are centrally appointed, workplaces and resources for particular tasks are centrally assigned. It is not those with the best ideas or qualifications for scholarly research who are given places at specialized centres (although it does sometimes occur), but those who have the necessary political prerequisites and the right influential friends. The progress of scientific research workers, their training and appointments are approved by superior Party bodies; here too political considerations go hand in hand with corruption and nepotism.

THE Czechoslovak health service has a well organized system of caring for mother and child, for both prophylaxis and treatment. Much educational research has been carried out involving several generations of mothers. Pregnant women are regularly checked, and in the first few years after the Second World War and later quite a number of maternity homes were built to ensure that most women should give birth in hospital. An adequate system for artificial feeding was also introduced; crèches and nursery schools were built. Since then, however, we have run out of steam, whilst progress outside Czechoslovakia continues. The introduction of modern methods such as rooming-in (allowing a mother to stay in one room with her new-born child, giving her the opportunity for contact with it as well as individual care for the baby) caused great economic, organizational and psychological problems. The system for artificial feeding is now out of date; it could cause allergies, and it cannot be guaranteed to work. We have failed to control all potential infections, particularly inflammations of the respiratory passages. Despite the care taken, many babies are born prematurely, or with congenital defects. Infant mortality has ceased to decline. In whole areas children are anaemic and suffer from inflamed respiratory passages, symptoms of allergies and poor resistance to infection. The rate of illness among children at crèches and nursery schools is quite high. It has become normal to try to make children more resistant, so that fewer mothers will have to be absent from work. The physical condition of army recruits continues to decline. As a result, young people's physical education is under review, but clearly it is difficult to find recreation and sports opportunities for children. The nutritional norms for children at various ages were once defined, but becuase of economic factors it is practically impossible to uphold them. Preventive methods such as lunch-time milk at school (served in repellant bags made from some synthetic material), are attempts to compensate for the appalling environment, unhealthy drinking water, and bad nutrition. Fresh fruit and vegetables aren't available in the shops for weeks on end, and parents cannot be sure that the food they are giving their children is not contaminated.

From early on, children are exposed to stresses imposed by the shortage of flats, their parents' tiredness and nervousness, and getting up early to be sleepily dragged off to crèches or nursery schools. Then come constant school reforms or changes of the school programme (children in the lowest years at elementary school are already working longer than the norms defined by the Labour Code for youths aged 15–16); next come the difficulties of getting into secondary schools. Even school-age children need written confirmation of illness from a doctor; pupils constantly spend long hours in waiting rooms just to get the required piece of paper to be allowed to go home to bed. Every time a child is ill, his/her mother has problems at work, causing the entire family irritation and more mental stress.

SOME old people with no one to care for them are sent to hospital as long-term patients, occupying beds on internal wards. Many of them are taken into hospital literally starving, their hygiene neglected—particularly lonely old ladies. The waiting time for admission to hospital for the long-term sick or to a home for pensioners is several months or even years, so that many people die before being admitted. These institutions are situated mainly within old monastery buildings or castles, or in redesigned hospitals. The standard of care is the social and medical minimum. Improved, specialized establishments for the elderly have been set up recently, but it is more expensive to stay in them and harder to gain admission.

There is a shortage of nurses to look after ailing old people at home. Recently, a separate branch for geriatric nursing was established. Geriatric nurses visit citizens over 65 years of age to look after their health and social welfare. At present one such nurse covers two health service districts, i.e. approximately 6,400 inhabitants. Care for the elderly is both mentally and physically exhausting and does not give much satisfaction. But it makes great demands on the few women who are prepared to devote themselves to it. The number of nuns who used to work in social care institutions is declining; motives are not admitted; even girls from religious families find it hard to gain admission to health-service training schools, especially in rural areas.

HEALTH care in our country has been pegged to a single, rigid standard. The only criterion for differentiating between patients ought to be the state of their health. Patients are examined and treated free of charge, including operations, care, food and medicines. Health care is administered according to one straightforward principle; patients have no opportunity to pay extra, for a private room for example, or for better food; nor can they choose to be treated by a particular surgeon. There is a shortage of modern diagnostic equipment, X-ray film, solutions for intravenous feeding, and hospital linen; assistants have to cope with the shortage of manpower. It is therefore the rule rather than the exception that sanitation problems are extreme, even in the best hospitals. Hospitals suffer from a permanent shortage of medicines, as do the ambulance services. Various institutions and commissions at all levels are responsible for distributing medicines; their prescriptions are strictly controlled so that every doctor and every department is obliged to stick to certain limits, or else they must produce good reasons for exceeding them.

The distribution of medicines on prescription is limited to particular district pharmacies, and doctors are not allowed to prescribe or recommend medicines that are not currently available at the local pharmacy. Lists of medicines in short supply are issued regularly. The import of medicines from abroad is set by plan, and it is impossible to place a realistic order for a new foreign medicine.

AS in other spheres of life, this chronic situation where everything is in short supply causes the black market to flourish. To get instruments and spare parts the doctor needs friends in the right places; to ensure that a piece of work is expertly done he has to bribe repairmen by offering them something in exchange, and to get medicines, books and reagents he has to do the same.

Enterprising citizens try to make acquaintances in the right places in advance in order to get better treatment, to see a different doctor, to be admitted to hospital sooner or to get a place in a hospital with a better reputation. The public knows which establishments are better and which worse, which specialists achieve better results and which surgeons are likely to accept bribes. Medicines are sold on the black market, and a corrupt system within hospitals ensures better care for some patients. Gifts are offered as an expression of satisfaction and thanks for care given, but they are partly intended and accepted as bribes. Official propaganda loudly condemns such activity, and thus successfully distracts attention from greater problems—but it does not admit that corruption is not purely an expression of selfishness, but a reflection of how poorly the system functions.

THERE are exceptions: there are special health-care services at large enterprises, the railways and the uranium industry. The armed forces and the Ministry of the Interior also have their own health services. Special health care was set up for employees of the Party apparatus and for leading figures in the state and Party. These institutions are equipped and financed in a different way. They have plenty of instruments, medicines and materials and face no problems in importing rare medicines from abroad. This care is also free of charge. These select categories have their own system of preventive treatment, their own spas, their own homes for disabled children and their own old people's homes.

Drink, Drugs and Corruption

Moonshining By Party Members

Excerpts from a report by I. Glanko, Pravda Ukrainy *correspondent in Chernigov oblast,* Pravda Ukrainy, *17 April 1987.*

In Chernigov oblast—or more precisely, in Repki rayon—there is a village called Novaya Budnya. Some time ago the inhabitants proclaimed the village alcohol-free. Quite recently, an inspection team from the rayon centre dropped in to have a look at the sober life the local people were living. What the controllers found was something else—"infernal machines" which, before their very eyes, ran sugar into brew and the brew into full-proof moonshine.

You would never guess who turned out to be the owner of the home-made miracle-working machines. It was M. M. Sodyl, Communist and leader of a crop-growing team, a member of the local organization of the Voluntary Society for the Struggle for Sobriety, and in addition a deputy on the Nedanchinsky Village Soviet. Believe it or not, at this "teetotaller's" premises the controllers found 80 litres of moonshine brew and 17 litres of 45°-proof first-brew moonshine (*pyervak*).

But something of a record in accumulating various types of equipment for raw moonshine distilling, barrels of brew and large bottles of moonshine was achieved by M. M. Sodyl's neighbours: M. F. Bilenok, a forester and, by the way, a member of the Sobriety Society and a Communist too; E. M. Yashchenko, a woman worker at the local Kotsyubinsky state farm; and P. V. Dekhtyarenko, a pensioner. On the day of the inspection, it was found that the aforementioned people had hidden in various places, all in all, 240 (!) litres of semi-finished moonshine and three sizeable bottles of drink ready for consumption.

If you like, I could tell you about another case, which has already been investigated by Repi people's court. The person involved was woman pensioner M. M. Yevtushenko who, as well as brewing moonshine, also supplied the builders of the town of Slavutich with her product in their township, the Yakor. How many trips she made from Kotsyubinsky state farm to the Yakor no one knows. But on one occasion the woman moonshiner and profiteer was unlucky: the militia caught her red-handed. The punishment prescribed by the people's court was a fine of 500 rubles. Wasn't it rather mild? . . .

One could cite many examples of moonshiners and moonshine dealers being exposed. Suffice it to say that from January to March of the current year alone, in Chernigov oblast 970 sources of moonshining were discovered, 2,500 sets of moonshining equipment were seized or voluntarily surrendered, and criminal or administrative proceedings were taken against 900 people. . . .

Alcohol as Solace and Barter

From an interview between A. V. Vlasov, the USSR Minister for Internal Affairs and an unnamed Izvestia *correspondent,* Izvestia, *11 March 1987.*

Correspondent: Aleksandr Vladimirovich, may I first ask what worries you particularly about alcohol-related crime today?

Vlasov: First of all I will say that more than one third of all crimes are directly linked to drunkenness. This amounts to one in five accidents or traffic accidents and one in nine fires; when it comes to crimes in the home, 60–70 per cent of them are the result of alcohol consumption. It is there—into flats, homes, and hostels—that drunkenness has crept from the streets and enterprises. This is its last firm bastion, which, unfortunately, is not being attacked with sufficient skill and energy. It is there that we find the rowdy drunk, the secret family drinker, the alcohol speculator, and the profligate who organizes binges with fellow drinkers.

I would like to talk frankly about the terrible danger of unrefined vodka and about the bootlegging which has recently come to light. Moonshining today—not only in the villages but in the cities too—has become a very dangerous refuge for alcoholism, is helping to turn people into drunks, and is a source of mercenary gain. It has a particularly strong hold in daily life.

Correspondent: Could you now explain about "unrefined vodka"—how widespread it is, how it is made, and so on?

Vlasov: I will try. Whereas in the recent past moonshining was typically a rural "criminal phenomenon," nowadays approximately 40 per cent of its "manifestations" are recorded in the cities. Along with alcohol speculators, bootleggers have begun to cause serious problems in urban residential areas and hostels. Geographically, the picture looks like this: moonshining is most prevalent in the RSFSR, particularly in large industrical centres in the Urals and Siberia where formerly there were no serious "hotbeds" of this sort. The RSFSR accounts for 72 per cent of all uncovered cases of moonshining, almost half of them in the Bashkir ASSR, Udmurt ASSR, Tatar ASSR, Altay and Krasnoyarsk krays, and Irkutsk, Kemerovo, Tyumen, Orenburg, Perm, Sverdlovsk, and Chelyabinsk oblasts. The "moonshine disease" is spreading in the Ukraine, Belorussia, Kazakhstan, Lithuania, and Moldavia.

Who are our modern moonshiners? According to our information, 50 per cent are workers and employees of urban and rural enterprises; 15 per cent are collective farm workers. 61 per cent of all moonshiners are women (it is deplorable that wives and mothers are drawn into the pernicious process of poisoning their relatives by turning them into drunks!) I must point out that both the producers and the consumers of moonshine have grown younger: 52 per cent of those sentenced are below the age of 30, and only 20 per cent are pensioners. Amongst those who had criminal charges brought against them last year, about 10,000 were people with higher or secondary specialized education, including 4,700 Communists and Komsomol members. . . .

Correspondent: And what kind of damage is all this doing?

Vlasov: Moonshine is extremely harmful and dangerous to health because, in addition to alcohol toxins, it contains a heavy concentration of highly poisonous fuel oils and spirits, metal oxides from the still, and all kinds of "special" additives—from tobacco to hydrochloric acid. In the last 18 months the militia has recorded 90 cases of group poisoning from alcohol substitutes. 200 people have died.

What other damage is caused by this problem? People become chronic alcoholics far more rapidly from moonshine, particularly teenagers . . . considerable economic damage is done, because valuable products—thousands of metric tons of sugar, beet, potatoes, and grain—are destroyed by being turned into toxic substances. The sharp increase in sugar sales in a number of regions of the country over the past year—a 14–16 per cent increase in Latvia and Moldavia, for example, and a 20 per cent increase in Kirghizia—require serious analysis, in particular.

Moonshiners often manufacture their "product" from stolen raw materials. The theft of sugar, grain, and beets for the purpose of unrefined vodka production has increased. A criminal group, led by the director of the Merkensky sugar refinery, which had embezzled sugar to the value of 140,000 rubles, has been broken up in Dzhambul, for example.

Moonshining has become a source of unearned income and illegal gain. In Kursk oblast citizen Korolkova systematically manufactured and sold hooch at the Kastornaya-Novaya station. She was found to be in possession of 1·5 metric tons of home-brewed beer. The court confiscated a Zhiguli car bought with dishonest "earnings" and also a large amount of money. . . . Tens of litres of unrefined vodka, 0·5 metric tons of sugar, and approximately 20,000 rubles were confiscated from the inveterate moonshiner Arzamasova. . . . The unrefined vodka profiteers are being identified and face inevitable punishment.

Correspondent: Why are people now joining the "clan" of moonshiners when they formerly had no such intention?

Vlasov: There can be no serious talk of combating drunkenness and moonshining until the matters of improving the organization of people's work and leisure time and satisfying popular demand for services and consumer goods are resolved alongside or, to be more precise, in close conjunction with this problem.

It is a well-known fact that in rural areas a bottle of moonshine is often the main form of payment for all manner of services rendered on the side. Have a bottle ready if you need firewood transported, your garden dug, or your house repaired. In Tula oblast, for example, more than half of all those sentenced for selling moonshine had manufactured it to pay for consumer services.

Correspondent: Would you please tell us about the role of the militia in the fight against moonshining?

Vlasov: It must be admitted that the militia has proved ill-prepared for the outbreak of moonshining, particularly in the cities. We are now making up for lost time. But we have not been sitting idle, of course. A number of measures have been implemented. In the last 18 months approximately 900,000 illicit stills have been either voluntarily handed in or confiscated and 2·6 million litres of home-brewed beer and moonshine have been destroyed. Since the change in legislative norms, the number of charges brought across the country as a whole has increased 2·6 times. Over the past year more than 130,000 people have been found guilty by civil courts and 70,000 have been punished.

These are strong measures. They are evidence of a more active fight against bootlegging and moonshine. This evil is not becoming less prevalent, however—on the contrary, in many regions of the country it is growing. This shows up the inadequacy of the preventive measures taken with the participation of the public, and reveals one-sidedness and formality in applying the punishments laid down by the law. The greater number of penalties cannot be automatically identified with the effectiveness of anti-alcohol measures. In some areas MVD [Ministry of Internal Affairs] organs are dazzled by figures showing a rise in punishments and have clearly slackened their preventive efforts.

I must say that the malicious moonshiner has rapidly reorganized his activity, has gone deep underground, so to speak, and is mastering new techniques. In the village of Grishentsy in Vinnitsa oblast the militia caught a certain V. Postupaylo, who had set up a distillery in a forest thicket with a watchtower so that he could keep a look out with a pair of binoculars. . . . In Khoyniksky rayon, Gomel oblast, they discovered a centre for the collective production of unrefined vodka; several families took it in turns to tend it. . . .

Alcoholism Leads to Venereal Disease

An excerpt from "Doctor's Advice," a talk by Irena Sivcillo, Deputy Chief Doctor at the Latvian Skin and Venereal Diseases' Treatment Centre; broadcast from Riga in Latvian on 13 November 1986.

Bad friends and drunken "heroes" boasting of their prowess to friends and women often forget the old truth that alcohol and Venus march in step.

In their everyday work venereologists encounter a great number of more or less vivid examples of this. There is no point in moralizing as it is boring and influences nobody. It would be better to give an example from real life, with the names and some facts altered. Perhaps this will inspire us to think about our behaviour.

There is a motor vehicle enterprise of our republic situated on the outskirts of town, where the administration office is located quite far away from the garages.

Because of this distance, hardly any of the bosses ever takes the trouble to go all that way in the mud to the garages.

But at the end of the working day the garages are the scene of lively activity. Some workers bring snacks, others share food round and put out plates and dishes on an improvised table. Almost every day there is a large or small drinking session at the garage.

Very often at the end of the working day three women friends, Antra, Liana and Amanda turn up at the garages. Antra is 27, flabby, carelessly dressed, and looks older than her age. The fact that two of her front teeth are missing does not make her any prettier. She is the mother of several small children, so she can afford not to work, and is dependent instead upon her parents, who are pensioners.

Antra's bosom-friend, Liana, is a slim, good-looking blonde, with very sincere, friendly blue eyes. Unfortunately, her external appearance is in complete contradiction to her past and present occupation. In the past she has been imprisoned for theft, and has abandoned her child to a maternity home. For two years Liana has not been able to settle in a job because she cannot find a suitable occupation and has been living with Antra.

The third girl, Amanda, is divorced. She does not work either, and is a close friend of the other two. When Amanda goes off for several days at a time she leaves her child with her mother. Her mother is sure to keep an eye on it and feed it. After all, no one is prepared to give up the pleasures of their personal life for a child's sake.

Usually one of the drivers from the motor vehicle enterprise, as he drives past, lets Antra know that there is a job coming up lasting several days. Antra gathers her team of women, and sometimes, if there is greater demand than usual, she invites an extra female friend along as well.

Then they travel with the drivers like butterflies, from one town to the next. If another driver is waiting along the road in his vehicle, he does not refuse services which are so easily obtainable; after a short time he hands the relay baton on to a third driver who is also thirsting for passionate love.

The women friends visit the garages frequently, because they can always be sure of getting a drink there. After the drink, they often stay overnight at the garage. It would be naive to think that none of the drivers ever stayed the night there too. On such nights their wives wait for their husbands in vain at home; their children wait for their fathers.

Perhaps all this would have gone on for a long time, but one day the wife of one of the drivers went to a dermatologist/venereologist. She was diagnosed as having syphilis. Then her husband was examined, and he too was found to be ill. Then his sexual contacts—Antra, Amanda and Liana—were examined. It turned out that these women had been suffering from syphilis for about six months.

Then began the difficult and unpleasant task of tracking down the drivers who had been in intimate contact with the women, from all over the republic, all of whom had to be examined. Those who were ill needed treatment. Many needed prophylactic therapy to prevent the disease from developing. Their wives and children had to be examined as well. Many people had to undergo some very unpleasant experiences, and let us hope that this will make some of them consider and perhaps change their lifestyles.

All the events described happened at a place of work, during working hours. A lot of people knew about the drinking garage. A couple of the more courageous wives went to the administration to ask for help, because their husbands frequently came home from work reeking of drink. The management of the enterprise, however, did nothing to wipe out this hotbed of alcoholism.

The struggle against two social evils as serious as alcoholism and venereal disease is beyond the powers of doctors if workmates, families and the general public will not help. Indifference and tolerance towards alcohol consumption encourage drinking, leading to alcoholism and its inevitable consequences, including venereal infection.

Drinking Behind Quiet Doors

Excerpt from an article by E. Isakova, Izvestia, *30 March 1987.*

Now, when heavy drinking is most safely done at home, behind the closed door of one's flat, the harm done by these "stay-at-home-drunkards" is especially clear. . . .

Not long ago, on assignment from my editors, I was "on duty" at an emergency medical aid sub-station. Three times that night, medical teams were called out to the same address: Flat 47, 23 Marina Raskova Street. A. Andreyeva, who lives there, did not need medical assistance. She only needed someone to listen to her unprintable cursing. Almost all of the sub-station's mobile-unit personnel are familiar with this patient. They have brought the police with them more than once. . . .

Virtually every sub-station has regular patients of this kind. It would be naive to think that the police officers don't know what's going on. However, they are in no hurry to apply really strict measures. A fine? But what should be done with the alcoholic? Assign him to a therapy-and-labour rehabilitation centre? Too much trouble. After all, first the person has to be registered with a doctor who specializes in addiction treatment; then, after a course of treatment, the patient must be kept under observation, and only if the desired results are not forthcoming can the drawing up of documents for the people's court begin. Only a court can commit an alcoholic to compulsory treatment. The whole procedure takes several months. Meanwhile, the stay-at-home drunkards have a carefree life—until, for instance, a drinking bout ends in injury.

On some days a line stretches from the first-aid vehicles to the admissions office of the Special Hospital for Injuries. And the fact that, although it's difficult now to drink on the job and people are afraid to drink on the street, this service is still busy, indicates that drunkenness is gaining ever greater "access" to the home. Hidden behind the doors of individual flats, it is less glaring. How can it be brought to light? Through the emergency medical service? The police? Neighbours? No, alas, neighbours are too tolerant of this evil. After all, we know when someone is drinking and becoming an inveterate alcoholic next door to us. Every day we say hello to these people, but helping them, advising them, reproving them—no, we feel that's none of our business. . . .

The editors receive a good many letters expressing concern for a son, a husband or some other relative who has taken to the bottle. But few people care about a neighbour.

Quite often relatives take an unprincipled position with respect to the drunkards and rowdies in their families. When a tipsy head of the family shouts, strikes out, and starts a row, after giving up all hope of persuading him to behave, his wife will call the police. But then she will refuse to make a written statement. "Give him a little scare, that'll be enough, but don't take him away." In fact, the police do not have the right to take such a person from his home without a statement from his relatives, so at the critical moment they are powerless. Besides words, they have no other means at their disposal to make the drunken hooligan see reason.

There is another problem, too. Let's say a statement is in fact given: take him, they say, protect the children. Then what? Where will he go? To the sobering-up station, of course. But he still has to be conveyed to the sobering-up station, and in what?

"It's very difficult to send a drunkard to a sobering-up station," says S. Soldatov, an officer in Moscow's Police Precinct Number 48. "Every vehicle assigned to pick up drunks is issued only 20 litres of petrol a day, so by evening it's no longer running. This means that sometimes we can't even pick them up off the street, much less from their flats". . . .

But why, strictly speaking, should the drunkards be transported free of charge using the state's petrol? Wouldn't it be more logical to abolish all allocations, not be concerned about economy here, but make the drunks themselves pay for the transport and the petrol? That would be fair.

So now, when, through the efforts of the Party and the people, drunkenness has been forcefully pushed out of the workplace and off the streets, it has begun hiding in courtyards and flats, where it is very hard to expose. But even when we succeed in doing so, the means for combating the evil itself are insufficient. And how much quiet, "creeping" drunkenness still exists—drunkenness that, although it may go unnoticed for the moment, will inevitably lead to emergencies and tragedies. The disease of alcoholism develops gradually, growing out of the occasional drink, but many of its social consequences are manifested even in the early stages. So let's not ignore them. Even when they occur "at home." . . .

"Society for the Struggle for Sobriety"

An interview by Anatoly Fedorov with Igor Astafyev, Deputy Chairman of the Central Council of the All-Union Society for the Struggle for Sobriety, Moscow home service, 4 May 1987.

Astafyev: The struggle for a sober way of life is one of the basic elements of restructuring. The results of two years' work, including that of the All-Union Society for the Struggle for Sobriety, bring one to the conclusion that a lot—and at the same time little—has been done.

These are the positive trends: consumption of pure alcohol has been reduced by half, the amount of money spent by the population on pure alcohol was down by 10·7 billion rubles last year, as compared with 1985, and the reduction in vodka production alone, it may be stated bluntly, has provided an additional one million tonnes of grain. Crime, road accidents, absenteeism and loss of working time have been reduced by a factor of 1·7.

There has been demographic progress as well. The birth-rate is up, and there has been a fall in the number of deaths. For the first time in the past 10 years, average life expectancy has increased, to 69 years.

Fedorov: The struggle for a sober way of life is a difficult matter, but what problems still remain unsolved?

Astafyev: We have not yet solved the main problem, that is, how to overcome the mentality of so-called "cultured wine consumption." A second serious obstacle to sobriety within our society is our own inconsistency and inconstancy: on the one hand we have a sharp reduction in the number of wine and vodka shops, and of the amount of time and number of days that they are open, but on the other we have a so-called experiment which extends the sale of alcohol in many regions of the country. The Party's aim of a rigorous struggle for a sober way of life is unwavering. All that is needed is for administrative steps to have greater support from educational quarters.

Fedorov: Perhaps it is actually true that the weakening of educational efforts helped the spread of such survivals from the past as the distilling of moonshine?

Astafyev: Yes, that is one of the reasons for the spread of moonshine distilling. If, in the first quarter of this year, in comparison with the same period last year, the reduction in sales of wine and vodka products through the retail network amounted to 35 per cent, then present-day bootleggers have more than compensated for this. Moonshine distillers have enriched themselves by more than two billion rubles—essentially, at the expense of our national income. You understand—a moonshine distiller doesn't exist in isolation. He commits his crimes against society right in front of his family and children, corrupting them in the process.

We have a strong force: 412 primary organizations, composed of almost 14 million members of the society. Our task is to ensure that each of them should not merely be a formal member of the society, but also active in the fight for the sobriety of every Soviet citizen.

Rationing Vodka

Excerpts from an article by T. Boikova, Sovetskaya Rossiya, *27 March 1987.*

The overall level of drunkenness dropped by more than 50 per cent in Kirov Province during the second half of last year.

This was achieved largely by an orders' system. All executives without exception—from the chairman of the local Soviet to the secretary of the province Party committee—diligently call it an "orders' system." But people queuing in shops, in livestock sections, or in factory stores, simply call it "Coupons."

How did this begin? When the people themselves were granted the exclusive right to decide—should there be an orders' system or not—public meetings and assemblies were held in each district, in all communities, at enterprises, on collective farms and state farms. These gatherings made decisions by open ballot, and immediately, they specified how the orders were to be distributed: to whom and in what quantity. Everywhere, alcoholics and "abusers" . . . were, as decided by the meetings, deprived of the right to buy alcohol. People who had undergone a course of treatment for alcoholism, who had returned from a therapy-and-labour rehabilitaton centre or a place of confinement, who had spent time in a medical soberting-up station, who had committed domestic disturbances, or who had been hooligans or violators of labour or public discipline were excluded. In some places pregnant women, young mothers and persons suffering from chronic illnesses were added to the list. At many of the meetings, a number of people publicly refused to take their coupons, decreeing a "dry law" for themselves. But only members of the Temperance Society considered refusal to be mandatory.

Clearly aware of the consequences of the slightest administrative fiat, the organizers tried to eliminate even the hint of any pressure. In short, the remaining people were given the right (the right, let us emphasize, not the command) to buy one or two bottles of alcohol per month (the exact amount varied according to district). . . .

This system is especially effective in small towns, settlements or villages, where everyone knows everyone else by sight. Many villages are managing without any coupons at all. In these places, lists of those who are not to be sold alcohol have been posted up inside the shops themselves. The lists put those prohibited to shame, as you can imagine. But they're very effective! . . .

There were arguments at some of the meetings, but only a handful of individuals complained to the "superiors." The "superiors" wrote prompt but polite replies: "Dear comrades! The decision of the labour collective can be reversed or revised only by the collective itself." The "comrades" scratched their heads, swore, and began to look for a way out of the situation. But they discovered, to their great chagrin, that all the easily accessible loopholes had been closed.

A person can go to a neighbouring province, of course. Or the yellow coupons can be resold. There have been instances in which local "businessmen" buy bottles of vodka and then put them back into circulation. But here the taut mechanism of public control, which because of its newness has not yet grown rusty, usually works. . . .

The results were made evident rather quickly: figures for crime, hooliganism, lawbreaking, traffic accidents, etc. began to creep downward throughout the province. . . .

Early in January a telegram was telephoned throughout the province, including those districts where the coupon system was already in effect: "Increase the sale of alcohol by 12 per cent." After several months of painstaking and laborious organizational and propaganda work involving hundreds of thousands of people, suddenly: "Increase the sale of alcohol." Why? It turns out that over 500,000 litres of locally produced wine which had accumulated in the warehouses of the consumers' cooperatives was beginning to spoil. People had suddenly stopped buying this wine; and not by accident. Under the orders' system, they were buying vodka or high-quality grape wines. The "stunner" [strong red vermouth] was to the taste only of the very people who had been deprived of the right to use orders. Now an effort was being made to salvage the stockpiles of this poison. The telephoned telegram had come from the province Soviet executive committee. It was carrying out an order of the Russian Republic Union of Consumers' Cooperatives.

Do you know what officials in most of the province's districts did when they received this telephoned telegram? They disobeyed it. But it did its work—it sowed the seeds of doubt: what if the next order was made binding?

Coupons for alcohol are, it goes without saying, a compromise intended to shut off the unrestricted flow of alcohol. They are meant to be a forced, temporary measure (let us emphasize this again), as a supplement to education, legal, administrative, medical and other measures for combating drunkenness. This compromise appears to be justified, and, as the Kirovites' experience shows, it is producing results.

Growing Your Own Drugs

From a report by V. Shcherban, Izvestia, *27 June 1986.*

The police have begun a massive operation to uncover secret crops of poppies, and to close off distribution channels for hashish in Central Asia.

Their helicopters and planes are airborne. Police detachments are combing the area on horseback and on foot. State Motor Vehicle Inspectorate posts have been reinforced. Specialists in combating drug addiction have flown to Kara-Kalpakia [Central Asia] where the poison fields have blossomed particularly luxuriantly in recent years.

We were soon standing by the side of a planted field, almost a hectare in size. I was told that even by the most conservative estimates its owners could have an almost six-figure income from it. . . . A representative of the public prosecutor's office drew up a list of charges. The "planter" will have to answer to the law.

"Look," said O. Burov, head of the criminal investigation department of the USSR Ministry of Internal Affairs. "This poppy is already past its prime, although it's still early for that. The growers have learned to regulate the time for blossoming. They obviously noticed what time we flew in last year. In other words, they try to shift the dates so that the crops don't get destroyed. If we had flown in a week later, the poison would have disappeared."

The crop's owner is 96 years old. He came out of his large brick house to meet us, leaning on a cane. He said he was growing the poppies for himself. "Teeth hurt, hands hurt, have to treat them." "So you tend the crops yourself?" "Myself, myself," he nodded.

His whole family (I counted 16 adults) nodded in agreement, affirming the sacred truth of his words. Apparently, the police run into situations like this constantly. The oldest person in the family assumes responsibility for the illegal crop. Like children, old people can get away with a lot. . . .

The more energetically the police fight the evil in this autonomous republic, the more feverishly the processors, or as they are still called locally, "botanists," seek new addresses. Nowadays many of them are off to the Chuya valley where wild hemp grows better.

They aren't just off to the valley, but to all the areas where hemp and poppies are grown as industrial crops on collective farms. They know full well that although these crops are actually guarded, the risk of being caught there is no greater than in the Chuya valley. Why? The law requires people who grow poppies and hemp to participate in guarding the crops. Farms are supposed to assign people to guard duty and build watchtowers in the fields. But it's too much trouble, so they don't bother. Since the fields are scattered throughout the countryside the cost of the guard service is too high. Hemp is grown in such densely populated areas as Krasnodar and Stavropol territories. The number of registered drug addicts is significantly higher in those areas than in the adjacent provinces where hemp is not grown. Wouldn't it be better to bring all the crops together into three or four areas? Guarding them would then be far less expensive. Meanwhile, the police are the only real force in this battle. . . .

"Wild hemp covers a large area in the Chuya valley," says L. Remez, Chairman of the Dzhambul Province Agro-Industrial Committee. "We attack it whenever we can; we cut it, burn it, treat it with herbicides and plough it under. We made all the farms promise to exterminate it. And we created special units to fight it. Over 500 hectares have already been treated. But none of these measures has been very effective."

The job of the police in the valley is both dangerous and difficult. They do night rounds and constantly patrol the railroad. There is constant tension.

"Our real work begins at night," says district inspector Kokchubai Dzheksambayev. "During the day the 'botanists' get their sleep or make hashish in nearby thickets. And at night they come out, like phantoms, with their loot. That's when we're waiting for them."

The police even work on trains, with specially trained dogs. I saw a dog named

Bulka at work. He took a dislike to the baggage of a passenger at Lugovaya Station, desperately scratching at the suitcase with his paws. When they opened it, there were eight kilograms of hashish inside. . . .

Dzheksambayev is in his second year as a district inspector. He replaced a colleague whom the "botanists" ran down with a car, crushing his feet. He told me that "visitors" from the Baltic republics, the Far East and Tomsk had already been caught in his district this season. . . .

More and more young people are falling victim to drug addiction. Teenage addicts who inhale various chemical substances have recently made their appearance. There have been cases of group deaths of children from such poisoning. Their first taste of the syringe and of "joints" (hashish cigarettes) happens in various ways. Sometimes it is simply through curiosity. But what terrible retribution can follow!

"Juvenile drug addicts turn into morons in two years," says N. Borovkova of the USSR Ministry of Public Health. "And drug addiction is much more terrible for girls. This vice also infects social life. The overwhelming majority of these children are educationally neglected."

I am focusing attention on juvenile drug addiction to show what deep roots it has put down. That is why the alarm must be sounded in time. Efforts are needed—major efforts—to close down the distribution channels for narcotics. . . .

Who Gives Them Narcotics?

A letter from I. Sergeyev, Pushkin, nr. Leningrad, Literaturnaya Gazeta, 14 January 1987.

Surely, when it has been so quick and so serious in its effort to root out alcoholism, our government can make an effective stand against the spread of drug addiction among young people? Even within the existing framework of the law the police, the public prosecutor's office and all the legal organs could take far more effective action in this direction, to preserve the young from the pernicious influence of drug addicts. And if additional laws are needed, they should be drawn up and brought into force. The first step is when someone gives a young man or woman some narcotic. Drug dealing and preparation should be regarded as the most heinous crimes against the state. But how do things really stand?

In this letter I shall refer only to facts which I know to be genuine and accurate. They relate to the town of Pushkin, a suburb of Leningrad, where I live.

Groups of drug addicts operate quite literally in the open, feeling that they are invulnerable and unpunishable. By various means they get hold of narcotics, prepare them, then exchange or deal in them. They have very well established information on what, where and from whom to get these drugs. The groups meet in flats, the addresses of which are well known, or else easily obtainable. A year ago a few addicts died from overdoses (Belobokov, Vorontsov and others).

It looks as if it would be quite easy to put a stop to this. However, the regional police department and its divisional inspectors try not to take any notice of the drug addicts, and do not interfere in their "business." Here is an illustrative example. In May last year I detained a certain Pavlenko and his girlfriend in my garden; they were both in a state of narcotic intoxication. I called for the police and asked the duty officer to make a medical examination.

However, these people were immediately released from the regional police station, without being examined, and no further action was taken.

Occasionally some of the more hardened drug addicts do end up in court and get comparatively light terms of imprisonment.

Drug addicts who are first offenders are sent to serve their sentence. No special treatment is provided to cure them, but they are cured by "abstinence." But the routes by which narcotics reach their goal are not closed off. Almost all those who serve a sentence are granted an "indulgence"—Article 62 of the Criminal Code is withdrawn. They are considered to be cured of drug addiction, and when they arrive at their permanent place of residence, they do not register either with the police or with a drug specialist.

There are cases where inveterate, incurable drug addicts have been released from prison before their time. In spring 1985 A. Zuyev, freed before his time, returned to Pushkin. He easily got himself registered and quickly became involved in a totally uncontrolled set-up, not only taking drugs himself but also energetically dealing in them. Finally, in the autumn of 1985 he was re-arrested and tried. But how many lives did he manage to ruin in the months of his freedom?

After they are released, those who have served their sentence are not sent back to the place they formerly lived in, but to different towns in the province (apparently, this is prescribed by some rule). However, practically all of them return to their former place of residence.

Naturally, they resurrect their old ties and acquaintances and start up their old tricks all over again. But what's more, the "veterans" are more refined operators, drawing new people into their circle. Policemen and divisional inspectors are completely uninterested in how former drug offenders live, whether they work, and how groups form around them.

I consider that all measures possible should be urgently taken to protect the rising generation from the terrible infection of drug addiction. However harsh and severe these measures may be, they would be fully justified. After all, if there is no hope of curing the sick, then it is essential to do everything possible to protect the healthy from their influence.

Drug Dealing Leads to Murder

An extract from "White Noose in an Ampule" by A. Vislyayev, Sovetskaya Rossiya, *6 August 1985.*

Today we will discuss several cases that deserve some contemplation from those who don't think the craving for narcotics presents a terrible danger.

A certain Troitsky, a resident of Lyubertsy, came under investigation on suspicion of murder. He needed a fair amount of money to hire a lawyer. Troitsky knew only one method of getting money—peddling narcotics. He sent two of his girlfriends to Central Asia for the "merchandise." After successfully completing their mission the women returned home. But somebody was waiting for them at the airport.

The investigation began, and the case became cluttered with new names and addresses. Police [*militsia*] officers managed to collar a certain Veldanov, also from Lyubertsy.

He was a very cautious person, so he always used his young son to deliver the "goods" to his clients. He also got his wife involved in his shady dealings. Veldanov's favourite amusement was to draw juveniles into drug addiction, and, after the "drug sessions" were over, to debauch them. . . .

Ivanov and Cherenovsky were not yet 25 years old. . . .

They were arrested in Pushkino for trying to sell goods found during a search of their premises. In the course of the investigation, it was ascertained that for the past six months neither of them had worked and that they had got money for food and drink, and most importantly, to buy narcotics, by making the acquaintance of some girls, moving in with them, and then disappearing with their belongings.

But these were the most inoffensive acts that they committed in leading their parasitic way of life. In Baku, where they had gone for narcotics, they attempted murder. It was only by a miracle that the victim survived. But there was no "miracle" in Moscow: while burgling a flat, they killed the woman who lived there.

Nina of Minsk

Excerpts from an article by special correspondent D. Mysyakov and Znamya Yunosti *[Banner of Youth] correspondent P. Yakubovich in* Komsomolskaya Pravda, *9 October 1986.*

We are talking about [a certain] category of [Minsk's] young women. They used to try to remain *incognito*, and if they failed, they vowed they "would never do it again." But as time passed, their timidity vanished. They feel absolutely invulnerable since they aren't violating anything. They ceremoniously exchange greetings with doormen and hail policemen in a familiar and friendly way. In the hotel, bar and restaurant they know everyone and everyone knows them too. For these damsels, there is no such thing as public opinion.

Their "business," as they see it, is no worse than any other, and is in many respects even better. The main advantage is security. . . . At worst, they will be called in to the police station for a warning. They will be shamed and admonished. But they will be released in any case. The problem here is by no means poor work on the part of the police. On the contrary, they deserve good mention. Mikhail Gapanovich, the officer in charge of criminal investigations at the Central Borough Internal Affairs Department, even keeps a special album containing photographs of all the "ladies" without exception. Mikhail can tell you everything there is to know about each and every one of them. But unfortunately, the law is powerless against these "business-women." True, from time to time some reason for serious talking arises. The ladies usually don't work in one place for very long. But as soon as they see the clouds gathering, they quickly get a job. They look for the sort of job where they don't have to strain themselves too much. If possible, they prefer to be officially listed as employed without actually holding a job. . . .

Nina had something that most of her friends did not—her own two-room flat fairly close to the centre of town. Whenever necessary, she "deposited" her school-age son on her neighbour's doorstep. Many of the ladies would take their new friends to her flat to continue the friendships struck up in the restaurant.

Services of another kind were also on offer. Since their guests were usually foreigners, the payment the ladies received from them for their night-time service was in foreign currency. Nina would convert it, retaining a commission. Through an acquaintance from a southern country who was for some reason called Paul although his name was really Mohammed, the enterprising woman bought and sold dollars, marks and kroner.

Nina got her just punishment for maintaining a house of ill repute, procuring girls for prostitution, speculation and violation of currency regulations. The charge brought against her younger friends was far more concise—illegal foreign-currency transactions. The measures applied to put a stop to their activities were also much less severe. A few days after the trial they could be seen once again, back in their usual places. What's more, only a few of those who might have ended up in the dock appeared there. What about the rest? Is there really no way of dealing with them? Will they really be able to continue their shameful trade with impunity like this, bringing greater discredit to our morality than to themselves? . . .

Minsk, by the way, is a relatively lucky city in this respect. The situation in Moscow, Leningrad, Riga and other major centres is far more alarming. . . . Let's admit it: this immoral "business" still exists. For many years now, we have pretended not to notice—not to know a thing about it. It's shameful, and it's not surprising that we keep it quiet. But these women are growing positively impudent. . . .

We do not intend simply to confirm the existence of these "ladies" and the places where they do business. By pooling the efforts of the police and the Young Communist League [*Komsomol*], we are going to rid our society of this pollution.

Strains and Stresses

Housing and Babies

Excerpts from the "Donahue in Russia" programme broadcast on Soviet Television on 14 March 1987.

Donahue: I would like to talk for a moment about family planning. How widely available are information and devices for preventing pregnancy? Are you satisfied with their availability? Why is the abortion rate so high in the Soviet Union? Suddenly I sense silence from this audience. Is it the woman's responsibility here? Are the men involved in solving this problem? Why is the number of abortions so high in the Soviet Union? [To man in audience] Yes, sir?

Man: I can give some professional information, because I am a professor of sociology and in addition to that my field is sexology. The fact is that we are a long way behind in this. This is now being talked about by doctors and demographers: the style of the propaganda is changing, but these subjects, so to speak, are regarded as being delicate in our country, and that's why your question really does provoke a rather sharp reaction. But as far as contraceptive devices are concerned, the situation is quite simply awful. There is a shortage of hormone pills and their quality is not good enough. They are now dealing with this; doctors and demographers are dealing with this. There is a high abortion rate because of the poor standard of contraceptive devices—the rate is much higher than in many other countries, although everyone knows it's a bad thing, because it is hard to think of anything worse than an abortion.

Donahue: Is abortion also provided free in the Soviet Union?

Same man: Yes.

Donahue: Thank you very much for your candour. Is there anyone else who would like to speak on this subject? Yes?

Woman: I would like to answer this question not simply as a woman, but as a specialist. I work in a chemist's shop as a pharmacist. The comrade has just said that things are difficult in our country as far as contraceptive devices are concerned. I would like to disagree. At present there is a wide range and a large amount of propaganda work being carried out amongst boys and girls in the higher classes. I, for example, work in the chemist's shop and can see for myself how many people buy these things. I can't talk about the abortion rate. But as

to whether or not these devices are in demand and are popular, well I can't say that they aren't. They are very much in demand. Both devices manufactured in the Soviet Union and imported ones.
Donahue: Who purchases the contraceptive, the man or the woman?
Same woman: Well, you know, it's chiefly the woman, of course.
Donahue: Does it matter to you if your child starts to be sexually active before marriage? Does that bother you?
Women: No, it does not bother me. [Donahue begins to clap, thereby suggesting that members of the audience in sympathy with this view should also clap; no-one in the audience is heard to clap, perhaps because not everyone has understood Donahue's intention]. Yes, it does bother me. [Some members of the audience clap]. I want my child, my daughter, to be a virgin before her marriage. [Some members of the audience clap, possibly fewer than the previous number]. I am sure that she will be a virgin until she gets married. [One of two members of the audience clap; laughter from the audience].
Donahue: I have noticed that as a rule Moscow families have just one child although, of course, my observation is not based on any scientific analysis. So couples of your age have one child; not all of them, of course, but most of them. And I have also been told that the state encourages families with more than one child, since the birth rate here in Russia is lower than in any of the other republics of the Soviet Union. Are you moved by any feeling of patriotic responsibility towards having two or more children?
Woman: I have two children, and I can't really say whether that is going to be all. Of course, we might have some more. And the state gave us a flat immediately, a two-room flat, within a year, because we had twins. If a family has three children the state immediately provides a three- or four-room flat, and the parents even have the right to choose which rayon in Moscow to live in, and they get a telephone, and masses of benefits of all kinds. They immediately receive help from the order departments of the food shops and Children's World and they get help everywhere. I regard this as a big concession, and for this reason people now consider having at least three children, because housing is in short supply in the Soviet Union.
Donahue: Why, then, are all these families with only one child waiting? Have more babies and you'll get an excellent flat.
Woman: Our American audience might think that we really are embellishing things; because that woman was not absolutely right in what she said. I have three children, and of course I receive benefits. I could describe them in detail for our American audience. But we do have a problem in our family; we live in a communal flat. How can I describe it? Our family, and another family too. We share a kitchen. Perhaps this isn't so typical now; but it really is a problem for our family, and we are going to be waiting for three years, that is the shortest time likely. And we'll see how we get on.
Donahue: Yes. Yes. Our time is coming to an end. Please go ahead.
Woman: I have been married for 12 years, but I only have one child, one child in 12 years. The child is eight years old. It isn't the material side of things that worries us, it's the housing issue. We live just like that woman, in a communal flat; they've already explained to you what that is—it means several families living in one flat. We have only one room. And it is precisely that which is stopping me from having more children, because a new child would grow up to the age of five—the most difficult age—and I still wouldn't be given a flat during that time. I think young families ought to be given flats from some kind of separate waiting list, perhaps. Generally speaking, housing policy ought to be changed a little in our country in

favour of families, the allocation of flats to families, and then families will have more children. I think that this problem can only be solved by means of housing. Everything rests on housing. I have bad housing conditions, and this stops me having more children.

The Truth is Not for Foreigners

D. Kosyrev, *Pravda*, 16 April 1987.

I shall attempt to give an account of some letters from viewers. Many contain questions like these: who allowed an American to try to extract information from Soviet people? And, the main thing, why did they tell him . . . the truth? Here are some lines I remember: "Everything was going well until one woman . . . said she had been on the waiting list for a flat for 10 years and because of that could not have children. Let her wait another 100 years and may she rot for telling an American that. In our country everyone lives in good flats."

Tramps and Hoboes

John-Thor Dahlburg reviews an article by a Soviet reporter who spent six months living as a tramp, Associated Press, *21 February 1987.*

Thousands of people have dropped out of Soviet society to become tramps and hoboes, living on the fringes of the law in freight cars and cemeteries and surviving off odd jobs like berry-picking and lumberjacking, a Soviet weekly reports.

The *exposé* in *Ogonyok* magazine, the result of an undercover investigation by reporter Alexei Lebedev, was in stunning contradiction to official claims that the problems of unemployment and homelessness have been virtually solved in the Soviet Union.

The story, published in the magazine's latest edition, was clearly linked to Mikhail Gorbachov's policy of *glasnost*, that permits wider discussion and debate on selected social issues.

Ogonyok painted a bleak picture of the life led by "many thousands" of vagrants who drift from one corner of the Soviet Union to another in search of food, shelter and part-time work.

Some, it said, have lost all self-respect and the ability to hold a job, and exist by foraging through garbage heaps for bottles they can sell back to stores.

Medical experts have established that tuberculosis and venereal diseases in the Soviet Union are largely spread by the vagrant population, *Ogonyok* said.

It noted that since vagrants do not carry the internal passport required of all Soviet citizens, they cannot receive medical care in state-run clinics. Doctors are often unable to save ailing vagrants because their diseases are too far advanced when they are finally examined, the report said.

"God forbid that the AIDS virus break out among them," *Ogonyok* added.

Soviet officials have said that there are only 20 cases of Acquired Immune Deficiency Syndrome in the Soviet Union, and that all are foreigners.

For six months, Lebedev wrote, he donned old clothes and went on the road in search of the Soviet Union's *bichi* (social outcasts) and *brodyagi* (tramps).

"The geography of the outcast is the whole country," Lebedev wrote. He said that Soviets from the frigid Far North to the Central Asian republics are living without official papers, finding shelter in cellars, attics, boiler rooms, cemeteries, railway carriages and public dumps.

Among the tramps he met, Lebedev wrote, were educated people, a Seventh-Day Adventist minister, a Russian Orthodox clergyman, a Zen Buddhist and members of the Hare Krishna sect.

The vagrants, travelling by rail and on "anything with wheels," slip through the fingers of Soviet authorities because there are employers who are willing to hire them illegally on a part-time basis, the article said.

Those who decide finally to forsake seasonal work as cranberry pickers or woodsmen and take a regular job are often shunned by managers who are reluctant to hire them, the magazine said.

Government officials detain vagrants and beggars in cities, towns and at railway stations to screen them for possible criminal backgrounds, *Ogonyok* said. Legislation authorizes detention of up to a month for purposes of verifying a vagrant's identity.

Officials must provide vagrants referred to them with a state-sanctioned job, the magazine said.

But it said that as soon as a vagrant receives a new passport and a certificate authorizing him for a job, he is often caught up in a bureaucratic tangle and referred from one agency to another in a clear attempt to get rid of him.

Because of all the hassles, some Soviet tramps and hoboes strike out again for the open road, preferring its hardships to bureacratic runarounds and social ostracism, the magazine said.

"I've lived for 15 years without any papers and I'm going to live for 15 more without any problem," one Soviet tramp who gave up attempts to get a regular job was quoted as saying as he cast his newly obtained documents into a hoboes' campfire.

On Non-Workers and Parasites

From a report of the Buro of the Uzbekistan Communist Party Central Committee, Pravda Vostoka, *15 May 1987.*

As a result of [. . .] an irresponsible attitude on the part of local Party, Soviet and economic bodies and the oblast Party and executive committees and their leaders, the number of non-working people is steadily rising. In 1986, only a little more than half of the increase in the able-bodied population was employed or engaged in study. The proportion of non-working people is particularly high in Kumkurgan, Denau, Baysu and Termez regions.

At the same time, the oblast does not use the existing real reserves. It was noted that more than 3,000 people could have been employed through bringing up manpower to full strength; about 1,000 through fulfilling plans for putting production capacities into operation; 2,500 through fuller use of industrial production capacities; 2,000 through raising the industrial shift coefficient to two; a total of 12,000 through developing the construction industry and raising the shift coefficient there to two; and another 15,000 or 20,000 through involving the population in work performed at home, fuller use of working places on state farms and more widespread family contract work.

The law-enforcement and administrative bodies manifest negligence and lack of commitment to take the necessary measures against parasites and those who live on non-labour incomes. There are many among the non-working population who lead a parasitical life.

The oblast Party and executive committees do not pay sufficient attention to relocating surplus population in other regions of the country.

In a resolution adopted in connection with this matter the Buro of the Uzbekistan CP Central Committee found unsatisfactory the work of Surkhandarya oblast Party and executive committees directed towards involving the non-working part of the able-bodied population in socially useful labour. S. M. Mamarasulov, First Secretary of the oblast Party committee, and K. E. Berdyyev, Chairman of the oblast executive committee, were told that their attitude towards resolving this paramount political and social problem was irresponsible. They were warned that if they do not revise their attitude to solving this problem, they will be held strictly responsible to the Party for their failure.

Down and Out in Poland

An underground monthly produced in Wroclaw describes the living conditions of some Poles and the efforts of the author, Jerzy Janoszka, to help the homeless in Wroclaw. The article is based on a speech made by Janoszka at a conference of the Social Movement Towards a Civilization of Love, held in Czestochowa on 17 May 1985. Biuletyn Dolnoslaski, *No. 6 (64), July 1985.*

In his article, Janoszka claims that although the authorities deny homelessness in Poland, more than 500,000 Poles have nowhere to live. He describes his work as a warden at the Blessed Brother Albert Refuge, the only hostel for the homeless in the entire country, run on charitable contributions. Janoszka urges that similar shelters should be set up in all major cities. He describes the problem:

> Who are the homeless? It is not true that homeless people are only alcoholics or degenerates (such is the common opinion, that only such people have no roof over their heads). And even if it were so, such people also deserve help. . . . The people who come to us are exhausted, old, in the last stages of cancer or tuberculosis, people without housing, people without pensions. In these last three years more than 800 people have passed through our centre. We have 50 beds, and 100, if not more, people sleep in them. They sleep on the floor, on chairs, wherever there is some free space.
>
> One man without a home is a former Polish sports champion, a [former] member of the national team, for whom the national anthem was once played and who has been deprived of a pension because disability acquired through sport does not qualify one for a pension. . . . [The homeless] are brought here in ambulances or in militia vans; the doors open, a sick old man is thrown out, the vehicle leaves.
>
> I have been describing the situation of homeless men, but there are about 250,000 homeless women sleeping in cellars and on garbage tips. Recently a woman came to us having spent her entire pregnancy in a cellar, and from the maternity hospital she had to go right back to it. Her baby got a bad [case of]

> pneumonia from the damp and had to go back to the hospital. The woman came to us asking for shelter otherwise she would have had to go back to the cellar. . . . The situation of homeless women in our country is really tragic. A man can still cope, but a woman, once she is pregnant or has suffered a mental breakdown, has to contend with much greater difficulties.
>
> [The Wroclaw shelter] is a wooden shed, on the verge of collapse, with no fire precautions. There are three rooms in which about a hundred people sleep. The staff sleep with them. We have a separate room for people in a very bad state, and I sleep there myself to give immediate aid if necessary. I have learned how to give injections—the Department of Health knows about these illegal practices, but provides no trained aid. I give them antibiotics too, I have learned how. . . . But we do know that the refuge lengthens people's lives because we have some [people] coming in who are being eaten alive by worms; it is really tragic.
>
> If you should ever come to Wroclaw, there is a wooden shed on Lotnicza Street. I invite you to come and look. It has to be seen.

Janoszka's invitation was taken up by the editors of *Biuletyn Dolnoslaski* who reported as follows.

> We did visit the Brother Albert Refuge. People do, indeed, live in nightmarish conditions there; darkened, sooty walls, stink, overcrowding, hopelessness. The beds are pushed so close together that one can hardly get through. The people lying on them were like us once, they believed that they could take care of their lives, that the world would do them no harm; they were young, strong, they could cope. Today they are the losers, they are forgotten, they wait for death as a delivery. And yet, they very badly want to live. We owe them our solidarity, they must feel our concern, they must know that they count for us.
>
> We appeal to doctors in Wroclaw (and not only there) to devote at least an hour a month to helping these poorest of the poor. We need skilled help to renovate the shelter (the shed really is falling apart). We need money and medicines (above all pain killers). We need hypodermic syringes, food, washing powder and so on. All gifts should be sent directly to the shelter (103 Lotnicza Street).

"Our Work is Our Strength!"

In 1985 the workers of the Sofia Locomotive Factory addressed an underground appeal to the working people of Bulgaria. The extracts below are translated from the French journal, La Nouvelle Alternative, *No. 1, April 1986.*

Young men and women!

The present regime in our country is preparing a gloomy future for you. The gates of universities and colleges are closed to the children of the people, open only to the sons and grandsons of the influential—the Party aristocracy. And even if, by hard work, the most gifted children of the people are successful in getting a higher education, they are doomed either to lead the miserable life of a petty official or to be humiliated as the lackey of some ungifted upstart. Every day the number of those forced to accept jobs below the standard of their qualifications, below their potential, grows. The only way to escape this fate is to have the support of the Party aristocracy.

The education reform has one single aim: to distance you, the youth of our nation, from the cushy, comfortable jobs reserved for the offspring of the privileged. From the classroom onwards they are preparing you to become cheap, docile labour. In the new schools science teaching is already being neglected in favour of studying Marxism–Leninism. Even history and literature lessons are turned into propaganda sessions. The crude dogma of the Party is imposed on you as if it were an exact science, and the imbecilic remarks of insignificant people are presented as prophetic utterances. The past is distorted and the present falsified. They are trying to deform your minds, to prevent you from acquiring the faculty of judgement. Isn't it for exactly the same reason that every year you are torn from the classroom and sent for a month or two to the so-called TKZC [collective farms] to help the peasants?

Young men, young women of the nation, struggle for your future; you have a sacred right to a proper education which will give you the chance to rise to positions of responsibility; do not let the Party aristocracy decide your destiny for you, don't let them make you slaves to their offspring. Stop learning that idiotic Marxist ideology and prepare yourselves instead for life by studying on your own, by helping each other in a spirit of solidarity.

Our oppressors will fall, and then your knowledge will find a vast area of application. Refuse the gloomy future they are preparing for you, refuse to be exploited!

Workers!

We must not let ourselves be exploited any more! We all know that today's "record production figures" will become tomorrow's obligatory norms.

This has to stop! Let us stop fulfilling the norms! The way work is now organized, the more eagerly we work the more we impoverish ourselves, and the more we enrich our exploiters.

That is why we must no longer work hard for nothing. Let this be our response to a system that relies on our manpower in order to exist. Let us be united in our efforts to get better living conditions. Only resistance, with no submission, can force the authorities to give in. Our brother workers in Poland have shown us the way.

In order to neutralize the passive resistance of our working class, the government has brought in workers from abroad. Right now 5,000 Vietnamese work in our factories, at our sites. We have nothing against these poor, starving wretches, but instead of trying to force us to work through fear of unemployment, the government would do better to improve our living and working conditions. Meanwhile, we are still the decisive element in production. Without us, nothing can be produced, and we must continue our struggle until the final victory.

Peasants!

Leave the countryside, stop working in the TKZC and DZC [state farms] where you are treated like slaves, where you are exploited and shamelessly robbed. Sell the produce from your personal allotments directly to the consumers. Don't sell anything to the state any more. You are the first people it robs paying you a pittance for the fruits of your labour, and then it cheats you, reselling it at a high price.

The passive resistance which you have carried on for dozens of years brings its rewards. This regime, established by force, is falling apart. You must hold on for just a bit longer to see it crumble for once and for all.

Faced with the success of your passive resistance, the authorities have resorted more and more to a cunning practice: in order to replace you, they appeal to categories of the population who have only a feeble class consciousness (gypsies, for example, among others); as for work in the fields (sowing, harvesting, etc.) they use compulsory labour brigades—schoolchildren, students, soldiers, office workers and even pensioners come and work for nothing against their will. Be indulgent towards these people, but make them understand that the Bulgarian peasant doesn't need their "help," that he is quite capable of cultivating his land all on his own and of feeding the people just as he has done for centuries, but that he refuses to be exploited. Explain to them that in agreeing to act as strike breakers they are betraying the interests of the Bulgarian peasantry, and that they would do better minding their own business rather than interfering in yours.

Officials, office workers!

It isn't your fault that the most gloomy, dirty work within our society falls to your lot. The Party aristocracy have made you the tools of their oppression and exploitation of the working people. But you are no less victims of injustice and exploitation than we are. Your pitiful salaries and your precarious existence do not justify the efforts your masters demand from you.

Come on then, believe us, put no more effort into executing your orders, stop being cruelly inflexible towards poor, defenceless people, and help them instead, protect them when the weight of injustice burdens them.

Let those who abuse their power in favour of the tyrants know that they will earn the just anger of the people. We, the democratic workers, have nothing but contempt for such unworthy people!

The small clique of Party pundits subjects the working people to oppression and exploitation, unrivalled in the past. Despite our exhausting work, systematic price rises reduce our living standards more and more. To provide properly for the needs of our families we need 1,000 leva a month, not just the 200–300 which they allot to us.

Ground down by need, there are many people who have to take the risk of breaking the law in order to get enough to live on. In the past few years delinquency has become far more common. Will the Bulgarian, known in the past for his honesty and hard work, suddenly become a thief and a good-for-nothing? What is certain is that there's no lack of examples among the Party big shots, even at the highest level, who use their power to heap up a fortune and get rich. Those are the real thieves and speculators. And so one can't help asking: if he's cheated and deprived by such wrongdoers, does the ordinary worker have a right to use illegal means to recover what belongs to him by rights, which has been stolen from him by criminals?

We reckon that at this gloomy juncture the Bulgarian worker has an incontestable moral right to secure his own survival by all possible means.

Robbing the robbers has always been moral and just. We are convinced that the democratic society of the future will agree to revise all sentences passed for deeds such as embezzlement, diversion of funds and other crimes, if these deeds were committed for the benefit of the public good, and if their author can prove that his monthly revenue does not exceed 1,000 levas.

Such a deed cannot be called a crime when it is committed in an extremely precarious situation. Can there be a greater hardship than the sort of privation, hunger and poverty to which the nation is subjected nowadays?

Bulgarians!

These days the Bulgarian Communist Party aristocracy lives in total isolation from the people; they go to exclusive shops where they can get a wide variety of high quality, inexpensive goods. The foodstuffs sold there are specially prepared to contain nothing carcinogenic. They have exclusive houses, private clubs, seaside resort homes, rest homes, hospitals and even their own cemeteries. As for their children, they study at special schools, and university places are reserved for them by priority.

The present regime usurps the title of a workers' state; it has confiscated all freedom from the workers; all legal resistance to injustice is rendered impossible.

The only thing that we are authorized to do is to work: to work without complaining, to work in conditions of poverty, slavery and lies.

It is off the labourers, the peasants, the clerks, the Bulgarian workers in general that the exploiters live and grow fat. It is we who feed them, clothe them, build their palaces and villas where they loll about like emperors. It is we who earn the money that they squander on banquets, orgies and trips abroad, not to mention the high salaries they award themselves which they hoard in banks here or abroad—they have always owed it all to us. We have become their lackeys since to enjoy all these benefits they condemn us to live a wretched existence. We are only aware of a tenth of the fruits of our labour, and we cannot even be certain of having enough for tomorrow, while their livelihood, and that of their children and grandchildren is assured for at least a century.

But the force we represent is greater than that of our oppressors.

It is time for all of us to believe it. It is time to understand that our salvation is in our own hands.

Stop working, and the parasites will fall! The sooner we put a stop to this economic mechanism of oppression and exploitation, the sooner will strike the hour of freedom and salvation for our people.

Our work is our strength!

We the workers of the Sofia railway factory call upon all our brothers, on all the working people of Bulgaria, to think about the need to act, so that every one of us, by the force of his strength, and all of us together, may take on the great task of public salvation.

Come, brothers, let's not wait any longer! The time has come for the people to be heard. Let all those who want the public good join us! Read, copy and distribute this appeal! Our cause is just, we shall be triumphant!

For the Initiative Committee, Dimitrov.

Waiting for a Roof, a Bed and Medicines

22 Years on Waiting List

The population of the Soviet republic of Tadzhikistan, the majority of whom are Muslims, has grown rapidly. Sixty-three years ago it totalled 595,000; today it has risen to over 4·8 million. The capital city of Dushanbe, which grew from nothing more than a village, now numbers 583,000 inhabitants, more than a third of whom live in crowded slums.

The Soviet journal Ogonyok, *No. 14, April 1987, carried a report by Eduard Yodkovskii.*

Accompanied by Viktor Konstantinovich Cheremushkin, Vice-President of the Dushanbe city council, I set off for Nazym Hikmet Street in the centre of town, next to the ultra-modern Hotel Tadzhikistan. The tumble-down, dilapidated houses and clay huts stand out like warts on the face of Dushanbe . . . . I enter house No. 81, the home of T. I. Zalmanova, a nurse at City Hospital No. 1. A dull little window hardly lets any light into the two adjoining rooms, where nine people live in a space of 28 square metres. "The regional executive committee tells me 'Go and live where you like, keep writing to us!' But where can I go? I've already been on the waiting list for 22 years!"

"We'll move you this year, before the October holiday . . .," says Viktor Konstantinovich, to comfort the weeping woman. "But they've said that before, they say that every year!"

Until recently 67 families lived in the clay huts on Nazym Hikmet Street, of whom 10 still remain. It has not been possible to resettle them because the city council was counting on getting 245,000 square metres of housing space, but got only 195,000. Every time the annual plan for new housing is not fulfilled, human lives are badly affected. Because the 1986 plan provided for less housing than the 1985 plan, and because the housing plan was not fulfilled by almost a third, about 9,000 people didn't get their new homes, including nurse Zalmanova's family . . . .

Yodkovskii describes the city council's reception centre for housing inquiries.

I spent a few evenings at public reception sessions held by Cheremushkin—an energetic man, promoted to the difficult position of Vice-President of the Dushanbe city council responsible for housing.

"There's a curious phenomenon here," he said, smiling youthfully. "If I am reminded by telephone about a particular flat, there's almost always some violation of the law behind it. People with a clear conscience who are getting their flat legally have no reason to make superfluous calls to the Vice-President."

People of all kinds come to his reception sessions. War heroes, their chests decorated with medals (there are 811 veterans of the Second World War still waiting for housing), and young people, including the occasional dizzy single mother; senile old ladies supported by their grandchildren, and people who have had a few drinks to steel themselves before coming to make complaints.

On the list of appointments today was Svetlana Ulko, coming to see about "getting material aid." (Incidentally, are many people aware of the following remarkable, wonderful rule: every Soviet citizen who finds himself, not by his own choice, without any money, can turn for help to his executive committee, wherever he is registered to live, where he will immediately be given 30 rubles?). But 20-year old Svetlana's situation was quite impossible. She had left her husband and returned from Pskov with two children, but her father had refused to give his permission for her to re-register at his address. Then some kind people had advised her to turn to Cheremushkin.

He had a look at her passport—there was a registration stamp for an address at a hostel on Nakhimov Street. With the precision of a psychologist, he asked her: "How much did you have to pay for this stamp?"

After some hesitation, Svetlana admitted that the passport official Shura had demanded 100 rubles, and had got them; but at the hostel she had been advised not to push it, or the deception would come to light. "Now write a statement about it," said Cheremushkin firmly, handing her some paper and a pen. The prosecutor's investigator, Muhammed Badalov, was called immediately. He explained to Svetlana that if she made a willing confession, she would be free of criminal responsibility as a bribe-giver, but that the bribe-taking passport official would be punished by the full force of the law. "She shared it with the head of the passport department, did she? He'll have to answer for it as well, then."

The Consumer Wants to Know

Extracts from readers' letters sent to Literaturnaya Gazeta, *14 January 1987, in reply to an article entitled "A Separate Flat for Each Family," 24 September 1986.*

. . . "In our little town there are several queues for housing: the general one (which doesn't move at all; the people at the front of it registered in 1960); the privileged queue (which moves at about the same pace—those first in line have been there since 1964). The privileged queue consists of war veterans, veterans of labour, sick people and large families. The third queue, consisting of 64 people, began in 1980, and is for Second World War invalids. Usually about four to five flats are allocated to it annually. There are other queues as well: for those on military service, but transferred to the reserve, for teachers and doctors, and *militia* (police) employees. All these queues move slowly, although houses are constantly being handed over, and there is always someone moving into a new flat without any queuing. And these aren't people moving from crowded communal flats, but from separate, parental flats, leaving lots of space for their mum and dad. Or else it's the other way around: the domineering parents assign their old flat to their children, and move into a new one of their own. In 1985, *Mosoblispolkom* drew up and issued its rules for registration of citizens in need of better living conditions, and for the allocation of housing. In these rules there is also a list of people with foremost priority. The authorities (and also their secretaries and chauffeurs, whom they patronize at the expense of those queuing) are not on this list . . ." (N. Shokhen, Stupino.)

Providing a comparable example, construction worker I. Lebedev of Gorky writes: "In our town a lot of housing is being built. As a result, the housing problem is losing its edge, but is assuming particular intensity. In the first place this intensity is really caused by injustice in allocation of the housing."

So what's the way out? *Glasnost*! Everyone uses the word without exception. "Complete, all-embracing *glasnost*, that wouldn't allow even one single flat to be hidden." (I. Lebedev). "Justice is not afraid of *glasnost*." (A. Zhuchkov, Pushkino, Moscow oblast). "There is an almost complete lack of information on housing matters at the regional executive committees and housing registration and allocation departments. How fast is the queue moving? Who will get a flat next year? Or a year later? When will such and such a house actually be vacated? There are dozens of questions, hundreds! And they result in a lot of talk, chatter and gossip." (The Maximov family, Moscow).

And here is a suggestion: "Lists should be posted not only of those queuing, but also of those who have received housing, and also a bulletin should be published once a year (listing the queue, giving dates for arranging registration, assignment of flats for the planned year, and privileges applying to particular queuers)." "A bulletin of registration and allocation of housing space must be published, in which a list of those in need is given, as well as complete information on the settlement of newly constructed houses, and also of vacated flats, data for the year and for the Five-Year Plan period on prospects for housing and construction. Such a bulletin would provide a reflection of social justice." (A. Gryazev, Krasnodar). "There should be a full, annual review of housing allocated, and its results should be published in the local press." (A. Mozgovoy, Saratov).

A question for those in charge of local authorities, arising from the letters: what changes are you planning to introduce in the near future to the system of control over the allocation of flats, to stop flats from being squandered?

A second lot of letters concentrates on communal flats. "What is one supposed to do if one lives in a communal flat with several neighbours, where the living space for one member of the family is bigger than the norm? They don't put us in the queue." (V. Vigirich, G. Larkina, Moscow oblast). "A large number of native Leningrad inhabitants still live in communal flats. And as we have realized, in the near future there's no light at the end of the tunnel for us. In any case, in reply to the question of the Civil War veteran's widow, T. A. Simbirtseva, the city's chief architect, G. N. Buldakov, said officially: by the year 2000 all families will live in separate flats.[1] And it never occurred to Comrade Buldakov that neither Comrade Simbirtseva nor many others will live to see the year 2000. Isn't it blasphemous to speak to old people like that?" (S. Rozinova, Leningrad.)

Readers are concerned that a large number of rooms (and even flats) are empty, but that the registration of this unoccupied space is badly arranged, and that no one is seriously involved in its systematic reallocation. As a result, in Leningrad, where in the central areas of town about 8,000 rooms are empty in large communal flats (the greater number of these are long term lets), a construction worker and his wife are being placed in a vacated flat, 10 square metres in size, (the kitchen is 5·5 square metres). And this did not happen 10 years ago, but in 1984, i.e. after the RFSFR Housing Code was issued, in which new, modern principles of housing allocation were set out. And in which it is clearly stated that a couple cannot be settled in a room 10 metres square. This is what those whose living space has been reduced are asking: what exactly can their families now expect?

And so the second question is: how exactly do the specialists envisage the process of transferring the inhabitants of communal flats into separate ones?

There are two other questions related to this one: can one consider a flat in which several family members of different generations are living to be separate? (V. Bobylev, Lyubertsii, Moscow oblast.) And what are single people supposed to do, who for one reason or another don't have a family? (G. Shkvarkov, Leningrad oblast.)

The cooperative flat: "Here's something worth considering in the plan for social justice. It is not enough that in the usual housing-office blocks the flats are free, and their inhabitants don't even have to bother about the upkeep of the entrances or roof. But the owners of cooperative housing, for which they have paid out thousands, have nowhere to turn to get it repaired. Everything is done 'on the side,' and all for big money. Thus, the cooperative is a deep abyss into

[1] *Leningradskii Rabochii*, 18 April 1986.

which you fall, by the nature of the thing, for the rest of your life. What sort of social justice is that?" (N. Shapchenko, Alma-Ata.)

Operation "Five-Storey Blocks of Flats"

In six Soviet cities an experiment has begun to reconstruct five-storey blocks of flats built in the early 1960s. The following excerpts are taken from an article by V. Shcherban in Izvestia, *15 October 1986.*

. . . The delight that the residents [of five-storey blocks of flats] experience upon moving into their "dream flats," with their cramped kitchens and their narrow hallways and entrances, like mountain passes where two people cannot get past each other without brushing shoulders, is long since past. One day a report got into the press stating that all the first examples of housing built using the assembly-line method were to be razed. And almost immediately newspaper editors and radio and television stations began receiving letters in which residents boldly wrote "We support the proposal!!!!" Meanwhile, the designers continue to claim that most of the buildings have held up well in terms of their physical condition. . . . [Even so,] residents are plagued by poor sound and heat insulation, constant leaks and breezes; tiny bathrooms in which lavatories were installed as well are also the subject of universal complaints.

It now appears that a solution has been found for renovating the blocks of flats. . . .

For the time being, this is being done as an experiment. And its objectives are rather modest. But the main reason why it has been undertaken is to ensure that, following renovation, flats in the five-storey residential buildings should be in no way inferior to housing in third-generation buildings, with the possible exception of ceiling height. City boroughs made up of these buildings will become outwardly more attractive.

Krasnodar is already prepared for the experiment. Blueprints for renovation in Kalinin have been approved. Work will get under way soon in Moscow, Minsk, Vorkuta and Leningrad. All the cities are making arrangements to relocate people from the five-storey buildings that have been selected. The experiment will reveal all the pluses and minuses of the commendable undertaking in two years' time. . . .

As the architects see it, after the reconstruction the residents themselves will choose where to live—either in the renovated flats or in new ones. And if some choose the latter option, it will no doubt be possible to turn some of the reconstructed five-storey blocks of flats over to cooperatives and young people's housing complexes. . . .

Housing Prospects in Poland

Summary of an article which appeared in the Polish Communist Party weekly, Polityka, *24 January 1987.*

Poland is facing such a severe housing shortage nationwide that the crisis is threatening to spark off new social tension among young people who have to wait years to move out of their parents' home, *Polityka* reported.

In a nation where three million people are waiting for new homes, according to official statistics, said *Polityka*, only 127,000 new flats were built last year—5,500 less than in 1985.

It is said that there was no prospect of improvement this year because of chaos in the state-run building industry and poor economic performance.

Observers noted that 267,000 weddings were recorded last year, indicating that the housing shortage is forcing more than half the nation's newly-weds to live with their parents in overcrowded accommodation.

Polityka said that 29 of the country's 49 provinces were unable to meet their 1986 housing construction quotas; the capital, Warsaw, was worst hit.

"There is no need to convince anybody what non-fulfilment of the housing construction plan means in social, political and economic terms, and what kinds of conflicts, dramas and tensions it arouses," *Polityka* said.

The official Polish media have reported that nowadays it is "normal" to wait at least 15 years for a new flat, and that in some areas the "average" wait is as long as 25 years.

Alfred Miodowicz, leader of the Communist Party-controlled unions that replaced the outlawed Solidarity labour union, went so far as to warn last year that young people in Poland could revolt unless the situation is remedied.

Noting that the best year in housing construction was 1978, during the rule of then Communist Party leader Edward Gierek, *Polityka* said that a steady decline had set in since his removal in 1980.

"Despite various efforts and programmes, fewer and fewer flats are being built," said *Polityka*. "It seems that housing construction has been hit by an incurable disease."

Polityka said that the "disastrous" performance in housing construction, caused by a lack of hard currency, manpower and building materials, was a reflection of the state of the economy.

The paper listed some of the key items of which the building industry is desperately short to illustrate its point: five million couplers for cast iron pipes, 300 kilometres (190 miles) of sewage piping, 200 kilometres (120 miles) of water piping, and 100,000 bathroom components.

Polityka said that an additional problem was caused by the fact that about 80 per cent of builders had returned to their homes in rural areas and had given up their city jobs for more lucrative work as farmers.

Punishing Old Age

Yurii Makartsev in Sobesednik, *No. 48, November 1986.*

In 1941, only 200,000 people received old-age pensions in our country. By 1961 the figure had risen to 5·2 million, by 1976 to 29·4 million, by 1981 to 34 million and by 1986 to nearly 40 million. . . .

As a result of our country's declining birth rate, the proportion of people aged 60 and older in 1975 stood at 13·3 per cent. In some areas—rural Pskov oblast, for example—the total amounted to 22·5 per cent of the overall population. An unexpectedly large number! The surprising thing is that old age has developed an intricate social structure. And we have only approximate knowledge, a rough outline, of its economic, social and moral dimensions. Even M. Ya. Sonin and A. A. Dyskin, who have written what I consider to be the most detailed work on the subject—"The Elderly Person in the Family and Society" [*Pozhiloi chelovek v semye i obshchestve*], published in 1984—were working with 10-year-old data.

When I contacted the relevant department of the USSR Central Statistical Administration and asked them to provide me with more recent data for my research, I was refused: the figures are not usually made available, I was told. "Why is that?" I asked. "It's not done," I was told. But if you want to know why, I can tell you myself.

One day my neighbour, a doctor by profession, came to my flat to call the emergency medical squad for her 70-year-old mother. In giving her mother's details on the phone, she lowered the patient's age to 50. She later explained: "Before coming out to assist an old lady, the ambulance might take care of other calls first. I used to work for the emergency squad myself and I know its procedures. The staff are held strictly accountable for failing to respond in time to a call involving a young patient."

I remembered this sad confession while paying a visit to my aunt. There she lay, pale and quite alone, on the couch, crying. "Where does it hurt?" I asked in alarm. "Everywhere," she replied. "And why are you crying?" She answered: "I barely managed to drag myself to the housing estate polyclinic. I waited in line. And then the doctor said, 'What are you doing here? I'm not even going to have time to examine the younger patients!'." . . .

Apparently, the ministries and departments responsible for the social situation of pensioners and old people have a stake in keeping the aforementioned data unavailable. Social norms for old people either haven't been worked out in our country or are lagging behind its present achievements. They do a poor job of measuring up to our concepts of humanity, philanthropy and charity. In withholding these data under the pretext of "state expediency"—as if to say "What will other countries think of us?"—these ministries and departments are in fact pursuing a different objective: they are shielding themselves from public criticism. . . .

For many elderly and very old people, pension-based living conditions do not meet current conceptions of social justice. I think *Sobesednik*'s readers will agree with me. As a result of the effects of the war and the difference in longevity between men and women, there are a good many single elderly women living out their lives in our country. Here are some typical features of their home life, especially in rural areas: old worn-out furniture, a refrigerator that has long outlived its natural life, a 20-year-old television. The old women wear their old clothing to threads.

In the shops they are pushed aside by pensioners holding coupon books entitling them to supplementary privileges. Can it be that our present public capabilities are so meagre that we must completely close our eyes to the way these old women live? Let's think whether we could pay at least some of them an additional 13th pension once a year. And provide others with occasional assistance in the form of a free coat, warm boots, a television, a refrigerator and so on, as if to say "this is for you, grandmother, from people who respect old age."

Unfortunately, the concept of respect for old age has yet to find its place in our restructuring efforts. . . .

Giving Birth in Tadzhikistan

Excerpts from "Extraordinary Event," by N. Kozlova, Kommunist Tadzhikistana, *25 January 1987.*

If you were to try to describe what you are likely to see at the maternity department of Tursunzade rayon hospital, you would be lost for words. It is frightening that such things are possible in the present day. As E. Babayeva, Chief Sanitary Inspector of Tursunzade rayon puts it, "At times when I look at all this, I want to cry."

The outer door leads straight into a small, dingy room, where the sheets are black and cobwebs hang in the corners. The improvised curtain made of torn oilcloth flaps in the cold wind which rushes in. Behind it old bedsteads and cramped folding beds stand close together. Babies are crying, someone is groaning, someone is shouting. As the babies cry, you can also hear water dripping into a dirty bowl from a leaky pipe along the ceiling. "This is what we call the first maternity ward," the doctors say bitterly.

The babies lie in a tiny room—two to a cot, which is strictly prohibited. Nearby stands a basin full of dirty nappies. The patients were recently transferred here from the building of the sanitary and epidemiological department, where sick pregnant women used to be kept. They were transferred from there because the drain had burst. This drain runs right down the middle of the ward (for some unknown reason, it was designed like that). The breakdown of the drain was not unexpected, as the system has been problematic since time immemorial. The rayon sanitary and epidemiological department has closed and reopened this ward seven times during the last year alone. [There are no proper lavatories or washing facilities.]

Lately, five commissions of various degrees of importance have visited this place. Before their arrival, the doctors were told to move some things together, separate others, or to hide something else in the corner—simply pathetic. Who could be satisfied like that?

The rayon central hospital was constructed in stages at various times: in the 1930s, 40s and 50s, and no "cosmetic" measures can hide the real state of affairs. A report sent by the rayon sanitary and epidemiological department to the chairman of the City Executive Committee and the head of the Sanitary and Epidemiological Directorate of Tadzhikistan's Ministry of Health noted that the maternity department of the rayon central hospital was put into service in an unfinished state, without its permission. Nevertheless, the maternity department was opened.

The difficulties at the maternity department, the only one in the whole rayon, are not a recent problem. Over the years only the thickness of the files containing instructions for the sanitary inspectors has changed. Of 63 medical workers on the staff of the department, 29 received various punishments last year; this year the sanitary and epidemiological department has already compiled 11 reports on the state of affairs at the maternity department; overcrowding is a particularly acute problem.

Because of the shortage of essential laundry, linen for mothers and babies is washed with all the other patients' bedding. It comes back from the laundry damp, and is dried wherever possible: in the street, on radiators, etc., and then it is deemed to be "sterile." Despite the funds allocated by the City Executive Committee, according to F. Abdullayev, deputy chief physician of the therapeutical department of the hospital, there is a shortage of pillows, mattresses, babies' night clothes and towels. [The Research Institute for the Protection of Motherhood and Childhood, established in November 1985, has issued instructions to the hospital, but "not a single one of the recommendations has been implemented. They remain on paper." A commission from the institute went to Tursunzade, accompanied by K. Abdushukurova, Deputy Minister of Health; she examined the chaos at the maternity department and left without waiting for the commission's conclusions.]

"Bring-Your-Own-Beds" Hospital

Extracts from an article by Marian Butrym, Zycie Warszawy, *31 January–1 February 1987.*

In this article I render tribute to the doctors of the Collective District Hospital of Lublin, who have announced to their patients that yes, indeed, they will receive them at their department, on condition that they bring their own beds with them.

This severe but sincere demand, proposed in a spirit of humanity, marks the latest and—let's not deceive ourselves—giant step in the process of educating the patients. The small step taken by the doctors of Lublin is still a giant step for mankind, showing dedication to the interests of the individual for the sake of the Great Cause of Medicine.

New ideas always have teething problems; not everyone understands what stakes they're playing for. There are even some who—shame to say—will start insulting the doctors, laughing at them or making ironical remarks, suggesting for instance that the doctors should try putting themselves into hospital beds, even in the special department. . . .

A sick person must know full well that being admitted to hospital is conditional not only upon bringing his own bed, but also upon bringing a set of scalpels, oxygen canisters, splints, syringes, rubber boots and gloves, hempen fibre, needles and thread, candles, bandages, stretchers, spatulas, or any other medical accessories. In nine out of 10 cases the potential patient immediately feels better and withdraws from the idea of going into hospital.

Of course, the idea of the doctors of Lublin still has its shortcomings. It doesn't envisage, for example, any reductions or mitigations for the impoverished; for not everyone can produce his own sheets, mattresses stuffed with this year's hay, or a scalpel sharpener.

In a Polish Hospital

Extracts from an unsigned article which appeared in the Polish bi-monthly Obraz, *No. 8/9, August–September 1986, published in Szczecin.*

The writer befriends a doctor in an unnamed hospital, and is told:

"This place brings to mind anything but a hospital. It looks like a cross between a prison and a government office. A sinister, ancient building, walls painted greenish-grey, a stink of chlorine and bad cooking, and hallways filled with people in winter coats, pyjamas, and white coats (we can tell visitors from patients and employees by their clothing.)"

The place is dirty, humid, and in one of the wards, passing among cabinets and medical equipment moved into the hall, we stumble onto a painter in his smock, with a ladder and pots of paint. The ward is being renovated: drafty air, the smell of drying paint, and in the midst of it all, they are trying to heal people . . . .

Patients are put everywhere. In rooms and hallways, in spaces originally planned to serve other purposes. The international norm is 12 square metres per patient, but the Polish Ministry of Health has reduced it to six square metres. In fact, patients are crammed into a space no greater than 3–4 square metres, a state of affairs that encourages, among other things, the spread of hospital-induced infections; there can be no question of comfort during convalescence or, more tragic still, during the process of dying.

"The conditions are such," says my doctor friend, "that most hospital patients should be paid danger money for putting up with them; they are harmful to health and life. Can you imagine what would happen here in case of a fire?" Indeed, we are looking down the corridor of a ward which is not being renovated but is still thickly stuffed with extra beds, leaving only a narrow passage.

Once a friend of mine was late for an appointment in a hospital, as a result of which he did not get the bed he had been promised but was placed in a hallway between two old men, one of whom snored and stank, while the other was dying. This was a doubly difficult position to be in, both physically and morally. Theoretically (but only theoretically) the problem of the smelly old man was easier to solve, it would have been enough to wash him or persuade him to wash himself. The problem lay in the fact that it was difficult to get into the bathroom, the space itself was filthy, the only water available was cold, with only one shower working (cold) and two washbasins. My friend suffered a much more serious dilemma in dealing with the dying old man. How should one behave? Read, hide one's head under the pillow, pray? Normal life went on in the hallway. The patients read, slept, had visitors, and the old man kept on dying.

Even hospital personnel, hardened by such conditions, are shocked when patients die in public and are then put on to trolleys in full view of everyone to be carted away to wherever space is available.

Depending on the quality of the hospital and the kind of disease or operation, the bribes range from 15–30,000 zlotys. This is what one hears, anyway. And even if this does not hold true for all hospitals and certainly not for all medical practices, there is quite a plausible story that made the rounds after the parliamentary elections, which was told to me by an employee of the health service. On 13 October [1985] patients who showed up for a urine test were met on one side of the room by a glass jar and on the other by a ballot box. The ward nurse, who was also a "regime nurse," brought the patient to both containers in turn, explaining that a patient who was being cured for free should at the very least give his vote to the state. One of the patients then disclosed how free his treatment was (a bribe of 50,000 zlotys), which threw a pall over the voting procedure in the hospital.

Generally speaking, patients do not boast of the bribes they pay, for no one knows when and to whom he might have to pay. For instance, the grandmother of one of my acquaintances broke her hip bone. After being taken to hospital, she was put in a plaster cast for three months. This was rather startling, because this kind of break was normally corrected with a steel pin. According to the hospital, there was a shortage of pins, and the grandmother would have to remain crippled for the rest of her life. Without much ado, her family put together an attractive package of coffee and cognac, added 20,000 zlotys as further encouragement and, by this simple means, quickly secured an operation for the grandmother and her full return to health. . . .

The hospitals are in no way sterile. There is a shortage of cleaning equipment, except for the traditional mop and bucket—the best way of spreading germs [if there is no disinfectant]. There are no sterilization chambers. Frequently, hospitals lack their own laundries. The orderlies push trolleys with dirty laundry down the same corridors along which other orderlies bring along the food trays and nurses transport the sick and the dead. . . . Often operating theatres open almost straight on the corridor, so that post-operative infections are no rarity.

In this madhouse—or so it appears to outsiders—sick people are being treated. The first question to arise is: with what?

"To a large extent," a doctor tells me, "we take advantage of drugs sent from abroad, either as charitable contributions or purchased by the Ministry of Health. I am speaking here of drugs that actually work, since we have enough drugs at our disposal that are not easily absorbed, not very effective, or with too many side effects. Or else we use placebos."

Thus an imaginative doctor ransacks gift packages and sends requests to the Ministry of Health for specific drug imports. Quite often drugs are imported for "dead souls," patients who have already been cured or almost cured, because in this way a doctor can continue to prescribe the drug or, under more favourable circumstances, create a personal stockpile. These are necessary either for the hospital's own use or for informal exchanges among hospitals. Few people realize this, but hospitals are great markets for bartering medicines. This is the noblest form of black market in Poland. For a specific drug one can obtain another drug or medical advice or a diagnostic investigation. . . .

My medical friend told me: "I spend 10–15 per cent of my time with my patients. The rest of the day is spent on administrative tasks, telephone calls, flattery, barter, trade, trips to town. In other words, I [have to] organize my work."

This is a shameful situation. Hospitals lack medicines. It is like time in field stations. . . . In 1984, 34·6 per cent of all drugs listed on an already reduced official drug list was in short supply. Under these circumstances, treating patients takes much longer, and nothing seems to promise future improvement, particularly as charitable aid, which previously covered about 40 per cent of hospital needs, is declining.

"Generally speaking," wonders one of my friends, "can one speak at all of hospital therapy? In each case, not just in the case of heart attacks, the conditions in our hospitals are not suitable for therapy and rehabilitation. It is [still] possible to operate, diagnose, order supplies, or even administer the appropriate medicines. What the hospital requires of the patient is psychological resilience, because in this matter he can hardly count on the support of hospital personnel. . . ."

And so we part, wishing each other iron-clad health.

The Final Hours of Jozef S.

Investigative journalists Grazyna Wroblewska and Tadeusz Filipkowski wrote this detailed report of Polish health care in Odrodzenie, *9 March 1986.*

Warsaw. "Mikowa Street speaking . . ."

"My neighbour has been vomiting for several hours, has a high temperature and stomach pains."

"I cannot accept your call. Please phone the night service on 22-57-36."

It was nearly 7 pm. Mrs Szustak, the sick man's neighbour, rang the number. She quickly told her story to the woman who answered. Unfortunately, she got almost exactly the same reply.

"Please wait until the morning. The doctor can't come."

"What should we do?" she asked. "Please listen. He's having a heart attack . . ." She said that deliberately. "They've got to take notice of that," she thought.

It had the right effect. A woman doctor came to the phone.

"How long has he been ill? What medicine has he taken? Has he seen a doctor?" the questions poured out.

"He's been vomiting since breakfast. He has a temperature of 40 degrees centigrade. His legs hurt. He's got heart trouble. The enterprise doctor prescribed vibramycin [an all-purpose antibiotic] and *necocardyna* [a herbal tranquillizer] and headache powders for his fever! He took them at 4 pm. We've also given him stomach drops, the usual kind."

"Please give him pyramidone. Every four hours. Those drugs won't have begun to work yet."

"What about his legs?"

"Massage them with a brush."

"Isn't anyone coming over, then?"

"What will you give the doctor to come?"

Today, Maria Szustak feels sure that if only she'd given them something . . . .

"We only keep records of calls which were accepted," they told us at the emergency department on Hoza Street.

"Do you make tape-recordings of telephone conversations, like the police or the fire brigade?" we asked.

"We haven't done so for years. Our central telephone exchange is being renovated. We're considering installing such a system."

The Regional Clinic is on Skarzynski Street, where from 7 pm onwards the Night Treatment Centre serves the entire Ochota district. From 8 pm onwards this centre has vehicles at its disposal, to take three doctors to visit the sick. But not one of them came to see Jozef S. There is no record of his neighbour's phone call in their book of messages received.

Who did Mrs Szustak call next? It turns out that the number given her by the emergency department wasn't the Night Centre's at all, but that of the daytime centre, which doesn't serve her street. At the emergency department on Skarzynski Street no one will admit that they spoke to Mrs Szustak.

8 am came. They gave the sick man pyramidone. He was still sitting on the couch, just as he was when he came back from work. His temperature did not go down until 10 am. He was turning brown. . . . What could they do? Call again? Call again. They might just get hold of someone who'd understand. . . .

This time Mrs Szustak's husband went to phone. It's always a different story if a man does the talking.

"They accepted the call. They're coming over."

But by midnight no one had turned up. The patient kept insisting, "call again, they didn't take it in." So they tried again. "Please hold on, the emergency service is on its way."

From a conversation afterwards with the director of the emergency rescue service, Henryk Zejdel, it emerged that the service received its first notification of the call at about 20 minutes past midnight.

No one could say what had happened to Mr Szustak's vanished notification of 10 am. They didn't even answer our questions about it.

At 2.30 am the rescue service came. A female doctor and an orderly immediately decided that the patient must go to the nearest hospital. The orderly and the neighbour helped the staggering man into the ambulance.

"To Barska Street." The driver switched on the siren and the flashing blue light.

"At the time of your visit to the sick man did you call an ambulance equipped for resuscitation, or ask for any additional help?" we asked the emergency doctor, Anna Drzazgowska-Zachary.

"No. The patient was in a serious, but not critical state. His blood pressure was average. And we were less than 20 minutes away from the hospital."

Before 3 am emergency team No. 62 stopped before the hospital gate. It was locked. The door-keeper's lodge was empty. The driver wrestled with the gate. Several minutes passed. The reception was a short way off, up 13 steep steps. The patient no longer had the strength to walk up them. The orderly and driver carried him up to the reception waiting room and sat him down on a trolley. Besides them, there wasn't a living soul in the reception.

"I raised the alarm," says Dr Drzazgowska. "I shouted and beat at the doors. No one replied. Finally, in one of the rooms in the accommodation area I found a man in white overalls. He was asleep. He woke up and was abusive. He was an orderly. I could smell vodka. At that moment the hospital nurse appeared. I screamed at her to call for the duty doctor.

'The internal phones don't work,' she replied. 'I'll have to call from the municipal phone.' The nurse ran towards some doors. They were locked. As it later transpired, there really was a municipal phone on the other side of them, and beside it another drunken orderly was fast asleep.

Then I heard my colleague, the team orderly, calling: 'The patient's at a standstill,' which means he's dying.

We began to resuscitate him. The driver helped us. We did it very professionally. We're a good team. I shouted for the nurses: resuscitation crew—at once! In a couple of minutes, maybe several, I heard: 'What do you mean by bringing me corpses? He's been dead for at least two hours!'

The first and only doctor whom I saw in the hospital said that. He was the anaesthetist, Mieczyslaw Januszewski. There was no duty doctor.

'But I give you my word of honour that just a moment ago he was alive,' I said. We were shocked. Several minutes before I had taken the man's pulse. He was sitting in an armchair at that time, and he was breathing.

Then we went to Hoza Street to tell the senior emergency doctor the whole story, and then we went on to visit other sick people. We were on duty, after all."

"Didn't you inform the police?"

"No."

At 3.40 am police officers arrived at the Barska Street hospital. The porter reeked of beer. Three orderlies were also drunk. Tests showed that they had from 1·2–1·7 mils of alcohol in their blood. The orderly M.G., educated to second class at elementary school, had worked in the hospital for 19 years. J.G., educated to fourth class, also an orderly, had been there for 16 years. The third one had worked at Barska for 23 years. So they were old, experienced employees who knew their duties well. In December 1985 the first two were caught drinking alcohol during working hours. In conformity with the regulations they should have been sacked. But this had not happened. They had asked for a mild punishment. They had got it. They had themselves offered to resign, but only a reprimand remained on record.

It is an open secret that the health service suffers from a dramatic shortage of personnel. In that same hospital on Barska Street they are waiting to take on 20 permanent employees. And so when the matter quietened down, these nurses were allowed to withdraw their resignations and remained at work.

27 February was a double cause for celebration—not just because it was payday, but also because they had managed to stay on in the place where they had worked for so many years. In their evidence they said they hadn't drunk much—half a litre and any number of beers. The porter was drinking separately.

"Mr Director," we asked the director of the Ochota Health Department, Dr Stanislaw Oledzki, "why are you so liberal?"

"I'll reply with a question. Do you know anyone who would do hard and thankless work, for from 5·7–10 thousand zlotys? We accept everyone who comes forward. Last year we took on 95 people, and just as many left, giving up the hardest jobs."

"Drunken orderlies is one thing. But isn't communication the nerve centre of every hospital? The critical night phones didn't work. And as if that was nothing, in the duty room, locked from the inside, there was a working telephone, and a drunken orderly fast asleep. Couldn't the duty doctor have foreseen that earlier? We're told that he's an outstanding specialist, a doctor who cares about his patients, until now a man of irreproachable professional repute."

"We made great efforts for a long time to get that doctor at Barska Street, and we pinned great hopes on his arrival. In our district, which is larger than most, it is essential to have a physician of his standard. At the time when the emergency happened, that doctor was on the ward with his patients.

Communication? Yes, we know it is scandalous that the phones didn't work. Not just the phones. Not long ago we had a major disaster at Barska Street. The wards were flooded. We have to repair an entire floor. But where can we put the patients?"

Jozef S.'s workmates found out about his death from the press. On Thursday he had been working as usual. Just after breakfast he had felt ill. A temperature and vomiting had overcome him. He went to the enterprise doctor. Then he went back to the factory floor with his prescriptions and a discharge note allowing him to leave at 5 pm. For six days. But his mates weren't happy about him. They knew he wasn't shamming—he hadn't missed a single day's work for years on end. And they knew he had a bad heart.

"Jozef, don't worry about the discharge note. Go home, go to bed," said the foreman.

So he went. For the last time he left the factory and went home on the No. 173 bus.

"Do you have a rule that if a worker is extremely ill you send him home by car or call an ambulance?" we asked Grazyna Zamorska, the enterprise doctor.

"Of course we do. But in this case I didn't see the need. He was complaining of a cough and a temperature."

"What about his heart?"

"He had hollow tones."

"Didn't that alarm you?"

"He didn't generally like being treated."

On the evening of Friday 28 February the Warsaw Television Courier carried an extensive report of the circumstances surrounding Jozef S.'s death. It was repeated on two successive TV news transmissions. That was enough to alert the public. How could such a tragedy occur?

The Ochota district prosecutor ordered the arrest of the three nurses and the porter who had slept in a drunken stupor while on duty.

The doctor on duty in the Barska Street hospital on the night of 27–28 February was suspended from his duties as head of the internal ward.

The Ministry of Health and Public Safety is appointing a special commission to investigate the circumstances surrounding such incidences.

Jozef S.'s relatives are arranging his funeral.

It is too early to make judgements. But inevitably a number of questions come to mind. After all, this doesn't just concern orderlies, porters, nurses and doctors, but a human being who, from the first moment when he fell ill, didn't get effective help at the right time. This matter also concerns the inadequacy of communication links within the health service. We think it should be analyzed and evaluated in this light.

We went round collecting the facts. The picture of events continually grew more complex and more diverse in significance. We saw individuals entangled in a situation in which their capacity for effective action was limited. Unquestionably the health service has needs and potential. There is a painful shortage of material resources. There are fewer personnel than there should be, and the technology is not up to scratch—it's out of date, impossible to get at, or missing. The lack of responsibility is appalling.

It is not an experienced doctor who is the first contact, who decides when and whom to call in the first place for help, but often it is someone from the central emergency service—who actually is trained, but who is not responsible in the medical sense—or else it is a girl at the registration reception booth. In our opinion the drama of Jozef S. really took place when the anonymous woman answering the 999 call did not accept his friend's message but passed her on to the receptionist. And the drama deepened in the course of the conversation with the receptionist, who also made little of the call. From hour to hour the patient lost his chances, and because there were no tape-recordings, and because of the medical supervisor, there aren't even any records of those first calls!

Of course, we could say that the people who receive the calls are powerless to do anything. Even when there are ambulances, there often aren't enough doctors, and when there is a doctor, there's no orderly. And so they've learned to sift out notifications of illness, and in the battle for attention those who shout loudest win.

Death is inevitable. But in every case where life is threatened we want and have the right to expect help with full assurance. Every incident similar to the one described here shatters our reliance and destroys long recognized authority, undermining the good work of thousands of honest health workers.

Medical treatment always costs an awful lot. Treatment of the health service itself does too. We must be fully conscious of that, because if we aren't, more than one patient will pay the highest price.

★ ★ ★ ★ ★

Trybuna Ludu, *17–18 May 1987, carried a report of the final court hearing on the Barska Street hospital case:*

On 16 May 1987 the trial of four employees of the Municipal Hospital on Barska Street took place. They were the orderlies Marian Galazka and Jan Galazka, the porter Mieczyslaw Sulich and the cloak-room attendant Jan Dziugiel. They were accused of having, on 28 February 1987, been incapable of performing their work obligations through drunkenness, and by so doing of directly risking the danger of the loss of health and life of patients brought to the hospital, under Article 147, paragraph 2 of the Criminal Code.

The Warsaw District Court found the accused guilty of the charges brought against them and sentenced them as follows: M. Galazka to one year of imprisonment; J. Galazka to one year and three months' imprisonment; M. Sulich and J. Dziugiel to ten months' imprisonment each.

Fringe Medicine

Sect Offers Cure-All

Condensed from an article by Special Correspondents E. Manucharova and S. Tutorskaya, Izvestia, *24 July 1986.*

Viktor Konstantinovich Kobyakov is a former patient in the alcoholism-treatment programme conducted in Leningrad by a certain Stolbun. He describes his initial doubts about the programme: "At first . . . they didn't even question the fact that the treatment included ethyl chloride, a substance that produces a serious narcotic effect." During the first few days, he felt good after the chemical-chill procedure. . . . But later he noticed that the ethyl chloride left him feeling keyed up and told his wife about it. "Her response really surprised me. Apparently the 'doctors' had warned her that I was a schizophrenic. They claimed that schizophrenia was my primary ailment, and that my addiction to drink was secondary. Suppodedly, our son was also suffering from schizophrenia. They said that if he didn't receive the same treatment I was getting (which had to be administered by them), the child would stop talking! I didn't believe them, but my wife would no longer listen to me."

The situation grew increasingly baffling. Kobyakov could not understand why during the ethyl chloride treatments (it was applied to parts of the body that are not usually mentioned in polite company) other half-dressed men and women were made to lie beside him. What role did Stolbun's lectures about phallic cultures and the origin of obscenities play in the treatment? How could the so-called "psychologists" abuse their patients in crude, public displays of aggression? And if patients were to say something like "well, really, now" in the course of a conversation, fold their arms across their breasts or cross their legs, why was their behaviour considered to be a gross infraction that could result in a suspension of treatment?

Let's interrupt Kobyakov's story (he refused to continue the treatment in any case) and let the other side have their say. Here are some typical excerpts from a letter that the group's leaders wrote to higher authorities:

"Our collective has developed a method of psychophysiological treatments that tone the brain's functional systems down to normal levels." This was followed by a brief description of their method of using ethyl chloride, applied to the skin to treat the brain, and a list of the various possibilities this opens up—possibilities incomparably greater than any offered by medical science. Even that was not enough for the authors. They maintained that their method stimulates "the nerve centres that create feelings of love for the homeland and for the opposite sex." They proposed that it be used "for mass work with the younger generation," and also to "rehabilitate much-needed workers."

The authors were not given permission to carry out their proposals, naturally. But for all practical purposes they had been experimenting on gullible people on a semi-legal basis for about 10 years in Dushanbe and Dimitrov. Finally, in 1983, over-ruling the objections of psychiatrists and scientists specializing in addiction treatment, the USSR Ministry of Public Health allowed them to conduct a two-year experiment based at Leningrad's Psychiatric Hospital Number Six, and let them work with volunteer patients who were listed as incurable alcoholics. But—and we stress this point—only on condition that the work would be open to scrutiny, constantly monitored by psychiatrists and addiction-treatment specialists. . . .

D. M. Chedia—the "laboratory director"—is a paleontologist by training.

V. D. Stolbun, the true head of the "project," trained to be a teacher (by correspondence course) and does not have a medical degree (he was dismissed from Moscow Medical Institute Number Two for consistently poor performance). The second most important person is his wife, V. P. Streltsova, the only physician in the group. There are two psychologists with higher education. Their assistants are mainly first- or second-year students at various institutes in departments unrelated to biology or psychology. They include a film director, an engineer, and a former police officer. The team's lack of medical education was carefully concealed from the patients and their relatives, as well as from the many volunteers. . . .

It is worth noting that roughly half the team consisted of people who were closely related to one another. . . .

Who are the followers of Stolbun and Streltsova? Their chief characteristic is an obedience to and complete lack of criticism of the group's leader. Stolbun's and Streltsova's assistants are selected over a period of time. They follow their "prophet"—to Dushanbe, Dimitrov, Leningrad, and recently to yet a fourth city, Brezhnev. As a rule, they live together in a kind of commune, or at least that is how they attempt to live. We talked with one of Stolbun's and Streltsova's adherents. He accompanies them from one city to the next. He has indeed stopped drinking, but is clearly already addicted to ethyl chloride. When asked what benefit he derives from this drug, he admitted: "It takes away the fear, the uncertainty, the feeling of guilt about drinking, and makes me feel as if everything in my life will turn out fine." And another devotee happily reported: "I feel good, I'm going to Brezhnev."

Stolbun is the sole master of the "commune." He demands unquestioning submission from his entire entourage. . . . There are attractive sides to the group's life (hiking, invigorating work in the fields, concerts, rehearsals), but there is another sinister side that is hidden from outsiders. Absence from the commune without leave for personal reasons is punished; money is pooled; patients may only watch television broadcasts recommended and selected by Stolbun; and although he rarely puts in an appearance, shrouding himself in secrecy, Stolbun likes to know everything about both his assistants and his patients. . . .

We have . . . letters from Dushanbe, Dimitrov and Moscow describing the physical punishments administered [to patients]. It is hard to believe it, but Stolbun would place a person he was beating at the centre of a circle of onlookers and ask: "Am I right to administer this beating?" And the victim, like those around him, is supposed to answer: "You are right." Incredible? Yes, but it happened, as our letters from three cities attest. Individuals would be subjected to group humiliation—binding the participants more securely than an iron chain. Binding them to what? To the sect. We aren't the first to use this word for Stolbun's group. It is used by his former patients, and by scientists, doctors and those who have studied the group's activities. . . .

So why on earth is this group flourishing? "They know how to maintain their cover," say the patients. They also make claims to cure every disease, be it cancer, schizophrenia or depression. The latter-day medicine men persistently and deliberately seek out, as publicizers and defenders of their work, people whose professional interests lie in other spheres. Without a hint of embarrassment, members of Stolbun's retinue reel off the names of celebrities in the art and literary world and high-ranking officials who supposedly support the "experiment." . . . In their "reports," Stolbun and Streltsova use the names of scientists who are alleged to be their teachers and advocates of their method. But here is what the scientists actually think. Professor N. N. Ivanets, Professor I. P. Anokhina and Professor A. N. Ivanitsky, members of the commission that investigated the experiment, conclude: "Clinical and experimental results lead us to believe that the 'method' proposed by V. P. Streltsova and V. D. Stolbun for treating alcoholics is ineffective. Therefore its use in public-health practice is inadvisable." The commission's findings were approved by Academician G. V. Morozov of the USSR Academy of Medicine. These and many other views and documents are fully accessible and available for inspection.

Perhaps the most surprising thing about this story is the attitude taken by the USSR Ministry of Public Health. Although they condemn, sometimes quite sharply, the "work" of Stolbun and Streltsova, the ministry's officials hem and haw ominously when it becomes a question of using their authority. Even now, in the wake of the evaluation of the group's work in Leningrad the Russian Republic Ministry of Public Health is letting the whole story start all over again in the city of Brezhnev.

We visited Brezhnev. A rumour is already going round about the "doctors" who can cure any craving for alcohol in a single day. . . .

The Uses of Quack Medicine

Extracts from an article entitled "Why are they thriving?" by V. Shtirts, Kazakhstanskaya Pravda, *10 April 1987. It quotes from readers' letters and investigates the practices of herb doctors.*

In their letter the Kuznetsov family gave several addresses. One of them is in Alma-Ata: Kamenskoye Plato, the "Shop" bus stop, where you ask for Pavel Zinovyevich.

"Well, it is easy to find him without asking anyone," the Kuznetsovs continue: "On Saturdays and Sundays, when he holds a surgery, people go to him in droves. They go to see him with empty jars, and return from him with full ones. The 'doctor' charges 200 rubles for six half-litre jars of decoction. He treats cancer with kerosene, and all other diseases with decoctions. . . ."

The Kuznetsovs had a telephone call from their relatives in Krasnodar kray. They gave the Kuznetsovs the addresses of Alma-Ata quacks over the telephone and asked them to find out if such people really existed.

"We did not want to refuse to do them this favour, and we wasted more than one weekend paying 'visits' to these addresses. We were shaken by what we saw. We were hurt and embittered by the fact that our beautiful city has become famous for such charlatans. . . ."

Shtirts visited one "Dr Ayzhan" at the Uzhet settlement near Alma-Ata; the "doctor" received his patients in an extension resembling a shed.

Dr Ayzhan was about 70. He wore leather overalls, which despite their enormous width were hardly big enough for his stomach. His round, clean-shaven head seemed to sprout straight from his stomach.

The doctor turned out to be chatty. I told him that I wanted to bring my sick sister to him. Having found out that I was not a patient, he probably decided that in that case I should become his audience. He immediately declared that he was "not just any doctor, but an educated one." In his absolutely absurd and improbable stories he presented qualified doctors as complete idiots and dunces and told me that he, who had been sent by nature itself to cure people, invariably exposed them successfully.

While listening to him, I examined the premises. The space was divided into two. The part in which we were sitting did not exceed five square metres in size, and the area behind the partition was about the same. Through a tiny window and a low door I could see two iron bedsteads with rags heaped up on them. Jars and bottles containing some liquid were standing on the window sill.

The Kuznetsovs' letter said: "It was a dirty and dilapidated shed where some 12 or 15 people were lying on their own bedding."

The success of the self-styled doctors, undisguised charlatans, cries out for a question: Why do people turn to them? These people are not put off either by scandalous filth, or uneducated chatter, or the fantastic fees or prices of the "medicines."

Of course, health is a very precious thing. Desire for good health overpowers mistrust. And, by the way, advertising is well organized by these "doctors." The rumour of "miracles" performed by the "healers" spreads faster than any scientific or technical information, and people believe it, however fantastic it may be. . . .

You don't have to explain to the reader that the root of the matter is in the quality of medical care; and this depends on the doctors themselves, in the first place. It is enough to mention a situation in which everyone has found himself more than once. You arrive at the polyclinic for a 10.25 appointment. 11.00 arrives, but the queue is not getting any shorter. You have made your calculations and asked for an hour off work. You start getting nervous, but the doctor won't see you before 12.00. . . .

There are also occasions, reader, when you at last get into the doctor's room, and he will not pay the slightest attention to you.

You also get plenty of outright rudeness.

But under no circumstances will the Ayzhans display such discourtesy. When I went to see that doctor in Uzhet, I told him that I had not come for treatment; he did not snap at me, "What do you want then?" but invited me to come in. He may have been talking nonsense, but he showed me courtesy. And that's how he wins you over.

4. Rights—Seen From Below

Eye-Witness Accounts from the Soviet Union*

The General State of Soviet Health Care

Because of the shortage of hospitals and hospital beds, people have to wait months for an operation. Even seeing a doctor means spending half a day in line. There are lines for X-rays and lines to get analyses done. And by the time the analyses are ready, they are already out of date. How can you treat patients in a situation like that? Medicine is difficult to obtain. When you do find some, the expiry date is often past. Someone from the Ministry of Health told me that new medicine goes into the military stores, while older products are put on the market. Speculation in medicines is flourishing. The hospitals are filthy and smelly. The bed linen is full of holes, the beds are old and uncomfortable because of all the broken springs, there is a shortage of wheelchairs and a shortage of crutches. There are 15–20 people in the general wards and more lying in the corridors. Terminal patients are not separated from the others, and there aren't enough post-operative wards. The surgical instruments are old and often rusty. Needles are often sharpened by the patients themselves and they also have to wash surgical instruments because no one can be found to do the work of hospital attendants and assistants at the extremely low pay of 60 rubles a month. Relatives bring food to the patients since they would literally starve without it. Patients have to make extra payments for everything, although medical care is theoretically free, since none of the doctors, nurses or lab workers will do anything at all without it. Bribes even have to be paid to obtain a prosthesis after an amputation. Normally there is a waiting period of several months, and patients go out to the factory and pay over a bribe to get the work speeded up.

Physician in his 50s from Kalinin, February 1983

Although penicillin and cotton wadding are available in hospitals, other medicines and bandages are not. This means that bandages are often dispensed with completely, or else washed out and used again. The more complex antibiotics have disappeared and there are no imported ones either. Patients who need them are dying. Medicines are available in the Kremlin hospital (reserved for thc *nomenklatura* and foreign "comrades") and can be obtained through connections at an exorbitant rate. Yugoslav antibiotics cost 10 or 20 rubles a bottle although their official price is 4·65 rubles. Birth control pills from Germany, Finland and France can only be obtained on the black market or through special outlets. Even not to produce another soldier for the Soviet army is a privilege.

Nurse in her 40s from Moscow, February 1983

An increase in the number of deaths caused by sickness and a drop in the average life span attest to the decline of medical services and social aid to the Soviet population. The quality of medical workers has slumped because admission to institutions of higher education is regulated through nepotism and bribery.

* Collected from *émigrés* in the 1983–87 period by the Soviet Area Audience and Opinion Research Department of Radio Liberty.

Hospitals have only one-third of the medicines and equipment they need. Bribe-taking among doctors and other medical personnel is widespread.

Physician in his 60s from Pavlovsk; former CP member, February 1983

Hospital patients are very poorly cared for. This is because the nurses are so poorly paid. They only get 80–120 rubles a month, and one can't expect good work for that price. If neither the patient nor his relatives can afford to pay for a private nurse (private nursing consists mainly of observing the patients, for a fee of two rubles a day or 10 rubles a week), they bribe the regular nurses and attendants. This doesn't work very well, however, since there aren't enough nurses to go round anyway. The doctors also take bribes for operations and for extending sick leave. The minimal fee for an operation performed by a professor or department head is 1,000 rubles, and a good surgeon takes 600 rubles. Removal of a gall bladder costs 1,200 rubles for the professor or 800 for the surgeon. An oncological abdominal operation costs 2,000 rubles. Every extra day in the clinic costs 10 rubles.

Pensioner and hospital employee in her 50s from Zaporozhye, August 1983

As a hospital nurse, I was caught between the patients on the one hand and the hospital administration on the other. The administration wanted us to try and extort payment for deficit medicines from the patients, with the lion's share [of the medicines] being given to those who paid up. The patients, however, would create a scandal if they were deprived of medicines because they had no money to pay for them. Not only was this a terrible strain on the staff's nerves, it could even end with imprisonment in the worst cases.

Nurse in her 30s from Kaliningrad, August 1983

The level of medical service was very bad in the polyclinic where I worked. The doctors, being anxious to obtain food products, would often see as many as 20 patients in an hour (the patients often paid in food). The medical equipment was old and in need of repair. One item or another was constantly lacking. There were no sheets for the beds and not enough medicines for injections. Minor operations were done without anaesthetics. Epidemics were constantly breaking out in the city, but nobody did anything to stop them.

Nurse in her 40s from Leningrad, August 1983

I was responsible for inspecting small regional hospitals in Voronezh oblast. I usually found unsanitary conditions, rusty instruments, and a lack of needles and certain drugs, such as Rovocaine. The hospitals were overcrowded; they often had to take in twice the number of patients they had been designed for. The food was of very low quality. Instead of meat, there were tiny frozen fish and half rotten vegetables. The hospital staff was mainly concerned with the pigs and poultry they were allowed to keep in the hospital yard as an incentive to stay on at the hospital. The *nomenklatura* do not use these hospitals; they are taken either to Voronezh or to Moscow.

Physician in his 60s from Voronezh, June 1984

In the nursery school where I worked, hygiene levels were low because there was a shortage of service personnel. There was a lot of intestinal disease among the children. Mothers were supposed to supply five rolls of toilet paper for their child, but of course that was impossible because there was none on sale. There were also frequent cases of food poisoning, due to the low quality of the foodstuffs supplied to the nursery school. In any case, the teachers used to eat the children's food, and they sometimes took food home too—even though some of the mothers used to bring the teachers butter, sausage, eggs and other foodstuffs in the hope of obtaining preferential treatment for their children. . . . There is a shortage of nursery school places in Riga, and even when you get a place there are a great many other requirements to be satisfied. Mothers have to provide several sets of clothes and shoes for their child, for instance, and they don't always have them. And then, when the child gets sick, they have to keep him at home to avoid infecting the other children.

Nursery teacher in her 40s from Riga, June 1984

Unhealthy Living

Up to 1983, I worked as a radiologist in Khabarovsk. Part of my job was to make medical inspections in the outlying districts. I recall one such trip, to the Muchnaya railway station in Chernigov rayon, Maritime kray. The medical team consisted of myself, my assistant, a paediatrician, and a gynaecologist. We examined the railway workers and their families as well as local *sovkhoz* workers. Most of the patients had poor living conditions and bad eating habits. Standards of hygiene were low, and the rate of alcoholism was high. I discovered tuberculosis in about 10 per cent of the people we examined. Several schoolchildren showed preliminary signs of the disease. Paediatric examinations indicated that around 25 per cent of the children under three were suffering from rickets, and many of them also had scrofula and chronic respiratory diseases. A lot of children had skin diseases. These problems stemmed from the fact that many of these children were born to alcoholic parents. Poor heredity reduced their chances of living healthy lives, especially in such unfavourable conditions. The infant mortality rate (that is, deaths before the age of one year) was also very high. Gynaecological examinations showed that many of the married women had had one or two miscarriages. One reason for this was again chronic alcoholism, which was as common among women as among men. Another reason was that miscarriages are especially frequent among women who do hard physical work, and this is very common on the railways, where most of the maintenance workers are women. A typical railway maintenance group consists of one or two men and five to 10 women.

Radiologist from Kishinyov, May 1986

Corruption and Morale in the Health Service

The pharmacy where I worked never received adequate quantities of the most widely prescribed medicines—and we came in for a lot of abuse from clients because of this. There was some speculation in medicines on the black market, but since the products were often sub-standard or imitation, they sometimes led to rather nasty side-effects. Often people brought in medicines they had purchased on the black market and asked us to check them, but we were forbidden to do this.

Pharmacist in her 30s from Moscow, January 1983

I worked as a nurse in a polyclinic, which was a good position for making money. The patients gave money to the nurses in order to receive medicine, and they in turn gave part of it to the head doctor. This was standard practice and took place quite openly. The patient was unable to object. If he tried to argue, he wouldn't get any medicine at all unless he bought it on the black market, where the quality would be dubious and the price double.

Nurse in her 30s from Sukhumi, April 1983

Spectacles and lenses are very scarce in the USSR. There are several factories producing low-quality lenses, while somewhat better ones are supplied by the Zeiss factories in the DDR. Opticians keep the latter "under the counter." Frames are even harder to find. Soviet-made frames are ugly and unreliable. Better-quality frames are supplied by East European countries but these are scarce too. Contraband glasses get into the country via Odessa and other seaports. They are sold at extremely high prices and can only be obtained through connections [*po blatu*]. They go in priority to the Party bosses. Trading in these black market goods makes it possible to earn some extra money. I used to make a profit of 400–500 rubles after I had paid out all the necessary bribes and reimbursed my suppliers. Frames and lenses could also be exchanged for foodstuffs.

Optician in his 30s from Lvov, June 1984

For the last two or three years there have been no bandaging materials, no cotton-wool, and very few antibiotics available in Samarkand pharmacies. Everything goes to the military hospitals, which are full of wounded. There are many drug addicts among the soldiers who have come back from Afghanistan, and they are getting younger and younger. I saw the list of addicts myself when I went to the hospital for my work.

Pharmacologist in his 50s from Samarkand, June 1984

In October 1983, two dentists were executed in Stavropol for illegal gold trafficking. Their crime consisted in obtaining gold from private sources in Siberia and Central Asia and using it to make dentures. They did this because it's impossible to get gold from legal sources, and no alternative materials such as china and plastics are available.

Dentist in his 40s from Mineralniye Vody, Stavropol Kray, June 1984

Dr Kaverin, the physician in charge of the Moscow ambulance service, is due to go on trial on a variety of charges including bribe-taking, corruption and blackmail. Ambulances allegedly were used to move people's furniture, transport commercial goods, even take people on picnics to the country. Meanwhile, there weren't enough ambulances in the city to respond to emergency calls. According to former colleagues whom I talked to shortly before leaving, Gorbachov hopes to turn this into a sort of show trial since members of the City Executive Committee, the Oblast Party Committee, and even the Central Committee appear to be implicated in the affair along with Kaverin. It is hoped that the trial will serve as a deterrent to those who might be tempted to follow in Kaverin's footsteps.

Retired lawyer from Moscow, November 1986

Poor Quality Prostheses

I worked for a prosthesis factory which serviced almost half the USSR. It was a huge place and the atmosphere there was awful. People have to wait from 1–3 years before receiving their application to come for a fitting. When they come, they're left waiting for months. Invalids have nowhere to stay. Hotels in the city are for foreigners, so they sleep at the station in winter and in public gardens in summer and they go without food. They keep pleading to speed up the manufacture of their prostheses and give bribes even though they have no money left for food. They are treated like animals because they form a large crowd and keep pestering the administration with questions nobody can answer. The quality of the prostheses is very low. Models are obsolete, and there are no spare parts. The invalids live hundreds or even thousands of kilometres away, and with a broken prosthesis they can't do anything.

With the war in Afghanistan the number of invalids has greatly increased. Soldiers and officers don't have to queue up. They are very depressed, and go about as though they were hypnotized. Sometimes they make terrible rows, beating up doctors or technicians out of nervous frustration.

Prostheses with custom details are ordered via special channels. These are brand new models from Germany, France and Sweden and are delivered directly to the factory director. They are duplicated in special work-shops. They are for important people and ordered by Moscow or Party Obkoms. Fittings are made in special rooms.

Prosthetician from Odessa, July 1985

Hospital Food

I worked for many years as a dietician in the city hospital as well as a ward nurse in various departments. Patients' food was never especially good, so their relatives usually brought them food from home which they kept on their bedside tables. We tried to fight this practice because it attracted cockroaches and mice, but scandals arose each time we took food away. The patients complained with good reason that the hospital food was bad, and nothing was left for them to do but receive provisions from home. Finally the hospital acquired refrigerators in which patients were obliged to keep their food. Even then, patients couldn't always find their food, and we had to put up notices saying that the hospital was not responsible. Problems also arose when relatives of a seriously ill patient brought him food that was harmful to him—for example, right after an operation. There are several reasons behind this situation. First, the hospital could only spend 50 kopecks per day per patient on food, and it's impossible to feed anybody on such a sum. Second, hospital cooks are very badly paid, so qualified cooks find work elsewhere, leaving the hospital with an incompetent staff. Third, the cook, the kitchen workers, and anyone else who has to do with patients' food tries to steal whatever he can, and it's impossible to keep an eye on them all the time. As a dietician I raised this question repeatedly, but it was impossible to change things.

Nurse from Chernovtsy, July 1985

I worked in the computer centre of the Zaporozhye health department where we processed data on health statistics for the oblast. Between 1975 and 1985 the number of deaths attributable to alcohol-related liver cirrhosis in the Zaporozhye region increased by 150 per cent. Cases of tuberculosis increased by 36 per cent and infant mortality rates went up by 18 per cent. Inversely, expenditures on food and medicine in hospitals decreased. Rations of *tvorog*, poultry, eggs, milk, and sour cream were reduced by 20–30 per cent. Expenditures on hypodermic needles decreased even though the number of medicines which can be administered only by injection increased. Basic items such as mustard plasters, ether, alcohol, and local anaesthetics were constantly in short supply.

Programmer from Zaporozhye, August 1986

Rotten Meat for the Workers

I worked in the canteen at the Baku Petroleum industrial complex. We received two kinds of meat: one for the directors, and one for the workers. The meat for directors was good frozen meat, but there was so little of it that no one dared to steal it. The meat for workers originally came from military depots. No one stole that meat either. When the carcasses were delivered, they were already green with mould. They were thrown into a bathtub and scrubbed with brushes. The stench was so intense that the men who did the job wore special masks. They were paid well to ensure that they wouldn't talk too much. Sometimes each of them even received a kilo of good meat from the distributor but they sold it to buy vodka. They would only work when they were drunk: it wasn't the kind of job you could do sober. After being thoroughly washed and rinsed, the carcasses were sent to be cut up. By that stage the meat was slimy. It was used to make goulash, cutlets, and beefsteaks. It was cooked with plenty of garlic and pepper to remove the smell of carrion.

Cook from Baku, July 1986

Abortion in the USSR

In the Soviet Union, contraception is still at the Stone Age level, and it is common for a woman to have a vast number of abortions. To stop an unwanted pregnancy Soviet women drink iodine, poison, or herbs or use any object they think can help. Many of the young women who came to me were very ill. Inflammation of the reproductive organs is a common phenomenon. They end up in hospital with a blood infection or serious inflammation.

Gynaecologist in his late 60s from Voronezh, May 1984

A neighbour of mine used to practise abortion. Her husband had died leaving her with a three-room flat. She was a former nurse and she did abortions there for women who were afraid to go to the hospital. In Soviet hospitals abortions are done without anaesthetics. My neighbour had somehow got hold of some sort of imported preparation with which she injected her patients. It kept them drowsy for 24 hours after the operation. They were conscious all the time, but didn't feel anything. She was very much afraid of being caught by the OBKhSS or the Office of Public Prosecution, believing that she risked a 15-year sentence. She charged 80 rubles for an abortion, which was not particularly expensive. Most women were ready to pay anything she asked to avoid having to go to an overcrowded hospital. My neighbour always had a gynaecologist on call in case anything went wrong. If she called, he would get there within 15 minutes. She worked like that for seven years.

Pensioner from Kishinev in her 70s, May 1984

Maternity Clinics—Elite and Non-Elite

In Leningrad there are at least two maternity clinics reserved exclusively for the *nomenklatura*. They are connected to the Obkom and KGB polyclinics. The standard of medical care and cleanliness is much higher in these clinics than in an ordinary hospital, and instead of being 10 to a room, the new mothers are only two to a room. In the ordinary maternity clinic where I worked, there was an epidemic of staphylococcus infection and infectious hepatitis. To make matters worse, the kitchen workers responsible for preparing the babies' formula took the milk powder home with them and substituted ordinary milk and water for the newborn babies. Of course they were dismissed for this, but two babies died as a result of their negligence and a number of others were seriously ill for a long time. When children were born in this hospital with serious brain damage or other deformities, the parents were informed that the child was stillborn or that it had succumbed to post-natal infection (which was actually not uncommon). Then the child was taken to a special research institute belonging to the USSR Ministry of Health where experiments would be carried out on him.

Midwife from Leningrad, July 1985

Women Labourers

When I began work as a gynaecologist, I noticed a large number of prolapses of the uterus and rectum, and hernias. These are disorders caused by systematic lifting of weights and excessive muscular strain, especially of the abdomen. They were found both in women who had had several children—who are the most likely to have such ailments; and those who had only one or two children, or even none. Upon investigation, it almost always turned out that the women in the latter category were engaged in hard physical labour. In the Soviet Union, women are often used in road work. You often see a work brigade consisting of men working with a steam roller, men driving trucks full of gravel and asphalt, and a man and several women unloading and spreading out the asphalt and gravel with shovels. The same sort of system prevails on the railways: the women carry the ties and drive in the spikes with heavy sledge-hammers. In factories women are used as unskilled labour. Often, women suffering from hernias and the like continue to do heavy work, even though this is contra-indicated. In many cases, they also go on working after becoming pregnant; this often leads to a miscarriage. According to labour legislation in the USSR, the members of certain professions can retire at the age of 35. But retirement age is the same for women who work in offices as for those who do physical labour. I often had to struggle with the medical commission to get a woman certified to receive her pension before she had attained the legal retirement age. Medical commissions in the USSR are more inclined to protect the interests of the government than those of the patient.

Gynaecologist from Berdichev, May 1985

When I visited a *kolkhoz* near Kharkov, I found that the majority of the women there had some kind of health problem. Many of them were suffering from "women's diseases," ranging from prolapse of the uterus caused by lifting heavy weights, to fungus infections caused by communal washing in small wash basins. Other problems resulted from self-performed abortions in insanitary conditions. Many of the women had had miscarriages caused by heavy physical work and drinking bouts. They also tended to suffer from inflammation of the ovaries, since there was a shortage of warm underclothes on the *kolkhoz*, and they worked mostly in unheated buildings or out of doors. All my attempts to point out to the authorities that heavy work was a threat to women's health met with the response that the sexes are equal in the USSR, and that the *kolkhoz* women were "heroines of labour" who were capable of doing any work given them.

Gynaecologist from Kharkov, February 1987

Radiation Sickness

There are many uranium mines near Zhitomir, and many prison camps too, since it is prisoners who are used for labour in the mines and the uranium-processing plants. Because of the high radiation levels, there are few civilian workers in the mines and factories, even though both pay and provisions are excellent. There are frequent cases of radiation sickness in the area, and even the workers on the local *sovkhozy* are reluctant to stay. When I visited the "Bolshevik" and "Red Ray" *sovkhozy*, which are located near the uranium mines, I learned that the vegetables grown there give off an abnormally high amount of radiation. In spite of this, they are sent to the stores in Zhitomir, and there, of course, they are all snapped up.

Agronomist from Zhitomir, October 1986

Radioactive Pollution

From friends living in different areas of the USSR, we heard about harmful radiation in Karelia, Novosibirsk and Dnepropetrovsk. In the north of Karelia are harmful radio waves which not only interfere with Western radio broadcasts, but are also a threat to people's health. There are many closed military zones in Karelia, as well as radio stations and all sorts of radiation equipment. There are some sort of nuclear factories in the Severny Poselok district of Novosibirsk. They are built partly underground. There is a high incidence of deaths from leukaemia among people working in the factories and the inhabitants of the district, but this fact is kept secret by the authorities. Similar nuclear radiation affects the houses in the area surrounding the nuclear warhead factory "Yuzhnoye Mashinostroeniye." Every morning you can see the *zeks* [prisoners] being transported to the factory under guard; it is they who do the most dangerous jobs in the plant. We had friends who worked at a factory which manufactures equipment for the European gas pipeline. When they visited Syktyvkar (in the Komi ASSR), they saw that the pipeline was being built by *zeks*; the only civilians present being the gas technicians.

Engineer in her 50s from Leningrad, May 1983

Since a nuclear power plant was built in Kandalaksha, there has been a deterioration in public health. There have been several cases of leukaemia in children, and an increased incidence of miscarriages and impotency.

Geologist in his 50s from Kandalaksha, Murmansk oblast, May 1984

A friend of mine worked in a restricted hospital in Tallinn which specialized in treating people who had been exposed to radiation. The hospital was built to cater for 200 people and was always overcrowded, even though the death rate was very high. It was patrolled by plain-clothes KGB agents and you needed a pass to get in and out. Habitual patients included leukaemia sufferers from the atomic submarine base at Paldiski. They were both prisoners and ordinary sailors who had been responsible for cleaning the atomic reactors on the subs. However, according to my friend, it was "less a hospital than a laboratory." Experimental methods and untested medicines are commonly tried out on the patients under the guidance of medical research scientists who told the resident doctors what to do. When my friend tried to leave his job, the personnel office told him that this would be "inadvisable," since the government had "entrusted him with secrets." Apparently, there are several such hospitals in the Soviet Union. People from this hospital had talked with employees from similar institutions in order to "share their experiences."

Hairdresser from Tartu, October 1986

Chemical Pollution

In Kolpino, industrial waste is simply taken outside the city and dumped. In October 1985, School No. 7 conducted a military game in the woods called "Summer Lightning." After a few hours the teachers noticed that one group of students was missing. They began to search for them, and found the entire group of 25 children lying unconscious in a cave. An ambulance was called immediately and the children were saved. The children later recounted how they had gone into the cave to hide from the "enemy." This cave was about a kilometre away from the chemical factory, and there was a lake of chemical refuse on the floor of the cave. After a few minutes, the children began to notice that they couldn't breathe, but their 14-year-old "commander" ordered them to lie down and wait it out, saying, "Your duty is the most important thing!" It was fortunate the children were found so soon, or there would have been no way to save them. I heard this story from one of the teachers who was involved in the outing. Her comment was: "We are bringing up a generation of partiotic robots with a twisted sense of duty."

Engineer from Leningrad, October 1986

Polluted Air and Water

My work in a geological oversight group concerned with the preservation of natural resources gave me a good picture of pollution in the USSR. Factories are emitting poisonous waste into the rivers, and the quality of drinking water is increasingly a problem. In villages, polluted water is seeping into the wells and being drunk unfiltered. I know from sanitary inspectors that there have been numerous incidences of intoxication affecting whole villages. There is a shortage of good quality drinking water in both large and small towns. Things have reached such a state that private homes are affected by water restrictions day and night. Factories are given quotas, and fines are levied for surpassing the quota. Another problem concerns industrial waste dumps. No steps are taken to decontaminate them, and so they are a threat to the lives of the population.

Geologist in his 40s, September 1984

Drinking water is of very poor quality in Sverdlovsk. It is said to be irradiated, and it is heavily chlorinated. The air is polluted with factory gases. Industrial plants are not adequately equipped to prevent radioactive waste from escaping into the atmosphere. Many people are trying to leave the city.

Engineer in his 40s from Sverdlovsk, June 1984

The inhabitants of Tomsk have for many years been drinking water that contains a concentration of carbonic acid and other toxic substances 10 times higher then the legally permitted amount. And during the so-called "accidental" dumpings from the Kemerovo chemical plants, located upstream on the Tom river, the concentration of carbonic acid exceeds the norm by a factor of more than 100. Once, in December 1978, it was 200 times higher than the permitted norm. As a result of the increase of liver, stomach and kidney ailments, particularly among children, the inhabitants of Tomsk started drinking water from artesian wells. Lines began to form near them. After the December 1978 dumpings and the resulting increase in the infant mortality rate, people really began to panic. Meetings were held in all the enterprises in Tomsk to reassure the population that the water was of very high quality, and that the rumours of toxicity were the work of subversives. Directors of scientific establishments were summoned to a special session of the regional committee, where the Second Party Secretary implored them to do everything possible to suppress the rumours being spread by enemies of the USSR. Meanwhile, it was common knowledge that the regional committee and other Party officials had been drinking specially supplied water the whole time.

Geneticist in his 30s from Tomsk, April 1983

The air in Sverdlovsk is unbelievably filthy and the skyline is spiked with factory smokestacks. We complained about this to the sanitary authorities, but they claimed there was nothing they could do because of the military factories. A doctor friend told me that there was a worse problem than pollution. According to him, the inhabitants of certain areas of the city are exposed to radiation from factories manufacturing nuclear warheads. Of course, no one is aware of this, and my friend was afraid to give me more details.

Engineer in his 30s from Sverdlovsk, April 1983

Human Guinea Pigs

I heard from an impeccable source that children with congenital defects are not given to their parents to raise. They are kept apart till they reach a certain age and then passed on to secret institutes of the Ministry of Defence, where they are used for experiments. Similarly, both children and adults with brain trauma are "given" to the government so that it can "take care" of them. Their families are ordered not to inquire about them and not to ask for meetings. I also heard that the Ministry of Defence conducts experiments on soldiers and political prisoners.

Physician in his 50s from Zhitomir, May 1984

My boss, who was the head of the biochemistry lab in the Novosibirsk oblast clinic and also worked in Akademgorodok, told me that they experiment on people in Akademgorodok. Research is being carried out into areas such as the treatment of malignant tumours, methods of radiation diagnosis and hormonal treatment of burns. *Zeks* [prisoners] and soldiers are used as guinea pigs for this research.

Medical worker in her 40s from Novosibirsk, June 1984

Sick people in the hospital where I worked were intentionally infected with hepatitis to allow researchers to study the effectiveness of new medicines designed to combat the disease. A doctor told me this in secrecy.

Nurse from Donetsk, July 1985

My former assistant was transferred to a research department where experiments were conducted on sick people with no relatives. Various toxins were tried out on them. My former assistant said to me, "In our institute, we do things that the Nazis never even dreamed of."

Cardiologist from Leningrad, July 1985

Medicine Shortages

It's always been difficult to get medicines in the USSR, but recently things have become even worse. No doubt priority is being given to those wounded in Afghanistan, and the average Soviet citizen is consequently feeling the pinch. I worked in an ambulance service where we received our supplies once a month. By the third week of each month we had run out of many medicines, and without the proper supplies, it was obviously difficult to give emergency help! I had a pharmacist friend who provided ampules, cotton wool and other items; my assistant and I pilfered supplies where we could, and bought others. Neither of us had a family, so we spent our money on black market medicines for our patients.

Cardiologist from Leningrad, July 1985

Black Market Medicine

Medicines and narcotics are frequently brought into Latvia and Lithuania by foreign sailors. They are sold to middlemen, and from there make their way into the pharmacies. Because of the enormous risks involved, the prices of these goods are astronomical. A month's supply of birth control pills costs 300 rubles, for instance. Drug addiction has risen considerably, and pharmacies are robbed daily. Besides narcotics, the thieves will take any kind of pill containing morphine or codeine.

Pharmacist in his 50s, September 1984

Radiotherapy is still on a very primitive level in the USSR, and many modern techniques are not yet available there. X-ray film is also in very short supply. Doctors keep it for their own friends, and there is never enough for ordinary people, although the *nomenklatura* naturally have no problems. Part of my job was to try and obtain X-ray film from military factories, special clinics for Party workers, and even the black market. Since an X-ray costs between seven and 15 rubles, many diseases remain untreated, especially cancerous tumours and other internal diseases.

Technician in her 30s, September 1984

Alcohol as a Tradition

I worked in a textile plant as deputy head of the fabric-dyeing laboratory. The dyeing procedure required the use of pure alcohol, of which we had considerable quantities available. The lab assistants often used to take some home with them, explaining that they needed it to pay repairmen. Alcohol is gold in Russia. The only way to get a plumber to mend a leaking tap is to offer him alcohol. Even at the lab, we used alcohol to pay electricians, plumbers, and painters, in order to ensure that the job would get done quickly. In the factory itself, alcoholism was a scourge. It was at the root of a great deal of absenteeism, hooliganism and mechanical breakdowns. However, it wasn't punished very severely, because the managers were hard drinkers themselves. In the dyeing laboratory, we had one male assistant who drank pure alcohol. Although he was often absent on drinking binges, he was a good worker with 20 years' experience, and so he managed to get away with it.

All this changed when Gorbachov came to power. The *raykom* sent a commission to inspect the factory, and a section head was fired after he came to work with his face swollen from one of his regular drinking bouts. Our alcoholic lab assistant was fired too. The entry in his labour book read as follows: "Dismissed for chronic alcoholism. May only be re-employed after undergoing treatment, and upon presentation of a written statement from the clinic."

Chemist from Moscow, May 1986

For a couple of days after pay day, my brigade of construction workers stayed idle. They didn't start work again until they had "drunk" their way through all their money. I tried a variety of measures to lessen the toll taken by alcoholism. For instance, I instructed the cashier not to give the inveterate alcoholics their money until their wives arrived, so the men wouldn't spend it all on drink. Then I tried replacing part of the brigade with women, hoping that the women wouldn't drink. My hopes were unfounded; the women drank up their pay and landed in the sobering-up stations just like the men. Encountering wives who had come to pick up the pay of their alcoholic husbands, they sometimes came to blows with them. After that, I tried bringing in young people from the technical institute. But it turned out that girls and boys alike were already well schooled in the art of consuming large quantities of alcohol. In the end, I gave up. Alcoholism is part of the system. It's a tradition; what can you do about it? Everyone drinks, both Party members and workers. The only difference between them is where and what they drink. The workers drink in halls, alleyways, bathrooms, and stores, either alone or with two or three others, downing a half-litre [of vodka] at a time; whereas the Party *apparatchiki* drink cognac at home or in restaurants.

Builder from Luga, May 1985

Alcohol as a Cause of Accidents

Before emigrating, I worked at an ambulance station. The doctors there were inclined to drink heavily between calls. One night, towards the end of February 1986, there was a call around three o'clock in the morning. An old woman had had a heart attack. The doctor and his driver were dead drunk, but there was no one else to take the call, so we woke them up and they set out. They were gone for a good hour and a half, and when they got back, there was no old woman with them. They had lost her. Going round a corner somewhere, the back door had opened and the stretcher on wheels had rolled right out of the ambulance, taking the old lady with it. Fortunately she was strapped on to the stretcher, so she survived. Even so, the doctor was forced to retire when the story came to light. This incident didn't stop anybody from drinking on the night watch, but at least they make sure the ambulance doors are properly closed now.

Nurse from Leningrad, November 1986

Krivoi Rog is a miners' city noted for drunkenness and hooliganism. At the entrance to factories, bottles of spirits were confiscated on the way in in the mornings. If someone returned after the shift to claim his property and found it gone, then the guard would get a bloody nose. Miners showed more resourcefulness than workers in camouflaging their supplies. They filled hot-water bottles with alcohol and tied them to their stomachs. But this tactic led to five miners being blown up at the Proletarsky mine in May 1984. After drinking the contents of their "little water bottles" they settled down to sleep in an area where dynamiting was taking place.

Crane operator from Krivoi Rog, March 1985

Drying-out Station

Before applying for my exit visa I was offered the post of head doctor in an experimental clinic for alcoholics. The new system, which is now being tried out, is a mixture of psychology and medication reinforced by stiff discipline. The clinics are under the full jurisdiction of the Ministry of Health and the militia. The treatment is compulsory. Militiamen have the power to send any drunk they find to the clinics without prior legal proceedings or administrative decisions. Family members or neighbours can ask the militia to send an alcoholic to the clinics. Patients are kept in barracks, called "blocks" and put under constant supervision. The whole area around the clinic is closed off to prevent any escape, just like a prison camp. Patients get up at six o'clock. They are given one hour to tidy up the "blocks," to have breakfast and to receive their first injection (not pills). It's a brand new treatment and I wasn't allowed to write down the formula. All I know is that it induces violent vomiting if the patient has a drink afterwards. After that first hour, patients are shown films and given lectures on the harmful consequences of alcoholism. After lunch and some rest they are taken out for two hours of intense exercice just to show them what poor condition they're in. One hour of rest is followed by another injection and more dissuasive talks. All in all a very intense day. I heard that the army is very much in favour of this programme because it fears that many reservists are not ready for combat.

Physician from Orenburg, July 1985

Bribery as a Way of Life

The only way to get things done these days is to grease someone's palm. You have to pay to get your child into a better school, to make sure your mother is put in a hospital ward and not left to lie in the corridor, to see that she is given proper medical examinations. . . . What's more, payment has to be made with food or other goods; no one wants money these days. When we wanted to travel to Kiev, it was impossible to get train tickets until we gave the cashier a packet of American cigarettes. He then immediately produced the tickets.

Accountant in his 40s from Minsk, February 1983

To try and get food, I and some acquaintances used to borrow a truck and drive out to a *sovkhoz* or *kolkhoz*. For a bribe of 30 rubles they would sell us products which it was impossible to buy in the city, such as butter, sunflower oil, meat, fruit and eggs. They took these from their "consumer-cooperation" [*potrebkooperatsii*] warehouses. We didn't know for whom these products were destined, but they weren't intended to go on the market.

Mechanic in his 40s from Kakhachkala, Dagestan ASSR, February 1983

Wholesale bartering has become the norm. Bribes are paid for food products or deficit goods, and people trade food or consumer goods for refrigerators or other things. Everything in the country is based on *blat* [influence]. Workers from food *kombinats* and consumer goods factories steal things (instant coffee, meat, soap) and sell them to their neighbours. Recently there have been interruptions in the supply of vodka, and people have been selling it in their flats for a large profit—particularly late at night and early in the morning when no vodka is on sale in the shops. On the other hand, people from the regional committee, the KGB, the Procurator's office, the OBKhSS and so on, can simply walk into the stores and ask for what they want, and it's more than your job's worth to refuse them.

Sales' clerk in his 60s from Lvov, April 1983

A lot of people come into Baku to buy food and carry it out by the sackload to other areas of the USSR. Inversely, people from Baku rent trucks and transport vegetables and fruits to Siberia and the Urals. This is dangerous, especially now that the police have begun to crack down. You can't get away with it unless you give them a bribe amounting to 30 per cent of the value of the goods, or 50 per cent of the earnings. People who have insufficient ready money to pay the bribe send a coded telegram to friends in Baku ("Grandmother is sick" or "Send medicine" or "Bagrat flew to Riga" etc.) and the friends telegraph a money order to a previously agreed post office or the address of an acquaintance. The bribe goes all the way to the head of the local OBKhSS, and money is also distributed among all the staff of the OBKhSS to prevent them from talking. This precaution is necessary because there is a special police department charged with investigating bribe-taking among the police.

Pensioner in his 60s from Baku, April 1983

I used to work in private houses. I took 5–7 rubles from a member of the leadership for a massage, but only 2–3 rubles from ordinary people. The leaders are stealing thousands of rubles, so I didn't consider it dishonourable to take more money from them.

Physical therapist in her 50s from Riga, April 1983

At the repair shop where I worked, we bought defective colour television sets from the factories. They cost us 35 rubles each, plus 20 rubles to ensure that they were sold to us whole, not in parts. Then we fixed them, and sold them for 250 rubles, with a one-year guarantee. A large part of the revenue went into the pockets of the shop director, the Party and the police, to ensure "mutual comprehension." Another source of income for me was the sale of spare parts which I stole from the shop.

Television repairman in his 40s from Chernovtsy, April 1983

Although the workers often failed to show up for compulsory work on Saturdays and Sundays, there was nothing the management could do about it. The fact of the matter was that workers and management had reached a tacit agreement whereby the workers overestimated their production output and bribed the technicians to accept lower amounts; the technicians in turn bribed the department heads, and the department heads bribed the factory management. Thus it was in the interest of the management to prevent conflicts from escalating lest this bring about its own downfall.

Technician in his 50s from Ulyanovsk; former CP member, February 1983

Cover-up

Working with the ambulance service, I sometimes answered calls from the "drying out" stations or the police to aid victims of police brutality. They had their own doctor on hand, and we were only called in when the doctor feared for the person's life. But even if it seemed likely that he would die, we were almost never allowed to take the person into intensive care. At most he would be taken to the prison hospital. The most usual incident was internal bleeding caused by beatings; they have a special technique of beating that leaves hardly any trace until the victim begins vomiting blood or has a bloody discharge and goes into shock. Many of them are admitted to prison hospitals with ruptured spleens; there must have been 18–20 cases of this a year. I don't know how many of them died.

Physician in his 50s from Kishinev, January 1983

Until 1983, I sometimes did some extra work as a pathologist for judicial inquests in Kishinev. We often had to deal with the corpses of people who had died from internal hemorraging as a result of being systematically beaten. If we tried to inform the Prosecutor that they had clearly been bludgeoned to death, the police would claim that they had fallen from a train or frozen to death in the street. Although this did not correspond to the clinical analysis, the Prosecutor would say, "The chief of police wouldn't lie, would he?" If the deceased was known to have been in a drying-out centre, the pre-trial detention cell [KPZ], or prison, we were instructed to write simply "convict" on the certificate, so as to avoid questions or complaints from the dead man's relatives. In these cases, the police usually said that the person had "fallen," "slipped in the shower," etc. Once a doctor wrote down "industrial accident" for a prisoner who had been beaten to death.

Physician from Kishinev, December 1984

A police lab technician, whose job is to measure the alcohol content in the blood of people who have been arrested, told me that his work was frequently interfered with by the police, either because they were taking bribes, or because they were trying to protect the relatives of highly-placed people. Thus, in the autumn of 1983 tests were run on a 20 year-old man who had run over an elderly woman. They showed clearly that he was intoxicated. A few days later, the test results "disappeared" and then "reappeared," but in altered form, made out in handwriting which was not that of the technician who had done the analysis. It turned out that the young man was the son of the Chernovtsy Regional Committee Secretary. Another incident involved an actress from the Chernovtsy Theatre of Drama who was arrested for possession of hashish. Her lover was the head of the supply department of a local electronics factory, and he was able to offer a large bribe to the police analyst. A report was prepared stating that the analysis had been "inconclusive," and that it was "impossible to assert that the confiscated substance was in fact a narcotic."

Lab technician from Chernovtsy, December 1986

In Vladimir Jail

One of the nurses who worked with me had spent two years (1983–84) working in Vladimir prison. She said that most of the prisoners are kept in solitary confinement. Some of them are "secret" prisoners whose names are unknown to the workers, and who are referred to only by numbers. One old man told her that he had been in prison since he was a young boy. As a shepherd boy, he had seen KGB officers shooting Polish officers in Katyn Forest. For this, he had been sentenced to life imprisonment. There were some foreigners in the prison, but since they knew no Russian, she never talked to them. Some prisoners were forbidden to leave their cells, and when they needed medical assistance, the doctors had to visit them there. The lower floors of the prison were so poorly heated that they froze in winter and this caused many people to fall ill. When a prisoner died, his head was cut off and cremated, while the rest of the body was sent to the medical institute for students to practise on.

Nurse from Vladimir, December 1986

Fixing the Statistics

Contrary to the claims of the Ministry of Health, tuberculosis has not been eradicated in the Soviet Union. It cannot be eradicated so long as drunkenness and poor living conditions continue to exist. I specialized in eye tuberculosis in the city tuberculosis clinic. The various city clinics would send me sick people with suspected ocular tuberculosis, and I had to diagnose and treat them. Up until seven years ago, when I began working as a specialist in this field, there had been no such speciality nor any persons sick with it. According to the figures, Barnaul was one of the most fortunate cities in the USSR as far as ocular tuberculosis was concerned. However, as soon as I started to work in this area, it became clear that many people *were* suffering from this disease, but that it was neither recognised nor treated. However, this was not what the city authorities wanted to hear. I was repeatedly summoned by the head doctor and the health department, which first tried to persuade me that I was mistaken and then threatened me. In the end they called in a "scientific commission" which spent three weeks studying my patients and "taught" me how to liquidate eye tuberculosis in the city. The commission decreed that chronic cases which did not react to the usual anti-tuberculosis treatments were no longer to be considered as tuberculin. Only cases which responded to treatment within a period of four months were to be counted as tuberculin for statistical purposes. Although ordinary cases of tuberculosis are currently entitled to go on drawing their salaries for nine months while under treatment before being declared invalids, my suggestion that these provisions should be extended to victims of ocular tuberculosis were rejected. It was explained to me that people can die from tuberculosis, whereas ocular tuberculosis "merely" makes them blind. Since I couldn't agree with such "advanced" methods of "fighting" tuberculosis, I left and went to work as a regular ophthalmologist in an ordinary clinic. The tuberculosis clinic found a more "copoerative" doctor to replace me, and the city is once again in the forefront of ocular tuberculosis treatment.

Opthalmologist in his 40s from Barnaul, September 1984

The Housing Shortage

I lived alone in a room in a communal flat. There were three other rooms besides mine. Two of them housed two elderly couples, and in the third lived a family of workers with two children aged seven and 13. They had had the room for 15 years, and had been glad to get it. Previously they had been lodged in some barracks, where their first son had died. Because of his death they were rehoused, while many of their friends remained in the barracks for another 7–10 years. The family had been waiting for an apartment for eight years, but they obviously didn't hold out much hope of ever getting it.

Pensioner in her 70s from Leningrad, January 1983

The two million or so inhabitants of Zaporozhye oblast have only an average of four square metres of living space each. Four thousand families are on the waiting list for flats. Even if we could freeze the number of people in need of housing at the present level, it would still take five years to deal with the backlog. Although we build 8,000 new housing units a year, all this does is keep step with the number of new families.

Ukrainian engineer and CP member from Zaporozhye, Soviet citizen, May 1983

Visiting people's homes in the course of my work, I saw many cases of acute misery. I visited communal flats with 6–10 families sharing the same kitchen and bathroom, and dormitories where 10–15 rooms gave on to the same corridor, and the same kitchen and bathroom were used by everybody. In places like this, there were constant fights and continual drinking. I also met pensioners trying to eke out their existence on an income of 8–12 rubles a month. Many of them were reduced to begging for scraps of food and cigarette butts in cafes. Sometimes war veterans had to sell their ration tickets because they had no money to buy the food to which they were entitled. Two clients of mine hanged themselves out of sheer desperation recently, and they were not exceptional cases.

Insurance agent from Kaluga, February 1987

Poorly Constructed Housing

Whole new housing areas have been built in the countryside around Moscow. It took years for the construction work to be completed. The roads are not asphalted, and the mud comes up to the axles of the cars in spring and fall. Transport into Moscow leaves a great deal to be desired; it used to take me one and a half hours to get to the centre of Moscow from my house in the Salkhozvystavka region. There was a shortage of buses and trolleys, and the crush during the morning and evening peak periods was horrendous. As for the houses themselves, they defied all the normal construction standards. The floors and frames were made of boards that were still damp. When they dried, gaps of 4–5 centimetres appeared between them. They warped so badly that it was impossible to walk across the floor without stumbling. Even worse: the houses were constructed from slabs of reinforced concrete held together by electrically welded iron rods cemented into the concrete. But the iron rusted, the rods came apart, and in the end the house would simply fall apart like a house of cards. Although attempts to correct this weakness were made (when a split appears the wall is hollowed out and new iron rods welded into place), catastrophes are inevitable. But people live in these buildings in spite of all their defects because there is nowhere else to live. . . .

Physician in his 30s from Moscow, April 1983

Desperate for a New Home

One day, the workers living in a barracks near my home decided to burn the building down. Many of them had been living there for several years while they waited for flats. They arranged the "fire" very carefully. Everyone in the building had an electric stove, and they all turned them on at the same time. The wiring in the barracks was old and could not withstand the electric surge, and it caught fire. Once the flames had taken hold, everyone raced outside with their pre-packed belongings. The barracks burned to the ground, and all the inhabitants were taken to court. After threatening to have them all imprisoned for arson, the judge finally backed down and the case was closed. In due course, everyone was allocated new living quarters.

Tailor from Vladimir, February 1987

Dangerous Housing

In the late 1970s the workers at my paper-manufacturing factory were given the opportunity to construct flats for their own use. The factory supplied the materials and the workers supplied the labour. It took seven years to construct a block of flats containing 64 units. At the end of that time, the housing office refused to pass the flats for residents, since they failed to meet required security and construction standards. However, a 7,000 ruble bribe was paid to the appropriate person, and the flats received the necessary approvals. One of the tenants was a friend of mine, and I visited his flat. It was in an incredible state. The ceiling was crumbling away; the walls were crooked; the chimneys were constantly getting clogged up because they had used improper connecting joints. Shortly before we left the USSR, one of the balconies collapsed and five people were killed. No investigation was made to determine who had approved the building for residents, and the factory didn't even send a representative to the funeral of the people who died.

Technician from Bukhara, December 1986

Private Housing-Policy

Thanks to good connections with the city council and city cooperatives, I was able to set up some good housing deals. For example, someone might exchange a room in a communal flat for a cellar or flat in a house scheduled for demolition. Then he would submit an application for new housing to the city council. Housing is allocated according to family size and sometimes health. The normal floor space allowance per person is 7–9 square metres, but people suffering from certain diseases, such as tuberculosis and nervous and psychological disorders, are entitled to more. So I had several physicians standing by to deliver the necessary certificates to ensure the new flat was a large one. Finally, I would bribe someone at the city council or the cooperative to authorize new housing or the purchase of a vacated flat in a cooperative. I took 800–900 rubles for each of these deals. With just two such "arrangements" a month, my family and I were able to live in comfort and take vacations in the Crimea, the Caucasus or the Baltic area. I only left the country because I was afraid of getting caught. Operations like this have become more difficult since Gorbachov came to power.

Housing administrator from Chernovtsy, May 1986

Every summer, I and some other guys went round the *kolkhozy* in Moscow, Vladimir and Kalinin oblasts doing building work. There were 6–8 people in our work force and we built calf-sheds, remodelled chicken coops, and so on. We were paid by the job: 1,000 rubles for a calf-shed, 800 for a vegetable storage shed, etc. The *kolkhozy* obtained the building materials themselves; we weren't interested in doing this. We wouldn't start a job unless all, or almost all, the materials were available. Of course I had to take time off my regular job to do this, which meant paying a doctor 100 rubles for a certificate to a hospital for three weeks, plus another 300 rubles to the building department so that they wouldn't make a fuss about it. However, I made between 1,200 and 1,600 rubles for the summer, so it was still worthwhile, especially as I always brought back chickens and vegetables from the *kolkhozy* in addition to the money.

Building technician in his 30s from Moscow, April 1983

When he could obtain the necessary materials, my husband used to tile bathrooms and kitchens. French and Italian tiles are very fashionable among the leadership right now. He got 250 rubles for labour alone just for tiling a kitchen.

Sales' clerk in her 30s from Tbilisi, April 1983

Living Conditions Compared

As a member of the CPSU, I frequently participated in health and sanitation committees. This led me to visit many student and worker dormitories, where people live in deplorable conditions. In student dormitories, there are often 8–10 people living in a single room. The beds have no sheets, and the mattresses are frayed and dirty. Official policy is to issue one bed to two people, which means that they have to take turns sleeping. With stipends of only 40 rubles a month, many of the students don't have enough money for food, although they always manage to get hold of vodka. Drunkenness and hunger generally go hand in hand. All kinds of people go to the dormitories, including criminals and drifters who "purchase" a place to stay for the night with vodka. Prostitution is common among female students anxious to earn a little extra money. In winter the dormitories are cold and smoke-filled, and in summer they are extremely stuffy. Naturally, they are also filthy. It is hard to get janitors since no one wants to work for 50 rubles a month.

Even worse are the workers' dormitories, which are located in former prison camp barracks. Families do not have their own rooms, and there are no separate quarters for men and women. Instead everyone sleeps together in an area housing 100–150 people, partitioned only with torn blankets hung from the ceiling, or plywood boards. There are lots of dirty, unkempt little children running around. The air is thick with screams and obscenities day and night. Prostitution and drunkenness are rife. Generally, there are no toilet facilities, and in winter there are always lumps of frozen excrement to be found on the street outside.

In sharp contrast to this are the dormitories which are placed at the disposal of Arabs and blacks. There are only two people to each room, and everyone has his own bed with sheets and blankets. There are janitors to keep everything clean, working toilets, and hot and cold running water. What's more, they receive a monthly stipend of 90 rubles. There is a lot of resentment over this special treatment, and the foreign students frequently get beaten up.

On one occasion I also saw the dormitory of a special KGB school. Everything was set up very pleasantly, with two students to a room. The place was clean and warm, there was radio and television, the bathrooms were nicely kept, and there were plenty of teapots. The students here had a stipend of 120 rubles per month.

Dentist from Vladimir, December 1986

Adolescent Girls Driven to Prostitution

Neurological diseases—including sexually transmitted infections—are increasing among young people. Although this fact is officially acknowledged by the Ministry of Public Health, censorship prevents it from being mentioned in the press. However the issue has been take up at medical conferences and measures are being taken to try and resolve the problem. I was involved in tracing sources of infection, and in the course of this activity I came across young girls aged 14–15, living in a dormitory for technical students, who were engaged in prostitution. Although the existence of prostitution is not officially recognized, there is a procedure in dispensaries designed to uncover sources of infection and provide the necessary treatment. The dispensary is entitled to use the militia to bring in infected people who are avoiding treatment. It is particularly difficult to bring in these young girls because sleeping with a minor is prohibited and is punishable with a prison sentence. So unless the girl is of age, it is hard to discover her identity. I had a chance to discuss the phenomenon of adolescent prostitution with several directors of professional/technical institutes. They ascribed it to the fact that these young students, who live in dormitories because their families are too poor to take care of them, have such meagre stipends that they are obliged to sell themselves to get money to live on. The girls are half-starved and sell themselves for virtually nothing—three rubles a time. Many get pregnant; others get venereal disease; from time to time there are cases of suicide.

Neurologist in his 40s from Moscow, September 1984

Parapsychology

There is a spiritual vacuum in the USSR. Nobody believes what the authorities say and people are searching for food for the soul. There is immense interest in parapsychology and religion. More than 2,000 young people visited my art studio in Leningrad, which was a meeting place for those interested in such matters. There was a huge demand for the journal *Tainovedeniye* [literally "Conduct of Mystery"] which is published in Israel. Bibles are also very sought after; they fetch 150–200 rubles on the black market. The KGB has a department of "bioenergetics" (as it calls parapsychology) which uses modern technology to verify the abilities of mediums. This is done openly in the "House of Culture" and hordes of young people try to attend. Those who prove themselves as mediums are diverted to the KGB's special laboratories. The KGB long ago took over parapsychological research, officially announcing that it is "not a science." Those involved with it are recruited for work in the KGB's secret labs, and life is made intolerable for those who refuse to cooperate. In my case, my studio was taken away from me, and I was excluded from the Artists' Union before being finally thrown out of the USSR. Other parapsychologists who refused to work with the KGB are Varvara Ivanova-Kissin, Mikhail Sergeev and Nikolai Kozyrev, to name only three. All were forbidden to lecture. Ivanova-Kissin was threatened with arrest and/or a psychiatric hospital for giving lectures at her home and in public parks in defiance of the order and for putting out a bulletin entitled *Parapsychology News*, which was distributed through *samizdat*.

Artist and self-styled parapsychologist–philosopher in his 50s from Leningrad, January 1983

Apathy

My fellow workers were apathetic and indifferent to everything except vodka. They weren't seriously interested in the prospect of changes in the leadership. All they did was tell anecdotes, even in front of the stool pigeons. Usually there are two or three of the latter in every department; everyone knows who they are, and no one is afraid of them. I never heard of anyone I knew having trouble with the KGB; these days they don't put you in jail for anything, even telling anecdotes. (On the other hand, there were sometimes rumours about department heads having problems, but that didn't concern us.) The only thing that bothered people was the food situation, but if that improves they'll be quite content. Nobody I knew worried about the international situation. They felt secure because, "Our army is the strongest in the world," and "We give way to nobody, but if anyone dares to fool with us, you won't even be able to find the bones afterwards." On the subject of Afghanistan, there was a widespread feeling that "it was necessary" because "the Chinese and Americans wanted to sneak in there." Few of the soldiers killed in Afghanistan were buried in Elektrostal.

Adjuster in his 40s from Elektrostal, January 1983

Talking to simple Soviet people, such as workers and low level service staff, you get the impression that nothing interests them outside of material problems. People have totally lost the desire to change anything. Soviet ideology has ceased to affect them; all they want is to get hold of something. The workers have a very negative attitude to the dissidents, blaming them for all kinds of real or imaginary crimes; while they look on the departure of the Jews as nothing more than an attempt to better themselves.

Engineer in his 60s from Sestroretsk, Leningrad oblast; former CP member, January 1983

"Forbidden Fruit"

I bought 2,000 rubles' worth of Western photographic equipment and used it to copy pictures from Western pornographic magazines, which I then resold. The clients who bought the photos off me fell into three categories. First there were people working in the Far North where money is plentiful but women are scarce. Second, people from Central Asia and the Caucasus who are interested in white women. Finally, the Party activists in search of "forbidden fruit" from the "decadent West." Respectable family men, with considerable standing in the Party, would appear in my studio and eagerly pay out 100 rubles for a pornography album. While the Asians used to like fluffy blondes, the Party people preferred unnatural pictures; group sex, boys and other perversions.

Photographer in his 40s from Leningrad, June 1984

5. As the Kremlin Sees Us

The Soviet View of the State of Human Rights in the United States and Western Europe

Human Rights in the West

Extract from Mikhail Gorbachov's speech at the official dinner held in honour of Mrs Thatcher's visit to the Soviet Union. From Pravda, *31 March 1987, in which both leaders' speeches were published in full.*

A representative humanitarian forum, which we have suggested should take place in Moscow, could make an active contribution to the common European process. But here we find an interesting point. As soon as we invite them to discuss human rights in a serious and business-like manner, to make mutually frank comparisons of how people live here and in the capitalist countries, they seem to grow nervous, and once again try to relate the entire theme to two or three particular cases, refusing to consider all the others.

We are ready to consider personal cases as well in the spirit of humanity, but we are resolutely prepared to talk about the entire nature of the problem openly and frankly. So that we should be heard in the West by the millions of unemployed; by the homeless and by those living in poverty; by those who are beaten up by the police and oppressed by the courts; by those whose civil rights and human value are subjected to scandalous discrimination simply because of the colour of their skin; so that we should be heard by the unions whose rights to defend their members have been taken away, infringing on their very reason for existence; by the workers and other labourers deprived of the ability to participate in the management of the enterprises to which they have belonged throughout their lives.

If we are going to speak about human rights, then let us speak about all rights, and particularly about rights which concern millions of people.

Westminster Should Move Closer to Soviet Freedoms

This article by S. Andreyev, entitled "Why the British Parliament is discussing non-existent 'problems'," appeared in Sovetskaya Rossiya, *on 12 March 1987.*

Even before the new "Public Order" Act came into force in Britain, a man was arrested and subsequently charged for saying "Boo" to a police dog. The incident has become a joke, but the British do not find it so funny. "How the concept of freedom is gradually being eroded in Britain"—this is a headline from the conservative journal, *The Economist*. The article itself discusses the threat to civil rights posed by the new legislation. It is "a threat to freedom," in the opinion of Lord Salmon, who has held high office in the country for many years.

In the light of facts and opinions like these (and there are a great many of them), it seems quite natural that the British Parliament should take up the matter of human rights. But, while these rights are being violated every single day in the

British Isles, Parliament is discussing the situation in . . . the Soviet Union. What is more, emulating the American practice of unceremonious interference from Washington in the internal affairs of other states, the organizers of these wordy debates have arranged to hold them just before Prime Minister Margaret Thatcher's visit to our country. They obviously intend them to serve as a means of conveying their parting wishes.

According to one of the speakers, London will give Moscow its "vote of confidence" only when the USSR aims in its domestic policy for the high standards set on the banks of the Thames. It is clear that Westminster should reserve its unsolicited vote of confidence for debates on British domestic policy issues. This reminds me of something once said by Gerry Adams, leader of one of the parties in Northern Ireland, who was elected to Parliament from Belfast but refused to take the seat offered. When Soviet journalists asked him why he did not wish to discuss in Parliament the scandalous transgressions of the law committed by British security forces in Ulster, he replied: "I cannot discuss Irish affairs in the parliament of an alien country. It would be the same as discussing them in the FRG Bundestag. It would be useless anyway." But, as we can see, this very same Parliament regards political stratagems, which do not contribute to the successful development of relations between our countries, as useful.

So who needs them and why? First of all, a recent historical analogy springs to mind. We all remember how interference in socialist countries' internal affairs began on a large scale, with the aid of the "human rights" master key, soon after the signing of the Final Act in Helsinki. And exactly at a time when *détente* was able to take the form of practical disarmament measures. Today, with the Soviet Union's proposal to resolve the problem of medium-range missiles, opponents of nuclear disarmament in the USA and Western Europe have found themselves in an unusually difficult position. It requires special efforts to blur the issue. And so, once again, "rights" that are in fact mythical, but which are being linked with quite specific disarmament issues, are being dragged out of the bag of anti-Soviet tricks.

Another reason is that Conservative Members of Parliament want to reduce the pressure in their own social pressure cooker with the help of an escape valve. The move towards the thorough democratization of all social life in our country and the increasingly consistent practical fulfilment of Soviet citizens' rights and freedoms is in fatal contrast to the British trend towards limiting its own democratic freedoms.

British MPs may not be throwing stones inside a glass house, but they are throwing stones in a building from whose tall Gothic windows one can see the homeless bedding down for the night beneath a bridge of the Thames. There are approximately 100,000 homeless people in Britain. Those without a roof over their heads are mainly representatives of the four million unemployed, subsisting on a miserable pittance.

"We are talking about freedom—not poverty," could be London's reply. But the two are connected. In Britain, police repression is becoming the chief physician in the fight against social ills. Strikes by print workers and miners have demonstrated a relatively new and extremely unattractive side of life in Britain. Thousands of policemen had to be deployed—not to maintain order but to suppress picketing workers and break up demonstrations. The same response has been given to British people's demands for the removal of American nuclear missiles from their country. The police have so far arrested 10,000 people in connection with this. The police are becoming omnipresent. They have been bursting into a newspaper's editorial offices and BBC studios. They are tapping the telephones of peace movement activists. They beat up the country's coloured inhabitants if they protest against racial discrimination, and a number of people have actually died in police custody under unexplained circumstances.

"Why are the British police so willing to beat people up?" This question headed an article in another British journal, *The New Statesman*, which was also subjected to a police raid recently. Why does Westminster not give some thought to this matter, discuss it and then do something about it? This is phrased as a question, because we do not give advice to other legislators.

Thatcher's Britain: No Example

Excerpts from a commentary by Yurii Kornilov, TASS *in Russian and English, 27 March 1987.*

A process of restructuring and renewal is going on in the Soviet Union, and the Soviet people consider it to be a major task of that process to give even greater meaning to socialist democracy, and to develop and translate into practice the fundamental principles of the socialist rule of the people to a fuller extent. A "recipe" for accomplishing that goal has all of a sudden come from—London. British Prime Minister Margaret Thatcher, going for an official visit to Moscow, told the House of Commons that "Britain will have full confidence and trust in the Soviet Union if we feel it treats its people more the way we treat ours than is the case now." Unfortunately, Mrs Thatcher has not backed her words with specific facts. We shall try to help her.

As is well known, socialism stamped out unemployment and not only proclaimed but guaranteed in practice the right to work for all the citizens of the socialist state, and the Soviet people have every justification to view this fact as a major accomplishment of our revolution. The situation in Britain is different: in the seven years of the Conservatives' rule unemployment has more than trebled, and 3·2 million people, or 11 per cent of the employable population, are without employment today. So what would it mean for the USSR to emulate Britain, as Mrs Thatcher urges? A simple calculation shows that the Soviet Union would end up with an army of unemployed numbering almost 30 million (since the population of the Soviet Union is over 280 million and that of Britain 57 million). What sort of model is this?

Moreover, according to the British press, there are over 100,000 homeless in Britain, while the number of people living in premises which are totally unsuitable for habitation is 1·2 million. What would Mrs Thatcher's "recipe" mean for our country? Clearly, if the Soviet government pursued a domestic policy similar to that of the "free" capitalist Britain, it would have at least 600,000 homeless. What sort of model is this?

While urging Moscow "to treat its people more the way we treat ours," and holding up London as a staunch champion of "human rights and liberties," Mrs Thatcher for some reason persistently omits to mention such commonly known facts as the cancer of racialism, which is eating deeper and deeper into Britain, the harsh persecution of "dissident" trade union activists, and the terror conducted against participants in the anti-war struggle. And it is also well known that, according to press reports, in the past few years over 10,000 British citizens have been arrested by the authorities for participation in demonstrations protesting against the siting of nuclear weapons on British soil.

Following the "British model," this country with a population of 280 million should imprison at least 50,000 participants in the anti-war campaign. Is this what Mrs Thatcher is advocating, deliberately or inadvertently? Are these the "accomplishments" of British "democracy" which they are proposing we should borrow from the banks of the Thames?

No, Mrs Prime Minister, your "advice" and "recipe" in the sphere of democracy do not suit Soviet people at all. We in the USSR do not recognize and do not consider the reality of capitalist society to be an example of ensuring human rights, for it is a society based on social inequality and injustice, racial and national oppression, trampling on the civil rights of national and social minorities, discrimination against women and young people, propaganda of depravity and amorality. And if one is to speak of democracy and trust, then it must be said straight out: the Soviet people cannot trust those who shamelessly claim that black is white. On the contrary, Soviet public opinion is depressed, seriously depressed by the fact that the human rights' situation in Britain is not only not improving, but on the contrary is arousing increasing alarm. . . .

West Violates Human Rights

Excerpts from unsigned article, Pravda, *3 March 1987.*

"How can one deal with the leaders of a country who accuse all and sundry of violating human rights, while preaching the cult of force both in their own country and in its relations with other states, a country that exports to the rest of the world a warped culture cultivating hatred of other nations? How can one deal with those who break elementary human rights at home, while lecturing others non-stop in a mentor's tone about the need to respect human rights?"

The Soviet national daily *Pravda* said today that those legitimate questions were being asked in their letters to it by numerous readers who said that the human rights situation in the West, most notably in the USA, had not shown any change for the better for a long time and that, naturally enough, that circumstance could not but have a bearing on the Soviet Union's relationship with that country.

Such letters expressing concern about violations of human rights in the West came in nearly every day, the paper continued. It said they spoke about the position of blacks, the harassment of dissidents, the high number of jobless people, rampant crime, the cult of violence and wide-spread drug abuse in the USA.

The Soviet people in their letters voiced outrage also over police brutality against civil rights campaigners in Ulster, the practice of *Berufsverbot* (denial of jobs for political reasons) in West Germany, and discrimination against immigrant workers in France and other so-called developed capitalist countries, *Pravda* said.

Recalling how the staff of the bus-building RAF factory in Soviet Latvia had elected their director themselves after discussing several dozen candidates for the post, it added: "Try and name a country, company or firm in the West where this would be possible today."

Pravda went on to say: "The Soviet people will only believe assertions about the democratism of Western societies when the directors of banks and the owners and managers of factories there also begin to be elected in the same free way and when the mass media there start freely and regularly criticizing corporations and their heads and banks and their masters—in short, all those who have always proved above criticism for the mass media in the West, which have given vent to their bile as a rule by blasting unimportant figures and politicians, more often than not just men of straw.

"One needs to have the moral right to talk about democracy. But ruling quarters in the West, where millions and even tens of millions of people are denied the right to work and where the people's natural and universally shared aspiration for peace is callously and completely ignored, do not have this right.

"In Western countries hardened mercenary-mindedness, lust for profit, impenitent immorality and pornography are becoming tools for spiritual aggression against the really human, civilized principles of conduct. Money and the right of strength in the merciless fight for existence are being made into a cult.

"It is in capitalist countries that they flagrantly meddle in people's private lives, tamper with their mail, wiretap their telephone conversations and pry open the drawers of their desks to examine the contents.

"Take, finally, the most fundamental of human rights—the right to life. In the White House they can see from its windows a fasting man who is sacrificing his life so that the masters of the USA should grant this paramount right to their compatriots and to all people on earth by renouncing a policy that threatens mankind with self-immolation.

"This man is well-known American scientist Charles Hyder. The US administration has responded [to his act of self-sacrifice] by appropriating further billions of dollars for the arms race."

Pravda then expressed the opinion that "If the USA and its leaders really want improvements in international relations, they should end the propaganda of hatred of other nations and take a careful look at how the human rights' situation in their own country could be radically improved across the board, including such aspects as unemployment, racialism, preaching of violence, social inequality freedom of speech and freedom of conscience."

The paper said it believed that the resolution of all those issues, that is, the attainment of genuine democracy, not only in the USA but in all capitalist "democracies" would help to improve substantially the international climate in general and strengthen mutual trust.

"Blood-Splashed Pavements" in the West

From a statement by Yurii Kashlev, Head of the USSR Delegation at the Vienna CSCE Conference, 19 December 1986.

A considerable and important place in the [CSCE] debate belongs to international legal issues pertaining to principles and humanitarian cooperation. Unfortunately, their discussion has been confrontational, reflecting the desire of several delegations to distort the essence of the CSCE process. Leading the way in that confrontation have been the delegations of the United States, Canada and the United Kingdom.

The representatives of the USA, the country which has committed flagrant acts of direct aggression against Libya, Grenada and Nicaragua, which has crushed underfoot the Helsinki Declaration's principles by which the participating states pledged to be guided, not only in their mutual relations but also in relations with other states of the world; the country which ignores the decisions of the International Court of Justice and systematically commits gross and mass violations of human rights and fundamental freedoms on its own territory, have not hesitated to don a prosecutor's cloak and to pose at our meeting as champions of international law and order.

What's more, for 20 years now the US has boycotted the International Covenants and other major human rights' instruments such as the conventions on the suppression of genocide and racial discrimination, on the equality of women, and many others. At the 41st UN General Assembly session which came to an end just a few days ago the US delegation was the only one to vote against many resolutions on human rights.

The destructive line followed by the delegation of the United States and those who have sided with it has made itself felt with particular force during the discussion of human rights' issues and humanitarian problems.

The representatives of the country which is unequalled in the West in terms of its prison population—in December this year [1986] the number of inmates in its jails totalled 723,000—has expatiated more than anyone else at our meetings on the state of Soviet prisons. It is well-known that a survey conducted by the US public health association came to the conclusion that conditions in jails throughout US territory are inhuman, and meanwhile the head of the US delegation here has staged a cheap demonstration in connection with the death of one prisoner [Anatoly Marchenko] in the USSR.

The US delegation is very fond of talking about criminals in the Soviet Union whom it refers to only as "political prisoners." In so doing, it pretends there are none in the US at all. But the world should know the names of American religious figures who recently staged a protest against nuclear weapons and have been given prison sentences of 8–18 years for political reasons. They are Carl Cabit, Paul Cabit, Lawrence Claud Morgan, Martin Halliday and Helen Woodson. The struggle against the threat of war is viewed in the USA as a grave crime.

The representative of the United Kingdom, for his part, while expressing grief over the death of one prisoner in the Soviet Union, was quite calm when he gave the figure of those killed in Ulster—2,521 men. And no Western delegation showed any emotions on hearing that figure. While the representative of one country tells us about someone else's blood stained windows, it is in his own country that mass demonstrations with thousands of participants are being broken up, resulting in hundreds of casualties, blood-splashed pavements, and the police beating to death a student fighting for his right to education.

The US representative has said that among the rights enjoyed by his fellow-countrymen there is a right to sleep on a subway grate. This right, if one might use that word, is being exercised in that country by some three million people. Already dozens of thousands of homeless children have been born to homeless parents. We have no such "right." The USSR Constitution enshrines the obligation of the state to provide housing for all citizens.

Incidentally, a few words about housing. I should think everybody well remembers the time when the US authorities bombed and burnt a whole black neighbourhood in Philadelphia. 11 people, including women and children, were killed.

Why is it then that the US delegation is so patently indifferent to the lot of its fellow-countrymen? And why do some other Western delegations worry only about the fate of citizens of socialist countries, while ignoring the facts of lawlessness and the lack of rights in their American ally? Obviously, because in reality human rights and humanitarian issues on their own are of no concern whatever either to the US or to its closest allies.

Soviet Public "Greatly Concerned" About "Anti-Semitic Acts" in Canada

Extracts from the Soviet response (2 December 1986) to a plenary statement by Ambassador William Bauer, head of the Canadian delegation to the CSCE Conference in Vienna (24 November 1985).

The Canadian representative's explanations do not convince us that his country does not grossly violate the provision of the seventh principle of the Final Act:

> The participating States on whose territory national minorities exist will respect the right of persons belonging to such minorities to equality before the law, will afford them the full opportunity for the actual enjoyment of human rights and fundamental freedoms and will, in this manner, protect their legitimate interests in this sphere.

In the Subsidary Working body we showed that during the last year anti-semitic acts were on the increase in Canada and we adduced concrete facts about the blowing up of a synagogue in Vancouver. With reference to this, the Canadian representative can take a look at the *House of Commons Debates*, 30 January 1985, pp. 1814–15.

In order to square accounts with our Canadian colleague, we observe in passing that in the Soviet Union synagogues are not blown up, nor are Jews insulted; these things only happen in countries which call themselves part of the "free world."

There is particular public anxiety over our observation that in Canada group racialist activities go mostly unpunished.

A sense of unease arises when the distinguished Canadian colleague fails to react to our statement that in his country groups of war criminals who have the blood of European people on their hands live freely. . . .

With the best will in the world, we cannot consider the answer of the Canadian representative to the question about relations between his authorities and trade unions to be satisfactory. Can it be that we are not specific enough? We can easily put that right. We see concrete examples which provide evidence that the Canadian authorities use fines and imprisonment in the fight against the trade unions. Thus, members of the transport workers' trade union of Montreal were fined 50,000 dollars for an alleged violation of "the interdiction against a general strike" in May 1983; the leaders of this trade union were given various prison sentences.[1] In 1985, the police broke up the demonstrations of striking trade union workers after which, as we have already mentioned, 10 demonstrators were arrested. And that is not something we invented. On 23 December 1985 it was reported in the *Canadian Tribune*. . . . This is only a drop in the ocean of facts available to us attesting to Canadian violations of the provisions of the Helsinki Final Act, and the Concluding Document of Madrid, international agreements on human rights and the conventions of the ILO. . . .

In answer to our criticisms the Canadian representative explained that in his country the authorities do not suppress dissidents, especially in the anti-war movement, but that, on the contrary, they encourage them in every way. But indeed, the facts prove otherwise. Could it be that in some way we are being misled? We would be obliged to our Canadian colleague if he would explain especially why in July 1983 14 organizers of the peace camps in Toronto were thrown into prison? Why in the autumn of 1984 were 16 peace sympathizers arrested in Halifax? These cases were reported in the *Globe and Mail* on 8 August

[1] See *Canadian News Facts*, No. 11, 1984, p. 3086.

1983 and 2 January 1985. How should we interpret the fact that because of provocative explosions of homemade bombs by the terrorist group "Direct Action" during a demonstration near the enterprises of the company Litton Industries in 1982, some 10 members of the anti-war groups "Union for Non-Violent Actions" and "Reject the cruise missile" were arrested. . . .

We are especially worried that we have received no answer to the concrete examples we have adduced concerning widespread psychiatric malpractices in Canada. The Soviet delegation showed that, according to the *Toronto Star*, there are a minimum of 145 known cases in which Canadian psychiatrists experimented on Canadian citizens without their agreement, using electric shocks as well as methods which induce hallucinations and insomnia. At the same time, we drew attention to the severe after-effects of experiments conducted by the Canadian Dr Cameron on nine patients at the Allan Memorial Institute in Montreal, as well as the malpractice and violent acts of doctors and personnel at the psychiatric hospital in Rivière-des-Prairies. All of this was reported in the *Toronto Star* and *Le Devoir* on 7 January 1986 and 11 January 1986. We would like to ask the Canadian representative directly what measures the Canadian authorities intend to take in order to bring an end to psychiatric abuses in Canada. We are waiting for a reply to this question which is of great concern to the Soviet public.

Our Contributors

STEPHEN ASHLEY has been a Bulgarian analyst at Radio Free Europe since October 1985. Born and educated in Leeds he received his MA and DPhil in Modern History at Oxford University.

ANNELI UTE GABANYI is the Chief of Romanian Research at Radio Free Europe. She was born in Bucharest and studied at the universities of Cluj (Romania), Clermont-Ferrand, Southern California and Munich. She is the author of a book on post-war Romanian cultural policy and has written articles for *Osteuropa*, *Suedost-Europa*, *Index on Censorship* and *Die Zeit*, amongst others.

DAN IONESCU, born in Romania, is an analyst on Romanian affairs at Radio Free Europe. He graduated from the Academy of Economic Sciences and the Fine Arts Institute in Bucharest. From 1980 to 1984 he studied East European History at the University of Muenster, West Germany. He has worked as a researcher at the Institute for World Economics and at the Institute for South East European Studies in Bucharest.

VLADIMIR V. KUSIN, born and educated in Czechoslovakia, is the Deputy Director of Research of Radio Free Europe. He has filled a number of academic posts in Czechoslovakia, Great Britain and Japan and is the author *The Intellectual Origins of the Prague* Spring (1971), *Political Grouping in the Czechoslovak Reform Movement* (1972) and *From Dubcek to Charter 77* (1978).

SOPHIA M. MISKIEWICZ is a coordinator of the East European Economic and Social Rights' programme at Radio Free Europe. Born and educated in the United States, she has given lectures and contributed articles on Poland to a number of publications.

JUDITH K. PATAKI has been an analyst of Hungarian affairs at Radio Free Europe since 1980. Born in Hungary, she received her PhD from the University of Southern California in Los Angeles. She specializes in Hungarian social affairs, education and literature.

AARON TREHUB has worked in Radio Liberty Research since 1985. He is a graduate of McGill University and the Johns Hopkins University School of Advanced International Studies.

LINDA VALENTINE is an analyst of Polish affairs for Radio Free Europe. Born and educated in the United States, she is a specialist in modern Polish history and social conditions.